AETIUS

LCL 555

AETIUS

PLACITA

EDITED AND TRANSLATED BY

JAAP MANSFELD
DAVID T. RUNIA

HARVARD UNIVERSITY PRESS

CAMBRIDGE, MASSACHUSETTS

LONDON, ENGLAND

2023

Library of Congress Control Number 2023002935
CIP data available from the Library of Congress

ISBN 978-0-674-99759-2

*Composed in ZephGreek and ZephText by
Technologies 'N Typography, Merrimac, Massachusetts.
Printed on acid-free paper and bound by
Maple Press, York, Pennsylvania*

CONTENTS

CONTENTS

CONTENTS

PREFACE

In July 2020 the authors of the present volume published an edition of the *Placita* of Aëtius, together with a commentary and a collection of related texts. As will be set out in more detail in the General Introduction, this four-volume work was the end result of a thirty-five-year project, which had the aim of replacing the monumental edition of Hermann Diels, dating back to 1879.

A key feature of the new edition was that it provided a unified text in a single column. The original treatise is incompletely preserved and has to be reconstructed from evidence in two main authors (with further assistance from a third). Diels had produced his reconstruction in two columns and was thus unable to provide a single authoritative text. For this reason it was never translated into any modern language, with the exception of a double-column Italian version (Torraca, *I dossografi greci*). The new edition also contains an English translation. But for technical reasons this version could not be placed side-by-side (or below) the Greek text. It was located in a separate volume at the end.

At the conclusion of the General Introduction to the edition and commentary we expressed the intention to produce an *editio minor* of the larger work. It seemed to us that the methodology used in the new edition made it particularly suitable for inclusion in the Loeb Classical Library. We were thus delighted when our proposal was accepted by the Editor and Trustees of the series.

The text in this Loeb edition faithfully reproduces the text in the larger work, retaining the same line division, as indicated by vertical bars. Only a minimum of changes have been introduced, indicated in each case in the textual notes and also collected together in an Appendix. An additional change is the inclusion of the Arabic text of Qusṭā ibn Lūqā for those passages that his Arabic translation preserves but that are lost in the transmission of the Greek text. In contrast, the translation on the facing page deviates quite considerably from that published in the earlier work. It is less literal and, following the conventions of the Loeb series, aims to render the telegrammatic style of the *Placita* with a reasonable degree of fluency. The General Introduction and the Introductions to the five individual books of the work have the purpose of introducing the user to the main features, background, and context of the treatise and its constituent parts. In these sections of the volume we emphasize strongly the dialectical features of the work that set it apart from most other philosophical works from antiquity. In the translation a very brief guide is given to these dialectical features at the beginning of each chapter. As is usual in the Loeb series, notes to the translation have been kept to a minimum. For a more detailed guide to the contents of the work, the reader is referred to the extensive commentary in the larger edition.

PREFACE

When the founder of the Loeb Classical Library, James Loeb, explained his reasons for establishing the series in a prefatory statement published in the first volume in 1912, he also announced that he had appointed an Advisory Board of "eminent scholars." Among these was "Hermann Diels Ph.D., of the University of Berlin, Secretary of the Royal Academy of Science, Berlin." It is fitting that this volume of Aëtius' *Placita*, which builds on and replaces Diels' celebrated edition, be published in the same series more than a century later.

The authors express their gratitude to the General Editor of the Loeb Classical Library, Jeffrey Henderson, and to its Managing Editor, Michael B. Sullivan, for the generous and efficient assistance that they gave the project during the preparation of this volume. Their guidance in the difficult task of adapting the original work to the requirements of a very different kind of presentation is greatly appreciated. The authors are also indebted to Glenn W. Most for support, especially in the early stages. The present volume, though focusing on a single treatise of a very different kind, may be seen as a companion piece to the nine volumes of *Early Greek Philosophy* that he and his co-editor, André Laks, produced for the same series. We also thank Robert Turnbull (Melbourne) and Alexander Treiger (Halifax) for their assistance with the Arabic text of Qusṭā ibn Lūqā. Finally, warm thanks must be extended to Louise Schouten, Senior Editor at Brill Leiden, the publishers of the larger edition, for granting permission to publish this reduced version three years after the appearance of the earlier work.

As was the case for all the volumes of the *Aëtiana* series, the authors, Jaap Mansfeld and David Runia, have written this work in full collaboration and accept joint responsibility for its contents.

Jaap Mansfeld
Bilthoven, The Netherlands

David Runia
Melbourne, Australia

October 2022

GENERAL INTRODUCTION

1. THE COMPENDIUM

1.1. *The Lost Original and Its Author*

The *Placita* of Aëtius is one of the more remarkable works that has come down to modern times from antiquity. The original is lost, and of the author we know nothing except his name, and even that has been challenged by scholars. Ever since, however, the great German scholar Hermann Diels (1848–1922) proved the work's existence and reconstructed its contents from three key ancient witnesses, it has made a fundamental contribution to the study of ancient philosophy, particularly for the period from the sixth to the first centuries BC. In 2020 the editors of the present volume produced for the first time a complete reconstruction and edition of the text in a single column based on all the ancient evidence.[1] This edition is the basis for the text and translation produced for the Loeb Classical Library.

In the period from the second to the fifth century AD, three ancient authors made use of a compendium setting out the opinions of the philosophers in response to questions and topics in the domain of natural philosophy. Two of these authors, the one named Plutarch but not to be

---

[1] Mansfeld and Runia, *Aëtiana V* (abbreviated MR 5).

identified with the famous Plutarch of Chaeronea (so thus called Ps.-Plutarch), the other named John of Stobi (or Stobaeus), made extensive *verbatim* excerpts from the original work. The third author, the Christian church father Theodoret of Cyrrhus, also drew on the work, paraphrasing its contents in such a way that much of the original text could still be identified. Taken together, these three witnesses allow the greater part of the original work to be reconstructed. From the mid-fifth century onward, after Stobaeus and Theodoret ceased their literary activities, the original compendium disappears from view. The abridged version produced by Ps.-Plutarch continued to enjoy a rich reception throughout the Byzantine period. But the access that this tradition provides to the original work is always mediated via the initial process of abridgment carried out in the second century.[2]

The name of the author of the compendium can be deduced from cross-references in Theodoret. Three times the bishop refers by name to the sources of the information he has on the doctrines of the philosophers, on one occasion also adding the titles of the works he used:[3]

Cur. 2.95: Πλούταρχος δὲ καὶ Ἀέτιος τὰς τῶν φιλοσόφων ἐκπαιδεύουσι δόξας· τὸν αὐτὸν δὲ καὶ ὁ Πορφύριος ἀνεδέξατο πόνον, τὸν ἑκάστου βίον ταῖς δόξαις προστεθεικώς. (Plutarch and Aëtius give a thorough exposition of the opinions of the

---

[2] On the tradition and reception of the work, see further sections 1.6 and 2.1.2 below.

[3] Texts at 62.4–7, 108.27–9.4, and 126.21–22 in Raeder's edition.

philosophers. Porphyry too took up the same task, adding the life of each philosopher to the opinions.)

Cur. 4.31: Εἰ δέ τις οἴεται κἀμὲ συκοφαντῆσαι τοὺς ἄνδρας, τὴν παμπόλλην αὐτῶν διαφωνίαν ἐλέγξαντα, ἀναγνώτω μὲν Ἀετίου τὴν Περὶ ἀρεσκόντων ξυναγωγήν, ἀναγνώτω δὲ Πλουτάρχου τὴν Περὶ τῶν τοῖς φιλοσόφοις δοξάντων ἐπιτομήν· καὶ Πορφυρίου δὲ ἡ Φιλόσοφος ἱστορία πολλὰ τοιαῦτα διδάσκει. (If anyone thinks that I am slandering the men when I refute their copious dissension, let him read Aëtius' compendium *On Placita*, let him read Plutarch's epitome *On the Opinions of the Philosophers*; in addition, Porphyry's *Philosophical History* also teaches many such things.)

Cur. 5.16: Ἃ δέ γε ξὺν Θεῷ λέξω, ἐκ τῶν Πλουτάρχῳ καὶ Πορφυρίῳ καὶ μέντοι καὶ Ἀετίῳ ξυγγεγραμμένων ἐρῶ. (What I now shall state with God's help, I shall take from the writings of Plutarch and Porphyry, and of course Aëtius.)

"Plutarch" in these extracts refers to the author of the abridged version.[4] The *Placita* cannot be identified with Porphyry's work, which as Theodoret tells us also contained biographical accounts of the philosophers and, as we know from other sources, did not treat philosophers later than Plato. Since the opinions that Theodoret records contain material not found in Ps.-Plutarch, the deduction, first made by Diels, that Aëtius was the primary

---

[4] Theodoret also knew of the work via the *Praeparatio evangelica* of Eusebius of Caesarea.

author of the doxographical opinions recorded by Theodoret is convincing.[5]

No ancient author with the name Aëtius is known who
can plausibly be connected with the compendium.[6] As for
the date of the work, the latest time of composition, i.e.,
its *tempus ante quem*, is furnished by Ps.-Plutarch's *Epitome*,[7] which from the evidence of the Christian apologist Athenagoras, must have been completed by about AD
150. For the earliest time of composition, i.e., its *tempus
post quem*, we have to use the evidence of its contents.
The last philosopher to be mentioned is the Peripatetic
philosopher Xenarchus of Seleucia, whose death occurred
in the final years BC.[8] Other prominent first-century BC
philosophers such as Antiochus and Eudorus are not cited.
As we shall see,[9] the *Placita* show evidence of the beginnings of the Middle Platonist movement, which is to be
dated to the period 50 BC to AD 50. However, a learned
writer, Philo of Alexandria (ca. 15 BC–AD 50), who was
certainly acquainted with early Middle Platonist writings,

[5] Diels, *Doxographi*, 45–49; see further MR 1.73–87. Doubt
has been cast on Diels' hypothesis by Frede, "Rev. Mansfeld-
Runia," and Gourinat, "Diels' Whodunit." For a refutation of
these doubts see MR 5.9–15; Mansfeld, "Theodoret."

[6] On the identity of the author, see further MR 1.320–23,
5.15–16, 5.119–20.

[7] As we shall often refer to this work, though the term ἐπιτομή
may not have been in the title of the work as a whole; see further
below, at nn. 10 and 25.

[8] Cited in 4.3.10. Note also the mention of Timaeus the astrologer at 5.18.2, who has been dated to the second half of the
first century BC.

[9] Below, section 1.5 at n. 54.

uses a doxographical manual very similar to the Aëtian *Placita* but does not know the compendium itself. The evidence thus seems to point in the direction of a date in the middle of the first century AD. As for the place of composition, the work itself gives no clues of any kind. Alexandria has been suggested, but this is no more than an educated guess. All that can be said is that the author must have had access to a considerable body of information on the doctrines of ancient philosophers. Further insight is obtained when we examine his method of composition, particularly the extent to which he relied on earlier doxographical traditions.

1.2. *Reconstruction of the Original Text*

The contribution that the three primary witnesses to the original text, Ps.-Plutarch, Stobaeus, and Theodoret, each makes to our knowledge of the compendium is dependent on the use that they made of it for their own purposes. Each witness therefore needs to be analyzed separately before the work can be reconstructed.

A practically complete Greek text of Ps.-Plutarch's Περὶ τῶν ἀρεσκόντων τοῖς φιλοσόφοις φυσικῶν δογμάτων (*On the Physical Tenets Accepted by the Philosophers*),[10] is extant in several Byzantine manuscripts, and also in a complete Arabic translation. Papyrus snippets of an early copy were found at Antinoopolis in Upper Egypt. The final pages of the Greek archetype were damaged. Fortunately, the Arabic translation has preserved lemmata

---

[10] On the title, see further below, section 1.3 at n. 25; on the textual witnesses, see further section 2.1.1 below.

that were later lost. A later further reduced version of the work made by Ps.-Galen adds a little more information.

A fundamental premise of the reconstruction is that the abridged version preserves the compendium's original structure in books and chapters with very little change. That this premise is justified can be proven through a comparison of the *Epitome* with the evidence of Stobaeus. The latter does not preserve the original structure to the same degree, but the order of his excerpts converges to such an extent with that of Ps.-Plutarch that, from a statistical point of view, it is vanishingly improbable that this occurred by chance. Moreover, it belongs to the general practice of ancient epitomators to reproduce the essential structure and contents of the original work while reducing the full extent of its length, although how this process was exactly carried out in each case depended on the particular kind of material contained in the original, as well as the purposes of the epitomator.

Further analysis of the *Epitome* reveals that Ps.-Plutarch preserves the structure of five books and almost all of their chapters. As a result it is best to retain this numbering in the reconstruction of the original.[11] It appears, however, that he deleted at least three chapters, which in the present edition receive the numbers 2.2a, 2.5a, and 4.7a. The main form of abridgment occurs within the individual chapters, and mostly through the deletion of lemmata within them. When lemmata are retained, they are usually written out verbatim and in full, but some-

---

[11] On a puzzling chapter number in the papyrus text, see the note to 5.4.

times long lemmata are reduced to a shortened form, and on rare occasions they are (not very successfully) combined. The epitomator also often shortens lists of name-labels, replacing them with inclusive formulae, e.g., in 2.1.1 "Thales" followed by ten names is replaced with "Thales and his followers" (the full text is preserved by Stobaeus). It is important to note, however, that generally speaking the dialectical structure of the chapters (to be discussed below) is preserved.[12]

The methods used by Stobaeus are different but complementary to those of Ps.-Plutarch. The first book of his mighty anthology with the title Ἐκλογῶν, ἀποφθε-γμάτων, ὑποθηκῶν, βιβλία τέσσαρα (Selected Passages, Sayings, Precepts, Four Books)[13] is almost entirely devoted to physics or natural philosophy. This book contains virtually all the material excerpted from the compendium, but it is not completely preserved. The introductory section containing the procemium is for the most part lost and its second half, from chapter 32 onward, was drastically bowdlerized by Byzantine editors, who for many chapters did little more than copy out the doxai of Plato and Aristotle, omitting the rest. Fortunately, these losses are partially compensated by another surviving anthology, the so-called Florentine sacro-profane Florilegium, which preserves six chapters of the book that are incomplete in

---

[12] For a full analysis of Ps.-Plutarch's abridgment techniques, see MR 1.182–95; also MR 5.3–6.

[13] This is the title found at Photius Bibl. cod. 167. It is called the Ἀνθολόγιον (Anthology) in the Suda. The first two books are also known by the title Eclogae, the final two books by the title Florilegium.

the two main directly transmitted manuscripts, as well as other evidence allowing us to gauge the extent of its original contents.[14]

On the basis of the preserved excerpts it can be concluded that Stobaeus, when he draws on the compendium, tends to copy it out *verbatim* and in full. But he does this in his own manner. He utilizes material from about 115 chapters out of Aëtius' original 135, but compresses it into fifty-two of the sixty chapters that his own book contains. The titles of many of these chapters are directly based on his source. But as a result of various interventions, the Aëtian material that he records is often substantially reorganized. For example, certain lemmata are replaced with material drawn from elsewhere. Platonic doxai may give way to quotations from the dialogues, those of Aristotle and the Stoics to excerpts from the handbook of Arius Didymus. Moreover, doxai with the same name-label but spread out over several chapters are coalesced together into a single cluster. Such methods mean that the order of lemmata in individual chapters can be seriously disturbed. Nevertheless, it is important to recognize that such clusters of coalesced Aëtian abstracts from several chapters constitute in each case an *enclave*, a micro-environment that is Aëtian. Accordingly, typically terse doxographical lemmata concerned with the topic(s) at issue in this environment can be safely attributed to Aëtius, even when they are irreducible in the sense that parallel lemmata in the other witnesses are lacking. This also occurs when he writes out an entire chapter that is missing elsewhere, e.g.,

14 On this manuscript (L), see further below, section 2.1.3.

at 4.7a. Occasionally, and notably at 2.28–32, he appears to tire of his normal methods of reorganization and writes out a sequence of chapters seemingly without any modification. Here we may be confident that we have direct access to the compendium's original text. For the most part, however, the editors must engage in detailed analysis, which can be compared to doing a jigsaw puzzle.[15] The results are not completely certain (unlike in a jigsaw puzzle, the pieces do not always perfectly interlock), but in most cases it is possible to credit them with a reasonable degree of confidence.

The procedure of the third witness, Theodoret, differs markedly from that of the other two. The purpose of his treatise Ἑλληνικῶν θεραπευτικὴ παθημάτων (*Cure of Greek Maladies*) was to defend the Christian faith against its opponents, among whom the pagan philosophers of the Greek tradition were prominent. Like his predecessor Eusebius (who also made extensive use of the *Placita*, but via Ps.-Plutarch's abridged version), he likes to cite the actual words of the thinkers he attempts to refute, but does not do this *verbatim*, preferring to produce a more literary product. The *Placita* were of course an ideal source for providing information on the many and varied doctrines of the philosophers. In four of the twelve books of the treatise, he includes extracts from the compendium: Book 2, "On the *archê*"; Book 4, "On matter and the cosmos"; Book 5, "On human nature"; and Book 6, "On divine providence." Following ancient custom, Theodoret prefers not

---

[15] For a detailed analysis of Stobaeus' methods, see MR 1.213–37, 5.6–9.

to name his source while actually quoting him, but, as we saw earlier,[16] he does include his name in a number of more general statements. The actual citations can be identified through comparison with the other two witnesses. Theodoret too in his excerpts preserved to a considerable degree the order attested by Ps.-Plutarch's abridged version.

The chief method that Theodoret uses to set out his borrowed material is the paraphrase.[17] He adapts the contents of the *Placita* to his purpose, introducing the topics of chapters in general terms and then rewriting the doxai in a compact reduced form, though occasionally adding extra details from his own knowledge when he thinks it suitable. Like Stobaeus, but in his own way, he thus produces clusters and enclaves of Aëtian material. This makes it possible from time to time to identify doxai that are not present in either of the other two witnesses, for example in 2.2a and 4.3–4. Theodoret's paraphrases are not of much value for determining the exact Greek text of the compendium. His priceless contribution to our knowledge is that he enables us to prove that there must have been a common anterior work utilized by all three witnesses, and that that text can be identified by its name and its author.[18]

The research on which the reconstruction and edition of the work is based allows us to determine the exact

16 See text above at n. 3.

17 For a detailed analysis of Theodoret's methods, see MR 1.276–84, 5.9–15.

18 See above, n. 5 and the references to MR 5.9–15, and Mansfeld, "Theodoret."

number of lemmata that each witness contributes to our knowledge of the work. The lemmata can be divided into seven categories:

in all three witnesses	55
in Ps.-Plutarch and Stobaeus	265
in Stobaeus and Theodoret	28
in Ps.-Plutarch and Theodoret	21
in Ps.-Plutarch only	222
in Stobaeus only	174
in Theodoret only	7

The total of the lemmata that have survived is 772. Ps.-Plutarch contributes 563, which is 73 percent of the whole; the remains of Stobaeus' excerpts reveal 522, which makes up 68 percent; while Theodoret discloses 111, which is 14 percent of the total.[19]

For chronological reasons Ps.-Plutarch cannot depend on the other witnesses. The independence of Stobaeus and Theodoret is demonstrated by the fact that they record lemmata that are not paralleled by lemmata in the other witnesses. As can be seen in the table above, Stobaeus and Theodoret share 28 lemmata that are not paralleled by lemmata in Ps.-Plutarch, so they cannot depend on the epitomator, and Theodoret shares 21 lemmata with Ps.-Plutarch that are not paralleled by lemmata in Stobaeus, so he cannot depend on Stobaeus. And it is hardly necessary to point out that the 265 lemmata shared by Ps.-Plutarch and Stobaeus that are not paralleled by lem-

---

[19] For these and other statistics, see MR 5.99–100. Because we have added chapter 2.2a to this edition, the numbers vary just a little from those presented in the larger edition.

mata in Theodoret show that Stobaeus does not depend on Theodoret. Our three chief witnesses are indisputably independent of each other.

We must add, however, that there is an eighth category that cannot be ignored but at the same time poses a seemingly insoluble problem: how many lemmata were present in the original compendium but were *not* taken up by *any* of the three witnesses? At this point, however, unexpected assistance is provided through the research undertaken by Edward Jeremiah. The Australian scholar discovered that the unusual structure of the Aëtian text, with its multitude of small discrete textual units, makes it "strangely suitable to quantitative methods of exploration."[20] Using advanced statistical techniques, he was able to give a probable answer to the question. A distinction can be made between chapters in which there are multiple witnesses (i.e., two or three) and chapters for which Ps.-Plutarch is the only witness. For the former, 87 in number, there are about 42 lemmata missing; for the latter, which constitute the remaining forty-eight chapters, the missing number may be expected to be about 81. This yields a total number of 123 for the eighth category of lemmata not taken up by any of the witnesses. We are thus in all likelihood in possession of about 86 percent, or six-sevenths of the original work, which would thus have contained 892 lemmata.[21] There is

[20] Jeremiah, "Statistical Explorations," 279.

[21] See full details of methodology and results in Jeremiah, "Statistical Explorations." He very properly gives confidence bounds for these results: for the former group these are for a 68 percent confidence interval between 31 and 52, for a 95 percent confidence interval between 23 and 62; for the latter group they are 78 and 85, and 75 and 89, respectively. The results for the entire work are bounds of 109 and 138, and 98 and 151, respectively.

no other text from the ancient world that, although lost in its original form, can be so fully reconstructed.[22] In this respect, too, the *Placita* of Aëtius is indeed a unique work.

1.3. *Title, Structure and Contents*

As already noted above,[23] Theodoret, in the second of the passages in which he enumerates the books that he has used for the purpose of expounding and refuting the disagreements of the philosophers, goes to the trouble of citing their titles. For Aëtius' work he invites his reader to study the Περὶ ἀρεσκόντων ξυναγωγή (*Cur.* 4.31). The noun *xunagôgê* (collection, compendium) could be taken as part of the title,[24] but it is more natural to read it as a description of the work with the title *Peri areskontôn*, i.e., *On (the) Placita*. A similar construction is used to refer to the abridged version of Ps.-Plutarch: the reader should study the Περὶ τῶν τοῖς φιλοσόφοις δοξάντων ἐπιτομήν, i.e., the epitome *On the Tenets of the Philosophers*.[25] In all probability, therefore, the lost original work had the title

---

[22] Comparison with other attempts to reconstruct lost ancient writings at Runia, "Irreducible Texts," 66–70.

[23] Section 1.1 at n. 3.

[24] For examples and full discussions of the title of the work, see MR 1.323–27; also 5.115–19.

[25] The Byzantine manuscripts of the work furnish a considerable variety of titles for the various books, but often indicating that the *placita* concerned are φυσικὰ δόγματα, i.e., pertaining to natural philosophy. The term ἐπιτομή in the nominative is used only for Book 2; Books 3 and 5 read ἐν ἐπιτομῇ. On these titles, see further MR 5.116–19.

Περὶ τῶν ἀρεσκόντων, *On the Placita* (the Latin equivalent is *De placitis*).[26]

The compendium is divided into five books, each of which had the length of a single papyrus roll. In the prooemium of the first book, which serves as the introduction to the entire work, the author states that its aim is to hand down the *physikos logos* (account of physics or natural philosophy), and that for this reason it is first necessary to divide up the discipline of philosophy, so that we may know what philosophy is and where physics comes in the order of its parts. True to the method of the *Placita*, he then gives two opinions on the matter, of the Stoics, on the one hand, and of Aristotle, Theophrastus, and the Peripatetics, on the other (1.prooem.2–3). But, starting at Book 2 he also includes a number of additional brief prooemia that, taken together, indicate the subject matter of all five books. In the proem to Book 2 he first looks back to the previous book and says he has completed his account of "principles (*archai*) and elements and what is closely associated with them," and then says he will turn to "the account concerned with the products (*apotelesmata*), starting with the most comprehensive of all things," i.e., the cosmos. In the proem to Book 3, the same method is used. He first looks back at the previous book, which gave "the account of the things in the heavens (*ta ourania*)," and then announces that he will turn to "the things on high (*ta*

26 If the shorter title Περὶ ἀρεσκόντων is accepted, the article τῶν should be added, as in the title of Ps.-Plutarch as found in the manuscripts (and also in MR). It is possible that, just like in the case of the abridged version, the title of the original work made reference to the "physical tenets," but we consider this to be less likely.

metarsia)." It is further indicated that he is moving from the periphery to the center, and so he now starts with the meteorological phenomena in the sublunary part of the cosmos. Then, midway through the book, when these phenomena have been discussed (in 3.1–8), he interposes another authorial comment, stating that "the things on high" have been described and that the account will now proceed to "the things on earth (*ta prosgeia*)." These subjects occupy the remainder of the book (3.9–17). Book 4 then begins once again with a procemium: "the parts (*merê*) of the cosmos having now been treated systematically," i.e., in Books 2 and 3, and now he will move to the "particular phenomena (*ta kata merê*)." What these latter are is not further explained. After a chapter on the Nile, which continues the treatment of the previous book, the remainder of Book 4 discusses questions on the soul. Finally, in Book 5 topics are pursued in which the role of the body becomes more prominent. The division between the last two books is not very precise, as is perhaps only to be expected, since body needs soul in order to live, but soul also needs the instrumentation of the body in order to carry out many of its functions.[27]

The contents of the work can therefore be summarized as follows: Book 1, First Principles; Book 2, Cosmology; Book 3, Meteorology and the Earth; Book 4, Psychology; Book 5, Physiology. Like Plato's *Timaeus* and Aristotle's series of physical treatises, it begins with the first principles and related subjects, moves on to the physical world, starting with the universe as a whole, and then advances

[27] On the division between Books 4 and 5, see further the Introductions to the two books.

from the heavenly bodies on high to the earth here below. The final important distinction is between cosmic parts and particular things. The latter group mainly comes down to human beings and their key features, though a few chapters discuss living beings more generally.[28] The principal features of this pattern are already found in mythical cosmologies (e.g., Hesiod's *Theogony* and the biblical *Book of Genesis*): first, the environment, then, the human being.

The five books are further divided into chapters, each with its own heading indicating the particular topic or question being discussed. For these chapter headings a variety of formulas are used. By far the most common used is the umbrella type "about x" (*peri tou deina*), simply indicating the topic. Other formulas are more specific, e.g., inquiring about the essence or nature (what it is), the location (where it is), its quality (of what kind), its quantity (how big, how many), the cause (how), and so on. It will be recognized that these formulas make use of the schemata of the Aristotelian categories and question types, reflecting the origin of the *Placita*'s method, as will be discussed in the following subsection.

The chapters of each book generally follow a logical order in accordance with their subject matter, although there are a few oddities. There are, for example, series of chapters on particular subjects, such as the cosmos (2.1–8), the heavenly bodies (2.11–19), the sun (2.20–24), the moon (2.25–31), the earth (3.9–14), the nature and characteristics of the soul (4.2–7a), spermatology and conception (5.3–14), and so on. The chapters on the sun and

[28] Especially 5.19–20; see further the introduction to Book 5.

the moon very clearly illustrate the use of categories, discussing in sequence the topics of substance (*ousia*), size (*megethos*), shape (*schêma*), motion, as well as special features, such as eclipses, illuminations, distances, and the moon's face.

In order to guide the reader further, the author has placed a table of contents (pinax, index) of the chapter headings at the beginning of each book. These are found only in the manuscripts of Ps.-Plutarch's epitome,[29] so the question might be raised whether they were already found in the lost original of Aëtius. There is a good deal of evidence to show that by the first century AD, professional and didactic treatises as a rule included such tables of contents, so we consider it probable that this was case here too and we have included them in the text of the edition.[30]

The final step in the articulation of the compendium's contents takes place within the individual chapters themselves. These consist in a number of lemmata ranging from one (only in exceptional cases) to as many as twenty or more, but generally averaging between five to eight per chapter. It is by means of the arrangement of these lemmata that our author constructs and organizes the contents of the *physikos logos*, using a variety of methods and techniques. In order to understand these key features of the work, it will now be necessary to delve deeper into the method that it uses to achieve its aims.

[29] In most Byzantine manuscripts, and also in one manuscript of the Arabic translation, on which see MR 1.115–16.

[30] See discussion at MR 1.122–25; also Mansfeld, "Helping the Reader." On their treatment in Diels' edition, see below at n. 92.

1.4. *Chapters and Lemmata: The Role of Dialectic*

The lemma is the basic building-block of the *Placita*. At the micro-level of the individual chapter, the topics and questions of natural philosophy are discussed and answered through the formulation and ordering of a body of lemmata, each for the most part representing a distinct view on the subject. The lemmata themselves have two main components, the name-label and an accompanying *doxa* (view, opinion, tenet), or *placitum*.

The name-label is most often an individual philosopher, but scientists and doctors are also included, as well as group designations, such as schools or followers of a particular philosopher or anonymi. Names are also often grouped together in multiple name-labels, varying from two to as many as eleven thinkers who hold the same view. Early in the work philosophers are introduced with patronymic and ethnicon, and elsewhere further limited information is sometimes given on individual names.

The doxa is a brief statement of the opinion that the philosopher holds on the subject of the chapter. In the majority of cases the formulation is terse, even telegrammatic. Often a verb of saying or declaration is used, but no less often this verb is elided, and the subject matter of the doxa too is assumed from the indispensable heading that begins every chapter. At the extreme limit a lemma can consist of two words only, as is the case at 2.25.9, where in response to the subject of the moon's substance (*ousia*) we find a lemma stating no more than: "Thales earthy" (*Thales geôdê*), i.e., the name-label and a single adjective giving the doxa. In the translation a verb of saying and the subject have to be supplied: "Thales (says that) (it, i.e., the moon's substance, is) earthy." Most lemmata are of course longer, and there can even be quite lengthy examples in which detailed information is given on the view held by the philosopher(s) in question. Even in these cases, however, the content is nearly always thetically formulated, without argumentation of any kind.

Within the chapter a further ordering process takes place. Because lemmata in each case represent a single position on the subject, they have to be organized. For this purpose the author employs dialectical techniques that go back to the origins of doxography in the Peripatos of Aristotle and Theophrastus. Series of lemmata are structured in basic configurations involving diaeresis (division), opposition (diaphonia), and lists organized in various ways, which taken together give systematic answers to the topics and questions involved. In practice, therefore, the minimum number of lemmata in a chapter is two, giving a positive and a negative answer on a question if it poses a dilemma, or two main positions if it does not. Most chapters, of course, present a larger number of views, which are organized with greater or lesser success, resulting in a multidimensional perspective on the subject.

On some occasions chapters commence with a nominal definition, either unattributed or preceded by a name-label, in order to get the discussion underway.[31] The main positions on the subject are commonly indicated through a diaeresis, which can be further subdivided by other distinctions between views.[32] A very common technique is

[31] Examples: unattributed definition, 1.9 (matter), 1.10 (idea), etc.; attributed definition, 2.1 (Pythagoras on cosmos), 4.19 (Plato on voice), etc.

[32] Examples of chapters with main and subordinate diaereses: 1.7 (on theology), 2.9 (on void), 5.2 (on divination), and passim.

the diaphonia, which presents two views that are opposed to each other, whether exclusively (A and not-A) or just as two main options (A or B), with sometimes a third compromise view added.[33] In the case of a larger number of views, these may be structured by means of a list, which can be further organized, e.g., by number (ascending or descending), by location (from whole to part, top to bottom), by prominence (standard view placed first), and so on.[34] Often there are multiple diaereses in a single chapter, either the one nestled within another or presented in sequence. If there are unusual or ancillary views on the subject, these are mostly relegated to the chapter's end.[35] The upshot is that, by means of these techniques, a chapter presents a structured and (more or less) systematic overview of the answers that can be given on a particular topic or question. In the translation, at the head of each chapter, we give a brief summary of the main structural features that it contains.[36]

It is important to observe that historical information relevant to the development of views is by no means neglected. The presence of name-labels in almost every

33 Examples of diaphoniae: exclusive, 4.2–3 (soul); two main options, 2.20 (sun); with third compromise view, 3.13 (motion of earth).

34 Examples of lists: 2.2 (shapes of cosmos); organized by number, 1.23 (on kinds of motion), 4.4 (on parts of soul); by location, 4.5 (on regent part of soul) (top to bottom); by prominence, 2.3 (on providence), 2.24 (on solar eclipse).

35 Examples of unusual views at the end of chapters: 2.13 (on stars' substance, no view rejected), 2.24 (sun disappears into an uninhabited part of the earth), 5.16 (nourishment of embryo).

36 See further below, section 3.3.

lemma necessarily brings such features to the fore. Philosophers and other thinkers are introduced with their ethnicon,[37] with sometimes other details added, including occasional references to writings. The Ionic and Italian successions, beginning with Thales and Pythagoras, play a significant role, not only when explicitly adduced, but also more subtly in the organization of chapters.[38] On a number of occasions the motif of the "first discoverer" of a particular theory or doctrine or key term is noted, generally at the beginning of a chapter.[39] Chapters also reveal the influence of chronology in the ordering of their lemmata.[40] Indeed, a palpable tension between historical and systematic aspects of the philosophical enterprise pervades the entire work. There can be no doubt, however, that the latter have the upper hand. The compendium is not a historical account of the development of Greek philosophy, even though it supplies a good deal of material

[37] With the exception of Xenocrates in 1.7.21, patronymics are mentioned only in 1.3, on the *archai*.

[38] Successions (*diadochai*) are first mentioned in 1.3.1 (Thales, Ionic philosophy, repeated in 1.3.6, then further elaborated with the mention of the Italic school and Pythagoras in 1.3.8). They are most prominent in the structure of 1.3 and 1.7, but note for example the first position of Thales, Anaximander, and Pythagoras in many chapters, esp. in Book 2. See further the Introductions to individual books, where variation in the balance between historical and systematic aspects of the five books is noted.

[39] Examples at 1.3.7, 2.1.1, 2.12.2 (Pythagoras); 2.24.1, 2.28.5 (Thales).

[40] Chronological ordering is particularly prominent in 3.10–12, 3.15, and 4.1.

for such an account. This has everything to do with its own historical roots in earlier Greek philosophy.

1.5. *Origins and Anterior Traditions*

From the outset Greek philosophers engaged in discussion with each other. Famously, the first three Milesians credited with initiating the practice of philosophy had differing ideas on the principles of reality. Heraclitus attacked the views of all others when presenting his *logos*. Evidence suggests that the sophist Hippias already collected and made a start on organizing the views that were current in his day. Another sophist, Gorgias, presents us with examples of contrasting views. Traces of such organization can also be found in Plato, for example, in the oppositions he sees between the holders of views on key doctrines.[41] Aristotle was the first, as far as we know, to commence his treatments of a topic with a survey of views held on it by earlier thinkers. But this practice must be seen in a wider context.[42]

As a philosopher and a scientist, Aristotle regarded it as a chief aim of human endeavor to build up a body of true demonstrable knowledge that ideally could be formulated in terms of propositions linked together through the iron rules of categorical logic. However, this was not the

[41] Notably between Heraclitus and Parmenides in *Tht*. 152e, 180e, and between the "friends of the body" and the "friends of the forms" in *Soph*. 246a–d.

[42] For what follows see further MR 5.78–85; Mansfeld, *"Physikai Doxai"*; Runia, "What is Doxography?"; Mansfeld, "Doxography."

path to discovering that knowledge. For that process another method had to be followed, which we, using his own term, may call dialectical. Aristotle envisaged a process that would commence not only with observation but also with the analysis of knowledge that humans had already acquired, namely the so-called *endoxa*, "reputable opinions." These would also include the views of earlier philosophers.

In his treatise on dialectic and its methods, Aristotle sets out a program involving the selection and classification of propositions and problems:[43]

> We should also make selections from the literature and include these in separate lists for each set, with separate headings, for instance "On the Good," or "On the Living Being"—that is to say the Good as a whole, starting with (the question) "what is it?" One should cite the doxai of individual thinkers, e.g., that Empedocles said that the elements of bodies are four in number. . . . Of propositions and problems there are—to comprehend the matter in outline—three sets: some are ethical, others physical, others again logical. Ethical: for instance (the problem) whether one should obey one's parents or the law, when these disagree with each other. Logical: for instance (the problem) whether the knowledge of opposites is the same, or not. Physical: for instance (the problem) whether the cosmos is everlasting or not.

[43] *Top.* 1.14 105b12–25, cited at Mansfeld, *"Physikai Doxai,"* 73. For the Empedoclean doxa, cf. *Plac.* 1.3.19; for the example of the physical problem given at the end of the quote, cf. 2.4.

We can discern here the origin of the method of the *Placita* in a nutshell. Topics and problems should be investigated by means of the collection and analysis of doxai, views commonly held or developed by experts. The terminology of "problems" (*problêmata*) and "topics of investigation," or "questions" (*zetêmata, quaestiones*) goes back to Aristotle.[44] These were to be organized through the use of techniques such as the diaeresis and the application of the categories and question types in the formulation of problems. Such analyses could be used as a starting point for the exposition of the results of research.

A clear example is found at the beginning of Aristotle's treatise on the soul:[45]

> For our study of soul it is necessary, when formulating the problems of which in our further advance we are to find the solutions, to summon the doxai of our predecessors, so that we may profit by whatever is sound in their suggestions and avoid their errors. The starting-point of our inquiry is to put forward those features that have been thought to belong to it by its very nature.

The topics that he would have had in mind are precisely those that centuries later were distilled in Book 4 of the *Placita*. There is evidence to suggest that in the Peripatos, the school or research institute that he established, Aris-

---

[44] See for example *Top.* 1.14 104b18 (cited above), *de An.* 1.1 402a12, etc.

[45] *De An.* 1.2 403b20–25, cited at Runia, "What is Doxography?," 49.

totle and his chief collaborator Theophrastus set up a project in which the chief opinions of earlier philosophers were recorded and summarized, providing a documentary basis for the kind of research that he envisaged. It is certainly the case that the core of both the dialectical method and the information in the formulation of doxai of the *Placita* goes back to the Peripatos of Aristotle and Theophrastus. This explains, for example, the high proportion of material on the early Greek philosophers of the sixth and fifth centuries BC, much of which is uniquely preserved in Aëtius, sometimes even in Aristotle's own words.

A most interesting remnant of this early dialectical history is found in the rare places that Aëtius argues against a doctrine that he records. In the entire work he is almost always studiously neutral, just giving terse accounts of the philosophers' opinions and hardly ever mentioning arguments of any kind. But on four occasions he states that they are mistaken, or words to that effect.[46] The terminology of *hamartanein* (being mistaken) used each time goes back to Aristotle and Theophrastus, for whom "making objections" was part and parcel of the dialectical method.[47] No doubt Aëtius took these passages over from his source. Whether he himself agreed with them or not is something that we cannot know for certain.

[46] *Plac.* 1.2.2 (Thales on *archê* and *stoicheion*); 1.3.2–3 (Anaximander and Anaximenes on neglecting the efficient cause); 1.7.1[35] (against Anaxagoras' and Plato's demiurgic theology).

[47] See MR 5.196, where the phrase ποιεῖται τὰς ἐνστάσεις is quoted from Theophrastus *Phys.dox.* fr. 11a Diels = fr. 241A FHS&G.

The early history of how collections of early philosophical views were converted into works of doxography that
laid the foundation for later compendia such as the *Placita*
is obscure. Diels was convinced that the *Physikai doxai*
(views on nature) of Theophrastus, which he wrongly gave
the title *Physikôn doxai* (views of the natural philosophers), played a key role in this development.[48] But we do
not know enough about the work to be sure of this. The
two mentions of Theophrastus at *Plac.* 2.20.5 and 2.29.8
most likely refer to his *Physics*. In the *Letter to Pythocles*
of Epicurus there is evidence that, as early as the beginning of the third century BC, he used material of a doxographical kind for cosmological, meteorological, and psychological topics.[49] Later in the same century the Stoic
philosopher Chrysippus drew attention to the disagreements of the philosophers on the seat of the regent part
(cf. *Plac.* 4.5), a passage that indisputably relies on material similar to what we find in the *Placita*.[50]

In the meantime the landscape of Greek philosophy
had changed. New schools and new names of greater and
lesser fame had come to the fore, necessitating a process
of updating name-labels and doxai on a considerable scale.
This is most apparent in the case of the Stoic school. There
are parts of the work where Stoic influence is very strong,
taking up entire chapters, for example, on theology (1.6)
and epistemology (4.11–12, 21), and also forming a dominant presence in entire sections, for example, on first prin-

[48] Diels, *Doxographi*, 119–44; on the role of Theophrastus,
see further MR 5.82–85; on the title, MR 5.83.

[49] See MR 5.72 and Runia, "Epicurus and the *Placita*."

[50] See MR 5.72 and Mansfeld, "Chrysippus and the *Placita*."

ciples (1.18–29), psychology and epistemology (4.8–20), and heredity (5.10–14). In addition, comparison with the extended doxography of the Stoic *physikos logos* in Diogenes Laertius *VP* 7.132–59 shows that it too has exerted influence on the general structure of the *Placita*, not only in the introductory section (1.1–8) but also throughout the rest of the work.[51] One may in fact speak of a broad Stoic overlay that has been imposed on the original Peripatetic foundation of the compendium. The process of updating has also included names and doxai from other Hellenistic schools, notably Epicureans and later Peripatetics. Academic and skeptical influence appears to have been less marked but may have been felt in the extended use of diaphoniae and other techniques that illustrate the prevalence of extensive disagreement among the philosophers.

The process of updating with new material will have continued throughout the first century BC, but the inclusion of new name-labels starts to peter out. Very few philosophers or scientists (including doctors) are included who were active after 100 BC. One can point only to Posidonius, Asclepiades, and Xenarchus. What we do see are authors such as Varro, Philodemus, Cicero, and a little later on Philo of Alexandria, making extensive use of doxographical material that often parallels what is found in the *Placita*. Diels postulated that this evidence pointed to an earlier edition, which he dubbed the *Vetusta placita*, that would have formed the basis of Aëtius' compendium.[52] But there is no evidence for such an edition. It is

[51] On this influence, see further MR 2.1.97–110.

[52] Diels, *Doxographi*, 181–85; on this hypothesis, see MR 5.28–30.

better to think of a gradual process of updating that took place in dialectical-doxographical works of various kinds, some of which will have retained or further developed the method of using name-labels and doxai such as we find in the *Placita*.[53]

There is one further development in the compendium as we have it that still needs be pointed out. The prominence of the philosopher Pythagoras is striking. Not only is he, as already noted,[54] foregrounded as the instigator of the Italian succession of early philosophers, resulting in his being attributed with a doxa on first principles that is one of the longest in the whole work (1.3.7), he is also often associated with Plato for views that are based on the latter's cosmological dialogue, the *Timaeus*.[55] The prominence of the three first principles of God, matter, and idea in 1.7–11 is another striking innovation.[56] These features reveal clear affinities with the movements of Neopythagoreanism and Middle Platonism that were occurring around the beginning of our era, just preceding the composition of the work.[57] They can be regarded as constituting a second overlay, which like the first Stoic one was grafted on the original Aristotelian and Peripatetic stock, though far less extensive in its scope.

[53] See the evaluative comments at MR 5.76.

[54] See above, n. 38.

[55] Examples at 1.7.20 (theology), 2.6.4–6 (cosmology), 5.19–20 (genera of living beings).

[56] Also the use of "prepositional metaphysics" in 1.11, on causes.

[57] See comments at MR 2.52, 86, 99, etc.; 5.73. Detailed analysis in Runia, "The Reception of Plato in the Aëtian *Placita*."

1.6. *Purpose, Contemporary Context, and Later Reception*

At no stage does our author give any indication of the purpose he had in mind when composing his work. All he says in the opening words is that he intends to hand down the account of physics. This could indicate a scholastic context, but such a hypothesis is far from necessary and probably too narrow.[58] The intent is best taken in a very general sense. What the compendium provides is above all a multipurpose *resource*, a manual of neatly packaged material on a wide variety of topics—to be used for study and as an *aide-memoire*, for displays of erudition, for persuasion in rhetorical or apologetic contexts, and so on. Several treatises of this nature, namely Aëtius' continuations Ps.-Plutarch and the even shorter Ps.-Galen, are still extant, and they will not have been the only ones. The first book of Stobaeus, containing a wealth of abstracts on physics, serves a similar purpose.

The work should thus be placed in a broad dialectical-doxographical context that we have called its "proximate tradition."[59] There are at least fifty authors writing in both Greek and Latin in the period from the first century BC to the end of antiquity who utilize this tradition for their own various purposes. These include Varro, Cicero, and Philo, mentioned in the previous section. One particularly

---

[58] The reference in 2.23.8, to the "sphere," a model of the heavens, implies a teaching context, but in itself proves little. It could also have been taken over from a source.

[59] See the discussions at MR 5.43–44, 69–78.

interesting example is Achilles, the third-century AD author of a work *On the Universe* (*De universo*), which was recycled as an introduction to the astronomical poem of Aratus. Its forty chapters on cosmological topics overlap to such an extent with the contents of Aëtius' Book 2 that they can be called "cousin writings,"[60] drawing on the same tradition but not directly related. Another author writing at about the same time, Censorinus, drew on a richer version of the *Placita* through the mediation of Varro, exhibiting remarkable parallels to the contents of Book 5 (and also 2.32). By contrast Seneca, very likely an exact contemporary of Aëtius, in his meteorological work *Naturales quaestiones*, offers numerous parallels to the contents of Book 3, but these are nowhere near as close, so must have been based on a broader tradition that goes back to Aristotle's *Meteorology*. A quite different example is the prolific doctor and medical author Galen, a contemporary of the epitomator Ps.-Plutarch. He is well-acquainted with the dialectical method used by the wider tradition of the *placita* and often uses various *quaestiones* as examples in his medical and philosophical writings.[61] But for the specific contents of Book 5 on physiology, the parallels he offers are rather limited. Due to the limitations of the Loeb edition format, we cannot include refer-

[60] See the discussion at MR 5.65–66. The text of this little-known work has been edited by Di Maria, *Achillis quae feruntur*, but there are as yet no translations into modern languages. Because the doxographical traditions it uses are so close to the *Placita*, in MR it is cited as a secondary witness. See further section 2.1.4 below.

[61] See the discussion in Tieleman, "Presocratics and Presocratic Philosophy in Galen."

ences to these proximate and broader traditions in the present volume. The reader is referred to our fuller edition of Aëtius' work, which offers a full selection of such "further related texts."[62]

The broad multipurpose nature of the work will have facilitated its reception after its publication. As far as our knowledge extends, the direct reception of the work was limited to the three authors who are witnesses to the original text. The purposes for which they cited its contents have already been discussed.[63] The further reception of the work is limited to the tradition of Ps.-Plutarch's *Epitome*, which was widely utilized and disseminated for another millennium. Speaking in general terms, there are two main lines of reception. One of these has a positive appreciation of the information that it contains on the Greek philosophers and their views on natural philosophy. For Ps.-Plutarch, Ps.-Galen,[64] Stobaeus, and the translator Qusṭā, this motivation is obvious, and it also applies to the Byzantine authors Lydus, Psellus, and Simeon Seth in their selective use of the work. The other line of tradition is represented by Christian authors. They find the *Placita* a most useful collection for the purpose of demonstrating the hopeless and reprehensible disagreements of the ancient philosophers among each other, in emphatic contrast

---

[62] In section E of each chapter in the commentary sections of MR, as explained at 5.92–93.

[63] Section 1.2 above.

[64] In chapter 2 of his work, which is not based on Ps.-Plutarch, Ps.-Galen states that he is writing for lovers of learning, so that they will not be in need of further explanations but can get to know for themselves all the details of what has been said (sc. by the philosophers).

to the unified doctrine of the Christian faith. After the apologist Athenagoras, Eusebius cites large sections of the *Epitome* in his *Praeparatio evangelica*, followed by Ps.-Justin and his *Cohortatio ad Graecos* and Cyril and his *Contra Julianum*. This apologetic appropriation finds its apogee in the work of Theodoret, which proved so important for the survival of Aëtius' original compendium.[65]

2. HISTORY AND RECONSTRUCTION OF THE TEXT

2.1. *The Witnesses to the Text*

Because Aëtius' *Placita* has not been transmitted in its original form, reconstruction of its text must be based on the evidence of the three witnesses who made direct use of it. Each of these must first be studied separately, starting with Ps.-Plutarch, who is not only the oldest witness but also acquired a highly complex tradition involving both direct and indirect transmission. In the case of all three witnesses, we confine our discussion to those aspects that are relevant for the text as presented in this volume. For a much more detailed discussion, the reader is referred to the fuller edition.[66]

2.1.1. Ps.-Plutarch and His Tradition

The earliest directly transmitted text of the *Epitome* is the third-century AD papyrus found at Antinoopolis in Upper

[65] For an analysis of the use of the *Placita* by the church fathers, see Runia, "The Aëtian *Placita* and the Church Fathers."
[66] See MR 5.45–69

Egypt.[67] It consists of twelve small fragments from what was evidently a complete codex of the work. Regrettably, the surviving textual material is too scanty to be of much help for an edition of the text.

The full text of the work is transmitted in an almost complete form in about twenty Byzantine manuscripts. Of these only five are of independent importance:

Family	Manuscript and Siglum	Date
I	Mosquensis 339 (M)	12th c.
II	Marcianus 521 (m)	13th/14th c.
III	Planudean family	
	Ambrosianus 859 (a)	shortly before 1296
	Parisinus 1671 (A)	1296
	Parisinus 1672 (E)	shortly after 1302

All these manuscripts are derived from a single archetype to be dated to about AD 1000. It was damaged toward the end, but fortunately additional material is found in some indirect witnesses, as will be described below. The present edition notes variants in the Byzantine manuscripts only on rare occasions, using the sigla P^1 and P^2. Modern editions of the Byzantine text will be discussed below.

The earliest indirect witness to copy out substantial sections of the *Epitome*'s text is Eusebius of Caesarea (ca. 263–339). In his *Praeparatio evangelica* he copies out *verbatim* 187 lemmata from forty-one chapters, amounting to about a third of the entire work. Eusebius' citations

---

[67] Edited by Barns, "[Plutarch], *Epitome de Placitis Philosophorum.*"

are generally very accurate, but on occasions he tampers with the text or shortens it, for example in the chapter headings. For the text we use the excellent edition of K. Mras.[68]

At an unknown date, but not later than the fifth century AD, an unknown author produced a further epitomization of the *Epitome* as part of a work entitled the *Philosophos historia (Philosophical history)*, which was pseudonymously attributed to Galen and whose author is now referred to as Ps.-Galen. In the first part of the work, chapters 1 to 24, which is a general introduction to philosophy, the author cites only limited material from 1.1 and 1.30. The remainder of the work, chapters 25 to 133, is an abridged version of the five books of Ps.-Plutarch's manual, amounting to 110 of the total of 133 chapters, of which sixty-two are cited with all their lemmata intact. However, unlike Ps.-Plutarch himself (and also Eusebius), Ps.-Galen does not aim in his abridgment to retain the actual words of his source, but continually makes changes to them, as can be seen by comparing his text with its source. However, as a very early witness, he often preserves readings that are superior to the direct tradition of the Byzantine manuscripts. In addition, he also preserves a number of lemmata that fell away in those manuscripts, mainly toward the end of the work. Remarkably, there is no more recent edition of the whole work than that of Diels, in the *Doxographi graeci*, so it is the one we have to use.[69] Very recently M. Jas has edited fifty chapters of the work, com-

68 Mras, *Eusebius Werke* VIII.1–2.
69 Diels, *Doxographi*, 597–648.

paring them with the 1341 Latin translation of Nicolaus of Rhegium and demonstrating that for these chapters Nicolaus used a separate hyparchetype. We make use of these very thoroughly edited chapters when available.[70]

Many centuries later a complete translation of the work into Arabic was made by the Syrian Christian Qusṭā ibn Lūqā (in Latin, Constans Lucae filius, ca. 840–912). The translation is basically a faithful reproduction of the Greek text, though of course allowance must be made for all manner of minor modifications introduced by the translator. It is thus a valuable witness to the original text and also includes a number of lemmata at the end of the work that are missing in the Byzantine manuscripts. The translation has been carefully edited by H. Daiber, who also comments on aspects of the translation that are relevant for establishing the text of Ps.-Plutarch.[71]

The last writer that must be taken into consideration is the Byzantine humanist Michael Psellus. In his handbook *De omnifaria doctrina*, sixty-eight chapter headings are taken from the *Epitome*, and a limited amount of text is also copied out, though almost never the name-labels. For this work we use the excellent edition of L. G. Westerink.[72]

---

70 Jas, *Nicolaus Rheginus*. She was also able to make use of two further manuscripts that were not available to Diels.

71 Daiber, *Aetius Arabus*. The title of his edition, though mellifluous, is unfortunate, since Qusṭā translated the *Epitome* of Ps.-Plutarch, and not Aëtius' original text. On the changed manner of presentation of the Arabic text in this edition compared with MR, see below, section 3.2.

72 Westerink, *Michael Psellus*.

Most regrettably, there is no modern critical edition of the *Epitome* that takes proper account of the full extent of this complex tradition. Diels' edition was primarily based on the Byzantine manuscripts, but he understood the value of Ps.-Galen's evidence and quite often used it to improve the text. He did not, however, have access to the papyrus or to Qusṭā's Arabic translation. J. Mau's edition in the Bibliotheca Teubneriana is very disappointing.[73] He does not know Qusṭā,[74] scarcely uses Ps.-Galen, and adheres far too closely to the defective text of the Byzantine manuscripts, accepting many of the obvious errors without any attempt to emend them. The edition of G. Lachenaud in the Belles Lettres series is an improvement.[75] Though in many regards it follows its predecessor quite closely, it does take the evidence of the papyrus, Ps.-Galen, and Qusṭā into account. But it also displays too conservative an approach to the text. In the present edition, in lieu of using a single edition, we have evaluated all the components of the tradition afresh and given them their appropriate weight, in order to ensure that the evidence of this key witness is as fully and accurately utilized as possible.

2.1.2. Stobaeus

For the *Eclogae* of Stobaeus there are only three manuscripts of any significance:

[73] Mau, *Plutarchi Moralia*.
[74] He could have used Daiber's 1968 dissertation, on which the later edition was based.
[75] Lachenaud, *Plutarque Œuvres morales*.

Siglum	Manuscript	Date
F (Farnesinus)	Neapolitanus III D 15	14 c.
P	Parisinus gr. 2129	15 c.
L	Laurentianus Pluteus 8.22	14 c.

This work was most recently edited by C. Wachsmuth as long ago as 1884.[76] Fortunately, the editing was capably done.[77] It is primarily based on the two main manuscripts F and P, but it also fully incorporates the evidence of L, which, as noted above,[78] does not provide a complete text, but only some excerpts accompanied by sections of the original index of Stobaeus' *Anthology*. A feature of Wachsmuth's edition that must be taken into account is that it was strongly influenced by Diels' treatment of the Stobaean evidence in the *Doxographi graeci* that had appeared only five years earlier, agreeing with the main lines of his source analysis and even going so far as to include the numbering of the reconstruction of the *Placita* in the main body of the text. Only on very rare occasions do we refer to variants in the manuscript tradition.[79]

Valuable additional evidence for Stobaeus' work is also provided by the Byzantine patriarch Photius (ca. 810–ca. 895) in the *Bibliotheca*, a digest of his reading of ancient Greek writers up to his own time. Photius still had access

[76] Wachsmuth, *Ioannis Stobaei*. A new edition is being prepared by T. Dorandi.

[77] See the evaluation by Royse, "The Text of Stobaeus."

[78] See text above at n. 14.

[79] In 2.5.3 Stobaeus quotes the same lemma twice (the only time he does this). The variants this yields are indicated with the sigla S^1 and S^2.

to the *Anthology* in its complete form. He provides a full index to the work and also compiled long lists of the names of ancient authors mentioned in it. For his account in *Bibl.* 167 we use the edition of R. Henry.[80] The contribution of the dissertation of A. Elter should also be noted.[81] To his credit, he was able to decipher the rationale of Photius' quasi-alphabetical list of names. Elter also noted that the index of the second half of *Eclogae* Book 1 in the manuscript L was contaminated with a limited number of chapter headings and at least one lemma from Ps.-Plutarch's *Epitome*, which Diels had not realized when preparing his reconstruction and edition of the *Placita*.[82]

2.1.3. Theodoret and Other Witnesses

In comparison with the other primary witnesses, the textual transmission of Theodoret's treatise is much more straightforward. For the text we use the edition of J. Raeder that, although also published more than a century ago, is adequate for our purposes.[83] Raeder notes in his apparatus the sections of Theodoret's text that are based on the *Placita*, utilizing the results of the analysis of his earlier dissertation, which is heavily dependent on Diels' work.[84] The text and German translation pub-

---

80 Henry, *Photius*; text in 2.149–59.

81 Elter, *De Ioannis Stobaei codice Photiano*.

82 See Diels' response to Elter's study, "Stobaios und Aëtios."

83 Raeder, *Theodoreti* Graecarum affectionum curatio.

84 Raeder, *Quaestiones criticae*. But note that in the app. crit. of the edition he refers to the pages of Diels' text only, not to the individual chapters and lemmata based on Ps.-Plutarch, and also not to the parallel texts in Stobaeus.

lished recently by C. Scholten is based on Raeder's edition.[85]

Beside the three primary witnesses, the only other secondary witness to which we refer in this edition is Achilles. His doxographical extracts included in the treatise *De universo* are so close to the *Placita* that they can provide some assistance in the reconstruction of the latter. For this purpose we use the edition of Di Maria, which has now superseded the edition of Maass.[86]

2.2. *Previous Editions*

So far there have been only two editions of Aëtius' compendium, the trailblazing reconstruction and edition by Diels (1879), followed by that of Mansfeld and Runia (2020), on which the present edition is based. Though the two editions share a number of common features, and Mansfeld and Runia are very conscious of the debt they owe to their predecessor, the methodology of the two differs in a number of significant respects. This will become clear in the descriptions that now follow.

2.2.1. Diels' *Doxographi graeci*

The edition of the *Placita* is the centerpiece of Diels' *Doxographi graeci*.[87] The other texts that he collected and

[85] Scholten, *Theodoret*, who continues Raeder's practice of minimal reference in his app. crit. The edition of Canivet, *Théodoret de Cyr*, in the Sources chrétiennes series, scarcely differs from that of Raeder.

[86] Di Maria, *Achillis quae feruntur*; Maass, *Commentariorum in Aratum reliquiae*. See further above at n. 60.

[87] Diels, *Doxographi*, 273–444.

edited (and that justify the plural of the title) were included in order to complement the contents of the main work and further elucidate its wider context. The lengthy "Prolegomena" laid the foundation of the work, setting out in nineteen subsections, first, the textual traditions of the witnesses, then putting forward the hypothesis of Aëtian authorship, followed by lengthy analyses of the sources of the *Placita* and the broad extent of the doxographical tradition in which it must be situated.[88]

The key feature of the edition is that it is presented in two columns: on the left, Ps.-Plutarch, on the right, Stobaeus. Both texts are edited on the basis of their manuscript transmission, with an apparatus criticus containing all the important textual variants beneath. Lemmata shared by both witnesses are placed side by side as much as possible. The joint numbering of the lemmata is located in the narrow space between the two columns, the numbers themselves "interlocking like the teeth of a zipper."[89] At the top of each page a horizontal brace links up the columns, with the heading above it indicating the book and chapter in the reconstructed work. Below the left column there is a second apparatus entitled *testimonia Plutarchi* containing excerpts preserved in Achilles,[90] Nemesius,

88 Diels, *Doxographi,* 1–263. It is entirely written in scholarly Latin.

89 MR 5.31. But as noted there, the layout and the numbering had to give precedence to the *Epitome*, which means that the Stobaean text not only is dismembered but also does not always remain uncontaminated. This was the unavoidable result of his methodology.

90 Diels erroneously believed that parallel texts in this work were directly taken from the *Epitome*. He later realized his

and some scholia. Diels did not include the abridged version of Ps.-Galen here, no doubt for reasons of space, giving only a cross-reference to the separate edition next to the chapter heading in the left column. The second apparatus below the right column is entitled *aliorum ex Aetio excerpta*. It is here that he placed the texts in Theodoret containing material drawn directly from Aëtius. On the rare occasions that Theodoret supplied lemmata not found in the more copious witnesses, the lemmata numbers are placed in the middle with blank space on either side.[91]

There are two further aspects of Diels' edition that should be observed. First, the text of the five books is prefaced by two indices or tables of contents. The former lists the chapter headings of the *Epitome*, corresponding to the pinakes at the beginning of each book.[92] These are then not included within the reconstruction of the *Placita*. The index of Stobaeus Book 1 is put together from Photius and the Laurentianus manuscript. It was useful to do this, especially since the Stobaean chapter headings could not be included in the reconstruction. But, as noted above,[93] Diels did not recognize that parts of the index as he reconstructed it were contami-

---

mistake, but we know this only at second hand; see MR 5.65 n. 273.

[91] For example, at the end of 4.3, on the corporeal nature of the soul. But the three lemmata at the end of 4.7, on the soul's immortality, are wrongly included, because these texts were drawn by Theodoret from another source, namely Clement of Alexandria *Strom.* 8.10.3–4.

[92] On these *pinakes*, see text above at nn. 29–30.

[93] See text above at n. 82.

nated with material from Ps.-Plutarch. Second, Diels also had taken on the task of separating out other doxographical material in Stobaeus, mostly drawn from the handbook of Arius Didymus,[94] which was mixed together with the excerpts from the *Placita*. He did this based on mainly stylistic criteria commendably set out in the "Prolegomena." In case of doubtful material, he tended to be charitable and leave it in. The sifting process can be further refined.[95]

Diels' landmark edition, a work of incomparably brilliant scholarship, was the product of his early years. He never published a revised edition. Instead, he used it as a main pillar of his second great work, *Die Fragmente der Vorsokratiker*, first published in 1903, followed by three more editions in his lifetime, and still used as the edition of reference for the Presocratics in the sixth edition revised by W. Kranz.[96] It is fascinating to see that in this work Diels constantly cited his own edition of the *Placita*, but as a rule did so without reference to its witnesses, thereby necessarily producing a single synthesized text. Moreover, these texts quite often deviate from what is found in the *Doxographi graeci*. (Some readings of this later edition are occasionally noted in the apparatus to our text.) In recent times, however, scholars working with Presocratic texts have felt the deficiency of just the single reference to

---

94 On this work, which belongs to the Περὶ αἱρέσεων literature that uses a different method from the *Placita*, see Algra, "Arius Didymus as a Doxographer of Stoicism."

95 See further Runia, "Additional Fragments," the results of which have been absorbed into MR 5.

96 Diels (and W. Kranz), *Die Fragmente der Vorsokratiker.*

Aëtius, and so have started to separate out again the multiplicity of witnesses to the *Placita*, both primary and secondary.[97]

2.2.2. Mansfeld and Runia *Aëtiana V*

The new edition by Jaap Mansfeld and David Runia, published by Brill in 2020,[98] took Diels' work as its starting point with the explicit aim of updating and superseding it. Its publication was preceded by a comprehensive analysis of the Dielsian project and the development of the doxographical tradition from its beginnings in the Peripatos to the end of antiquity. These results were distilled in four preliminary volumes.[99] The edition is thus based on a full study and re-evaluation of the method of the *Placita*, with special attention being given to the role of dialectic as initiated by Aristotle, which Diels had overlooked.[100]

The chief innovation that separates the new edition from Diels' is that it offers a text in a single column, integrating the evidence of the witnesses into a unified whole. In an earlier volume a detailed analysis of Book 2 had demonstrated that such a reconstruction was possible and

---

[97] Notably in the Traditio Praesocratica series, e.g., Wöhrle (2009) on Thales. On this "concertina" process, see the comments at MR 5.32–34. But in the Reclam edition of the Presocratics edited by J. Mansfeld and O. Primavesi, *Die Vorsokratiker*, Diels' practice of citing a single text is continued, now updated with the text of the new edition.

[98] *Aëtiana V*.

[99] *Aëtiana I–IV*.

[100] On Aristotle's key role, see further Mansfeld, "Aristotle in the Aëtian *Placita*."

legitimate.[101] This innovation enables the new edition to overcome a number of the shortcomings of the Dielsian edition that have been noted above. In particular, it resolves the ambiguity as to what is to be regarded as the best text that can be determined on the basis of the compendium's transmission down to the present.

A further key feature of the new edition is that it aims to set out *all* the available evidence that can be used for the reconstruction of the lost original. Making a clear distinction between primary and secondary witnesses,[102] it lists them at the beginning of each chapter, and then takes into account all the textual evidence they provide. In so doing, it makes use of the best available critical editions of these texts, the most important of which have been discussed above. (It here differs from the practice of Diels, who provided his own critical editions of three main witnesses.[103]) But in the apparatus criticus to the reconstructed text, it sets out all the important textual variants by means of a positive apparatus,[104] including copious ref-

---

101 *Aëtiana II*, part 2 = MR 2.277–661. The edition was called a "specimen reconstructionis."

102 See MR 5.42–43. Primary witnesses are those authors and texts that in one way or another go back in a linear fashion to the original version of the *Placita*. Secondary witnesses are those authors and texts containing material that is very similar to the primary witnesses but not derived in a linear fashion from the original work. The most important examples of the latter are Achilles and Nemesius.

103 That is, for Ps.-Plutarch, Stobaeus, and Ps.-Galen, but not for Theodoret.

104 In contrast to the edition of Book 2 in MR vol. 2, which had only a negative critical apparatus.

erence to the Arabic translation not used by Diels. In the single column of the text, the editors have to opt in each case for one particular reading, but users have all the material needed to determine the text for themselves.

The resultant single text is further accompanied by a full commentary, in which all the major decisions taken in reconstructing the sequence of lemmata in each chapter and editing their text are set out and discussed. This is in contrast to Diels, who could insert only brief notes in the apparatus criticus or refer his user to discussions tucked away in the labyrinthine "Prolegomena." Analysis of the contents of individual chapters also has the benefit of insights into the method of *Placita* gained through an improved understanding of the role of dialectic in their structure. Users receive additional assistance from the English translation that is presented in a separate part of the work, allowing them to gain further insight into how the text is to be understood.

A final important feature of the new edition is the awareness it shows of its own limitations. As can be readily seen in the table set out above,[105] for a little less than half of the lemmata (369 out of 772) there are multiple primary witnesses. Here the edition often has to decide between a variety of readings. On occasions (fortunately fairly rare), two differing versions of a word, a phrase, or even a whole sentence cannot easily be led back or "reduced" to a single unambiguously superior text. This is the problem that Diels tried to solve with his two columns and further apparatus. For the remaining 403 lemmata, more than half of the total, there is only a single wit-

[105] See text above at n. 19.

ness available. Here the transmitted text must be accepted, unless emendation is required. The text is "irreducible" in the sense that it cannot be confirmed through reference to a particular lemma in another witness.[106] In the case of Ps.-Plutarch's shorter *Placita*, such lemmata have to be accepted, while in the case of Stobaeus and Theodoret, they are vindicated structurally by their location in an Aëtian enclave, as we have seen in section 1.2 above.

Even so, the edition recognizes that, because it is a reconstruction, it cannot have the same status as a fully critical edition of an ancient text transmitted through a direct path of transmission. It necessarily must exhibit a greater degree of uncertainty. Users are advised that they "will have to be content if the text it offers bears a well-reasoned resemblance to the lost original."[107] It is thus above all a text for practical use, aiming to provide a sound basis for reference to and study of the important and often unique material it contains on the topics of natural philosophy and the opinions that ancient philosophers held about them.

Another uncertainty of the edition is the extent to which it is incomplete. Here, as already noted,[108] it was possible to draw on the research of Edward Jeremiah and affirm that it contains by far the greater part of the original work, probably about 86 percent, or six-sevenths, of the

---

106 On these two kinds of "irreducible" texts, see further Runia, "Irreducible Texts."

107 MR 5.41; see further the discussion at 5.37–42.

108 Text above at n. 20.

total. It is thus much more complete than Diels thought.[109]
In the commentary the editors have tried to take into account the places where additional material is missing and must have got lost at some stage of the transmission process. In the text, however, it was obviously not possible to include that for which no evidence is available.

3. GUIDE TO THE PRESENT EDITION

The present edition is based on the *Aëtiana V* edition by the same editors but adapted to the practices and requirements of the Loeb Classical Library.[110] In essence, it is a reduced and slightly modified and updated version of the same edition. Its most significant innovation is that it places the Greek text and English translation together on facing pages, an ideal presentation for the user that was not possible in the case of the larger and much more detailed edition. Whenever users wish to obtain more information on any aspect of the text—its contents, the traditions out of which it grew, and the context in which it was produced, as well as the finer details of its reconstruction and of the witnesses on whose text it is based—, they are referred to the mother work. In the case of that edition, every care was taken in order to ensure that the reader

[109] He mistakenly thought that the evidence of Theodoret pointed to a much larger original. See MR 1.284–88. The same mistake was made by Frede, "Rev. Mansfeld-Runia," in his critique of *Aëtiana I*.

[110] In particular, these requirements have led to changes in the use of punctuation and quotation marks.

would be orientated as easily and fully as possible in the complexities and vast quantity of documentation that it contains.[111] It too has a full and detailed guide for the user.[112]

3.1. *Introductions to Books I–V*

The text and translation of each book is preceded by an Introduction that provides an overview of its main features, including the state of its transmission, its contents and structure, prevalence of name-labels and dialectical features, comparative material in other authors, and ultimate sources for the doctrines that it contains.

3.2. *Text*

The reconstructed text of the compendium is virtually identical to that of the *Aëtiana V* edition. A very few minor changes are indicated by the siglum MR² in the apparatus criticus. These are also listed in the Appendix at the end of the volume. The text of each chapter is preceded by the list of the main witnesses: Ps.-Plutarch (with Ps.-Galen added in parentheses when available); Stobaeus; and Theodoret. After each chapter heading and each lemma, it is

---

111 As duly recognized in the reviews of Bernabé, "Review *Aëtiana V*"; Inwood, "Review *Aëtiana V*." The allegation of the otherwise highly positive review of Moore, "More on Aëtius," 1, on 1.7.1[58] that "to know precisely which bits, it seems one must still go to the text of Theodoret," is not correct. The relevant texts are printed at MR 5.378 and explained at MR 5.383.

112 MR 5.85–95; summarized at 5.719–25, 1347–353.

indicated whether the text in question is available in these main witnesses (reference is only made to Ps.-Galen and Qustā when the lemma is missing in Ps.-Plutarch). A further change is the inclusion of the Arabic text of Qustā ibn Lūqā for those passages that his Arabic translation preserves but that are lost in the transmission of the Greek text. For the purposes of the apparatus criticus, however, reference continues to be made to Daiber's German translation.

The text of each chapter is accompanied by two apparatuses. The critical apparatus is restricted in scope. It contains major emendations to the text, notably when made by the editors themselves, but also those of other editors. For the sigla used and also explanation of the names and editions referred to, see the Abbreviations. Only a very few variants are given, such as those relating to name-labels and important cases when the text in Ps.-Galen and the Arabic translation of Qustā is superior to that of the Byzantine manuscripts of Ps.-Plutarch. For explanation of the Latin abbreviations used in the apparatus criticus, see the Abbreviations.

In the case of Books 2 and 5, there are a number of problematic passages that are discussed in Appendix II. These mostly involve either texts where the evidence in the witnesses cannot easily be reduced to a single version (on these "irreducible texts," see above, section 2.2.2) or texts toward the end of the work where there is damage to the archetype of the Ps.-Plutarchean text. These passages are indicated by a cross-reference in the apparatus criticus.

The text of each chapter also includes an apparatus testimoniorum. Since the provenance of most of the information in the *Placita* is lost, for each name-label we indicate the fragment collection in which the lemma in question has been taken up. For Presocratic authors this will in the first instance be H. Diels and W. Kranz, *Die Fragmente der Vorsokratiker*, sixth edition, but if not found there, other collections will be referenced. For other authors we refer to the most recent or complete collection. References to these collections are given in the Abbreviations. For those authors whose writings survive, for example, Plato and Aristotle, we indicate passages from which the opinion has been derived, whether directly or indirectly (in the latter case the reference is introduced by the abbreviation cf.).

3.3. *Translation*

The English translation on the facing page is for the most part identical to that in the *Aëtiana* V edition. Like that translation, it aims to give an accurate picture of the original Greek text as it has been reconstructed. It thus tends to the literal side, though wishing to avoid language that is artificial or unidiomatic. The following features should be noted.

1. The Greek text is often highly compressed. Many words and phrases have to be supplied in the translation, especially at the beginning of lemmata, where the Greek text often elides a word of saying and takes over the topic of the doxa from the chapter heading. In the *Aëtiana* V translation these additions were placed in parentheses, but in the present translation that practice has been discontinued.

2. Name-labels are rendered in the usual Latinate forms of the names. Where possible, collective names of

groups and schools are translated in a uniform manner, for example, in the following cases:

hoi apo tinos	the successors of X
tis kai hoi ap' autou	X and his successors
hoi peri tina	X and his followers

Unlike in the earlier translation, where the names in multiple name-labels are placed side by side without conjunctions (i.e., as *asyndeta*), commas and conjunctions are inserted as in normal English prose.

3. Conjectural additions to the transmitted text, when translated, are placed in angle brackets (just like in the text itself). Braces are also taken over from the text, indicating that the text is likely to be not authentic. An obelus (†) indicates a crux in the text. Three asterisks indicate a lacuna.

4. Although the aim is to achieve consistent one-for-one renderings of Greek terms in English to the extent possible, this cannot always be achieved because of the polyvalent meanings of certain words in Greek.

5. On some occasions it is best to use a transliterated equivalent of the Greek term. In such cases an English rendering of the term is added in parentheses, unless this is not needed, as for example in the case of the term *pneuma*. Such terms are generally explained in the Glossary at the end of the volume.

6. Only on rare occasions are alternative renderings supplied. These are introduced by "or:" and placed in square brackets.

7. Similarly, transliterated equivalents of Greek terms, indicated in parentheses, are usually added only for etymologies or plays on words.

8. Greek adjectives with the suffix *–eidês* are usually

translated by the phrase "like a," e.g., *sphairoeidês* in 2.2 is twice rendered "like a ball."

9. Passages that are preserved only in the Arabic translation of Quṣtā ibn Lūqā are printed in italics. These are confined to 1.21.2*a*, 5.27.2, and 5.29.1–3.

At the beginning of each chapter, we include a very brief guide to the main dialectical features that the structure of the chapter exhibits. These will assist the user in understanding how the chapter works. On the dialectical methods that underlie these features, see above, section 1.4. For each chapter the reader is referred to the fuller analysis found in section D(c) of the Commentary in the *Aëtiana* V edition.

The notes to the translation are kept to a minimum. They mainly give explanations for unusual aspects of the contents in need of further elucidation. No attempt is made to explain the doxai themselves. For more information the user is referred to the Commentary of the *Aëtiana* V edition. Brief notes on individual philosophers and other thinkers included in the translation, as well as on authors who are sources of or witnesses to the *Placita*, are presented in the Index of Name-Labels and Other Names at the end of the volume.

3.4. *Schematic Overview of the Tradition of the* Placita

The interrelationship of the main witnesses to the *Placita* tradition can be schematically represented in figure 1 (based on MR 5.98).

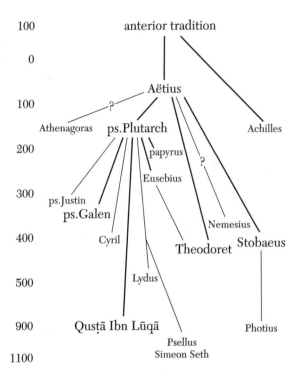

Figure 1. Main witnesses to the *Placita* tradition.

ABBREVIATIONS

APPARATUS CRITICUS

Sigla and Editors

The following list contains the sigla used in the critical apparatus to the text and sets out the details of all the editions referred to by the names of their editors.

{. . .}	words to be omitted from the text
⟨. . .⟩	words to be added to the text
[. . .]	letters missing in papyrus text
. . .]	all witnesses except
Ach	Achilles *De universo*. In *Achillis quae feruntur astronomica et in Aratum opuscula*, edited by G. Di Maria. Palermo, 1996.
Aët.	Aëtius *Placita*
Ant	Antinoopolis papyrus. Edited by J. W. Barns. In *The Antinoopolis Papyri Parts II & III*, edited by J. W. Barns and H. Zilliacus. London, 1960–1967.
Bst. DB	Baustein. In *Der Platonismus in der Antike*, edited by H. Dörrie, M. Baltes, and C. Pietsch. 8 vols. Stuttgart, 1987–.

corr. Voss.	corrector of ms. Ps.-Plutarch, Vossianus Q 2, University of Leiden Library
Corsinus	*Plutarchi De placitis philosophorum libri V*. Edited by E. Corsinus. Florence, 1750.
Diels *DG*	*Doxographi graeci*. Edited by H. Diels. Berlin, 1879.
Diels *VS*	*Die Fragmente der Vorsokratiker*. Edited by H. Diels. Berlin, 1903.
DK	*Die Fragmente der Vorsokratiker*. Edited by H. Diels and W. Kranz. 3 vols. Berlin, 1951 (6th ed.).
E	Eusebius, *Praeparatio evangelica*
Elter	Elter, A. *De Ioannis Stobaei codice Photiano*. Bonn, 1880.
G	Ps.-Galen, *Historia philosopha*
Kronenberg	Kronenberg, A. J. "Ad Plutarchi moralia (Continued)." *Mnemosyne* 10 (1941): 33–47.
Lachenaud	*Plutarque Œuvres morales* T. 12.2, *Opinions des philosophes*. Edited by G. Lachenaud. Paris, 1993.
Mau	*Plutarchi Moralia*. Vol. 5.2.1, *X oratorum vitae; Placita philosophorum*. Edited by J. Mau. Leipzig, 1971.
Meineke	*Ioannis Stobaei florilegium*. Edited by A. Meineke. 4 vols. Leipzig, 1855–1857.
MP	*Die Vorsokratiker. Griechisch/Deutsch. Ausgewählt, übersetzt und erläutert*. Edited by J. Mansfeld and O Primavesi. Stuttgart, 2021.

MR	*Aëtiana* V. Edited by J. Mansfeld and D. T. Runia. 4 vols. Leiden, 2020.
MR²	this edition (LCL 555)
P	Ps.-Plutarch *Placita*
P¹ and P²	variants in the manuscripts of Ps.-Plutarch
Ps	*Michael Psellus De omnifaria doctrina.* Edited by L. G. Westerink. Utrecht, 1948.
Q	Quṣṭā ibn Lūqā
Reiske	*Plutarchi Quae supersunt omnia.* Edited by J. Reiske. Vol. 9. Leipzig, 1778.
S	Stobaeus
S¹ and S²	variants in the manuscripts of Stobaeus
Simp.	Simplicius
T	Theodoret of Cyrrhus
Taylor	Taylor, A. E. *A Commentary on Plato's Timaeus.* Oxford, 1928.
Wachsmuth	*Ioannis Stobaei Anthologii libri duo priores qui inscribi solent Eclogae physicae et ethicae.* Edited by C. Wachsmuth. 2 vols. Berlin, 1884.
Xylander	*Plutarchi Chaeronensis Moralia.* Edited by G. Xylander (Holzmann). Vol. 2. Basel, 1574.

Latin Abbreviations

The following list sets out and translates all the Latin abbreviations used in the critical apparatus.

ad fin. (cap.)	*ad finem* (at the end) *capitis* (of the chapter)

ABBREVIATIONS

add.	*addidit* (added)
addend.	*addendum* (to be added)
adn.	*adnotatio* (annotation)
al.	*aliter* (differently)
ap.	*apud* (at)
app. crit.	*apparatus criticus* (critical apparatus)
attrib.	*attribuit* (attributed)
cap.	*caput, capita* (chapter, chapters)
coni.	*coniecit, coniecerunt* (conjectured)
coniunx. cum	*coniunxerunt cum* (joined up with)
conl.	*conlato* (comparing)
corr.	*correxit* (corrected)
crucif.	*crucifixit, crucifixerunt* (applied crux to, regarded as uncertain)
damn.	*damnavit* (condemned, deleted)
del.	*delevit, deleverunt* (deleted)
dub.	*dubitat, dubitavit* (uncertain whether correct)
dubium an	uncertain whether
ed., edd.	*editor, editores* (editor, editors)
emend.	*emendavit* (emended)
exhib.	*exhibit* (displays)
expect.	*expectes* (one would expect)
fort.	*fortasse* (perhaps)
gloss.	*glossa* (gloss)
hab.	*habet* (has)
lac.	*lacuna* (lacuna, missing text)
leg.	*legit* (reads)
mov.	*movit, moverunt* (moved)
ms., mss.	*manuscriptus, manuscripti* (manuscript, manuscripts)
nom.	*nomen, nomina* (name, names)

om.	*omisit, omiserunt* (omitted)
paraphr.	*paraphrasit* (paraphrases)
pos.	*posuit* (placed)
prob.	*probavit* (approved)
prop.	*proposuit* (proposed)
reconstr.	*reconstruxit* (reconstructed)
sc.	*scilicet* (namely)
sec.	*secutus, secuti* (following)
secl.	*seclusit* (bracketed)
stat.	*statuit* (established)
suppl.	*supplevit* (inserted)
susp.	*suspexit* (suspected)
tit.	*titulus* (title)
trad.	*traditio* (tradition)
transp.	*transposuit, transposuerunt* (displaced)
ut vid.	*ut videtur* (as it seems)
v.l.	*varia lectio* (alternative reading)
vel sim.	*vel simile, vel similia* (or similar)
vid.	*vide* (see)
vid. app. sec.	*vide appendicem secundam* (see Appendix II)

APPARATUS TESTIMONIORUM

Fragment Collections and Source Texts

The following list sets out the editions of fragments and testimonia used for the apparatus testimoniorum to the text, listed under the name of the author. For the Presocratic philosophers, as explained in the General Introduction, section 3.3, reference is made in nearly all cases to the collection of H. Diels and W. Kranz only.

Alcmaeon	Diels-Kranz 24
Anaxagoras	Diels-Kranz 59
Anaxagoras Gemelli Marciano	"Anaxagoras." In *Die Vorsokratiker*, edited by M. L. Gemelli Marciano, 3:6–103. 3 vols. Dusseldorf, 2007–2010.
Anaximander	Diels-Kranz 12
Anaximander Wöhrle	*Die Milesier: Anaximander und Anaximenes* Edited by G. Wöhrle. Berlin, 2012.
Anaximenes	Diels-Kranz 13
Anaximenes Wöhrle	*Die Milesier: Anaximander und Anaximenes*. Edited by G. Wöhrle. Berlin, 2012.
Antipater	*SVF* vol. 3
Antiphon	*Antiphon the Sophist. The Fragments*. Edited by G. J. Pendrick. Cambridge, 2002.
Apollodorus	*Die Fragmente der griechische Historiker*. Edited by F. Jacoby et al., §244. Berlin and Leiden, 1923–.
Apollophanes the Stoic	*SVF* vol. 1
Aratus *Phaen*.	Aratus, *Phaenomena*
Archelaus	Diels-Kranz 60
Archytas	*Archytas of Tarentum: Pythagorean, Philosopher and Mathematician King*. Edited by C. A. Huffman. Cambridge, 2005.
Aristarchus	Heath, T. *Aristarchus of Samos, The Ancient Copernicus*. Oxford, 1913.

Aristoph. *Nub*.	Aristophanes, *Nubes*
Arist. *Cael*.	Aristotle, *De caelo*
Arist. *Cat*.	Aristotle, *Categoriae*
Arist. *de An*.	Aristotle, *De anima*
Arist. *De phil*.	Aristotle, *De philosophia*
Arist. *de Pythag*.	Aristotle *De Pythagoreis*
Arist. *Div. somn*.	Aristotle, *De divinatione per somnia*
Arist. *EE*	Aristotle, *Ethica Eudemia*
Arist. *EN*	Aristotle, *Ethica Nicomachea*
Arist. *GA*	Aristotle, *De generatione animalium*
Arist. *GC*	Aristotle, *De generatione et corruptione*
Arist. *HA*	Aristotle, *Historia animalium*
Arist. *Iuv*.	Aristotle, *De iuventute*
Arist. *Met*.	Aristotle, *Metaphysica*
Arist. *Mete*.	Aristotle, *Meteorologica*
Arist. *PA*	Aristotle, *De partibus animalium*
Arist. *Phys*.	Aristotle, *Physica*
Arist. *Pol*.	Aristotle, *Politica*
Arist. *Rhet*.	Aristotle, *Rhetorica*
Arist. *Sens*.	Aristotle, *De sensibus*
Arist. *Somn.Vig*.	Aristotle, *De somno et vigilia*
Arist. *Top*.	Aristotle, *Topica*
Aristotle fr. Rose	*Aristotelis qui ferebantur librorum fragmenta*. Edited by V. Rose. Leipzig, 1886; repr., Stuttgart, 1967.
Aristotle fr. Ross	*Aristotelis fragmenta selecta*. Edited by W. D. Ross. Oxford, 1955.

Arius Didymus	*Epitomes fragmenta physica*, ed. H. Diels. *Doxographi graeci*, 447–72. Berlin, 1879.
Asclepiades	Vallance, J. T. "The Medical System of Asclepiades of Bithynia." In *Aufstieg und Niedergang der römischen Welt*, vol. II.37.1, edited by W. Haase, 693–727. Berlin, 1993–.
Atomists	Diels-Kranz 68
Berossus	*De Babyloniaca van Berossos van Babylon. Inleiding, editie en commentaar.* Edited by G. E. E. De Breucker. Groningen, 2012.
Boethus the Stoic	*SVF* vol. 3
Bst. DB	Baustein, Dörrie-Baltes *DPA*
Callimachus	*Callimachus*. Edited by R. Pfeiffer. 2 vols. Oxford, 1949–1953.
Chrysippus	*SVF* vol. 2
Cleanthes	*SVF* vol. 1
Crates	*Sphairopoiia. Untersuchungen zur Kosmologie des Krates von Pergamon.* Edited by H. J. Mette. Munich, 1936.
Critias	Diels-Kranz 88; see also Kannicht
Critias *Sisyph.*	Critias, *Sisyphus*
Critolaus	*Hermippos von Rhodos, Kritolaos und seine Schüler.* Edited by F. Wehrli. Basel, 1969.

Demetrius Laco	Puglia, E. *Demetrio Lacone: Aporie testuali ed esegetiche in Epicuro (PHerc. 1012)*, edited by M. Gigante, 11–23. Napoli, 1988.
Democritus	Diels-Kranz 68
Democritus Luria	*Democrito. Raccolta dei frammenti, interpretazione e commentario.* Edited by S. Luria. Milan, 2007.
Diagoras of Melos	*Diagorae Melii et Theodori Cyrenaei reliquiae.* Edited by M. Winiarczyk. Leipzig, 1981.
Dicaearchus	Mirhady, D. C., ed. "Dicaearchus of Messana: The Sources, Text and Translation." . In *Dicaearchus of Messana: Text, Translation, and Discussion*, edited by W. W. Fortenbaugh and E. Schütrumpf, 1–142. New Brunswick, 2001.
Diocles	*Diocles of Carystus: A Collection of the Fragments with Translation and Commentary.* Edited by P. J. Van der Eijk. 2 vols. Leiden, 2000–2001.
Diodorus Cronus	*Die Megariker: Kommentierte Sammlung der Testimonien.* Edited by K. Döring. Amsterdam, 1972.
Diodorus Tyrius	*Hermippos von Rhodos, Kritolaos und seine Schüler.* Edited by F. Wehrli. Basel, 1969.
Diog. Laert.	Diogenes Laertius, *Vitae philosophorum*

Diogenes of Apollonia	Diels-Kranz 64
Diogenes of Apollonia Laks	*Diogène d'Apollonie. Edition, traduction et commentaire des fragments et témoignages.* Edited by A. Laks. Sankt Augustin, 2008 (1st ed., Paris, 1983).
Diogenes of Babylon	SVF vol. 3
Diotimus of Tyre	Diels-Kranz 76
DPA	*Der Platonismus in der Antike.* Edited by H. Dörrie, M. Baltes, and C. Pietsch. Stuttgart, 1987–.
Ecphantus	Diels-Kranz 51
Empedocles (Emped.)	Diels-Kranz 31
Empiricists	*Die griechische Empirikerschule.* Edited by K. Deichgräber. Berlin, 1965 (1st ed., 1930).
Ephorus	*Die Fragmente der griechischen Historiker.* Edited by F. Jacoby et al., §70. Berlin and Leiden, 1923–.
Epicurus	*Epicurea.* Edited by H. Usener. Berlin, 1887.
Epicurus *Ep. Her.*	Epicurus *Letter to Herodotus*, Diogenes Laertius *VP* 10.35–83.
Epicurus *KD*	Epicurus, *Kuriai doxai*
Eratosthenes	*Eratosthenica.* Edited by G. Bernhardy. Berlin, 1822.
Erisastratus	*Erasistrati fragmenta collegit et digessit.* Edited by I. Garofalo. Pisa, 1988.

Eudemus	*Eudemos von Rhodos*. Edited by F. Wehrli. Basel, 1969.
Eudoxus	*Die Fragmente des Eudoxus von Knidos*. Edited by F. Lasserre. Berlin, 1966.
Euhemerus of Tegea	*Euhemeri Messenii reliquiae*. Edited by M. Winiarczyk. Stuttgart, 1991.
Euripides *Or.*	Euripides, *Orestes*
Euthymenes of Massilia	*Die Fragmente der griechischen Historiker*. Edited by F. Jacoby et al., §647. Berlin and Leiden, 1923–.
Hecataeus	Diels-Kranz 73
Heraclides	*Heraclides of Pontus. Texts and Translation*. Edited by E. Schütrumpf. New Brunswick, 2008.
Heraclitus	Diels-Kranz 22
Heraclitus Mouraviev	*Heraclitea* II: *Traditio* A.1–4. Edited by S. N. Mouraviev. 4 vols. Sankt Augustin, 1999–2003.
Herodotus *Hist.*	Herodotus, *Historiae*
Herophilus	*Herophilus: The Art of Medicine in Early Alexandria*. Edited by H. Von Staden. Cambridge, 1989.
Hesiod *Th.*	Hesiod, *Theogony*
Hestiaeus	*De Léodamas de Thasos à Philippe d'Opunte, témoignages et fragments*. Edited by F. Lasserre. Naples, 1987.
Hicetas	Diels-Kranz 50
Hippasus	Diels-Kranz 18
Hippo	Diels-Kranz 38
Hippocrates	Diels-Kranz 42

Hippocrates *Carn.*	*De carnibus* (Corpus Hippocraticum)
Hippocrates *Oct.*	*De octimestri partu* (Corpus Hippocraticum)
Homer *Il.*	Homer, *Iliad*
Homer *Od.*	Homer, *Odyssey*
Ion	Diels-Kranz 36
Kannicht	*Tragicorum Graecorum fragmenta.* Bd. 5, Euripides. Edited by R. Kannicht. 2 vols. Göttingen, 2004.
Leucippus	Diels-Kranz 67
Melissus	Diels-Kranz 30
Metrodorus	Diels-Kranz 70
Morb. sacr.	Corpus Hippocraticum, *De morbo sacro.* In *Œuvres complètes d'Hippocrate*, vol. 6, edited by E. Littré. Paris, 1849.
Ocellus	*"Ocellus Lucanus." Text und Kommentar.* Edited by R. Harder. Berlin, 1926; repr., Dublin, 1966.
Oenopides	Diels-Kranz 41; also Bodnár, I. *Oenopides of Chius: A Survey of the Modern Literature with a Collection of the Ancient Testimonia.* (Online at www.mpiwg-berlin.mpg .de, dated 2007.)
Orphics	*Orphicorum et Orphicis similium testimonia et fragmenta.* Edited by A. Bernabé. 2 vols. Munich, 2004–2005.

Parmenides	Diels-Kranz 28
Philip of Opus	*Academica: Plato, Philip of Opus, and the pseudo-Platonic* Epinomis. Edited by L. Tarán. Philadelphia, 1975. *See also* Hestiaeus
Philolaus	Diels-Kranz 44
Plato *Leg*.	Plato, *Laws*
Plato *Lys*.	Plato, *Lysis*
Plato *Phd*.	Plato, *Phaedo*
Plato *Phdr*.	Plato, *Phaedrus*
Plato *Phlb*.	Plato, *Philebus*
Plato *Soph*.	Plato, *Sophist*
Plato *Tht*.	Plato, *Theaetetus*
Plato *Tim*.	Plato, *Timaeus*
Polemon	*Polemonis Academici fragmenta*. Edited by M. Gigante. Naples, 1977.
Polybus	*See* Hippocrates
Posidonius (E.-K.)	*Posidonius. Vol. 1: The Fragments*. Edited by L. Edelstein and I. G. Kidd. Cambridge, 2005 (1st ed., 1972).
Posidonius Theiler	*Poseidonios: Die Fragmente* Edited by W. Theiler. 2 vols. Berlin, 1982.
Ps.-Arist. *MM*	Pseudo-Aristotle, *Magna moralia*
Ps.-Arist. *Mu*.	Pseudo-Aristotle, *De mundo*
Ps.-Plato *Def*.	Pseudo-Plato, *Definitiones*
Pythagoras	Diels-Kranz 14
Pythagoreans	Diels-Kranz 58
Pythagorean Golden Verses	*The Pythagorean Golden Verses*. Edited by J. C. Thom. Leiden, 1995.

Pytheas	*Pytheas von Massilia*. Edited by H. J. Mette. Berlin, 1952.
S.E. *M.*	Sextus Empiricus, *Adversus Mathematicos*
Seleucus	Russo, L. "Seleuco, Galileo e la teoria della gravitazione." *Quaderni Urbinati di Cultura Classica* 49 (1995): 143–60.
Simp. *in Cael.*	Simplicius *In Aristotelis de caelo commentaria*. Edited by J. L. Heiberg. Berlin, 1894.
Solon	*Iambi et elegi graeci*. Edited by M. L. West. 2 vols. Oxford, 1992.
Speusippus	*Speusippus of Athens: A Critical Study with a Collection of the Related Texts and a Commentary*. Edited by L. Tarán. Leiden, 1981.
Sphaerus the Stoic	*SVF* vol. 1
Stoics	*SVF* vol. 2
Stoics Hülser	*Die Fragmente zur Dialektik der Stoiker: neue Sammlung der Texte mit deutscher Übersetzung und Kommentaren*. 4 vols. Stuttgart, 1987–1988.
Strato	Sharples, R. W., ed. "Strato of Lampsacus: The Sources, Texts and Translations." In *Strato of Lampsacus. Text, Translation, and Discussion*, edited by M. L. Desclos and W. W. Fortenbaugh, 5–229. New Brunswick, NJ, 2011.

SVF	*Stoicorum veterum fragmenta*. Edited by I. von Arnim. 4 vols. Leipzig, 1905–1924.
Tertullian, *De an.*	Tertullian, *De anima. Quinti Septimi Florentis Tertulliani De Anima*. Edited by J. Waszink. Amsterdam, 1947.
Thales	Diels-Kranz 11
Thales Wöhrle	*Die Milesier: Thales*. Edited by G. Wöhrle, Berlin, 2009. (Enlarged ed., *The Milesians: Thales. Translation and Additional Material by R. McKirahan*. Berlin, 2014.)
Theodorus of Cyrene	*Diagorae Melii et Theodori Cyrenaei reliquiae*. Edited by M. Winiarczyk. Leipzig, 1981.
Theophrastus FHS&G	*Theophrastus of Eresus: Sources for His Life, Writings, Thought, and Influence*. Edited by W. W. Fortenbaugh, P. M. Huby, R. W. Sharples, and D. Gutas. 2 vols. Leiden, 1992.
Timaeus	*Die Fragmente der griechischen Historiker*. Edited by F. Jacoby et al., §566. Berlin and Leiden. 1923–.
Xenocrates	*Senocrate Ermodoro Testimonianze e frammenti: Edizione, tradizione e commento*. Edited by M. Isnardi Parente. 1982. Rev. ed. by T. Dorandi. Pisa, 2012.
Xenophanes	Diels-Kranz 21
Zeno of Elea	Diels-Kranz 29
Zeno the Stoic	*SVF* vol. 1

GENERAL BIBLIOGRAPHY

All works referred to but not referenced in the Abbreviations are included here.

Algra, K. "Arius Didymus as a Doxographer of Stoicism: Some Observations." In Mansfeld and Runia, *Aëtiana IV*, 53–102.

Arrighetti, G., ed. *Epicuro: Opere. Introduzione, testo critico, traduzione e note*. Turin, 1973.

Bakker, F. *Epicurean Meteorology. Sources, Method, Scope and Organization*. Leiden, 2016.

Barns, J. W. B. "[Plutarch], *Epitome de Placitis Philosophorum*." In *The Antinoopolis Papyri*, edited by J. W. B. Barns and H. Zilliacus, 2:74–83, 3:181–82. London, 1960–1967.

Bernabé, A. "Review *Aëtiana V*." *Bryn Mawr Classical Review* 2021.08.28.

Bianchetti, S., ed. *Pitea di Massilia*. Pisa, 1998.

Broggiato, M., ed. *Cratete di Mallo: I frammenti. Edizione, introduzione e note*. La Spezia, 2001.

Canivet, P. *Théodoret de Cyr*. Thérapeutique des maladies helléniques. 2 vols. Paris, 1958.

Coxon, A. H., ed. *The Fragments of Parmenides. A Critical Text with Introduction and Translation, the Ancient*

Testimonia and a Commentary. Assen, 1967. Revised reprint, Las Vegas, 2009.

Daiber, H. *Aetius Arabus. Die Vorsokratiker in arabischer Überlieferung*. Wiesbaden, 1980.

―――. "The *Meteorology* of Theophrastus in Syriac and Arabic Translation," In Fortenbaugh and Gutas, *Theophrastus*, 166–293.

De Falco, V., ed. *L'Epicureo Demetrio Lacone*. Naples, 1923.

Decleva Caizzi, F., and alii, eds. "17: Antipho." In *Corpus dei Papiri filosofici Greci e Latini*, edited by F. Adorno et al., vol. 1*, 176–236. Florence, 1989.

Delatte, A., ed. "Syméon Seth." In *Anecdota Atheniensia et alia. T. 2: Textes relatifs à l'histoire des sciences*, edited by A. Delatte, 1–125. Liège, 1939.

Di Maria, G. *Achillis quae feruntur astronomica et in Aratum opuscula*: De universo, De Arati vita, De Phaenomenorum interpretatione. Palermo, 1996.

Diels, H. *Doxographi graeci*. Berlin, 1879.

―――. "Stobaios und Aëtios." *Rheinisches Museum* 36 (1881): 343–50.

―――. *Die Fragmente der Vorsokratiker*. Berlin, 1903. Fourth rev. ed. in 2 vols. Berlin, 1922. Sixth ed., revised by W. Kranz. 3 vols. Berlin, 1951.

Dorandi, T., ed. *Diogenes Laertius: Lives of the Eminent Philosophers. Edited with an Introduction*. Cambridge, 2013.

Elter, A. *De Ioannis Stobaei codice Photiano*. Bonn, 1880.

Falcon, A. *Aristotelianism in the First Century BCE: Xenarchus of Seleucia*. Cambridge, 2011.

Fortenbaugh, W. W., and D. Gutas, eds. *Theophrastus:*

His Psychological, Doxographical and Scientific Writings. New Brunswick, 1992.

Frede, M. "*Aëtiana*." *Phronesis* 44 (1999): 135–49.

Giannantoni, G., ed. *Socratis et Socraticorum reliquiae collegit, disposuit, apparatibus notisque instruxit*. 4 vols. Naples, 1990.

Gigon, O. *Aristotelis Opera: vol. III Librorum deperditorum fragmenta*. Berlin, 1987.

Gourinat, J.-B. "Diels' Whodunit: The Reliability of the Three Mentions of Aëtius in Theodoret." In Mansfeld and Runia, *Aëtiana IV*, 17–52.

Heinze, R., ed. *Xenokrates. Darstellung der Lehre und Sammlung der Fragmente*. Leipzig, 1892. Reprinted, Hildesheim, 1965.

Henry, R. *Photius*: Bibliothèque. 9 vols. Paris, 1959–1991.

Hense, O., ed. *Ioannis Stobaei Anthologii libri duo posteriores*. 3 vols. Berlin, 1894–1912. Reprinted, Berlin, 1974.

Huffman, C. A., ed. *Philolaus of Croton: Pythagorean and Presocratic*. Cambridge, 1993.

Inwood, B. "Review *Aëtiana V*." *The Studia Philonica Annual* 33 (2021): 315–19.

Isnardi Parente, M., ed. *Speusippo Frammenti. Edizione, traduzione e commento*. Naples, 1980.

Jas, M. *Nicolaus Rheginus als Übersetzer der pseudo-Galenischen Schrift* De historia philosopha: *Ein Beitrag zur lateinischen Überlieferung des Corpus Galenicum*. Wiesbaden, 2018.

Jeremiah, E. T. "Statistical Explorations of the *Placita* of Aëtius." In Mansfeld and Runia, *Aëtiana IV*, 279–373.

Kollesch, J., ed. [*Galeni*] *Definitiones medicae*. Corpus Medicorum Graecorum 5/13,2. Berlin, 2023.

Lachenaud, G. *Plutarque Œuvres morales* T. 12.2, Opinions des philosophes. Paris, 1993.

Lammer, A., and M. Jas, eds. *Received Opinions: Doxography in Antiquity and the Islamic World*. Leiden, 2022.

Lang, P., ed. *De Speusippo academici scriptis, accedunt fragmenta*. Bonn, 1911. Reprinted, Frankfurt, 1964.

Leith, D. "Causing Doubt: Diodorus Cronos and Herophilus of Chalcedon on Causality." *Classical Quarterly* 64 (2014): 592–608.

Maass, E. *Commentariorum in Aratum reliquiae collegit recensuit indicibus instruxit*. Berlin, 1898.

Manetti, D., ed. *Anonymus Londiniensis* De medicina. Berlin, 2011.

Mansfeld, J. "Chrysippus and the *Placita*." *Phronesis* 34 (1989): 311–42. Reprinted in Mansfeld and Runia, *Aëtiana III*, 125–57.

———. "*Physikai Doxai* and *Problêmata Physika* from Aristotle to Aëtius (and Beyond)." In Fortenbaugh and Gutas, *Theophrastus*, 63–111. Reprinted with additions in Mansfeld and Runia, *Aëtiana III*, 33–97.

———. "Theodoret as a Source for the Aëtian *Placita*." In Mansfeld and Runia, *Aëtiana IV*, 174–95.

———. "Aristotle in the Aëtian *Placita*." In *Brill's Companion to the Reception of Aristotle*, edited by A. Falcon, 299–318. Leiden, 2016.

———. "Doxography of Greek Philosophy." In *The Stanford Encyclopedia of Philosophy*, edited by E. N. Zalta. Online at https://plato.stanford.edu/archives/win2016/entries/ doxography-ancient (last updated 2020).

————. "Helping the Reader: The Paratextual Elements in the *Placita* in the Context of their Genre." In Lammer and Jas, 33–50.

Mansfeld, J., and O. Primavesi. *Die Vorsokratiker. Griechisch/Deutsch. Ausgewählt, übersetzt und erläutert*. 3rd ed. Stuttgart, 2021.

Mansfeld, J., and D. T. Runia. *Aëtiana I: The Method and Intellectual Context of a Doxographer: The Sources*. Leiden, 1997.

————. *Aëtiana II: The Method and Intellectual Context of a Doxographer: The Compendium*. 2 vols. Leiden, 2009.

————. *Aëtiana III: The Method and Intellectual Context of a Doxographer. Studies in the Doxographical Traditions of Greek Philosophy*. Leiden, 2010.

————, eds. *Aëtiana IV: Towards an Edition of the Aëtian* Placita*: Papers of the Melbourne Conference 1–3 December 2015*. Leiden, 2018.

————. *Aëtiana V: An Edition of the Reconstructed Text of the* Placita *with a Commentary and a Collection of Related Texts*. 4 vols. Leiden, 2020.

Marcovich, M., ed. *Athenagoras* Legatio pro Christianis. Berlin, 1990.

————. *Heraclitus: Greek Text with a Short Commentary*. Sankt Augustin, 2001.

Mau, J. *Plutarchi Moralia*, vol. 5.2.1: X oratorum vitae; Placita philosophorum. Leipzig, 1971.

Moore, C. "More on Aëtius." *Classical Review* 72 (2022): 101–3.

Morani, M., ed. *Nemesius* De natura hominis. Leipzig, 1987.

Mras, K., ed. *Eusebius Werke* VIII.1–2, *Die* Praeparatio

Evangelica. 2 vols. Revised reprint edited by É. Des Places. Berlin, 1982–1983.

Parker, H. N. *Censorinus* The Birthday Book. Chicago, 2007.

Raeder, J. *De Theodoreti Graecarum affectionum curatione quaestiones criticae*, diss. Hauniae. Copenhagen, 1900.

———. *Theodoreti* Graecarum affectionum curatio. Leipzig, 1904.

Riedweg, C., and W. Kinzig, eds. *Kyrill von Alexandrien Werke I: Gegen Julian. Teil 1: Buch 1–5*. Berlin, 2016.

Royse, J. R. "The Text of Stobaeus: The Manuscripts and Wachsmuth's Edition." In Mansfeld and Runia, *Aëtiana IV*, 156–73.

Runia, D. T. "Additional Fragments of Arius Didymus on Physics." In *Polyhistor: Studies in the History and Historiography of Philosophy Presented to Jaap Mansfeld on His Sixtieth Birthday*, edited by K. A. Algra, P. W. van der Horst, and D. T. Runia, 363–81. Leiden, 1996. Reprinted in Mansfeld and Runia, *Aëtiana III*, 313–32.

———. "The *Placita* Ascribed to Doctors in Aëtius' Doxography of Physics." In Van der Eijk, *Ancient Histories of Medicine*, 191–250. Reprinted in Mansfeld and Runia, *Aëtiana III*, 515–75.

———. "What Is Doxography?" In Van der Eijk, *Ancient Histories of Medicine*, 31–55.

———. "Epicurus and the *Placita*." In Mansfeld and Runia, *Aëtiana IV*, 377–431.

———. "Irreducible Texts: The Implications for an Edition of the Aëtian *Placita*." In Lammer and Jas, 51–76.

———. "The Aëtian *Placita* and the Church Fathers: Creative Use of a Distinctive Mode of Ordering Knowledge." In *The Intellectual World of Late Antique Christianity*, edited by L. Ayres, M. W. Champion, and M. Crawford, 198–220. Cambridge, 2023.

———. "The Reception of Plato in the Aëtian *Placita*." In *Festschrift for Harold Tarrant*. Forthcoming.

Sallmann, N., ed. *Censorini* De die natali liber ad Q. Caerellium. Leipzig, 1983.

Scholten, C. *Theodoret* De Graecarum affectionum curatione–Heilung der griechischen Krankheiten. *Übersetzt, eingeleitet und mit Anmerkungen versehen*. Leiden, 2015.

Scott, L., ed. *Pytheas of Massalia. Texts, Translation, and Commentary*. London, 2021.

Sider, D., ed. *The Fragments of Anaxagoras. Introduction, Text, and Commentary*. Sankt Augustin, 2005.

Solmsen, F. *Aristotle's System of the Physical World. A Comparison with His Predecessors*. Ithaca, NY, 1960.

Tarán, L., ed. *Parmenides. A Text with Translation, Commentary and Critical Essays*. Princeton, 1965.

Tieleman, T. "Presocratics and Presocratic Philosophy in Galen." In Lammer and Jas, 120–50.

Torraca, L. *I dossografi greci*. Padua, 1961.

Van der Eijk, P. J., ed. *Ancient Histories of Medicine*. Leiden, 1999.

Wachsmuth, C. *Ioannis Stobaei Anthologii libri duo priores qui inscribi solent Eclogae physicae et ethicae*. Vols. 1–2. Berlin, 1884.

Wehrli, F., ed. *Dikaiarchos*. Basel. 1967.

———, ed. *Herakleides Pontikos*. Basel, 1969.

———, ed. *Straton von Lampsakos*. Basel, 1969.

Westerink, L. G. *Michael Psellus De omnifaria doctrina with Critical Text and Introduction*. Nijmegen, 1948.

Wöhrle, G. *Die Milesier: Thales*. Berlin, 2009. Enlarged English version by R. McKirahan. Berlin, 2014.

Wolfsdorf, D. "Empedocles and His Ancient Readers on Desire and Pleasure." *Oxford Studies in Ancient Philosophy* 36 (2009): 1–71.

Wright, M. R., ed. *Empedocles. The Extant Fragments*. New Haven, 1981.

PLACITA

BOOK I

FIRST PRINCIPLES

INTRODUCTION

Transmission

Book 1, by far the longest of the work, is relatively well-preserved by our witnesses. Stobaeus retains a higher number of lemmata than Ps.-Plutarch, even though he appears not to have included some early chapters (1, 4, 6). The contribution of Theodoret is quite modest. Ps.-Galen includes only just over a third of the whole, preferring other sources for the first part up to chapter 9. The book has an introductory procemium, followed by thirty chapters, each on a well-defined question in natural philosophy. This is the same number of chapters as Book 5, but less than what is found in Book 2 (thirty-four chapters), which is about 40 percent shorter in length. Yet Book 1 has only 183 lemmata, substantially less than the 217 of Book 2. This clearly demonstrates that on average individual doxai are longer in Book 1, resulting from the differing nature of its contents.

BOOK I: FIRST PRINCIPLES

Contents

Book 1 consists of two parts: (1) the introduction to the *physikos logos*, as the treatise is called in the opening lines, that is, chapters 1 to 8; and (2) the series of chapters 9 to 29 (with 30 as appendix), which sets out the basic concepts of theoretical physics. Together they lay the foundation for the remaining four books. The introductory part (1–8) in turn can be divided into two clusters. The first (1–5) deals with a definition of the subject and its constituent parts, followed by a historical and systematic overview given in a long list of *archai* (first principles) as determined by the philosophers as its chief practitioners. This is obligatory in technical/didactic literature. The second cluster (6–10) first treats the god(s) and connected questions, together with the concepts of "matter" and "idea." It is no coincidence that these topics combine the two principles of Stoicism with the three principles of Middle Platonism, showing that the redactor is a child of his time. The last two chapters of this cluster (9–10) form a bridge to the second major part of the book (11–29), dealing with the basic concepts of theoretical physics. After a chapter on causes (11), this part can be further subdivided into sections on bodies (12–17), incorporeals (18–22), motion (23–24), and, finally, important concepts in Hellenistic philosophy, that is, necessity, fate, and chance (25–29). The final chapter (30), on nature, forms a bookend with the opening chapter. It is noteworthy that in the seven sections bridging the first and second parts (9–15), all chapters except 13 commence with a nominal definition, introducing the everyday meaning of terms, before listing technical meanings given by the philosophers. In subsequent chapters the opening lemma also often plays the role of an initial definition, but it is in all cases attributed to one or more philosophers, and so is a real definition. A further observation is that all the chapters from 8 onward use the compact formula *peri* x ("On" plus subject), whereas in the preceding chapters it did not occur (in ch. 3 it is expanded).

Name-Labels

Most of the name-labels in Book 1 indicate philosophers, with only incidental references to scientists and doctors. But the diversity of different philosophers included (sixty-four) is greater than in any other book, as might be expected given the foundational nature of its subject matter. This is also the reason that the role of successions comes to the fore, especially in chapter 3, on the *archai*, showing the influence of priorities in Hellenistic philosophy. In fact, chronology is more influential in this book than in any other except Book 3. But it does not overrule the primary importance of the dialectical ordering of doxai, even if this ordering is not always easy to follow in the lengthy chapters 3 and 7.

Comparative Material

In assembling and analyzing the comparative material available for the study of Book 1, it is important to take into account its division into parts and clusters of chapters, as set out above, since for each of the subdivisions the situation tends to differ. In the proximate and wider doxographical traditions,[1] we find for the introductory chapters 1 to 10 adequate illustrative material in authors such as Cicero, Varro, Philo of Alexandria, Arius Didymus, Sextus Empiricus, Achilles, works of Galen that refer to philosophical concepts, and later authors, including Lactantius, Calcidius, and Augustine. For the combination of chapter 3, on the *archai*, and the theological chapters 6 and 7, Philo and Sextus Empiricus provide valuable comparative material, while Cicero, *De natura deorum*, and Philodemus, *On piety*, do so for chapters 6 and 7 in particular. For the cluster of chapters 7 through 10, the Middle Platonist background is illustrated by texts in Cicero, Seneca, Athenagoras, Ps.-Justin (*Cohortatio*), and Arius Didymus. For the foundational theoretical chapters, 11 through 29, the available material is uneven and lacking for many chapters. For the cluster of chapters 11 to 24, there is Achilles, Ps.-Galen *Historia philosopha* 1–24, and Nemesius. The last-named church father is also the source of the best parallels for chapters 25 through 29, with their specific Hellenistic focus.

Other Sources

When looking for other sources beyond the proximate and wider doxographical traditions, we find that, in the case of the introductory chapters 1 through 10, a rich crop of parallels can be harvested in scientific and didactic literature. There we find definitions of the subject matter and its divisions, and also historical overviews of the main rep-

---

[1] On these traditions, see further General Introduction 1.6.

resentatives (often connected via successions) and their contributions and discoveries. Rewarding material is located in Ps.-Galenic works and Celsus' *De medicina*, as well as the later Aristotelian commentators. Cicero and Sextus Empiricus too provide little-used comparative material. For the remainder of the book, there are a wide range of parallels found in various philosophical handbooks and authors such as Alexander of Aphrodisias, Clement of Alexandria, Sextus Empiricus, and other authors who know this material well and who utilize it for their various purposes.

Ultimate Sources

Finally, there is the question of the ultimate sources from which the contents of this book are drawn. In the first instance one must think of the Peripatos here, and in particular the otherwise lost sources used by Aristotle, Theophrastus, and their predecessors. Even before Plato, a process had started in which a set of physical questions were separated out from their original cosmological context. Examples of such themes are *genesis* (cf. ch. 24), motion (23), infinite divisibility (cf. 16), void (18), and mixture (17).[2] The account of the *archai* and the early philosophers in chapter 3 is ultimately dependent on the first books of Aristotle's *Physics* and *Metaphysics*, which built on earlier accounts. But when we reach the theological chapters (6–8), the influence of the Stoa and its

[2] Cf. MR 1.110 and the study of Solmsen, *Aristotle's System*, cited there, esp. 7–9, 51.

presentation of the *physikos logos* make its presence felt.[3] Indeed, a comparison with the Stoic doxography at Diogenes Laertius *VP* 7.132 reveals that the first main division of the *physikos logos*, when applied to Book 1, allows the identification of seven subparts: about bodies (12–17), principles (3), elements (2), gods (6–8), bounding entities (14), place (19–20), and void (18). Interestingly, the concept of nature is absent in this division. As already noted, the connection of theology with matter, idea, and causes reflects the influence of incipient Middle Platonism. Additional subjects not in the Stoic division but of great importance for Hellenistic philosophies are time (21–22), necessity (25–26), chance (29), and—most important for the Stoics but irrelevant for Aristotle—fate (27–28). Thus, the Peripatetic treatment of physics has been adapted to fit the requirements of the Hellenistic *koinê*, which goes back to the Stoa but may no longer have been felt to be particularly Stoic.

[3] See further General introduction 1.5.

⟨TITLE⟩[1]

ΑΕΤΙΟΥ ΠΕΡΙ ΤΩΝ ΑΡΕΣΚΟΝΤΩΝ
ΤΟ Α΄,[2] |

ἐν ᾧ κεφάλαια τάδε· |

⟨Index⟩

Ps.-Plut. *Plac.*

---

[1] Ps.-Plut. *Plac.* 1; Theod. *Cur.* 4.31, cf. 2.95, 5.16
[2] tit. T: Περὶ τῶν ἀρεσκόντων φιλοσόφοις φυσικῶν δογμάτων βίβλια ε΄ τὸ α΄ P

AETIUS
ON THE PLACITA[1]

BOOK I

in which the following chapter headings are found:

‹Index›[2]

Ps.-Plutarch, *Tenets*

[1] This is the title of the work as given in the description by Theodoret. Ps.-Plutarch for his abridged version has a different and longer title that varies a little between the five books and includes the term *epitomê* in the titles of Books 2, 3, and 5. See further General Introduction 1.3.

[2] The list of chapter headings, or pinax, is found only in Ps.-Plutarch but was originally present in Aëtius. See further General Introduction 1.3.

AETIUS

⟨Proœmium⟩

Ps.-Plut. *Plac.* procem.

1. Μέλλοντες τὸν φυσικὸν παραδώσειν λόγον ἀναγ-
καῖον ἡγούμεθα εὐθὺς | ἐν ἀρχαῖς διελέσθαι τὴν τῆς
φιλοσοφίας πραγματείαν, ἵν' εἰδῶμεν τί | ἐστι καὶ
πόστον μέρος αὐτῆς ἡ φυσικὴ διέξοδος. (P) |

2. οἱ μὲν οὖν Στωικοὶ ἔφασαν τὴν μὲν σοφίαν εἶναι
5 θείων τε καὶ ἀνθρωπίνων | ἐπιστήμην, τὴν δὲ φιλοσο-
φίαν ἄσκησιν ἐπιτηδείου τέχνης, | ἐπιτήδειον δ' εἶναι
μίαν καὶ ἀνωτάτω τὴν ἀρετήν, ἀρετὰς δὲ τὰς | γενι-
κωτάτας τρεῖς, φυσικὴν ἠθικὴν λογικήν· δι' ἣν αἰτίαν
καὶ τριμερής | ἐστιν ἡ φιλοσοφία, ἧς τὸ μὲν φυσικὸν
τὸ δ' ἠθικὸν τὸ δὲ λογικόν· καὶ | φυσικὸν μὲν ὅταν
περὶ κόσμου ζητῶμεν καὶ τῶν ἐν κόσμῳ, ἠθικὸν δὲ τὸ
10 | κατησχοληημένον περὶ τὸν ἀνθρώπινον βίον, λογικὸν
δὲ τὸ περὶ τὸν | λόγον, ὃ καὶ διαλεκτικὸν καλοῦ-
σιν. (P) |

3. Ἀριστοτέλης δὲ καὶ Θεόφραστος καὶ σχεδὸν πάν-
τες οἱ Περιπατητικοὶ | διείλοντο τὴν φιλοσοφίαν οὕ-

§1 —   §2 Stoics 2.35   §3 Aristotle cf. *EE* 2.1
1220a5, *EN* 2.1 1103a14–15, *Met.* α.1 993b19–23; Theophrastus
fr. 479

12

BOOK I: FIRST PRINCIPLES

⟨Prooemium⟩[3]

*Teaching physics, the purpose of the treatise, requires de-
fining physics qua part of philosophy. Views differ as to
the number of these parts. Physics, like ethics, deals with
problems, i.e., with different views of the topics treated.*

Ps.-Plutarch, *Tenets*

1. Since our objective is to teach [or: hand down] the
physical theory [or: theory of physics, account of nature],
we believe it to be necessary to divide up the discipline of
philosophy directly at the beginning, so that we may know
what philosophy is and where in the order of its parts the
detailed account of physics comes.

2. Now the Stoics said that wisdom is the knowledge of
divine and human matters, while philosophy is the prac-   5
tice of an appropriate technique. There is, they say, just
one virtue that is appropriate and supreme, while below
this there are three virtues that are most generic, namely
physical, ethical, and logical virtue. For this reason philosophy too consists of three parts: physics, ethics, and
logic. Physics is when we do research on the cosmos and
the things within the cosmos, while ethics is the part that   10
is thoroughly occupied with human life, and logic is the
part concerned with discourse, which they also call dialectic.

3. Aristotle and Theophrastus and almost all the Peripatetics divided philosophy as follows: the perfect [or: com-

[3] This proem is not paralleled in Stobaeus, who wrote one for
his own work.

13

τως· ἀναγκαῖον τὸν τέλειον ἄνδρα[3] καὶ | θεωρητικὸν
εἶναι τῶν ὄντων καὶ πρακτικὸν τῶν δεόντων· τοῦτο δ᾽
15 ἔξεστι | καὶ ἐκ τούτων συνιδεῖν, οἷον· ζητεῖται εἰ ζῷον
ἢ μὴ ζῷον[4] ὁ ἥλιος, εἰ | π⟨ῦ⟩ρ, ⟨εἰ τηλικοῦτος ἡλίκος⟩[5]
ὁρᾶται· ὁ τοῦτο δὲ ζητῶν θεωρητικός | ἐστι· οὐδὲ γὰρ
τι πλέον θεωρεῖται ἢ τὸ ὄν. ζητεῖται ὁμοίως εἰ ἄπειρος
| ὁ κόσμος ἐστὶ καὶ εἰ ἔξω τι τοῦ κόσμου ἔστι· ταῦτα
γὰρ πάντα θεωρητικά. | ζητεῖται πάλιν πῶς βιοτεύειν
20 καὶ πῶς προΐστασθαι τέκνων | προσήκει καὶ πῶς
ἄρχειν καὶ πῶς νομοθετεῖν· ταῦτα γὰρ πάντα ἕνεκα |
τοῦ πρᾶξαι ζητεῖται· καὶ ἔστιν ὁ τοιοῦτος πρακτικὸς
ἀνήρ. (P) |

1.1

Ps.-Plut. *Plac.* 1.1 (+ Ps.-Gal. *Hist. phil.* 20)

α΄. Τί ἐστιν ἡ φύσις (P) |

1. ἐπειδὴ πρόκειται ἡμῖν τὰ φυσικὰ θεωρῆσαι, ἀναγ-
καῖον ἡγοῦμαι δηλῶσαι, | τί ποτ᾽ ἐστὶν ἡ φύσις· ἄτο-

§1 —

3 ἄνδρα: Mensch Q = ἄνθρωπος ?
4 μὴ ζῷον: μείζων Q ut vid.   5 εἰ π⟨ῦ⟩ρ, ⟨εἰ τηλι-
κοῦτος ἡλίκος⟩ ὁρᾶται coni. MR: †εἴπερ ὁρᾶται P

14

plete] man should both theorize about the things that are and perform the acts that must be done. This can also be understood from these considerations as well: when re- 15 search takes place on whether the sun is a living being or not a living being, whether it is ‹fire, or whether it is just as large› as it is seen to be, the person who does this research is theorizing, for what is theorized about is nothing more than what is. Similarly research is done on whether the cosmos is infinite and whether there is anything outside the cosmos, for all these subjects are theoretical.[4] On the other hand, research is done on how one should live one's life and look after one's children and how to rule and 20 how to legislate. All these matters are researched with a view to conduct, and the person who does this is a man of action.

1.1

The chapter presents a real definition of nature and natural phenomena valid for the treatise, based on Aristotle.

Ps.-Plutarch, *Tenets* (+ Ps.-Galen, *Philosophical History*)

1. What nature is

1. Since our proposal is to study what belongs to nature, I consider it necessary to make clear what in fact nature is.

---

[4] Of the five research questions given as examples, the first is not treated in the book itself (but cf. 2.3 on the cosmos), the second at 2.20, the third at 2.21, the fourth at 2.1 (cf. 1.5), the fifth at 2.9. The questions that follow belong to the domain of ethics and are not dealt with in the treatise.

πον γὰρ πειρᾶσθαι μὲν φυσιολογεῖν, | ἀγνοεῖν δ' αὐτὸ
τοῦτο, τὴν τῆς φύσεως δύναμιν. (P) |

5 2. ἔστιν οὖν κατὰ τὸν Ἀριστοτέλην φύσις ἀρχὴ κινή-
σεως καὶ ἠρεμίας, ἐν ᾧ | πρώτως ἐστὶ καὶ οὐ κατὰ
συμβεβηκός· πάντα γὰρ τὰ ὁρώμενα, ὅσα | μήτε ὑπὸ
τύχης μήτε ὑπ' ἀνάγκης μήτ' ἐστὶ θεῖα μήτε τοιαύτην
αἰτίαν | ἔχει, φυσικὰ λέγεται καὶ φύσιν ἔχει ἰδίαν·
οἷον γῆ πῦρ ὕδωρ ἀὴρ φυτὰ | ζῷα· ἔτι δὲ ταῦτα τὰ
10 γινόμενα, ὄμβροι χάλαζαι κεραυνοὶ πρηστῆρες | ἄνε-
μοι· ταῦτα γὰρ ἔχει ἀρχήν τινα· οὐ γὰρ ἐξ αἰῶνος
ἕκαστον τούτων | ἐστὶν ἀλλ' ἀπό τινος ἀρχῆς γίνεται·
καὶ ταῦτα μέντοι, οἷον ζῷα φυτά, | ἀρχὴν γενέσεως
ἔχει· ἐν δὴ τούτοις ἡ φύσις ἀρχὴ ‹καὶ›⁶ τὸ πρῶτόν
ἐστι· | ἀρχὴ δὲ κινήσεώς ἐστι,⁷ καὶ οὐ μόνον κινήσεως
15 ἀλλὰ καὶ ἠρεμίας· ὅσα | γὰρ ἀρχὴν κινήσεως ἔλαβε,
ταῦτα δύναται λαβεῖν καὶ τελευτήν. διὰ | τοῦτο οὖν ἡ
φύσις ἀρχὴ κινήσεώς ἐστι καὶ ἠρεμίας. (P) |

§2 Aristotle cf. *Phys.* 2.1 192b8–193a8

⁶ καὶ add. MR²
⁷ ἀρχὴ δὲ κινήσεώς ἐστι om. edd.

16

For it is absurd to attempt to speak on the subject of nature but not to know this very thing, the meaning of "nature."

2. Now according to Aristotle nature is the principle 5 [*archê*] of movement and rest for the entity in which it exists primarily and not incidentally. For all things that are visible, which are not the result of chance or necessity, are not divine, and do not have such a (sc. divine) cause, are called "natural" and have their own particular nature. Examples are earth, fire, water, air,[5] plants, living beings.[6] In addition there are also these occurrences: rains, hailstorms, thunderclaps, tornadoes, winds.[7] These phenom- 10 ena have a certain origin [*archê*], for each of them does not exist from eternity, but comes to be from a certain origin. They too, just like living beings and plants, have a beginning [*archê*] of generation. In these entities, therefore, nature is the principle <and> what is primary. It is the principle of movement, and not only of movement, but also of rest, for all entities that have obtained a beginning 15 of movement can also obtain an end. For this reason, therefore, nature is the principle of movement and of rest.

[5] Treated in 1.2, 1.3, and passim.
[6] Treated in Book 5.
[7] Treated in Book 3.

Ps.-Plut. *Plac.* 1.2 (+ Ps.-Gal. *Hist. phil.* 21)

β΄. Τίνι διαφέρει ἀρχὴ καὶ στοιχεῖα (PS) |

1. οἱ μὲν οὖν περὶ Ἀριστοτέλην καὶ Πλάτωνα δια-
φέρειν ἡγοῦνται ἀρχὴν | καὶ στοιχεῖα. (PS) |
2. Θαλῆς δ᾽ ὁ Μιλήσιος ταὐτὸν νομίζει ἀρχὴν καὶ
5 στοιχεῖα. πλεῖστον δ᾽ | ὅσον διαφέρει ἀλλήλων· τὰ
μὲν γὰρ στοιχεῖά ἐστι σύνθετα, τὰς δ᾽ ἀρχάς | φαμεν
εἶναι οὔτε συνθέτους οὔτ᾽ ἀποτελέσματα· οἷον στοι-
χεῖα μὲν | καλοῦμεν γῆν ὕδωρ ἀέρα πῦρ· ἀρχὰς δὲ
λέγομεν διὰ τοῦτο, ὅτι οὐκ ἔχει | τι πρότερον ἐξ οὗ
γεννᾶται, ἐπεὶ οὐκ ἔσται ἀρχὴ τοῦτο, ἀλλ᾽ ἐκεῖνο ἐξ |
οὗ γεγέννηται. τῆς δὲ γῆς καὶ τοῦ ὕδατος[8] ἔστι τινὰ
10 πρότερα ἐξ ὧν | γέγονεν, ἡ ὕλη ἄμορφος οὖσα καὶ
ἀειδής, καὶ τὸ εἶδος ὃ καλοῦμεν | "ἐντελέχειαν," καὶ ἡ
στέρησις. ἁμαρτάνει οὖν ὁ Θαλῆς στοιχεῖον καὶ | ἀρ-
χὴν λέγων τὸ ὕδωρ. (PS) |

§1 Plato cf. *Tim.* 48b–c; Aristotle cf. *Met.* 5.1 1012b34, 5.3
1014a26, 12.4 1070b23   §2 Thales fr. 146, 343, 345 Wöhrle

[8] post ὕδατος: die Luft und das Feuer add. Q

BOOK I: FIRST PRINCIPLES

1.2

Two opposed views of the difference or not between principle and element.

Ps.-Plutarch, *Tenets* (+ Ps.-Galen, *Philosophical History*)

2. In what way principle and elements differ

1. Aristotle, Plato and their followers believe that a principle and elements differ from each other.
2. Thales of Miletus regards a principle and elements as the same thing. But there is a very great difference between the two. For we say that the elements are composite, but that the principles are neither composites nor products. For example, we apply the term elements to earth, water, air and fire. But principles we speak of for the following reason, because there is nothing prior to them from which they originate, since this would then not be a principle, but that from which it had originated. In the case of earth and water there is something from which they come to be, namely matter that is without shape or form, and also form which we call "entelechy," and privation.[8] Thales is therefore mistaken when he says that water is both an element and a principle.[9]

---

[8] Cf. the doxa of Aristotle at 1.3.21.

[9] Thales' view, representative of Preplatonic thought, is criticized. Evaluative comments on the part of the author are very rare, cf. 1.3.2, 1.3.3, 1.7.1[35]. They derive from Aristotle, e.g., *Cael.* 3.5 304b11–13. On these comments see General Introduction 1.5.

1.3

Division of principles (and/or elements) from one to infinitely many according to number, disturbed by later reordering according to chronological lines of succession

Ps.-Plut. *Plac.* 1.3; Stob. *Ecl.* 1.10.12, 14, 16ab; Theod. *Cur.* 4.11–12

γ΄. Περὶ τῶν ἀρχῶν, τί εἰσιν (PS) |

1. Θαλῆς ὁ Μιλήσιος ἀρχὴν τῶν ὄντων ἀπεφήνατο τὸ ὕδωρ—δοκεῖ δ᾽ ὁ | ἀνὴρ οὗτος ἄρξαι τῆς φιλοσοφίας καὶ ἀπ᾽ αὐτοῦ ἡ Ἰωνικὴ αἵρεσις προσηγορεύθη· | ἐγένοντο γὰρ πλεῖσται διαδοχαὶ φιλοσοφίας· φιλοσοφή-
5 σας δ᾽ | ἐν Αἰγύπτῳ ἦλθεν εἰς Μίλητον πρεσβύτε-
ρος⁹—ὃς ἐξ ὕδατος φησι πάντα | εἶναι καὶ εἰς ὕδωρ πάντα ἀναλύεσθαι· στοχάζεται δ᾽ ἐκ τούτου πρῶτον, | ὅτι πάντων τῶν ζῴων ἡ γονὴ ἀρχή ἐστιν, ὑγρὰ οὖσα· οὕτως εἰκὸς καὶ τὰ | πάντα ἐξ ὑγροῦ τὴν ἀρχὴν ἔχειν. δεύτερον, ὅτι πάντα τὰ φυτὰ ὑγρῷ | τρέφεται καὶ καρποφορεῖ, ἀμοιροῦντα δὲ ξηραίνεται· τρίτον,
10 ὅτι καὶ | αὐτὸ τὸ πῦρ τὸ τοῦ ἡλίου καὶ τὸ τῶν ἄστρων ταῖς τῶν ὑδάτων | ἀναθυμιάσεσι τρέφεται καὶ αὐτὸς ὁ

§1 Thales A11; Homer *Il.* 14.246

⁹ δοκεῖ . . . πρεσβύτερος om. S damn. Diels

1.3

from Thales and from Pythagoras. Formal introduction of persons using patronymic and ethnicon.

Ps.-Plutarch, *Tenets*; Stobaeus, *Anthology*; Theodoret, *Cure of Greek Maladies*

3. On principles, what they are

1. Thales the Milesian declared water to be the principle[10] of the things that exist—this man appears to have commenced the pursuit of philosophy and from him the Ionic school of thought took its name, for there have been quite a number of successions of philosophy; after practicing philosophy in Egypt, he came to Miletus as a senior per- 5 son—, he is the one who says that all things take their existence from water and all things are dissolved into water. He supposes this firstly from the fact that semen is the principle of all living beings and is moist. Hence it is likely that all things also have their principle from what is moist. Secondly, because it is by moisture that all the plants are nourished and bear fruit, while if they lack moisture they dry out. Thirdly, because the fire of the sun itself and of 10 the heavenly bodies is also nourished by the exhalations of

[10] Cf. 1.2.2.

κόσμος· διὰ τοῦτο καὶ Ὅμηρος | ταύτην τὴν γνώμην
ὑποτίθεται περὶ τοῦ ὕδατος·

Ὠκεανός, ὅσπερ γένεσις πάντεσσι τέτυκται. (PS) |

2. Ἀναξίμανδρος δὲ Πραξιάδου Μιλήσιός φησι τῶν
15 ὄντων τὴν ἀρχὴν εἶναι | τὸ ἄπειρον· ἐκ γὰρ τούτου
πάντα γίνεσθαι καὶ εἰς τοῦτο πάντα | φθείρεσθαι· διὸ
καὶ γεννᾶσθαι ἀπείρους κόσμους, καὶ πάλιν φθείρε-
σθαι | εἰς τὸ ἐξ οὗ γίνονται. λέγει γοῦν διότι ἀπέραν-
τον ἐστιν, ἵνα μηδὲν | ἐλλείπῃ ἡ γένεσις ἡ ὑφισταμένη.
ἁμαρτάνει δ' οὗτος μὴ λέγων τί ἐστι | τὸ ἄπειρον,
πότερον ἀήρ ἐστιν ἢ ὕδωρ ἢ γῆ ἢ ἄλλα τινὰ σώματα.
20 ἁμαρτάνει | οὖν τὴν μὲν ὕλην ἀποφαινόμενος τὸ δὲ
ποιοῦν αἴτιον ἀναιρῶν· τὸ | γὰρ ἄπειρον οὐδὲν ἄλλο
ἢ ὕλη ἐστίν· οὐ δύναται δ' ἡ ὕλη εἶναι ἐνεργείᾳ, | ἂν
μὴ τὸ ποιοῦν ὑποκέηται. (PS) |

3. Ἀναξιμένης Εὐρυστράτου Μιλήσιος ἀρχὴν τῶν
ὄντων ἀέρα ἀπεφήνατο· | ἐκ γὰρ τούτου πάντα γίνε-
25 σθαι καὶ εἰς αὐτὸν πάλιν ἀναλύεσθαι· οἷον ἡ | ψυχή,
φησίν, ἡ ἡμετέρα ἀὴρ οὖσα συγκρατεῖ ἡμᾶς, καὶ
ὅλον τὸν κόσμον | πνεῦμα καὶ ἀὴρ περιέχει· λέγεται
δὲ συνωνύμως ἀὴρ καὶ πνεῦμα. | ἁμαρτάνει δὲ καὶ
οὗτος ἐξ ἁπλοῦ καὶ μονοειδοῦς ἀέρος καὶ πνεύματος |
δοκῶν συνεστάναι τὰ ζῷα· ἀδύνατον γὰρ ἀρχὴν μίαν
τὴν ὕλην τῶν | ὄντων ὑποστῆναι, ἀλλὰ καὶ τὸ ποιοῦν
30 αἴτιον χρὴ ὑποτιθέναι· οἷον | ἄργυρος οὐκ ἀρκεῖ πρὸς

§2 Anaximander A14   §3 Anaximenes B2

the waters, and this applies to the cosmos too. For this reason Homer too assumes this view on the subject of water when he writes:

Ocean, who was the origin for all things.

2. Anaximander, the son of Praxiades, the Milesian says that the unlimited is the principle of the things that exist. For from this all things come into being and back to this all things perish. For this reason unlimited worlds are begotten and again perish back to that from which they originate. He also states the reason why it is without limit, namely that the underlying process of generation will never fail. But he goes astray when he declares matter to be the principle, but neglects the efficient cause.[11] For the unlimited is nothing else than matter. But the matter cannot be in a state of being actualized, unless the efficient cause has been postulated.

3. Anaximenes, the son of Eurystratus, the Milesian declared air to be the principle of the things that exist, for from this all things come to be and back to it they are dissolved again. Just as, he says, our soul, which is air, holds us together and dominates us, so also *pneuma* and air contain the entire cosmos. Air and *pneuma* are used synonymously. But this man too goes astray when he appears to compose the living beings out of simple and uniform air and *pneuma*,[12] for it is impossible for matter to subsist as the single principle of the things that exist. Rather it is necessary also to postulate the efficient cause. For example, silver is not sufficient for the generation of

[11] Evaluative comments on the part of the author are very rare; cf. note at 1.2.2.   [12] See previous note.

τὸ ἔκπωμα γενέσθαι, ἂν μὴ καὶ τὸ ποιοῦν ᾖ, | τουτ-
έστιν ὁ ἀργυροκόπος· ὁμοίως καὶ ἐπὶ τοῦ χαλκοῦ καὶ
τοῦ ξύλου καὶ | τῆς ἄλλης ὕλης. (PS) |

4. Ἀναξαγόρας Ἡγησιβούλου ὁ Κλαζομένιος ἀρχὰς
τῶν ὄντων τὰς | ὁμοιομερείας ἀπεφήνατο· ἐδόκει γὰρ
35 αὐτῷ ἀπορώτατον εἶναι, πῶς ἐκ | τοῦ μὴ ὄντος δύναταί
τι γίνεσθαι ἢ φθείρεσθαι εἰς τὸ μὴ ὄν· τροφὴν γοῦν
| προσφερόμεθα ἁπλῆν καὶ μονοειδῆ οἷον τὸν Δη-
μήτριον ἄρτον,[10] τὸ ὕδωρ | πίνοντες· καὶ ἐκ ταύτης τῆς
τροφῆς τρέφεται θρὶξ φλὲψ ἀρτηρία σάρξ | νεῦρα
ὀστᾶ καὶ τὰ λοιπὰ μόρια. τούτων οὖν γινομένων ὁμο-
λογητέον | ἐστὶν ὅτι ἐν τῇ τροφῇ τῇ προσφερομένῃ
40 πάντα ἐστὶ τὰ ὄντα καὶ ἐκ τῶν | ὄντων πάντα αὔξεται
καὶ ἐν ἐκείνῃ ἐστὶ τῇ τροφῇ μόρια αἵματος | γεννη-
τικὰ καὶ νεύρων καὶ ὀστέων καὶ τῶν ἄλλων· ἃ ἦν
λόγῳ θεωρητὰ | μόρια. οὐ γὰρ δεῖ πάντα ἐπὶ τὴν αἴ-
σθησιν ἀνάγειν, ὅτι ἄρτος καὶ τὸ ὕδωρ | ταῦτα κατα-
σκευάζει,[11] ἀλλ᾽ ἐν τούτοις ἔστι λόγῳ θεωρητὰ μόρια.
ἀπὸ | τοῦ οὖν ὅμοια τὰ μέρη εἶναι ἐν τῇ τροφῇ τοῖς
45 γεννωμένοις ὁμοιομερείας | αὐτὰς ἐκάλεσε καὶ ἀρχὰς
τῶν ὄντων ἀπεφήνατο· καὶ τὰς μὲν ὁμοιομερείας |
ὕλην, τὸ δὲ ποιοῦν αἴτιον τὸν νοῦν τὸν τὰ πάντα δια-
ταξάμενον. | ἄρχεται δ᾽ οὕτως· "ὁμοῦ πάντα χρήματα

§4 Anaxagoras A46, B1

[10] post ἄρτον: ἔδοντες prop. Mau
[11] 40–43 καὶ . . . κατασκευάζει om. S

the drinking cup, unless there is also the efficient cause, namely the silversmith. And similarly in the case of bronze and wood and other kinds of matter.

4. Anaxagoras, the son of Hegesibulus, from Clazomenae declared the *homoiomereiai* (things with like parts) to be principles of the things that exist. For it seemed to him most puzzling how anything could come to be from the nonexistent and perish back to the nonexistent. For instance, we consume simple and uniform food such as the bread of Demeter and when drinking water. From this food the nourishment occurs of hair, veins, arteries, flesh, tendons, bones and the remaining parts of the body. Since this nourishment occurs, it must be agreed that all the things that result are already present in the food we consume; and from the things that are present all things will grow and in that food there are particles that generate blood and tendons and bones and the other parts, particles that were only observable by reason. For it is not necessary to refer everything to sense perception in saying that bread and water produce these things, but rather to say that in them particles observable by reason are present. Thus from the presence in the food of particles similar to what is produced he called them *homoiomereiai* (things with like parts) and declared them to be the principles of the things that exist. In addition, the *homoiomereiai* are matter, while the efficient cause is the Intellect that brought all things to order. He begins his treatise as follows: "Together were all things, but Intellect divided and

ἦν, νοῦς δ' αὐτὰ διῆρε[12] καὶ | διεκόσμησε," "χρήματα"
λέγων τὰ πράγματα. ἀποδεκτέος οὖν ἐστιν, ὅτι | τῇ
ὕλῃ τὸν τεχνίτην προσέζευξεν. (PS) |

50 5. Ἀρχέλαος Ἀπολλοδώρου Ἀθηναῖος ἀέρα ἄπειρον
καὶ τὴν περὶ αὐτὸν | πυκνότητα καὶ μάνωσιν· τούτων
δὲ τὸ μὲν εἶναι πῦρ τὸ δ' ὕδωρ. (PS) |

6. οὗτοι μὲν οὖν ἐφεξῆς ἀλλήλοις ταῖς διαδοχαῖς
γενόμενοι τὴν λεχθεῖσαν | Ἰωνικὴν ἐκπληροῦσι φιλο-
σοφίαν ἀπὸ Θάλητος.[13] (P, cf. S) |

7. πάλιν δ' ἀπ' ἄλλης ἀρχῆς Πυθαγόρας Μνησάρχου
55 Σάμιος, ὁ πρῶτος | φιλοσοφίαν τούτῳ τῷ ῥήματι
προσαγορεύσας, ἀρχὰς τοὺς ἀριθμοὺς καὶ | τὰς συμ-
μετρίας τὰς ἐν τούτοις, ἃς καὶ "ἁρμονίας" καλεῖ, τὰ
δ' ἐξ ἀμφοτέρων | σύνθετα στοιχεῖα, καλούμενα δὲ
γεωμετρικά·

πάλιν δὲ τὴν μονάδα καὶ τὴν ἀόριστον δυάδα ἐν
ταῖς ἀρχαῖς. | σπεύδει δ' αὐτῷ τῶν ἀρχῶν ἡ μὲν ἐπὶ
60 τὸ ποιητικὸν αἴτιον καὶ εἰδικόν, | ὅπερ ἐστὶ νοῦς ὁ
θεός, ἡ δ' ἐπὶ τὸ παθητικόν τε καὶ ὑλικόν, ὅπερ ἐστὶν
ὁ | ὁρατὸς κόσμος.

§5 Archelaus A7   §6 Thales fr. 344 Wöhrle
§7 Pythagoreans B15; 72–73 cf. *Pythagorean Golden Verses*
47–48 Thom; 88 Homer *Od.* 5.306

[12] διῆρε coni. MR: διῆρε P (om. S)
[13] ἀπὸ Θάλητος P: οὕτω προσαγορευθεῖσαν διότι Μιλήσιος αὐτῆς κατῆρξεν ἀνὴρ ὁ Θαλῆς ἀπὸ τῆς τῶν Ἰώνων
μητροπόλεως paraphr. S ex §1

ordered them," by "things" meaning the realities that exist. It must be accepted, therefore, that he coupled the artificer with the matter.

5. Archelaus, the son of Apollodorus, the Athenian says the principles of the things that exist are unlimited air and the density and rarefaction associated with it; of these the one is fire and the other water.

6. Now these are the men who followed each other and comprised the above-mentioned Ionic philosophy starting from Thales.[13]

7. But next we have another beginning: Pythagoras, the son of Mnesarchus, from Samos, the first to call philosophy by this name, declared that the numbers and the relationships between them, which he also calls "harmonies," are the principles, while the compounds from each of these, the so-called geometricals, are the elements.[14]

There again, he places the Monad and the Undeterminate Dyad among the principles. Of his principles, the one strives toward the efficient and formal cause, which is God the Intellect, the other toward the passive and material cause, which is the visible cosmos.

[13] See the beginning of the chapter.
[14] The long account of Pythagoreanism that follows, personified by its founding father, is determined by Platonizing and Neopythagorean reception.

εἶναι δὲ τὴν φύσιν τοῦ ἀριθμοῦ δεκάδα· μέχρι γὰρ
τῶν δέκα πάντες | Ἕλληνες, πάντες βάρβαροι ἀριθ-
μοῦσιν, ἐφ' ἃ ἐλθόντες πάλιν ἀναποδίζουσιν | ἐπὶ τὴν
μονάδα· καὶ τῶν δέκα πάλιν, φησίν, ἡ δύναμίς ἐστιν
65 ἐν | τοῖς τέσσαρσι καὶ τῇ τετράδι· τὸ δ' αἴτιον, εἴ τις
ἀπὸ τῆς μονάδος κατὰ | πρόσθεσιν τιθείη τοὺς ἀριθ-
μούς, ἄχρι τῶν τεσσάρων προελθὼν ἐκπληρώσει | τὸν
δέκα ἀριθμόν· ἐὰν δὲ ὑπερβάληται τὸν τῆς τετράδος,
καὶ τῶν | δέκα ὑπερεκπεσεῖται· οἷον εἴ τις θείη ἓν καὶ
δύο προσθείη καὶ τρία καὶ | τούτοις τέσσαρα, τὸν τῶν
70 δέκα πληρώσει ἀριθμόν· ὥστε ὁ ἀριθμὸς κατὰ | μὲν
μονάδα ἐν τοῖς δέκα κατὰ δὲ δύναμιν ἐν τοῖς τέσ-
σαρσι. διὸ καὶ | ἐπεφθέγγοντο οἱ Πυθαγόρειοι, ὡς με-
γίστου ὅρκου ὄντος τῆς τετράδος, |

 οὐ μὰ τὸν ἁμετέρᾳ ψυχᾷ παραδόντα τετρακτύν, |
παγὰν ἀεννάου φύσεος ῥίζωμά τ' ἔχουσαν. |

καὶ ἡ ἡμετέρα ψυχή, φησίν, ἐκ τετράδος σύγκειται·
75 εἶναι γὰρ | νοῦν ἐπιστήμην δόξαν αἴσθησιν, ἐξ ὧν
πᾶσα τέχνη καὶ ἐπιστήμη καὶ | αὐτοὶ λογικοί ἐσμεν.
νοῦς μὲν οὖν ἡ μονάς ἐστιν· ὁ γὰρ νοῦς κατὰ | μονάδα
θεωρεῖται, οἷον πολλῶν ὄντων ἀνθρώπων οἱ μὲν ἐπὶ
μέρους εἰσὶν | ἀναίσθητοι ἀπερίληπτοι καὶ ἄπειροι,
ἀλλ' αὐτὸ τοῦτο ἄνθρωπον ἕνα | μόνον νοοῦμεν, ᾧ
οὐδεὶς ἔτυχεν ὅμοιος· καὶ ἵππον ἕνα μόνον νοοῦμεν,
80 οἱ | δ' ἐπὶ μέρους εἰσὶν ἄπειροι. τὰ γὰρ εἴδη ταῦτα
πάντα καὶ γένη κατὰ | μονάδας εἰσί· διὸ καὶ ἐπὶ ἑνὸς
ἑκάστου αὐτῶν τοῦτον τὸν ὅρον | ἀποδιδόντες λέγουσι

As for the nature of number, he says it is the decad; for all the Greeks and all the barbarians count up to the ten, and when they reach it they return back to the monad. And again, as for the number ten, he says, its power consists in the four and the tetrad. The reason is that, if one departing 65 from the monad were to posit the numbers by addition, by advancing to the four one completes the number ten. If, however, one goes beyond the number of the tetrad, one will also fall beyond the ten. For instance, if one were to posit one and two and to add three, and four to those, one will complete the number ten. The result is that number according to the Monad is located within the ten, but ac- 70 cording to its generative power within the four. For this reason the Pythagoreans made the following pronounce- ment, regarding the tetrad as their strongest oath:

No, by him, who bestows on our soul the *tetraktys*, possessing the fount of ever-flowing nature and its root.

Our soul too, he says, is composed of the tetrad. For there are intellect, knowledge, opinion, and sense percep- 75 tion; from these every skill and every science originates, and through them we ourselves are rational. Now Intellect is the Monad, for intellect contemplates in terms of the Monad. For example, if you take the multitude of human beings, the individuals cannot all be perceived or grasped and are unlimited in number, but this is the very thing that we intelligize, the single human being only, which no one fully resembles. Similarly we intelligize the single horse only, but the individual horses are unlimited in number. 80 For all these forms and genera are in accordance with the monads. Hence in the case of each of these, they formu-

ζῷον λογικὸν ἢ ζῷον χρεμετιστικόν. διὰ τοῦτο οὖν |
νοῦς ἡ μονάς, ᾧ ταῦτα νοοῦμεν, καὶ ἡ δυὰς δ' ἡ ἀό-
ριστος ἐπιστήμη, | εἰκότως· πᾶσα γὰρ ἀπόδειξις καὶ
85 πᾶσα πίστις ἐπιστήμης, πρὸς δὲ καὶ | πᾶς συλλο-
γισμὸς ἔκ τινων ὁμολογουμένων τὸ ἀμφισβητούμε-
νον | συνάγει καὶ ῥᾳδίως ἀποδείκνυται ἕτερον· ὧν ἡ
ἐπιστήμη κατάληψίς | ἐστι, διὸ εἴη ἂν δυάς. ἡ δὲ δόξα
τριὰς ἐκ καταλήψεώς ἐστιν, εὐλόγως, | ὅτι πολλῶν
ἐστιν ἡ δόξα· ἡ δὲ τριὰς πλῆθος, ὡς "τρισμάκαρες
Δαναοί." | διὰ τοῦτο οὖν ἐγκρίνει τὴν τριάδα
***.[14] (PS) |

90 8. ἡ δὲ τούτων αἵρεσις Ἰταλικὴ προσηγορεύθη διὰ τὸ
τὸν Πυθαγόραν ἐν | Ἰταλίᾳ σχολάσαι· μετέστη γὰρ
ἀπὸ Σάμου τῆς πατρίδος, τῇ Πολυκράτους | τυραννίδι
δυσαρεστήσας.[15] (P) |

9. Ἡράκλειτος καὶ Ἵππασος ὁ Μεταποντῖνος ἀρχὴν
τῶν πάντων τὸ πῦρ· | ἐκ πυρὸς γὰρ τὰ πάντα γίνε-
95 σθαι καὶ εἰς πῦρ πάντα τελευτᾶν λέγουσι· | τούτου δὲ
κατασβεννυμένου κοσμοποιεῖσθαι τὰ πάντα. πρῶτον
μὲν γὰρ | τὸ παχυμερέστατον αὐτοῦ εἰς αὐτὸ συστελ-
λόμενον γῆ γίγνεται, ἔπειτ' | ἀναχαλωμένην τὴν γῆν
ὑπὸ τοῦ πυρὸς φύσει ὕδωρ ἀποτελεῖσθαι, ἀναθυμιώ-
μενον | δ' ἀέρα γίνεσθαι· πάλιν δὲ τὸν κόσμον καὶ
πάντα τὰ | σώματα ὑπὸ πυρὸς ἀναλοῦσθαι ἐν τῇ ἐκ-

§8 —   §9 Heraclitus A5; Hippasus 18.7

[14] 74–89 om. S   [15] 90–92 om. S, exhib. P ad fin. cap.,
transp. edd. post 89 τριάδα (lac.)

late the definition as follows, speaking of a rational living being or a living being that neighs. For this reason, therefore, the Intellect, by which we intelligize these things, is the Monad, and the Indeterminate Dyad is knowledge, and this is quite likely, since every demonstration and every proof involving knowledge, and in addition every 85 syllogism, deduces what is in dispute and effortlessly demonstrates something else from agreed premises. Knowledge is the understanding of these factors and so would be the Dyad. Opinion, taking its starting point from understanding, is the triad, and this is quite reasonable too, because opinion deals with multiplicity. The triad is plurality, as in the case of the "thrice-blessed Danaans." For this reason, therefore, he includes the triad . . . (lacuna)

8. The school of thought of these men has been named 90 "Italic" because Pythagoras taught in Italy, for he moved away from his native land Samos after he became displeased with the tyranny of Polycrates.

9. Heraclitus and Hippasus from Metapontum say that the principle of all things is fire, for they state that all things originate from fire and all things terminate in fire; but 95 when it is quenched, all things are formed into the cosmos. For first its densest part is concentrated and becomes earth; then the earth is loosened by fire and naturally produces water, which in turn evaporates and becomes air. And then the cosmos and all the bodies within it are consumed again by fire in the conflagration. The principle of

100 πυρώσει. ἀρχὴ οὖν τὸ πῦρ, ὅτι | ἐκ τούτου τὰ πάντα·
τέλος δέ, ὅτι καὶ εἰς τοῦτο ἀναλύεται τὰ πάντα. | (PS) |
10. Διογένης δὲ ὁ Ἀπολλωνιάτης ἀέρα ἄπειρον. (S) |
11. Ξενοφάνης ἀρχὴν τῶν πάντων εἶναι τὴν γῆν· γρά-
φει γὰρ ἐν τῷ Περὶ | φύσεως· |

> ἐκ γῆς γὰρ πάντα καὶ εἰς γῆν[16] πάντα
> τελευτᾷ. (S) |

12. Φιλόλαος ὁ Πυθαγόρειος τὸ πέρας καὶ τὸ ἄπει-
ρον. (S) |
13. Λεύκιππος Μιλήσιος ἀρχὰς καὶ στοιχεῖα τὸ
πλῆρες καὶ τὸ κενόν. (S) |
14. Δημόκριτος τὰ ναστὰ καὶ κενόν. (ST) |
15. Μητρόδωρος Θεοκρίτου Χῖος τὰ ἀδιαίρετα καὶ τὸ
κενόν. (ST) |

110 16. Ἐπίκουρος Νεοκλέους Ἀθηναῖος κατὰ Δημόκριτον
φιλοσοφήσας ἔφη | τὰς ἀρχὰς τῶν ὄντων σώματα,
λόγῳ θεωρητά, ἀμέτοχα κενοῦ, ἀγέννητα, | ἀδιά-
φθαρτα, οὔτε θραυσθῆναι δυνάμενα οὔτε διαπλασμὸν
ἐκ τῶν | μερῶν λαβεῖν οὔτ' ἀλλοιωθῆναι· εἶναι δ' αὐτὰ
λόγῳ θεωρητά· ταῦτα | μέντοι κινεῖσθαι ἐν τῷ κενῷ
115 καὶ διὰ τοῦ κενοῦ· εἶναι δὲ καὶ αὐτὸ τὸ | κενὸν ἄπειρον

§10 Diogenes 64A7   §11 Xenophanes A36, B27
§12 Philolaus A9   §13 Leucippus A12
§14 Democritus A46   §15 Metrodorus A2
§16 Epicurus fr. 267

[16] γῆς S: γαίης edd. ex S.E. *M.* 10.313

the things that exist therefore is fire, because all things   100
originate from it; and it is the end as well, because all
things are dissolved into it.

10. But Diogenes of Apollonia says that the principle of
the things that exist is unlimited air.

11. Xenophanes says that the principle of all things is the
earth; for he writes in the work *On Nature*:

> From earth all things come and in earth all things
>   terminate.

12. Philolaus the Pythagorean says that the principles of
the things that exist are the limit and the unlimited.

13. Leucippus the Milesian says that the principles and
elements of the things that exist are the full and the void.

14. Democritus says that the principles of the things that
exist are the solids and the void.

15. Metrodorus, the son of Theocritus, from Chios says
that the principles of the things that exist are the undi-
visibles and the void.

16. Epicurus, the son of Neocles, the Athenian, who phi-   110
losophized in the line of Democritus, said that the principles of the things that exist are bodies that are observable
by reason, not containing any void, ungenerated, indestructible, unable to be crushed or have their parts
modified or be qualitatively altered. These bodies are observable by reason; and they move with the void and
throughout the void. The void itself is unlimited in size,   115

καὶ τὰ σώματα ἄπειρα. συμβεβηκέναι δὲ τοῖς σώμασι | τρία ταῦτα, σχῆμα μέγεθος βάρος. Δημόκριτος μὲν γὰρ ἔλεγε δύο, | μέγεθός τε καὶ σχῆμα, ὁ δ᾽ Ἐπίκουρος τούτοις καὶ τρίτον, τὸ βάρος, | ἐπέθηκεν· "ἀνάγκη γάρ," φησί, "κινεῖσθαι τὰ σώματα τῇ τοῦ βάρους | πληγῇ· ἐπεὶ οὐ κινηθήσεται." εἶναι δὲ τὰ σχήματα
120 τῶν ἀτόμων ἀπερίληπτα, | οὐκ ἄπειρα· μὴ γὰρ εἶναι μήτ᾽ ἀγκιστροειδεῖς μήτε τριαινοειδεῖς | μήτε κρικοειδεῖς· ταῦτα γὰρ τὰ σχήματα εὔθραυστά ἐστιν, αἱ δ᾽ | ἄτομοι ἀπαθεῖς ἄθραυστοι· ἴδια δ᾽ ἔχειν σχήματα λόγῳ θεωρητά. καὶ | εἴρηται ἄτομος, οὐχ ὅτι ἐστὶν ἐλαχίστη ἀλλ᾽ ὅτι οὐ δύναται τμηθῆναι, | ἀπαθὴς οὖσα καὶ ἀμέτοχος κενοῦ· ὥστε, ἐὰν εἴπῃ ἄτομον,
125 ἄθραυστον | λέγει καὶ ἀπαθῆ, ἀμέτοχον κενοῦ. ὅτι δὲ ἔστιν ἄτομα, σαφές· καὶ γὰρ | ἔστι στοιχεῖα ἀεὶ ὄντα καὶ ζῷα <ἄ>κενα[17] καὶ ἡ μονάς.[18] (PS, cf. T) |

17. Ἔκφαντος Συρακούσιος, εἷς τῶν Πυθαγορείων, πάντων τὰ ἀδιαίρετα | σώματα καὶ τὸ κενόν. τὰς γὰρ Πυθαγορικὰς μονάδας οὗτος πρῶτος | ἀπεφήνατο σωματικάς. (ST) |

130 18. Διόδωρος ἐπίκλην Κρόνος τὰ ἀμερῆ σώματα ἄπειρα, τὰ δ᾽ αὐτὰ λεγόμενα | καὶ ἐλάχιστα· ἄπειρα μὲν κατ᾽ ἀριθμόν, ὡρισμένα δὲ κατὰ μέγεθος. | (S) |

§17 Ecphantus 51.2
§18 Diodorus Cronus fr. 117A

17 <ἄ>κενα coni. Mras: κενα P crucif. alii
18 ὥστε . . . μονάς P: non hab. S, secl. Diels

and the bodies are unlimited in number. The bodies possess these three characteristics, shape, size, weight. Democritus stated that there were two, size and shape, but Epicurus added to these a third, weight. "For it is necessary," he says, "that the bodies are moved by the blow caused by weight, since they will otherwise not be moved."[15] The shapes of the atoms are inconceivably many, but not unlimited in number. They cannot have the form of a hook or a trident or a bracelet, for these shapes are easily crushed, whereas atoms are impassible and unable to be crushed. They have their individual shapes, which are observable by reason. The term atom is used, not because it is a smallest particle, but because it cannot be cut, being as it is impassible and not containing any void. As a result, when he speaks of an atom, he means what is uncrushable and impassible, not containing any void. That there is such as thing as an atom is clear. For there are elements that always exist, that is to say figures ‹without void›, and the unit.

17. Ecphantus of Syracuse, one of the Pythagoreans, says that the principles of all things are the indivisible bodies and the void, for this man was the first to declare that the Pythagorean monads were corporeal.

18. Diodorus, with the surname Cronus, says that the principles are the unlimited partless bodies, those that are also called the least in size. They are unlimited in number, but bounded in size.

15 Sc. not by their soul or a divinity.

19. Ἐμπεδοκλῆς Μέτωνος Ἀκραγαντῖνος τέσσαρα μὲν
λέγει στοιχεῖα, πῦρ | ἀέρα ὕδωρ γῆν, δύο δ᾽ ἀρχικὰς
135 δυνάμεις, Φιλίαν τε καὶ Νεῖκος· ὧν ἡ μέν | ἐστιν ἑνω-
τικὴ τὸ δὲ διαιρετικόν. φησὶ δ᾽ οὕτως· |

τέσσαρα τῶν πάντων ῥιζώματα πρῶτον ἄκουε· |
Ζεὺς ἀργὴς Ἥρη τε φερέσβιος ἠδ᾽ Ἀιδωνεύς, |
Νῆστίς θ᾽, ἣ δακρύοις τέγγει κρούνωμα
βρότειον. |

Δία μὲν γὰρ λέγει τὴν ζέσιν καὶ τὸν αἰθέρα, Ἥρην
140 τε φερέσβιον τὸν | ἀέρα, τὴν δὲ γῆν τὸν Ἀιδωνέα,
Νῆστιν δὲ καὶ κρούνωμα βρότειον οἱονεὶ | τὸ σπέρμα
καὶ τὸ ὕδωρ. (P, cf. S) |

20. Σωκράτης Σωφρονίσκου Ἀθηναῖος καὶ[19] Πλάτων
Ἀρίστωνος Ἀθηναῖος (αἱ | γὰρ αὐταὶ περὶ παντὸς ἑκα-
τέρου δόξαι[20]) τρεῖς ἀρχάς, τὸν θεὸν τὴν ὕλην | τὴν
ἰδέαν· ὑφ᾽ οὗ, ἐξ οὗ, πρὸς ὅ. ὁ δὲ θεὸς νοῦς ἐστι τοῦ
145 κόσμου, ὕλη δὲ | τὸ ὑποκείμενον πρῶτον γενέσει καὶ
φθορᾷ, ἰδέα δ᾽ οὐσία ἀσώματος ἐν | τοῖς νοήμασι καὶ
ταῖς φαντασίαις τοῦ θεοῦ. (PST) |

21. Ἀριστοτέλης δὲ Νικομάχου Σταγειρίτης ἀρχὰς
μὲν ἐντελέχειαν ἤτοι | εἶδος ὕλην στέρησιν· στοιχεῖα

§19 Empedocles A33, B6
§20 Socrates Plato Bst. 113.2 DB
§21 Aristotle cf. *Met.* 12.1 1069b32–34 etc.

[19] Σωκράτης . . . καὶ om. S, del. Diels
[20] αἱ γὰρ . . . δόξαι om. S, del. Diels

19. Empedocles, the son of Meton, from Agrigentum says
that there are four elements, fire air water earth, and two
principal powers, Love and Strife, of which the former is   135
unifying, the latter divisive. He speaks as follows:

> Hear first about the four foundational roots of all
>   things,
> clear-bright Zeus and life-bearing Hera and
>   Aidoneus,
> and Nestis, who with her tears dampens the mortal
>   wellspring.

By Zeus he means the seething heat and the ether, by life-
bearing Hera the air, by Aidoneus the earth, and by Nestis   140
and the mortal wellspring such as semen and water.
20. Socrates, the son of Sophroniscus, the Athenian,[16] and
Plato, the son of Aristo, the Athenian—after all, the opinions of each of them are the same on every matter—say
that there are three principles: god, matter, idea, these
being equivalent to by whom, out of which, toward which.
The god is the Intellect of the cosmos, matter the primary   145
substrate for generation and destruction, while the idea is
an incorporeal substance in the conceptions and the impressions of the god.[17]
21. But Aristotle, the son of Nicomachus, from Stagira says
that the principles are entelechy (*entelecheia*) or form,
matter, privation, and the elements are four, but there is

---

16 Socrates is included as the link in the succession in order
to connect Preplatonic and Postplatonic physics.

17 For the conceptions and perceptions of the god, cf.
4.11[19–21].

δὲ τέσσαρα, πέμπτον δέ τι σῶμα αἰθέριον | ἀμετά-
βλητον. στοιχεῖα δὲ τῶν γενητῶν κατὰ μὲν τὰς δυνά-
150 μεις θερμόν, | ψυχρόν, ὑγρόν, ξηρόν, κατὰ δὲ τὰς
οὐσίας, ἐν αἷς καὶ περὶ ἃς | ὑπάρχουσιν αὗται, τὰ
τέτταρα. (PST) |

22. Ξενοκράτης συνεστάναι τὸ πᾶν ἐκ τοῦ ἑνὸς καὶ
τοῦ ἀεννάου, ἀένναον | τὴν ὕλην αἰνιττόμενος διὰ τοῦ
πλήθους. (ST) |

23. Ζήνων Μνασέου Κιτιεὺς ἀρχὰς μὲν τὸν θεὸν καὶ
155 τὴν ὕλην, ὧν ὁ μέν ἐστι | τοῦ ποιεῖν αἴτιος ἡ δὲ τοῦ
πάσχειν, στοιχεῖα δὲ τέτταρα. (PST) |

24. Στράτων στοιχεῖα ⟨θερμὸν⟩[21] καὶ ψυχρόν. (S) |

§22 Xenocrates fr. 21   §23 Zeno 1.85
§24 Strato fr. 46

1.4

Ps.-Plut. *Plac.* 1.4 (+ Ps.-Gal. *Hist. phil.* 33)

δ΄. Πῶς συνέστηκεν ὁ κόσμος (P) |

1. ὁ τοίνυν κόσμος συνέστη περικεκλασμένῳ σχήματι
ἐσχηματισμένος τὸν | τρόπον τοῦτον. τῶν ἀτόμων σω-

§1 Leucippus 67A24, cf. Epicurus fr. 308
[21] ⟨θερμὸν⟩ add. edd.

also a fifth that is an etherial and unchangeable body. The elements of generated things are, in terms of their qualities, hot, cold, wet, dry, while in terms of their essential natures, in which and concerning which these qualities exist, they are the four (sc. mentioned above). 150

22. Xenocrates says that the universe is constituted from the One and the ever-flowing [or: negating unity],[18] with the term ever-flowing hinting at matter on account of its multiplicity.

23. Zeno, the son of Mnaseas, from Citium says that the principles are the god and matter, of which the former is the cause of action, the latter of passivity, but the elements 155 are four in number.

24. Strato says the elements are ⟨the hot⟩ and the cold.

1.4

An atomist view as example of cosmogony.

Ps.-Plutarch, *Tenets* (+ Ps.-Galen, *Philosophical History*)

4. How the cosmos was constituted

1. The cosmos therefore was constituted, configured with a curved shape, in the following manner. Since the indivis-

18 This alternative translation would reflect Diels' emendation of the manuscripts' *aennaos* to *aenaos*, which we have not adopted. For further details, see MR ad loc.

μάτων ἀπρονόητον καὶ τυχαίαν ἐχόντων | τὴν κίνησιν
συνεχῶς τε καὶ τάχιστα κινουμένων εἰς τὸ αὐτό,
5 πολλὰ | σώματα συνηθροίσθη διὰ τοῦτο, ποικιλίαν
ἔχοντα καὶ σχημάτων καὶ | μεγεθῶν. ἀθροιζομένων δ᾽
ἐν ταὐτῷ τούτων, τὰ μέν, ὅσα μείζονα ἦν καὶ | βαρύ-
τατα, πάντως ὑπεκάθιζεν· ὅσα δὲ μικρὰ καὶ περιφερῆ
καὶ λεῖα καὶ | εὐόλισθα, ταῦτα καὶ ἐξεθλίβετο κατὰ
τὴν σύνοδον τῶν σωμάτων εἴς τε | τὸ μετέωρον ἀνε-
φέρετο. ὡς δ᾽ οὖν ἐξέλιπε μὲν ἡ πληκτικὴ δύναμις |
10 μετεωρίζουσα, οὐκέτι δ᾽ ἦγεν ἡ πληγὴ πρὸς τὸ μετέω-
ρον, ἐκωλύετο δὲ | ταῦτα κάτω φέρεσθαι, ἐπιέζετο
πρὸς τοὺς τόπους τοὺς δυναμένους | δέξασθαι· οὗτοι
δ᾽ ἦσαν οἱ πέριξ, καὶ πρὸς τούτοις τὸ πλῆθος τῶν |
σωμάτων περιεκλᾶτο, περιπλεκόμενα δ᾽ ἀλλήλοις
κατὰ τὴν περίκλασιν | τὸν οὐρανὸν ἐγέννησεν. τῆς δ᾽
15 αὐτῆς ἐχόμεναι φύσεως αἱ ἄτομοι, | ποικίλαι οὖσαι,
καθὼς εἴρηται, πρὸς τὸ μετέωρον ἐξωθούμεναι τὴν
τῶν | ἀστέρων φύσιν ἀπετέλουν· τὸ δὲ πλῆθος τῶν
ἀναθυμιωμένων σωμάτων | ἔπληττε τὸν ἀέρα καὶ τοῦ-
τον ἐξέθλιβε· πνευματούμενος δ᾽ οὗτος κατὰ | τὴν κί-
νησιν καὶ συμπεριλαμβάνων τὰ ἄστρα συμπεριῆγε
ταῦτα καὶ τὴν | νῦν περιφορὰν αὐτῶν μετέωρον
20 ἐφύλαττε. κἄπειτα ἐκ μὲν τῶν ὑποκαθιζόντων | ἐγεν-
νήθη ἡ γῆ, ἐκ δὲ τῶν μετεωριζομένων οὐρανὸς πῦρ
ἀήρ. | πολλῆς δ᾽ ὕλης ἔτι περιειλημμένης ἐν τῇ γῇ,
πυκνουμένης τε ταύτης | κατὰ τὰς ἀπὸ τῶν πνευμάτων
πληγὰς καὶ τὰς ἀπὸ τῶν ἀστέρων αὐγάς,[22] | προσε-

---

[22] αὐγὰς EQ Usener: αὔρας P

40

ible bodies (*atoma sômata*) have a nonprovidential and random movement and are continually and at great speed moving toward the same place, many bodies manifesting 5 a diversity of both shapes and sizes were for this reason collected together. As these bodies gathered together in the same place, those that were larger and heaviest settled down entirely. But those that were small and round and smooth and mobile were squeezed out as the bodies collided and were carried upward to the higher region. As then the force of the shock that had lifted them upward 10 lessened, the shock no longer bore them toward the higher region and they were prevented from moving downward, they were pushed toward the places that were able to receive them. These places were on the periphery and it was against them that the mass of bodies was bent around. Entangling with each other in accordance with this bending, they gave rise to the heaven. The indivisibles (*atomoi*) that had the same nature were diverse, as has been said, 15 and on being pushed out toward the higher region they produced the nature of the heavenly bodies. But the mass of bodies that rose up in exhalations struck the air and compressed it. This then through its motion turned into wind and, taking up the heavenly bodies it led them along in its course, thereby preserving their present revolution on high. Then from the bodies that had sunk downward the earth arose, while from those that rose upward the 20 heaven, fire, and air were formed. Since a considerable amount of matter was still contained within the earth and it was compacted by the pounding of the winds and the fiery rays from the stars, the entire configuration of this

θλίβετο πᾶς ὁ μικρομερὴς σχηματισμὸς ταύτης καὶ
τὴν ὑγρὰν | φύσιν ἐγέννα· ῥευστικῶς δ' αὕτη διακει-
25 μένη κατεφέρετο πρὸς τοὺς | κοίλους τόπους καὶ δυνα-
μένους χωρῆσαί τε καὶ στέξαι, ἢ καθ' αὑτὸ τὸ | ὕδωρ
ὑποστὰν ἐκοίλανε τοὺς ὑποκειμένους τόπους. (P) |
2. τὰ μὲν οὖν κυριώτατα μέρη τοῦ κόσμου τὸν τρόπον
τοῦτον ἐγεννήθη. (P) |

1.5

Ps.-Plut. *Plac.* 1.5 (+ Ps.-Gal. *Hist. phil.* 32); Stob. *Ecl.*
1.22.3ad

ε΄. Εἰ ἓν τὸ πᾶν (PS) |

1. οἱ μὲν ἀπὸ τῆς Στοᾶς ἕνα κόσμον ἀπεφήναντο, ὃν
δὴ καὶ τὸ πᾶν ἔφασαν | εἶναι τὸ σωματικόν. (PS) |
2. Ἐμπεδοκλῆς δὲ κόσμον μὲν ἕνα, οὐ μέντοι τὸ πᾶν
5 εἶναι τὸν κόσμον ἀλλ' | ὀλίγον τι τοῦ παντὸς μέρος,
τὸ δὲ λοιπὸν ἀργὴν ὕλην. (PS) |

§1 Stoics 2.530
§2 Empedocles A47

matter with its small particles was compressed and produced the nature that is moist. Being in a fluid state, this matter traveled down to the places that were hollow and able to contain and hold it, or the water, deposited on its own, hollowed out the areas beneath it.

2. In this manner the most important parts of the cosmos were produced.[19]

1.5

Division of views on the number of kosmoi, whether one or infinitely many. "Cosmos" and "All" can be but are not necessarily identical.

Ps.-Plutarch, *Tenets* (+ Ps.-Galen, *Philosophical History*); Stobaeus, *Anthology*

5. Whether the All is unique[20]

1. The philosophers from the Stoa declared the cosmos to be unique, which they also identified with the corporeal All.[21]

2. Empedocles says that the cosmos is unique; he does not, however, identify the cosmos with the All, but says it is a small part of the All, the remainder being unworked matter.

---

[19] This chapter is not paralleled in Stobaeus (or Theodoret). It forms a convenient bridge between chapters 3 and 5 and preludes upon Book 2.

[20] On this subject see further 2.1, esp. §§8–9.

[21] That is, with the part of the All that is corporeal. The "All" comprises the cosmos and the empty space beyond the cosmos.

3. Πλάτων δὲ τεκμαίρεται τὸ δοκοῦν, ὅτι εἷς ὁ κόσμος καὶ ἓν τὸ πᾶν, ἐκ | τριῶν, ἐκ τοῦ μὴ ἔσεσθαι τέλειον, ἐὰν μὴ πάντα περιέχῃ· ἐκ τοῦ μὴ | ἔσεσθαι ὅμοιον τῷ παραδείγματι, ἐὰν μὴ μονογενὴς ᾖ· ἐκ τοῦ μὴ ἔσε- σθαι αὐτὸν ἄφθαρτον, ἐὰν ᾖ τι ἐξωτέρω αὐτοῦ. πρὸς δὴ τὸν Πλάτωνα | ῥητέον, ὅτι οὐ τέλειος ὁ κόσμος·

10 οὐδὲ γὰρ ⟨εἰ⟩ πάντα περιέχει· | καὶ γὰρ ὁ ἄνθρωπός ἐστι τέλειος, ἀλλ' οὐ πάντα περιέχει· | καὶ πολλὰ παραδείγματα ἔστιν, ὥσπερ ἐπ' ἀνδριάντων καὶ οἰ- κιῶν καὶ ζῳγραφιῶν. πῶς δὲ εἶπεν ἔξωθέν τι αὐτοῦ οὐκ ἔστι; περιδινεῖσθαι γὰρ οὐκ ἐδύνατο. ἄφθαρτος δ' οὐκ ἔστιν οὐδὲ δύναται εἶναι, γενητὸς ὤν. (PS) |

15 4. Μητρόδωρος ὁ καθηγητὴς Ἐπικούρου φησιν ἄτο- πον εἶναι ἐν μεγάλῳ | πεδίῳ ἕνα στάχυν γεννηθῆναι καὶ ἕνα κόσμον ἐν τῷ ἀπείρῳ. ὅτι δ' | ἄπειρο⟨ι⟩[23] κατὰ τὸ πλῆθος, δῆλον ἐκ τοῦ ἄπειρα τὰ αἴτια εἶναι· εἰ γὰρ | ὁ μὲν κόσμος πεπερασμένος, τὰ δ' αἴτια πάντα ἄπειρα, ἐξ ὧν ὅδε ὁ | κόσμος γέγονεν, ἀνάγκη

20 ἀπείρους εἶναι. ὅπου γὰρ ἀπέραντα τὰ αἴτια, | ἐκεῖ καὶ τὰ ἀποτελέσματα· αἴτια δ' ἤτοι αἱ ἄτομοι ἢ τὰ στοι- χεῖα. (PS) |

§3 Plato cf. *Tim.* 30c–31b, 33a–d
§4 Metrodorus A6

[23] ἄπειρο⟨ι⟩ corr. Meineke prob. edd.: ἄπειρος PS antiquum mendum in trad. Aetii

3. Plato bases his belief that the cosmos and the All are unique on three considerations: (1) from the fact that it would not be complete, if it did not contain all things within itself; (2) from the fact that it would not be similar to the model, if it were not alone in its sort; (3) from the fact that it would not be indestructible, if there were anything exterior to it. But against Plato[22] it must be stated that the cosmos is not complete, and it need not be so even if it did contain all things; after all, the human being is   10
complete (i.e., full-grown), but he does not contain all things (cf. (1)). There are moreover many models, as in the case of statues and buildings and paintings (cf. (2)). How could he say there is nothing outside it, for if that were the case it could not be whirling around (cf. (1))? Moreover, it is not indestructible and cannot be so, since it has come into being. (cf. (3)).

4. Metrodorus, the teacher of Epicurus, says that it is   15
equally absurd that a single stalk should have sprung up on a large plain and that a single cosmos should have done the same in the Infinite. That the *kosmoi* are infinite in their multiplicity is clear from the fact that the causes are infinite in number. For if the cosmos is limited, while all the causes from which the cosmos originated are infinitely many, then necessarily the *kosmoi* are infinitely many. After all, where the causes are without limit, there the prod-   20
ucts [or: effects] are infinite in number or without limit also. These causes are either the atoms or the elements.

[22] See note at 1.2.2.

45

Ps.-Plut. *Plac.* 1.6 (+ Ps.-Gal. *Hist. phil.* 34)

ς'. Πόθεν ἔννοιαν ἔσχον θεῶν ἄνθρωποι (P) |

1. ὁρίζονται δὲ τὴν τοῦ θείου οὐσίαν οἱ Στωικοὶ οὕτως· πνεῦμα νοερὸν καὶ | πυρῶδες οὐκ ἔχον μὲν μορφήν, μεταβάλλον δ' εἰς ἃ βούλεται καὶ συνεξομοιούμενον | πᾶσιν.

5   ἔσχον δ' ἔννοιαν τούτου πρῶτον μὲν ἀπὸ τοῦ κάλλους τῶν ἐμφαινομένων | προσλαμβάνοντες· οὐδὲν γὰρ τῶν καλῶν εἰκῆ καὶ ὡς ἔτυχε | γίνεται, ἀλλὰ μετά τινος τέχνης δημιουργούσης. καλὸς δ' ὁ κόσμος· | δῆλον δ' ἐκ τοῦ σχήματος καὶ τοῦ χρώματος καὶ τοῦ μεγέθους καὶ τῆς | περὶ τὸν κόσμον τῶν ἀστέρων ποι-
10 κιλίας. σφαιροειδὴς γὰρ ὁ κόσμος, ὃ | πάντων σχημάτων πρωτεύει· μόνον γὰρ τοῦτο τοῖς ἑαυτοῦ μέρεσιν | ὁμοιοῦται· περιφερὴς δ' ὢν ἔχει τὰ μέρη περιφερῆ·

§1 Stoics 2.1009 (5–37 = Posidonius fr. 364 Theiler); 2–4 Posidonius fr. 101 E.-K; 11–12 cf. Plato *Tim.* 44d; 20–24 Aratus *Phaen.* 545–49; 27–28 Euripides, actually Critias *Sisyph.* 1.33–34 Kannicht = B25.33–34; 56 Hesiod *Th.* 134

1.6

The main distinction is between nature and culture. The first half explains the origins of the conception of the divine in a natural way, the second half as mediated through teaching and tradition.

Ps.-Plutarch, *Tenets* (+ Ps.-Galen, *Philosophical History*)

6. From where did human beings obtain a conception of gods

1. The Stoics define the substance of the divine as follows: it is an intelligent and fiery breath, which does not have a specific form, but changes to whatever things it wishes and assimilates itself to all things.[23]

They obtained a conception of this divine being in the   5
first place by taking as their starting point the beauty of what becomes visible in it. For nothing that is beautiful originates at random and by chance, but with the aid of a skill that works as a craftsman. The heaven[24] is beautiful. This is evident from its shape, its color, its size, and the variety of the heavenly bodies that adorn it. The heaven is spherical, a shape that takes the first place among all   10
shapes, for it alone corresponds to its own parts, since it is round and so are its parts. This is the reason according to

23 Very similar formula at 1.7.10, where it is attributed to Posidonius.

24 The Greek term is *kosmos*, but its meaning here is "heaven," as is evident from what follows.

(διὰ τοῦτο γὰρ κατὰ | τὸν Πλάτωνα ἐν τῇ κεφαλῇ τὸ
ἱερώτατον συνέστηκε νοῦς). καὶ τὸ | χρῶμα δὲ καλόν·
κυανώσει γὰρ κέχρωσται, ὃ πορφύρας μέν ἐστι |
μελάντερον στίλβουσαν δ᾽ ἔχει τὴν ποιότητα· καὶ διὰ
15 ταύτην τὴν αἰτίαν | τῷ τῆς χροιᾶς συντόνῳ διακόπτον
τηλικαύτην ἀέρος σύστασιν ἐκ | τοσούτων διαστη-
μάτων θεωρεῖται. καὶ ἐκ τοῦ μεγέθους καλός· πάντων
| γὰρ τῶν ὁμογενῶν τὸ ὑπερέχον καλὸν ὡς ζῷον καὶ
δένδρον. ἐπιτελεῖ τὸ | κάλλος τοῦ κόσμου καὶ ταῦτα
τὰ φαινόμενα· ὁ μὲν γὰρ λοξὸς κύκλος ἐν | οὐρανῷ
διαφόροις εἰδώλοις πεποίκιλται·

> τῷ δ᾽ ἔνι Καρκίνος ἐστί, Λέων δ᾽ ἐπὶ τῷ, μετὰ δ᾽
> αὐτὸν |
> Παρθένος, ἠδ᾽ ἐπί οἱ Χηλαὶ καὶ (ἐπ᾽ αὐτῷ)
> Σκορπίος αὐτὸς |
> Τοξευτής τε καὶ Αἰγόκερως, ἐπὶ δ᾽ Αἰγόκερωτι[24] |
> Ὑδροχόος· δύο δ᾽ αὐτὸν ἐπ᾽ Ἰχθύες ἀστερόεντες, |
> τοὺς δὲ μέτα Κριός, Ταῦρος δ᾽ ἐπὶ τῷ Δίδυμοί
> τε. |

25 μυρία δ᾽ ἄλλα καθ᾽ ὁμοίας τοῦ κόσμου περικλάσεις
πεποίηκεν· ὅθεν καὶ | Εὐριπίδης φησί· |

> τό τ᾽ ἀστερωπὸν οὐρανοῦ σέλας, |
> χρόνου[25] καλὸν ποίκιλμα, τέκτονος σοφοῦ. |

---

[24] Αἰγόκερωτι P: αἰγοκερῆι edd. ex Arato
[25] χρόνου corr. Beck ex S.E. M. 9.54: χρόνον P

Plato that the most sacred component (sc. of the human being), the intellect, has been established in the head. Its (sc. the heaven's) color is beautiful too, for it has been colored with blueness, which is darker than purple but still has the quality of brightness, and it is for this reason that 15 with its intense color it traverses so great a body of air and is visible at such large distances. It is also beautiful because of its size, for with all entities of a same species what excels is beautiful, as in the case of a living being or a plant. The following visible signs also contribute to bringing the beauty of the sky to perfection, for the ecliptic circle in heaven is decorated with a variety of graphic pictures (i.e., constellations):

> In it there is the Crab, followed by the Lion, and after it
> the Maiden, and then the Claws and after it the Scorpion himself,
> and the Archer and the Capricorn, and after the Capricorn
> the Water-carrier, and following him the two starry Fishes,
> and after them the Ram, and next the Bull and the Twins.

Countless other features he has created corresponding to 25 similar twistings of the cosmos. Hence Euripides too says:[25]

> . . . and the star-faced brilliance of heaven,
> a beautiful embroidery of time, by a wise builder.

[25] On the name-label and the source of the poetic lines, see the note at 1.7.1[10].

ἐλάβομεν δ' ἐκ τούτου ἔννοιαν θεοῦ· ἀεί τε γὰρ
30 ἥλιος καὶ σελήνη | καὶ τὰ λοιπὰ τῶν ἄστρων τὴν
ὑπόγειον φορὰν ἐνεχθέντα ὅμοια μὲν | ἀνατέλλει τοῖς
χρώμασιν, ἴσα δὲ τοῖς μεγέθεσι καὶ κατὰ τόπους καὶ
| κατὰ χρόνους τοὺς αὐτούς. |

διόπερ οἱ τὸν περὶ τῶν θεῶν παραδόντες σεβασμὸν
διὰ τριῶν | ἐξέθηκαν ἡμῖν εἰδῶν, πρῶτον μὲν τοῦ φυ-
35 σικοῦ, δεύτερον δὲ τοῦ μυθικοῦ, | τρίτον δὲ τοῦ τὴν
μαρτυρίαν ἐκ τῶν νόμων εἰληφότος. διδάσκεται δὲ τὸ
| μὲν φυσικὸν ὑπὸ τῶν φιλοσόφων, τὸ δὲ μυθικὸν ὑπὸ
τῶν ποιητῶν, τὸ δὲ | νομικὸν ὑφ' ἑκάστης ἀεὶ πόλεως
συνίσταται.

διαιρεῖται δ' ἡ πᾶσα διδαχὴ εἰς εἴδη ἑπτά· καὶ
πρῶτον μὲν τὸ ἐκ | τῶν φαινομένων καὶ μετεώρων·
40 θεοῦ γὰρ ἔννοιαν ἔσχον ἀπὸ τῶν φαινομένων | ἀστέ-
ρων, ὁρῶντες τούτους μεγάλης συμφωνίας ὄντας αἰ-
τίους καὶ | τεταγμένους ἡμέραν τε καὶ νύκτα καὶ χει-
μῶνα καὶ θέρος, ἀνατολάς τε | καὶ δυσμάς,[26] καὶ τὰ
ὑπὸ τῆς γῆς ζῳογονούμενα καὶ καρπογονούμενα. διὸ
| πατὴρ μὲν ἔδοξεν αὐτοῖς οὐρανὸς ὑπάρχειν, μήτηρ
δὲ γῆ· τούτων δ' ὁ | μὲν πατὴρ διὰ τὸ τὰς τῶν ὑδάτων
45 ἐκχύσεις σπερμάτων ἔχειν τάξιν, ἡ δὲ | γῆ μήτηρ διὰ
τὸ δέχεσθαι ταῦτα καὶ τίκτειν· βλέποντες δὲ τοὺς
ἀστέρας | ἀεὶ θέοντας αἰτίους τε τοῦ θεωρεῖν ἡμᾶς
ἥλιον καὶ σελήνην "θεοὺς" | προσηγόρευσαν. εἰς

[26] ἀνατολάς . . . δυσμάς glossema susp. Diels, γιγνόμενα
leg. Q

50

We also obtained a conception of God from the following: it is the case that the sun and the moon and the remaining heavenly bodies, after pursuing their course under the earth, rise again with the same colors, not varying in their sizes, in the same places, and at the same times.

Hence those people who have handed down reverence for the gods have done so by means of three kinds of exposition, first through natural philosophy, secondly through the mythical kind, and thirdly through the kind that takes its evidence from the laws [or: customs]. Natural philosophy is taught by the philosophers, the mythical kind by the poets, while what is lawful [or: customary] is established each time by the particular city.

The entire teaching on the gods is divided into seven kinds. The first is based on the visible signs and heavenly occurrences. People obtained a conception of God from the visible heavenly bodies, observing that these are the cause of a mighty harmony and have brought about the ordered state of day and night and winter and summer, risings and settings, as well as the births of living beings and plants produced by the earth. Hence it seemed to them that heaven had the role of father and earth that of mother. The former was father through the outpourings of rain that had the role of seeds, while the earth was mother by receiving these seeds and giving birth. When they saw that the heavenly bodies always followed their courses (*aei theontas*) and that the sun and moon were the cause of our ability to contemplate (*theôrein*), they called them "gods" (*theous*). They divided the gods into a second

30

35

40

45

δεύτερον δὲ καὶ τρίτον τόπον τοὺς θεοὺς διεῖλον, εἴς |
τε τὸ βλάπτον καὶ τὸ ὠφελοῦν· καὶ τοὺς μὲν ὠφελοῦν-
τας Δία Ἥραν | Ἑρμῆν Δήμητραν· τοὺς δὲ βλάπτον-
50 τας Ποινὰς Ἐρινύας Ἄρην, τούτους | ἀφοσιούμενοι
χαλεποὺς ὄντας καὶ βιαίους. τέταρτον καὶ πέμπτον |
προστεθείκασι τοῖς πράγμασι καὶ τοῖς πάθεσι, καθά-
περ Ἔρωτα | Ἀφροδίτην Πόθον, πραγμάτων δ᾽ Ἐλ-
πίδα Δίκην Εὐνομίαν. ἕκτον δὲ | τόπον προσέλαβε τὸ
ὑπὸ τῶν ποιητῶν πεπλασμένον· Ἡσίοδος γὰρ | βου-
λόμενος τοῖς γενητοῖς θεοὺς[27] πατέρας συστῆσαι εἰσ-
55 ήγαγε τοιούτους | αὐτοῖς γεννήτορας· |

Κοῖόν τε Κρεῖόν θ᾽ Ὑπερίονά τ᾽ Ἰαπετόν τε· |

διὰ τοῦτο καὶ μυθικὸν κέκληται. ἕβδομον δὲ καὶ
ἐπὶ πᾶσι τὸ διὰ τὰς | εἰς τὸν κοινὸν βίον εὐεργεσίας
ἐκτετιμημένον ἀνθρώπινον δὲ γεννηθέν, | ὡς Ἡρακλέα
ὡς Διοσκόρους ὡς Διόνυσον. ἀνθρωποειδεῖς δ᾽ αὐτοὺς
60 | ἔφασαν εἶναι, διότι τῶν μὲν ἁπάντων τὸ θεῖον
κυριώτατον, τῶν δὲ ζῴων | ἄνθρωπος κάλλιστον καί,
κεκοσμημένον ἀρετῇ διαφόρως κατὰ τὴν τοῦ | νοῦ
σύστασιν, τὸ κράτιστον. τοῖς οὖν ἀριστεύουσι τὸ
κράτιστον ὁμοίως | καὶ <κάλλιστον ἐπιτιθέναι>[28] κα-
λῶς ἔχειν διενοήθησαν. (P) |

27 θεοὺς corr. Diels: θεοῖς P
28 κάλλιστον ἐπιτιθέναι suppl. Mau prob. Lachenaud

and third category, namely that which harms and that which assists. Those who assist are Zeus, Hera, Hermes, and Demeter, while those who cause harm are the Avengers, the Erinyes, and Ares, whom they regard as holy even   50
though they are responsible for hardship and violence. The fourth and fifth kinds they applied to states of affairs and feelings, such as for the former Eros, Aphrodite, and Desire, and for states of affairs Hope (*sic*), Justice, and Good Order. As a sixth category were added the fictions of the poets. For example, Hesiod wanted to create gods as fathers of the beings that came into existence and so introduced the following as their begetters,   55

Coeus and Crius and Hyperion and Iapetus.

For this reason this category is also called mythical. The seventh and final kind of gods was the one that was especially honored for its beneficent contributions to the public good, but was born in human form, such as Heracles, such as the Dioscuri, and such as Dionysus. The reason they said these gods were of human form is that the   60
divine is the most excellent of all beings and the human being the most beautiful of living beings, and, adorned as he is with virtue especially through the formation of his intellect, also the most capable. Similarly, therefore, they thought it was good <to attribute the greatest beauty> to those who excelled with the highest capability.[26]

[26] This chapter is not paralleled in Stobaeus (or Theodoret). The proximate tradition shows that the origin of the concept should accompany the issue of existence as dealt with in ch. 1.7.

1.7

The primary division is between those who deny the existence of the divinity or at least of providence (§1), and those who posit existence but differ as to substance or number (§§2–25). The latter are listed according to various

Ps.-Plut. *Plac.* 1.7 (+ Ps.-Gal. *Hist. phil.* 35); Stob. *Ecl.* 1.1.29b

ζ′. Τίς ὁ θεός (PS) |

1. ἔνιοι τῶν φιλοσόφων, καθάπερ Διαγόρας ὁ Μήλιος²⁹
καὶ Θεόδωρος ὁ | Κυρηναῖος καὶ Εὐήμερος ὁ Τε-
γεάτης, καθόλου φασὶ μὴ εἶναι θεούς· τὸν | δ᾽ Εὐήμε-
ρον καὶ Καλλίμαχος ὁ Κυρηναῖος αἰνίττεται ἐν τοῖς
5 Ἰάμβοις | γράφων· |

§1 2 Diagoras of Melos fr. 47; Theodorus of Cyrene fr. 35;
3 Euhemerus fr. 16; 4–8 Callimachus fr. 191.9–11 Euhemerus fr.
1a; 9 Euripides, actually Critias *Sisyph.* fr. 19 Kannicht = B25;
13–14 Critias 19.1–2; 17–18 Critias 19.26; 19–20 Critias 19.17–
18; 21–23 Callimachus fr. 586; 24–25 cf. Arist. *Cat.* 10 12b40–41;
27–28 cf. Plat. *Tim.* 29e, 30c, Diog. Laert. 3.72; 28–29 cf. Aristoph.
Nub. 398; 29 Anaxagoras A48, B12; 31 cf. Pl. *Tim.* 30a, Diog.
Laert. 3.70; 34–40 Epicurus fr. 361, cf. *KD* 1; 54–55 Homer *Il.*
3.178–79

²⁹ Μήλιος G: Μιλήσιος P

*subdivisions, mainly between corporealists and incorpore-
alists, and between monists and pluralists. As in 1.3 a rearrangement according to succession also plays a part.*

Ps.-Plutarch, *Tenets* (+ Ps.-Galen, *Philosophical History*);
Stobaeus, *Anthology*

7. Who the deity is

1. Some of the philosophers, such as Diagoras of Melos,
Theodore of Cyrene, and Euhemerus of Tegea say that the
gods do not exist at all.[27] Euhemerus is also hinted at by
Callimachus of Cyrene when he writes in his *Iambi*:   5

[27] According to Aristotle, the question "whether it exists" precedes that of "what it is."

εἰς τὸ πρὸ τείχευς ἱερὸν ἀλέες δεῦτε, |
οὗ τὸν πάλαι χαλκέον[30] ὁ πλάσας Ζᾶνα |
γέρων ἀλαζὼν ἄδικα βιβλία ψήχει,[31] |

ταῦτ' ἔστι τὰ περὶ τοῦ μὴ εἶναι θεούς. καὶ Εὐριπίδης
10 δ' ὁ τραγῳδοποιὸς | ἀποκαλύψασθαι μὲν οὐκ ἠθέλησε,
δεδοικὼς τὸν Ἄρειον πάγον, ἐνέφηνε | δὲ τοῦτον τὸν
τρόπον· τὸν γὰρ Σίσυφον εἰσήγαγε προστάτην ταύ-
της τῆς | δόξης καὶ συνηγόρησεν αὐτοῦ ταύτῃ τῇ
γνώμῃ· |

ἦν γάρ χρόνος, φησίν, ὅτ' ἦν ἄτακτος ἀνθρώπων
βίος |
καὶ θηριώδης ἰσχύος θ' ὑπηρέτης· |

15 ἔπειτα φησὶ τὴν ἀνομίαν λυθῆναι νόμων εἰσαγωγῇ·
ἐπεὶ γὰρ ὁ νόμος τὰ | φανερὰ τῶν ἀδικημάτων εἴργειν
ἐδύνατο κρύφα δ' ἠδίκουν πολλοί, τότε | τις σοφὸς
ἀνὴρ ἐπέστησεν, ὡς δεῖ "ψευδεῖ λόγῳ τυφλῶσαι τὴν |
ἀλήθειαν" καὶ πεῖσαι τοὺς ἀνθρώπους

ὡς ἔστι δαίμων ἀφθίτῳ θάλλων βίῳ, |
ὃς ταῦτ' ἀκούει καὶ βλέπει φρονεῖ τ' ἄγαν· |

[30] χάλκεον P: Παγχαῖον coni. Bentley ex Callimacho, prob.
edd.
[31] ψήχει Q Bentley, cf. S.E. M. 9.51: ψύχει P

Come hither to the temple in front of the wall,
where the old man who fabricated the ancient
    bronze Zan
scribbles his unrighteous books like the charlatan
    he is.

These books are the ones on the subject that the gods do
not exist. Euripides[28] too, the tragic poet, though he did   10
not wish to disclose this view for fear of the Areopagus,
did make his position known in the following way. He introduced the character of Sisyphus as defender of this
opinion, and so pleaded his cause by means of this man's
judgment:

For there was a time, he says, when human life was
    disordered,
beast-like, and at the mercy of violence.

Then, he says, the lawlessness was dissolved through the   15
introduction of laws. Since, however, the law was able to
curb overt acts of injustice, but many people continued to
practice them in secret, at that point a wise man ordained
that it was necessary "to blind the truth with a false account" and persuade mankind

how there is a deity flourishing with imperishable life,
who hears and sees and takes good note of these
    deeds.

[28] It is generally agreed that the following passage and its
quotations are taken from the play *Sisyphus* of Critias, as indicated in the parallel passage in Sextus Empiricus M. 9.50–54, and
so are here mistakenly attributed to Euripides.

ἀναιρείσθω γάρ, φησίν, ὁ ποιητικὸς λῆρος σὺν Καλ-
λιμάχῳ τῷ λέγοντι· |

   εἰ θεὸν οἶσθα, |
   ἴσθ᾽ ὅτι καὶ ῥέξαι δαίμονι πᾶν δυνατόν. |

οὐδὲ γὰρ ὁ θεὸς δύναται πᾶν ποιεῖν· ἐπεί τοί γε, εἰ
25 θεὸς ἔστι, ποιείτω τὴν | χιόνα μέλαιναν τὸ δὲ πῦρ
ψυχρὸν τὸ δὲ καθήμενον ὀρθὸν καὶ τὸ | ἐναντίον. |

   καὶ γὰρ Πλάτων ὁ μεγαλόφωνος εἰπών ὁ θεὸς
ἔπλασε τὸν κόσμον | πρὸς ἑαυτὸν ὑπόδειγμα ὄζει
λήρου βεκκεσελήνου κατά γε τοὺς τῆς | ἀρχαίας κω-
μῳδίας ποιητάς· πῶς γὰρ αὐτῷ ἀτενίζων ἔπλασεν; ἢ
30 πῶς | σφαιροειδῆ τὸν θεόν, ὄντα ταπεινότερον ἀνθρώ-
που; ὁ δ᾽ Ἀναξαγόρας | φησὶν ὡς εἰστήκει κατ᾽ ἀρχὰς
τὰ σώματα, νοῦς δὲ αὐτὰ διεκόσμησε | θεοῦ καὶ τὰς
γενέσεις τῶν ὅλων ἐποίησεν. ὁ δὲ Πλάτων οὐχ ἑστη-
κότα | ὑπέθετο τὰ πρῶτα σώματα, ἀτάκτως δὲ κινού-
μενα· διὸ καὶ ὁ θεός, | φησίν, ἐπιστήσας ὡς τάξις
35 ἀταξίας ἐστὶ βελτίων, διεκόσμησε ταῦτα. | κοινῶς οὖν
ἁμαρτάνουσιν ἀμφότεροι, ὅτι τὸν θεὸν ἐποίησαν ἐπισ-
τρεφόμενον | τῶν ἀνθρωπίνων ἢ καὶ τούτου χάριν
τὸν κόσμον κατασκευάζοντα· τὸ γὰρ μακάριον καὶ
ἄφθαρτον ζῷον συμπεπληρωμένον τε | πᾶσι τοῖς ἀγα-
θοῖς καὶ κακοῦ παντὸς ἄδεκτον, ὅλον ὂν περὶ τὴν
συνοχὴν | τῆς ἰδίας εὐδαιμονίας τε καὶ ἀφθαρσίας,
40 ἀνεπιστρεφές ἐστι τῶν | ἀνθρωπίνων πραγμάτων· κα-
κοδαίμων δ᾽ ἂν εἴη ἐργάτου δίκην καὶ | τέκτονος ἀχθο-
φορῶν καὶ μεριμνῶν εἰς τὴν τοῦ κόσμου κατασκευήν. |

Let such poetic nonsense be done away with, he says, together with the words of Callimachus:

> if you recognize God,
> be aware that for the deity it is possible to achieve everything.

For not even God can do everything. If the divinity indeed exists, let him then make snow black, fire cold, what is 25 sedentary upright and vice versa.

And when the grandiloquent Plato says that God formed the cosmos by looking at himself as model, he reeks of archaic moonstruck nonsense, to use the language of the ancient comic poets. For how did he create while looking to himself? And how can Plato say the deity is 30 spherical in shape, humbler in status than man? Anaxagoras says that at the beginning the bodies were at rest, but the Intellect of God gave them an orderly arrangement and brought about the births of all things. Plato on the other hand supposed that the primary bodies were not at rest but moving in a disorderly fashion. Therefore, he says, the deity, ordaining that order is better than disorder, gave them an orderly arrangement. Both thinkers thus have this 35 mistake in common, namely that they made the deity pay attention to human affairs or even creating the cosmos for this reason. After all, the blessed and indestructible living being, who is replete with all good things and not receptive of any evil, being wholly focused on the maintenance of his felicity and indestructibility, is not involved with hu- 40 man concerns, for otherwise he would be wretched in the manner of a workman and a builder, burdened with care and fretting about the construction of the cosmos.

καὶ πάλιν ὁ θεὸς ὃν λέγουσιν ἤτοι τὸν ἔμπροσθεν
αἰῶνα οὐκ ἦν, ὅτ' | ἦν ἀκίνητα τὰ σώματα ἢ ἀτάκτως
ἐκινεῖτο, ἢ ἐκοιμᾶτο ἢ ἐγρηγόρει ἢ | οὐδέτερον τούτων.
καὶ οὔτε τὸ πρῶτον ἔστι δέξασθαι, ὁ γὰρ θεὸς |
45 αἰώνιος· οὔτε τὸ δεύτερον, εἰ γὰρ ἐκοιμᾶτο ἐξ αἰῶνος
ὁ θεός, ἐτεθνήκει· | αἰώνιος γὰρ ὕπνος θάνατός ἐστιν·
ἀλλ' οὐδὲ δεκτικὸς ὕπνου θεός, τὸ | γὰρ ἀθάνατον τοῦ
θεοῦ καὶ τὸ ἐγγὺς θανάτου πολὺ κεχώρισται. εἰ δ' ἦν
| ὁ θεὸς ἐγρηγορώς, ἤτοι ἐνέλειπεν εἰς εὐδαιμονίαν ἢ
πεπλήρωτο ἐν | μακαριότητι· καὶ οὔτε κατὰ τὸ πρῶτον
50 μακάριός ἐστιν ὁ θεός, τὸ γὰρ | ἐλλεῖπον εἰς εὐδαιμο-
νίαν οὐ μακάριον· οὔτε κατὰ τὸ δεύτερον, μηδὲν | γὰρ
ἐλλείπων κεναῖς ἔμελλεν ἐπιχειρεῖν πράξεσι. |

πῶς δέ, εἴπερ ὁ θεός ἔστι καὶ τῇ τούτου φροντίδι
τὰ κατ' ἄνθρωπον | οἰκονομεῖται, τὸ μὲν κίβδηλον
εὐτυχεῖ τὸ δ' ἀστεῖον τἀναντία πάσχει; |

Ἀγαμέμνων τε γάρ, |
ἀμφότερον βασιλεύς τ' ἀγαθὸς κρατερός τ'
   αἰχμητής, |

ὑπὸ μοιχοῦ καὶ μοιχάδος ἡττηθεὶς ἐδολοφονήθη· καὶ
ὁ τούτου δὲ συγγενὴς | Ἡρακλῆς πολλὰ τῶν ἐπιλυ-
μαινομένων τὸν ἀνθρώπινον βίον καθάρας | ὑπὸ Δηια-
νείρας φαρμακευθεὶς ἐδολοφονήθη. (P) |
2. Θαλῆς νοῦν τοῦ κόσμου τὸν θεόν, τὸ δὲ πᾶν ἔμ-

Another argument is that the god of whom they speak either did not exist in the previous age when the bodies were either at rest or in disorderly movement, or he was asleep, or he was awake, or neither of these. The first option is unacceptable, for the deity is eternal. The second 45 too is unacceptable. If God were sleeping from eternity, he would be dead, since eternal sleep is tantamount to death. But God is also not receptive of sleep, for God's immortality and a state close to death are separated by a great distance. If, however, God was awake, either there was a deficiency in his felicity or he was wholly fulfilled in his blessedness. But neither according to the first option is he blessed, because a deficiency in felicity is incompat- 50 ible with blessedness, nor is he blessed according to the second option, because then, though in no way deficient in happiness, he would embark on deeds that were to no purpose.

How does it happen then, if the deity indeed does exist and human affairs are administered through his fore-thought, that what is fraudulent flourishes and what is noble suffers the opposite fate?

> Agamemnon, for example, was
> both an excellent king and a mighty warrior,

but he was overpowered and murdered by an adulterer and an adulteress. And this man's relative, Heracles, who had cleaned up many of the evils that infest human life, fell prey to the sorcery of Deïanira and was murdered.[29] 2. Thales says that the deity is the Intellect of the cosmos,

[29] The entire first lemma is not paralleled in Stobaeus (cf. n. 25 on 1.6). This account of atheism has a clear Epicurean coloring.

60 ψυχον ἅμα καὶ δαιμόνων | πλῆρες· διήκειν δὲ καὶ διὰ
τοῦ στοιχειώδους ὑγροῦ δύναμιν θείαν κινητικὴν |
αὐτοῦ. (PS) |

3. Ἀναξίμανδρος τοὺς ἀπείρους[32] οὐρανοὺς θεούς. (PS) |

4. Ἀναξιμένης τὸν ἀέρα· δεῖ δ᾽ ὑπακούειν ἐπὶ τῶν
οὕτως λεγομένων τὰς | ἐνδιηκούσας τοῖς στοιχείοις ἢ
τοῖς σώμασι δυνάμεις. (S) |

65 5. Ἀρχέλαος ἀέρα καὶ νοῦν τὸν θεόν, οὐ μέντοι κοσμο-
ποιὸν τὸν νοῦν. (S) |

6. Ἀναξαγόρας νοῦν κοσμοποιὸν τὸν θεόν. (S) |

7. Δημόκριτος νοῦν τὸν θεὸν ἐν πυρὶ σφαιροει-
δεῖ. (PS) |

8. Διογένης καὶ Κλεάνθης καὶ Οἰνοπίδης τὴν τοῦ
κόσμου ψυχήν. (S) |

9. Πυθαγόρας τῶν ἀρχῶν τὴν μὲν μονάδα θεὸν καὶ
70 τἀγαθόν, ἥτις ἐστὶν ἡ | τοῦ ἑνὸς φύσις καὶ αὐτὸς ὁ
νοῦς, τὴν δ᾽ ἀόριστον δυάδα δαίμονα καὶ τὸ | κακόν,
περὶ ἥν ἐστι τὸ ὑλικὸν πλῆθος, ἐστὶν δὲ καὶ ὁ ὁρατὸς
κόσμος. | (PS) |

10. Ποσειδώνιος πνεῦμα νοερὸν καὶ πυρῶδες, οὐκ
ἔχον μὲν μορφήν, μεταβάλλον | δὲ εἰς ὃ βούλεται καὶ
συνεξομοιούμενον πᾶσιν. (S) |

§2 Thales A23   §3 Anaximander A17   §4 Anaximenes
A10   §5 Archelaus A12   §6 Anaxagoras A48
§7 Democritus A74   §8 Diogenes of Apollonia A8;
Diogenes of Babylon 3.31 Cleanthes 1.532; Oenopides 41.6
§9 Pythagoras —   §10 Posidonius fr. 101

32 ἀπείρους GQ: ἀστέρας PE

and that the universe is ensouled and at the same time full of demons. In addition, the divine power also pervades the 60 elementary moist substance and causes it to move.[30]

3. Anaximander says that the unlimited [or: infinitely many] heavens are gods.

4. Anaximenes says that the deity is the air. Statements such as these (i.e., of Anaximenes) should be understood as referring to the powers that pervade all parts of the elements or the bodies.[31]

5. Archelaus says that the deity is air and Intellect, but the 65 Intellect does not make the cosmos.

6. Anaxagoras says that the deity is an Intellect that makes the cosmos.

7. Democritus says that the deity is an Intellect that resides in fire with spherical form.

8. Diogenes, Cleanthes, and Oenopides say that the deity is the soul of the cosmos.

9. Pythagoras says that of the principles, the Monad is the deity and the Good, which is the nature of the One and 70 identical to the Intellect, but the Undetermined Dyad is a demon and what is evil, around which the plurality of matter resides, and is also the visible cosmos.[32]

10. Posidonius says that the deity is an intelligent and fiery Spirit, which does not have a single form, but changes into what it wishes and assimilates itself to all things.

[30] This responds to the criticism at 1.3.2.
[31] This responds to the criticism at 1.3.3.
[32] See n. 23 above on 1.6.

75 11. Σπεύσιππος τὸν νοῦν, οὔτε τῷ ἑνὶ οὔτε τῷ ἀγαθῷ τὸν αὐτόν, ἰδιοφυῆ δέ. | (S) |

12. Κριτόλαος καὶ Διόδωρος ὁ Τύριος νοῦν ἀπ᾽ αἰθέρος ἀπαθοῦς. (S) |

13. Ἡράκλειτος τὸ περιοδικὸν πῦρ ἀίδιον, εἱμαρμένην δὲ λόγον ἐκ τῆς | ἐναντιοδρομίας δημιουργὸν τῶν ὄντων. (S) |

80 14. Ζήνων ὁ Στωικὸς νοῦν κόσμου πύρινον. (S) |

15. Μνήσαρχος τὸν κόσμον, τὴν πρώτην οὐσίαν ἔχοντα ἀπὸ πνεύματος. | (S) |

16. Βόηθος τὸν αἰθέρα θεὸν ἀπεφήνατο. (S) |

17. Παρμενίδης τὸ ἀκίνητον καὶ πεπερασμένον σφαιροειδές. (S) |

85 18. Μέλισσος καὶ Ζήνων τὸ ἕν καὶ πᾶν καὶ μόνον ἀίδιον καὶ ἄπειρον {τὸ ἕν}.[33] | (S) |

19. ⟨Ἐμπεδοκλῆς τὰ στοιχεῖα καὶ τὰς ἀρχὰς καὶ⟩[34] τὸ ἕν, καὶ τὸ μὲν ἕν τὴν | ἀνάγκην, ὕλην δὲ αὐτοῦ τὰ τέσσαρα στοιχεῖα, εἴδη δὲ τὸ Νεῖκος καὶ τὴν | Φιλίαν. λέγει δὲ καὶ τὰ στοιχεῖα θεοὺς καὶ τὸ μῖγμα τού-
90 των τὸν | {κόσμον} ⟨σφαῖρον⟩, καὶ πρὸς τ⟨οῦτο τὸν

§11 Speusippus fr. 58   §12 Critolaus fr. 16; Diodorus Tyrius fr. 2   §13 Heraclitus A8   §14 Zeno the Stoic 1.157   §15 Mnesarchus —   §16 Boethus 3.2
§17 Parmenides A31   §18 Melissus A13; Zeno of Elea A30
§19 Empedocles A32

33 {τὸ ἕν} pos. post 87 ⟨Ἐμπεδοκλῆς . . . καὶ⟩ Wachsmuth
34 ⟨Ἐμπεδοκλῆς . . . καὶ⟩ coni. MR, alii alia

11. Speusippus says that the deity is the Intellect, which is   75
not identical to either the One or the Good but has a nature of its own.

12. Critolaus and Diodorus of Tyre say that the deity is an
Intellect derived from impassive ether.

13. Heraclitus says that the deity is the eternally recurrent
everlasting fire, and fate is reason (*logos*), producer of the
things that exist by turning in contrary directions.

14. Zeno the Stoic says that the deity is the fiery Intellect   80
of the cosmos.

15. Mnesarchus says that the deity is the cosmos, which
derives its primary existence from spirit (*pneuma*).

16. Boethus declared that the ether is God.

17. Parmenides says that the deity is the unmoved and
limited spherical being.

18. Melissus and Zeno say that the deity is the One and All   85
and solely everlasting and unlimited.

19. ‹Empedocles says that the elements and the principles
and› the One are gods, and that the One is necessity, but
that its matter is the four elements, while its forms are
Strife and Love. He also calls the elements gods, and the
mixture of these the ‹Sphere›, and says that the ‹cosmos›   90

κόσμον>[35] ἀναλυθήσεσθαι τὸ | μονοειδές· καὶ θείας
μὲν οἴεται τὰς ψυχάς, θείους δὲ καὶ τοὺς μετέχοντας
| αὐτῶν "καθαροὺς καθαρῶς." (S) |

20. Πολέμων τὸν κόσμον θεὸν ἀπεφήνατο. (S) |

21. Ξενοκράτης Ἀγαθήνορος Καλχηδόνιος τὴν μο-
95 νάδα καὶ τὴν δυάδα | θεούς, τὴν μὲν ὡς ἄρρενα πατρὸς
ἔχουσαν τάξιν, ἐν οὐρανῷ | βασιλεύουσαν, ἥντινα
προσαγορεύει καὶ Ζῆνα καὶ περιττὸν καὶ νοῦν, | ὅστις
ἐστὶν αὐτῷ πρῶτος θεός· τὴν δὲ ὡς θήλειαν μητρὸς
θεῶν δίκην, | τῆς ὑπὸ τὸν οὐρανὸν λήξεως ἡγουμένην,
ἥτις ἐστὶν αὐτῷ ψυχὴ τοῦ | παντός. θεὸν δ' εἶναι καὶ
100 τὸν οὐρανὸν καὶ τοὺς ἀστέρας πυρώδεις | Ὀλυμπίους
θεούς, καὶ ἑτέρους ὑποσελήνους δαίμονας ἀοράτους. |
ἀρέσκει δὲ καὶ αὐτῷ <θείας εἶναι δυνάμεις>[36] καὶ ἐν-
διήκειν τοῖς ὑλικοῖς | στοιχείοις. τούτων δὲ τὴν μὲν
<διὰ τοῦ ἀέρος> ἀειδοῦς <Ἅιδην>[37] | προσαγορεύει,
τὴν δὲ διὰ τοῦ ὑγροῦ Ποσειδῶνα, τὴν δὲ διὰ τῆς γῆς
| φυτοσπόρον Δήμητραν. ταῦτα δὲ χορηγήσας τοῖς
105 Στωικοῖς τὰ πρότερα | παρὰ τοῦ Πλάτωνος μεταπέ-
φρακεν. (S) |

§20 Polemon fr. 121
§21 Xenocrates fr. 133

35 {κόσμον} <σφαῖρον> . . . τ<οῦτο τὸν κόσμον> coni. MP,
alii alia
36 <θείας . . . δυνάμεις> coni. MR, lac. stat. edd.
37 <διὰ τοῦ ἀέρος> . . . <Ἅιδην> coni. MR, alii alia

will be dissolved into this uniform entity. He moreover thinks that the souls are divine, and that those "pure ones" who share in them "purely" are divine as well.

20. Polemon declared that the cosmos is God.

21. Xenocrates, the son of Agathenor, from Chalcedon says that the Monad and the Dyad are gods, the former as   95 male having the rank of father and ruling in heaven, which he also calls Zan and odd and Intellect, who for him is the first god, the latter as female having the role of Mother of the gods, presiding over the region under the heaven, who for him is the soul of the universe. He says too that the heaven is a god and that the fiery stars are Olympian   100 gods, as well as other sublunary demons who are invisible. It is also his view that there are divine powers, and that these penetrate the material elements. Of these the one that passes through the invisible (*aeidês*) air he calls Hades, the one that passes through the moist substance Poseidon, and the one that passes through the earth plant-sowing Demeter. These doctrines he bequeathed to the Stoics, but the views described earlier he took from Plato   105 and reformulated.

22. Σωκράτης καὶ[38] Πλάτων δὲ τὸ ἕν, τὸ μονοφυές,
τὸ μοναδικόν, τὸ ὄντως ὄν, | τἀγαθόν· πάντα δὲ τὰ
τοιαῦτα τῶν ὀνομάτων εἰς τὸν νοῦν σπεύδει. νοῦς | οὖν
ὁ θεός, χωριστὸν εἶδος, τὸ δὲ "χωριστὸν" ἀκουέσθω
τὸ ἀμιγὲς πάσης | ὕλης καὶ μηδενὶ τῶν σωματικῶν
110 συμπεπλεγμένον, μηδὲ τῷ παθητῷ τῆς | φύσεως συμ-
παθές. τούτου δὲ πατρὸς καὶ ποιητοῦ τὰ ἄλλα θεῖα
ἔγγονα | νοητὰ μέν (ὅ τε νοητὸς λεγόμενος κόσμος),[39]
παραδείγματα δ᾿ ἐστὶ τοῦ | ὁρατοῦ κόσμου, πρὸς δὲ
τούτοις ἐναιθέριοί τινες δυνάμεις (λόγοι δ᾿ εἰσὶν |
ἀσώματοι), καὶ ἐναέριοι καὶ ἔνυδροι, αἰσθητὰ δὲ τοῦ
115 πρώτου θεοῦ | ἔγγονα ἥλιος, σελήνη, ἀστέρες, γῆ καὶ
ὁ περιέχων πάντα κόσμος. | (PS) |
23. Ἀριστοτέλης τὸν μὲν ἀνωτάτω θεὸν εἶδος χωρι-
στόν ὁμοίως Πλάτωνι, | ἐπιβεβηκότα τῇ σφαίρᾳ τοῦ
παντός, ἥτις ἐστὶν αἰθέριον σῶμα, τὸ | πέμπτον ὑπ᾿
αὐτοῦ καλούμενον. διῃρημένου δὲ τούτου κατὰ σφαί-
ρας, | τῇ μὲν φύσει συναφεῖς τῷ λόγῳ δὲ κεχωρισμέ-
120 νας, ἑκάστην οἴεται τῶν | σφαιρῶν ζῷον εἶναι σύνθε-
τον ἐκ σώματος καὶ ψυχῆς, ὧν τὸ μὲν σῶμά | ἐστιν
αἰθέριον κινούμενον κυκλοφορικῶς, ἡ ψυχὴ δὲ λόγος
ἀκίνητος | αἴτιος τῆς κινήσεως κατ᾿ ἐνέργειαν. (PS) |

§22 Socrates Plato —
§23 Aristotle —

[38] Σωκράτης καὶ om. S del. Diels
[39] post κόσμος coni. Usener καὶ αἱ ἰδέαι, prob. edd.

22. Socrates and Plato say that the deity is the One, the single-natured, the monadic, the true Being, the Good. All such names immediately refer directly to the Intellect. The deity, then, is an Intellect, that is, a separate Form; by "separate" let that be understood which is free of all matter, not entwined with any of the bodily entities, and also not subject to affection by anything in nature that is 110 passible. Of this God as Father and Maker the other divine beings are the descendants; they are intelligible (as is also the so-called intelligible cosmos), but they are the models for the visible cosmos. In addition to these, there are ethereal powers (these are incorporeal *logoi*), and powers that inhere both in air and in water, as well as the sense-perceptible descendants of the first god, sun, moon, stars, 115 earth and the all-embracing heaven.[33]

23. Aristotle says that the highest god is a separate form, mounted on the sphere of the universe, which is the ethereal body, also called by him the fifth element.[34] This body is divided into spheres that are contiguous in reality but separated by reason. Each of these spheres he regards as 120 a living being composed of body and soul. Of these the body is ethereal and moves in a circular fashion, whereas the soul is unmoved reason and cause of movement in actuality.

[33] This lemma shows unmistakable signs of Middle Platonist revision.

[34] Famously, Aristotle actually never calls his highest element, the ether, "fifth." This is most likely a doxographical invention.

24. οἱ Στωικοὶ νοερὸν θεὸν ἀποφαίνονται, πῦρ τεχνι-
κόν ὁδῷ βαδίζον ἐπὶ | γενέσει κόσμου, ἐμπεριειληφὸς
125 πάντας τοὺς σπερματικοὺς λόγους, | καθ᾽ οὓς ἕκαστα
καθ᾽ εἱμαρμένην γίνεται· καὶ πνεῦμα μὲν ἐνδιῆκον δι᾽
| ὅλου τοῦ κόσμου, τὰς δὲ προσηγορίας μεταλαμβά-
νον διὰ τάς τῆς ὕλης, | δι᾽ ἧς κεχώρηκε, παραλλάξεις,
θεοὺς δὲ καὶ τὸν κόσμον καὶ τοὺς | ἀστέρας καὶ τὴν
γῆν· ἀνωτάτω δὲ πάντων νοῦν ἐναιθέριον εἶναι θεόν.
| (PS) |

130 25. Ἐπίκουρος ἀνθρωποειδεῖς μὲν τοὺς θεούς, λόγῳ δὲ
πάντας θεωρητοὺς[40] | διὰ τὴν λεπτομέρειαν τῆς τῶν
εἰδώλων φύσεως. ὁ δ᾽ αὐτὸς ἄλλας[41] | τέσσαρας φύ-
σεις κατὰ γένος ἀφθάρτους τάσδε· τὰ ἄτομα, τὸ
κενόν, τὸ | ἄπειρον, τὰς ὁμοιότητας· αὗται δὲ λέγονται
ὁμοιομέρειαι καὶ στοιχεῖα. | (PS) |

§24 Stoics 2.1101
§25 1–3 Epicurus fr. 355

40 θεωρητοὺς P: διαρητοὺς sive διαρήτους S
41 ἄλλας P[1]QS: ἄλλως P[2]E

24. The Stoics declare that God is intelligent, a designing fire that proceeds methodically to the generation of the cosmos, encompassing all the seminal *logoi* according to 125 which each thing comes to be in accordance with fate. It is also a spirit that pervades the whole cosmos, taking on the names that correspond to the alterations of the matter through which it has passed. In addition, they regard as gods the cosmos, the heavenly beings, and the earth, and what is at the summit of everything, the Intellect in the ether, is also a god.

25. Epicurus says that the gods are human in form and are 130 all observable by reason only because of the fine particles of which the nature of their images consists. The same philosopher says there are four other classes of natures that are indestructible: the indivisibles, the void, the infinite, and the similarities; these natures are called *homoiomereiai* (things with like parts) and elements.[35]

[35] The long chapter ends with full accounts of the theology of the four chief Hellenistic schools, indicative of redaction during the Hellenistic period.

1.8

Ps.-Plut. *Plac.* 1.8 (+ Ps.-Gal. *Hist. phil.* 36)

η′. Περὶ δαιμόνων καὶ ἡρώων (P) |

1. Παρακειμένως δὲ τῷ Περὶ θεῶν λόγῳ τὸν Περὶ δαι-
μόνων καὶ ἡρώων | ἱστορητέον. (P) |
2. Θαλῆς Πυθαγόρας Πλάτων οἱ Στωικοὶ δαίμονας
5 ὑπάρχειν οὐσίας | ψυχικάς (εἶναι δὲ καὶ ἥρωας τὰς
κεχωρισμένας ψυχὰς τῶν σωμάτων)· | καὶ ἀγαθοὺς
μὲν τὰς ἀγαθὰς κακοὺς δὲ τὰς φαύλας. (P) |
3. Ἐπίκουρος δ᾽ οὐδὲν τούτων ἐγκρίνει. (P) |

§2 Thales fr. 150 Wöhrle; Pythagoras cf. Diog. Laert. 8.32;
Plato —; Stoics 2.1101
§3 Epicurus fr. 393

1.8

Division between those who believe that demons and heroes exist, and those who do not.

Ps.-Plutarch, *Tenets* (+ Ps.-Galen, *Philosophical History*)

8. On demons and heroes

1. Appended to the account On the gods we must record the one On demons and heroes.[36]

2. Thales, Pythagoras, Plato, and the Stoics say that demons are psychic beings; the heroes too are souls that have been separated from their bodies; and they (sc. the demons) are good if the souls are good, but wicked if the souls are wicked.

3. But Epicurus admits none of these as demonic.

5

[36] *logos*, "account," here practically means "chapter."

Ps.-Plut. *Plac.* 1.9; Stob. *Ecl.* 1.11.1, 3, 5b; Theod. *Cur.* 4.23

θ′. Περὶ ὕλης (PS) |

1. ὕλη ἐστὶ τὸ ὑποκείμενον πάσῃ γενέσει καὶ φθορᾷ
καὶ ταῖς ἄλλαις μεταβολαῖς. | (PS) |

2. οἱ ἀπὸ Θάλεω καὶ Πυθαγόρου,[42] λέγω δὲ τοὺς μέχρι
5 τῶν Στωικῶν καταβεβηκότας | σὺν Ἡρακλείτῳ, τρε-
πτὴν καὶ ἀλλοιωτὴν καὶ | μεταβλητὴν καὶ ῥευστὴν
ὅλην δι᾽ ὅλης τὴν ὕλην. (PST) |

3. οἱ ἀπὸ Δημοκρίτου[43] ἀπαθῆ τὰ πρῶτα, τὴν ἄτομον
καὶ τὸ κενὸν τὸ | ἀσώματον. (PST) |

4. Πλάτων[44] τὴν ὕλην σωματοειδῆ ἄμορφον ἀνείδεον
10 ἀσχημάτιστον ἄποιον | μὲν ὅσον ἐπὶ τῇ ἰδίᾳ φύσει,

§1 cf. Arist. *GC* 1.4 320a2–4   §2 Thales fr. 151 Wöhrle;
Pythagoras —; Stoics 2.324; Heraclitus T410–11 Mouraviev
§3 Democritus frs. 193, 214 Luria
§4 Plato cf. *Tim.* 49a, 50b–d, 52d

42 καὶ Ἀναξαγόρας add. T
43 καὶ Μητρόδωρος καὶ Ἐπίκουρος add. T
44 ante Πλάτων pos. Ἀριστοτέλης καὶ PEQ, non hab. ST

1.9

The primary division is between those who see matter as continuous, flexible, and determinable, and those who see it as discrete and impassible.

Ps.-Plutarch, *Tenets*; Stobaeus, *Anthology*; Theodoret, *Cure of Greek Maladies*

9. On matter

1. Matter is the substrate for all generation and destruction and the other kinds of changes.[37]
2. The successors of Thales and Pythagoras, I mean those (sc. philosophers) descending as far as the Stoics together with Heraclitus, say that matter is wholly and completely 5 changeable and alterable and mutable and fluid.
3. The successors of Democritus say that the first things are impassible, i.e., the atom and the incorporeal void.
4. Plato says that matter is body-like, without figure, without form, fully shapeless, without quality as far as its own 10

[37] A few chapters (mainly Book 1.9–12 and 14–15) commence with an anonymous definition of the principle to be discussed. Here we have an anonymous nominal definition of the meaning of the word *hylê* (wood in everyday speech), in its technical sense of "matter."

δεξαμενὴν δὲ τῶν εἰδῶν οἷον τιθήνην καὶ | ἐκμαγεῖον
καὶ μητέρα γενέσθαι. (PST) |

5. Ἀριστοτέλης δὲ σωματικήν. (PT) |

6. οἱ δ' ὕδωρ λέγοντες ἢ πῦρ ἢ ἀέρα ἢ γῆν τὴν ὕλην
οὐκέτι ἄμορφον αὐτὴν | λέγουσιν ἀλλὰ σῶμα· (PS) |

15 7. οἱ δὲ τὰ ἀμερῆ καὶ τὰς ἀτόμους ἄμορφον. (PS) |

8. οἱ Στωικοὶ σῶμα τὴν ὕλην ἀποφαίνονται. (ST) |

§5 Aristotle cf. *GC* 1.5 320b23, 2.1 329a9–10
§6 anonymi —   §7 anonymi —   §8 Stoics cf. 2.324

1.10

*The primary division is between those who posit the idea
[or: Idea; form: or Form] as existing in itself and separate,
and those who see it as related to or inseparable from*

Ps.-Plut. *Plac.* 1.10 (+ Ps.-Gal. *Hist. phil.* 25); Stob. *Ecl.*
1.12.1a

ι΄. Περὶ ἰδέας (PS) |

1. ἰδέα ἐστὶν οὐσία ἀσώματος, αἰτία τῶν οἷά ἐστιν
αὐτὴ καὶ παράδειγμα | τῆς τῶν κατὰ φύσιν ἐχόντων
αἰσθητῶν ὑποστάσεως,[45] αὐτὴ μὲν ὑφεστῶσα | καθ'
ἑαυτήν, εἰκονίζουσα δὲ τὰς ἀμόρφους ὕλας καὶ αἰτία
5 γιγνομένη | τῆς τούτων διατάξεως, πατρὸς ἐπέχουσα
τοῖς αἰσθητοῖς τάξιν. | (PS) |

[45] αἰτία . . . ὑποστάσεως om. P

76

nature is concerned; but by receiving the forms it became like a nurse and a mold and a mother.

5. But Aristotle says that it is corporeal.

6. Those who state that matter is water or fire or air or earth no longer regard it as without figure but as body,

7. whereas those who say it is things without parts and the atoms say that it is without figure. 15

8. But the Stoics declare matter to be body.

1.10

bodies. A subsidiary division is between the Ideas as thoughts in the mind of the divinity, and those who see them as human concepts.

Ps.-Plutarch, *Tenets* (+ Ps.-Galen, *Philosophical History*); Stobaeus, *Anthology*

10. On the idea

1. The idea is an incorporeal substance. It is itself the cause that makes things to be such as they are and the model of the existence of the natural sense perceptibles. It exists by itself, but makes the formless materials into images of itself and becomes a cause of their arrangement, 5 occupying the role of a father toward the sense perceptibles.[38]

[38] This real definition is limited to the first alternative of the primary division.

2. Σωκράτης καὶ[46] Πλάτων χωριστὰς τῆς ὕλης οὐσίας
τὰς ἰδέας ὑπολαμβάνει, | ἐν τοῖς νοήμασι καὶ ταῖς
φαντασίαις τοῦ θεοῦ, τουτέστι τοῦ νοῦ, | ὑφεστώ-
σας. (P) |

10 3. Πυθαγόρας τὰ λεγόμενα εἴδη καὶ τὰς ἰδέας ἐν τοῖς
ἀριθμοῖς καὶ ταῖς | ἁρμονίαις αὐτῶν καὶ τοῖς καλου-
μένοις γεωμετρικοῖς ἐτίθετο ἀχώριστα | τῶν σωμά-
των. (S) |

4. Ἀριστοτέλης δ᾽ εἴδη μὲν ἀπέλιπε καὶ ἰδέας, οὐ μὴν
κεχωρισμένας τῆς | ὕλης, ἔξω γεγονὼς τοῦ ὑπὸ τοῦ
θεοῦ.[47] (P) |

15 5. οἱ δὲ ἀπὸ Ζήνωνος Στωικοὶ ἐννοήματα ἡμέτερα τὰς
ἰδέας ἔφασαν. (P) |

§2 Socrates —; Plato —   §3 Pythagoras —
§4 Aristotle —   §5 Stoics 1.65, 2.360

1.11

Ps.-Plut. *Plac.* 1.11; Stob. *Ecl.* 1.13.1abd

ιαʹ. Περὶ αἰτίων (PS) |

1. αἴτιόν ἐστι δι᾽ ὃ τὸ ἀποτέλεσμα ἢ δι᾽ ὃ συμβαίνει
τι· ἀρκεῖ γὰρ ὑπογραφικῶς.[48] | (PS) |

§1 —

46 Σωκράτης καὶ om. G, del. Diels
47 ἔξω . . . θεοῦ coni. Xylander
48 ἀρκεῖ . . . ὑπογραφικῶς om. P

2. Socrates and Plato understand the ideas as substances separate from matter, existing in the conceptions and impressions of God, that is to say, the Intellect.

3. Pythagoras placed the so-called forms and the ideas in the numbers and in their harmonies and what are named the geometricals, regarding them as inseparable from the bodies.

4. Aristotle preserved the forms and ideas, but as not in fact separated from matter, thereby placing himself outside the view that they are put into matter by God.[39]

5. The Stoics who were the successors of Zeno say that the ideas are our own conceptions.

1.11

The divisions are according to number, to corporeal vs. incorporeal, and for the first cause to mobility vs. immobility.

Ps.-Plutarch, *Tenets*; Stobaeus, *Anthology*

11. On causes

1. A cause is that through which the product [or: effect] is completed or through which something occurs; for a descriptive definition suffices.[40]

---

[39] The text of the final part of the doxa is garbled in the manuscripts of Ps.-Plutarch and his tradition. We print and translate the conjecture of the German humanist Xylander (Wilhelm Holzmann) with little confidence.

[40] A combination of two anonymous nominal definitions.

2. Πλάτων τριχῶς τὸ αἴτιον· φησὶ γὰρ ὑφ᾽ οὗ ἐξ οὗ
5 πρὸς ὅ· κυριώτερον δ᾽ | ἡγεῖται τὸ ὑφ᾽ οὗ· τοῦτο δ᾽ ἦν
τὸ ποιοῦν, ὅ ἐστι νοῦς.⁴⁹ (PS) |

3. Πυθαγόρας Ἀριστοτέλης τὰ μὲν πρῶτα αἴτια
ἀσώματα, τὰ δὲ κατὰ | μετοχὴν ἢ κατὰ συμβεβηκὸς
τῆς σωματικῆς ὑποστάσεως· ὥστ᾽ εἶναι | τὸν κόσμον
σῶμα. (PS) |

4. οἱ Περιπατητικοὶ τῶν αἰτίων εἶναι τὰ μὲν αἰσθητά,
τὰ δὲ νοητά. (S) |

10 5. οἱ Στωικοὶ πάντα τὰ αἴτια σωματικά· πνεύματα
γάρ. (P) |

6. Θαλῆς καὶ οἱ ἐφεξῆς τὸ πρῶτον αἴτιον ἀκίνητον
ἀπεφήναντο. (S) |

7. οἱ Στωικοὶ τὸ πρῶτον αἴτιον ὡρίσαντο κινητόν. (S) |

§2 Plato cf. *Tim.* 28a–29a, 46c–e, 50c–d
§3 Pythagoras —; Aristotle cf. *Met.* 12.4, 12.7
§4 Peripatetics —
§5 Stoics 2.340
§6 Thales fr. 347 Wöhrle
§7 Stoics 2.338

⁴⁹ ὅ . . . νοῦς om. S

2. Plato understands the cause in three ways, for he says by which [or: whom], out of which, toward which.[41] But more properly he regards the by which as the cause. This is the agent, i.e., Intellect.

3. Pythagoras and Aristotle say that there are first causes that are incorporeal, and there are causes by participation in or as property of the corporeal subsistence, with the result that the cosmos is body.

4. The Peripatetics say that of the causes some are sensible and others intelligible.

5. The Stoics say that all the causes are corporeal, for they are *pneumata* (currents of warm air).

6. Thales and his successors declared that the first cause is unmoved [or: unchanging].

7. The Stoics defined the first cause as movable [or: changing].

[41] The formulation in terms of so-called "prepositional metaphysics" shows Middle Platonist influence, though it has its roots in the writings of Plato and Aristotle.

1.12

The primary division is between those who attribute weight to bodies as an intrinsic property and those who believe weight to be adventitious and dependent on cir-

Ps.-Plut. *Plac.* 1.12; Stob. *Ecl.* 1.14.1adfh

ιβ'. Περὶ σωμάτων (PS) |

1. σῶμά ἐστι τὸ τριχῇ διαστατόν, πλάτει βάθει μήκει· ἢ ὄγκος ἀντίτυπος | ὅσον ἐφ' ἑαυτῷ· ἢ τὸ κατέχον τόπον. (PS) |

2. Πλάτων μήτε βαρὺ μήτε κοῦφον εἶναί τι φύσει ἔν
5 γε τῷ οἰκείῳ τόπῳ | ὑπάρχον· ἐν δέ γε τῷ ἀλλοτρίῳ γενόμενον τότε νεῦσιν ἴσχειν, ἐκ δὲ τῆς | νεύσεως ῥοπὴν ἤτοι πρὸς βαρύτητα ἢ κουφότητα. (PS) |

3. Ἀριστοτέλης βαρύτατον μὲν εἶναι τὴν γῆν ἁπλῶς, κουφότατον δὲ τὸ | πῦρ· ἀέρα δὲ καὶ ὕδωρ ἄλλοτ' ἄλλως. μηδὲν δὲ πῦρ κυκλοτερῶς φύσει | κινεῖσθαι, μόνον δὲ τὸ πέμπτον σῶμα. (PS) |

10 4. οἱ Στωικοὶ δύο μὲν ἐκ τῶν τεσσάρων στοιχείων κοῦφα, πῦρ καὶ ἀέρα, | δύο δὲ βαρέα, ὕδωρ καὶ γῆν· κοῦφον γὰρ ὑπάρχει φύσει, ὃ νεύει ἀπὸ τοῦ | ἰδίου

§1 —   §2 Plato cf. *Tim.* 62c–63e
§3 Aristotle cf. *Cael.* 1.1 269a15–b6, 4.4 311a15–b27
§4 Stoics 1.101, 2.571

cumstances. A subdivision according to number is between finitists and infinitists.

Ps.-Plutarch, *Tenets*; Stobaeus, *Anthology*

12. On bodies

1. A body is that which extends in three directions, width, depth, and length. Or it is a mass that of itself is resistant. Or it is that which occupies a place.[42]

2. Plato says that body is something neither heavy nor light by nature when it actually exists in the place proper to it. 5 But when it has come to be in an alien place, then it obtains inclination, and from this inclination there is a turning either to heaviness or lightness.

3. Aristotle says that earth is the heaviest body in absolute terms, and fire is the lightest, while air and water differ in weight according to circumstances. He also says that fire by nature never moves in a circular fashion, but only the fifth body does this.[43]

4. The Stoics say that two of the four elements are light, 10 fire, and air, and that two are heavy, water and earth. For light by nature is that which inclines away from the own

---

[42] Three anonymous definitions of the word *sôma*, "(human) body" in everyday speech, in the technical sense of "mathematical body," and as "physical body."

[43] See n. 34 on 1.7.23.

μέσου, βαρὺ δὲ τὸ εἰς μέσον. καὶ τὸ μὲν περίγειον
φῶς κατ᾽ | εὐθεῖαν, τὸ δ᾽ αἰθέριον περιφερῶς κινεῖ-
ται. (PS) |

5. Ἐπίκουρος ἀπερίληπτα εἶναι τὰ σώματα, καὶ τὰ
15 πρῶτα δὲ ἁπλᾶ τὰ δὲ | ἐξ ἐκείνων συγκρίματα πάντα
βάρος ἔχειν. κινεῖσθαι δὲ τὰ ἄτομα τότε | μὲν κατὰ
στάθμην, τότε δὲ κατὰ παρέγκλισιν· τὰ δὲ ἄνω κινού-
μενα | κατὰ πληγὴν καὶ ἀποπαλμόν.[50] (PS) |

6. Δημόκριτος τὰ πρῶτά φησι σώματα (ταῦτα δ᾽ ἦν
τὰ ναστά) βάρος μὲν | οὐκ ἔχειν, κινεῖσθαι δὲ κατ᾽
20 ἀλληλοτυπίαν ἐν τῷ ἀπείρῳ. δυνατὸν εἶναι | κοσμι-
αίαν ὑπάρχειν ἄτομον.[51] (S) |

7. Στράτων μὲν προσεῖναι τοῖς σώμασι φυσικὸν
βάρος, τὰ δὲ κουφότερα | τοῖς βαρυτέροις ἐπιπολά-
ζειν, οἷον ἐκπυρηνιζόμενα. (S) |

§5 Epicurus frs. 275, 280
§6 Democritus A47
§7 Strato fr. 50A

[50] ἀποπαλμόν emend. Diels: ὑπὸ παλμόν S, κατὰ παλμόν P
[51] ἄτομον S: fort. ἄτοπον

center (sc. of the cosmos), whereas heavy is that which moves to the center. In addition the light (sc. of the sun etc.) on earth moves in a straight line, whereas the etherial variety moves in a circle.

5. Epicurus says that the bodies are inconceivably many [or: inconceivable in number], and that the first bodies, which are simple, as well as all the bodies that are com- 15 posites of these, possess heaviness. He also says that the atoms at one time move perpendicularly, at another time with a swerve. But the bodies that move upward do so through impact or rebounding.

6. Democritus says that the first bodies (these are the solid bodies) do not have heaviness, but move by reciprocal impact in the infinite space. He also says that it is possible that an atom of cosmic proportions exists.[44] 20

7. Strato says that natural heaviness attaches to bodies, and that the lighter ones float on the surface of the heavier ones, like stones in fruit that are squeezed out.

[44] This translates the received text. But it makes better sense if *atomon* is emended to *atopon*, i.e., "that it is absurd that one of cosmic proportions exists."

Ps.-Plut. *Plac.* 1.13 (+ Ps.-Gal. *Hist. phil.* 26); Stob. *Ecl.* 1.14.1k

ιγ΄. Περὶ ἐλαχίστων (PS) |

1. Ἐμπεδοκλῆς πρὸ τῶν τεσσάρων στοιχείων θραύσματα ἐλάχιστα, οἱονεὶ | στοιχεῖα πρὶν στοιχείων, ὁμοιομερῆ, ὅ ἐστι στρογγύλα.[52] (PS) |

2. Ἡράκλειτος πρὸ τοῦ ἑνὸς δοκεῖ τισι ψηγμάτιά τινα εἰσάγει<ν>.[53] (PS) |

5   3. Ξενοκράτης καὶ Διόδωρος ἀμερῆ τὰ ἐλάχιστα ὡρίζοντο, (S) |

4. Ἡρακλείδης θραύσματα. (S) |

§1 Empedocles A43
§2 Heraclitus T405–7 Mouraviev
§3 Xenocrates fr. 68; Diodorus Cronus fr. 117B
§4 Heraclides fr. 62

[52] ὅ . . . στρογγύλα PQ, non hab. SG, secl. edd.
[53] εἰσάγει<ν> coni. MR

1.13

Diaeresis in the form of a list of various views concerned with corporeal minima.

Ps.-Plutarch, *Tenets* (+ Ps.-Galen, *Philosophical History*); Stobaeus, *Anthology*

13. On minimal bodies

1. Empedocles says that prior to the four elements there are minimal fragments, like elements before elements, which elements are *homoiomerê* (things with like parts), i.e., globular.[45]
2. Heraclitus, as some believe, introduces little filings prior to the one (sc. element).
3. Xenocrates and Diodorus defined the minima as part- 5 less entities,
4. Heraclides as fragments.

[45] The final phrase seems odd. It is not present in Stobaeus (and also not in Ps.-Galen). It may be a gloss that has entered the text.

1.14

Ps.-Plut. *Plac.* 1.14 (+ Ps.-Gal. *Hist. phil.* 28); Stob. *Ecl.*
1.15.3b, 6a

ιδ΄. Περὶ σχημάτων (PS) |

1. σχῆμά ἐστιν ἐπιφάνεια καὶ περιγραφὴ καὶ πέρας
σώματος. (PS) |
2. οἱ ἀπὸ Πυθαγόρου σφαιρικὰ τὰ σχήματα[54] τῶν τετ-
τάρων στοιχείων, | μόνον δὲ τὸ ἀνώτατον πῦρ κωνοει-
δές. (PS) |
5 3. Ἀναξαγόρας τὰ ὁμοιομερῆ πολυσχήμονα. (S) |
4. οἱ ἀπὸ Λευκίππου τὰ ἄτομα πολυσχήμονα. (S) |
5. Κλεάνθης μόνος τῶν Στωικῶν τὸ πῦρ ἀπεφήνατο
κωνοειδές. (S) |

§2 Pythagoreans —
§3 Anaxagoras A51
§4 Leucippeans cf. A43
§5 Cleanthes 1.498

[54] τὰ σχήματα Q Diels: κατὰ σχῆμα S, τὰ σώματα P

1.14

A diaeresis of elementary particles according to shape.

Ps.-Plutarch, *Tenets* (+ Ps.-Galen, *Philosophical History*);
Stobaeus, *Anthology*

14. On shapes

1. A shape is a surface and an outline and a limit of a body.[46]

2. Pythagoras and his followers say that the shapes of the four elements are spherical, and that only the very highest element, fire, is cone-like.[47]

3. Anaxagoras says that the *homoiomerê* (things with like 5 parts) are of many shapes.

4. The successors of Leucippus say that the atoms are of many shapes.

5. Cleanthes alone of the Stoics declared that the element fire is cone-like.

---

[46] An anonymous nominal definition of the meaning of the word *schêma* (shape).

[47] The shape of the four elements pertains to concentric cosmic layers, that of fire to atomic structure.

1.15

Ps.-Plut. *Plac.* 1.15 (+ Ps.-Gal. *Hist. phil.* 27); Stob. *Ecl.* 1.16.1

ιε΄. Περὶ χρωμάτων (PS) |

1. χρῶμά ἐστι ποιότης σώματος ὁρατή προηγουμένως.[55] (PS) |

2. οἱ Πυθαγορικοὶ "χροιὰν" ἐκάλουν τὴν ἐπιφάνειαν τοῦ σώματος.[56] (PS) |

3. Ἐμπεδοκλῆς τὸ τοῖς πόροις τῆς ὄψεως ἐναρμότ
5 τον·[57] τέτταρα δὲ τοῖς | στοιχείοις ἰσάριθμα, λευκόν, μέλαν, ἐρυθρόν, ὠχρόν.[58] (PS) |

4. Πλάτων φλόγα ἀπὸ τῶν σωμάτων σύμμετρα μόρια ἔχουσαν πρὸς τὴν | ὄψιν. (PS) |

5. Ἀρίσταρχος Σάμιος μαθηματικός, ἀκουστὴς Στράτωνος, φῶς εἶναι τὸ | χρῶμα τοῖς ὑποκειμένοις ἐπιπίπτον. (S) |

§1 —   §2 Pythagoreans B42, cf. Arist. *Sens.* 3 439a31
§3 Empedocles A92   §4 Plato *Tim.* 67c
§5 Aristarchus ap. Strato fr. 7

[55] προηγουμένως om. P   [56] post σώματος add. S 12–15
τὰ δὲ γένη . . . ἀέρων, om. infra   [57] τὸ . . . ἐναρμόττον,
al. etwas ist, worauf die Sehstrahlen fallen Q
[58] ὠχρόν: χλωρόν coni. Diels

1.15

The primary division is between color as adventitious in relation to light or vision, or as an intrinsic property.

Ps.-Plutarch, *Tenets* (+ Ps.-Galen, *Philosophical History*); Stobaeus, *Anthology*

15. On colors

1. Color in the primary sense is the visible quality of a body.[48]
2. The Pythagoreans called the surface of the body "color."
3. Empedocles declares color to be what is fitting for the passages of sight.[49] And there are four, equal in number to the elements: white, black, red, ocher (i.e., yellow). 5
4. Plato says that color is a flame emanating from the bodies, which has particles commensurate with the organ of sight.
5. Aristarchus of Samos the astronomer, disciple of Strato, says that color is light falling on what it falls upon.

[48] An anonymous nominal definition of the meaning of the word *chrôma* (color).

[49] That is, the theory of intromission, the effluences from the objects of sight reaching the eyes. The variant reading in Quṣṭā, "something on which the visual rays fall," assumes the opposed theory of extramission.

10   6. Ζήνων ὁ Στωικὸς τὰ χρώματα πρώτους εἶναι σχη-
ματισμοὺς τῆς ὕλης. | (PS) |

7. οἱ ἀπὸ Πυθαγόρου τὰ γένη τῶν χρωμάτων λευκόν
τε καὶ μέλαν, | ἐρυθρόν, ὠχρόν·[59] τὰς δὲ διαφορὰς τῶν
χρωμάτων παρὰ τὰς ποιὰς μίξεις | τῶν στοιχείων· τὰς
δὲ τῶν ζῴων παρὰ τὰς ποικιλίας τῶν τροφῶν[60] καὶ |
15   τῶν ἀέρων. (PS) |

8. Δημόκριτος φύσει μὲν μηδὲν εἶναι χρῶμα, τὰ μὲν
γὰρ στοιχεῖα ἄποια, | τά τε ναστὰ καὶ τὸ κενόν· τὰ δὲ
ἐξ αὐτῶν συγκρίματα κεχρῶσθαι· "διαταγῇ" τε καὶ
"ῥυθμῷ" καὶ "προτροπῇ," ὧν ἡ μέν ἐστι τάξις, ὃ δὲ
σχῆμα, ἡ | δὲ θέσις· παρὰ ταῦτα γὰρ αἱ φαντασίαι.
20   τούτων δὲ τῶν πρὸς τὴν | φαντασίαν χρωμάτων
τέτταρες αἱ διαφοραί, λευκοῦ, μέλανος, ἐρυθροῦ, |
ὠχροῦ. (S) |

9. Ἐπίκουρος καὶ Ἀρίσταρχος τὰ ἐν τῷ σκότῳ σώ-
ματα χροιὰν οὐκ ἔχειν. | (S) |

10. Ἀριστοτέλης πέρας ἐν ὡρισμένῳ διαφανεῖ, δια-
25   φανὲς δὲ ὕλην εἶναι | διηθημένην καθαρὰν καὶ ἀμιγῆ,
τούτου δὲ αὐτοῦ τὸ κινητικὸν[61] χρῶμα | ὑπάρχειν· ἐν
δὲ τῷ σκότῳ τὰ σώματα χροιὰν δυνάμει μὲν ἔχειν,

§6 Zeno the Stoic 1.91   §7 Pythagoreans —
§8 Democritus A125   §9 Epicurus fr. 29; Aristarchus —
§10 Arist. *Sens.* 3 439b11–12, *de An.* 2.7 418a31–b3

59 ὠχρόν: χλωρόν coni. Diels
60 τροφῶν S: τροπῶν P, τόπων GQ
61 κινητικὸν corr. Diels: κινητὸν S

6. Zeno the Stoic says that the colors are first configura- 10
tions of matter.

7. The successors of Pythagoras say that the kinds of the
colors are white and black, red, and ocher (i.e., yellow).
The differences between the colors come from the qualitative blendings of the elements, and those of the living
beings from the variations of the foodstuffs[50] and the airs 15
(sc. they breathe).

8. Democritus says that no color exists by nature, for the
elements are without quality, being the solids (i.e., atoms)
and the void. But the compounds formed from these are
colored by "intercontact," by "rhythm" and by "turning,"
of which the first results in order, the next in shape and
the last in position. For it is on the basis of these that the
impressions on the senses arise. Of these colors that relate
to the impression on the senses there are four differentia- 20
tions: white, black, red, and ocher (i.e., yellow).

9. Epicurus and Aristarchus say that the bodies in the dark
do not have color.

10. Aristotle says that color is a limit in bounded transpar-
ency, that the transparent is filtered matter that is pure and 25
unmixed, and that color exists as that which moves this
matter. In the dark bodies have color potentially, but never

[50] This is the reading in Stobaeus; the reading "locations" in
Ps.-Galen and Qusṭā is also possible.

ἐνεργείᾳ | δὲ μηδαμῶς· πολὺ δὲ τὸ μεταξὺ τοῦ τε μὴ
ἔχειν καὶ μὴ ὁρᾶσθαι. (S) |

11. οἱ μὲν ἄλλοι τὰ στοιχεῖα κεχρῶσθαι φυσικῶς, (S) |

12. οἱ δὲ τὰ ὁμοιομερῆ ποιότητος μετέχειν τὰ
πρῶτα, (S) |

30 13. οἱ δὲ τὰ ἄτομα πάντα συλλήβδην ἄχροα, ἐξ
ἀποίων δὲ τῶν λόγῳ | θεωρητῶν τὰς αἰσθητὰς ὑπο-
φαίνουσι γίγνεσθαι ποιότητας. (S) |

§11 Stoics 2.419   §§12–13 anonymi —

1.16

Ps.-Plut. *Plac*. 1.16; Stob. *Ecl*. 1.14.1bgi

ιϛʹ. Περὶ τομῆς σωμάτων (PS) |

1. οἱ ἀπὸ Θάλεω καὶ Πυθαγόρου παθητὰ ⟨τὰ⟩[62]
σώματα καὶ τμητὰ εἰς | ἄπειρον, καὶ πάντα τὰ συν-
εχῆ, γραμμὴν ἐπιφάνειαν στερεὸν σῶμα | τόπον χρό-
νον. (PS) |

§1 Thales frs. 152, 348 Wöhrle; Pythagoras —
[62] ⟨τὰ⟩ add. edd.

actually. There is, however, a great difference between not having color and color not being seen.

11. Other thinkers say that the elements are naturally colored,

12. but others say that the primary *homoiomerê* (things with like parts) participate in quality,

13. and yet others say that all the atoms taken together are without color, and they indicate that it is from entities without quality that are observable by reason that the visible qualities arise.   30

1.16

Diaeresis between bodies as infinitely or finitely divisible, with a third compromise view added.

Ps.-Plutarch, *Tenets*; Stobaeus, *Anthology*

16. On cutting of bodies

1. The successors of Thales and Pythagoras say that the bodies are passible and divisible to infinity. And all of the following are continuous: line, surface, solid (i.e., three-dimensional) body, place, time.

5   2. οἱ τὰς ἀτόμους ‹εἰσάγοντες›[63] περὶ τὰ ἀμερῆ ἵστα-
σθαι καὶ μὴ εἰς ἄπειρον | εἶναι τὴν τομήν. (PS) |
3. Ἀριστοτέλης δυνάμει μὲν εἰς ἄπειρον ἐντελεχείᾳ δ᾽
οὐδαμῶς. (PS) |

§2 Atomists 68A48   §3 Aristotle cf. *GC* 1.2 316b20–23

1.17

Ps.-Plut. *Plac.* 1.17 (+ Ps.-Gal. *Hist. phil.* 29); Stob. *Ecl.*
1.17.1

ιζ΄. Περὶ μίξεως καὶ κράσεως (PS) |

1. Θαλῆς καὶ οἱ ἀπ᾽ αὐτοῦ[64] τὰς τῶν στοχείων μίξεις
κατ᾽ ἀλλοίωσιν. (PS) |
2. οἱ δὲ περὶ Ἀναξαγόραν καὶ Δημόκριτον κατὰ
παράθεσιν. (PS) |
3. Ἐμπεδοκλῆς καὶ Ξενοκράτης ἐκ μικροτέρων ὄγκων
5   τὰ στοιχεῖα συγκρίνει, | ἅπερ ἐστὶν ἐλάχιστα καὶ οἱο-
νεὶ στοιχεῖα στοιχείων. (PS) |

§1 Thales A13a   §2 Anaxagoras A54; Democritus fr. 341
Luria   §3 Empedocles A43; Xenocrates fr. 71

63 ‹εἰσάγοντες› add. Mau   64 Θαλῆς καὶ οἱ ἀπ᾽ αὐτοῦ
S: οἱ μὲν ἀρχαῖοι PQ, οἱ μὲν παλαιότεροι G

2. Those thinkers who introduce the atoms say that the   5
cutting stops at the partless entities and that there is no
cutting to infinity.
3. Aristotle says that the cutting of bodies occurs potentially to infinity, but in actuality never.

1.17

The primary division is between mixing as alteration of
substance and as juxtaposition of particles.

Ps.-Plutarch, *Tenets* (+ Ps.-Galen, *Philosophical History*);
Stobaeus, *Anthology*

17. On mixing and blending

1. Thales and those following him say that the mixings of
the elements occur through alteration.
2. Anaxagoras, Democritus, and their successors say that
they occur through juxtaposition.
3. Empedocles and Xenocrates combine the elements out
of smaller masses, which are least in size and as it were   5
elements of elements.

4. Πλάτων τὰ μὲν τρία σώματα (οὐ γὰρ θέλει κυρίως αὐτὰ εἶναι στοιχεῖα ἢ | προσονομάζειν) τρεπτὰ εἰς ἄλληλα, πῦρ ἀέρα ὕδωρ, τὴν δὲ γῆν εἴς τι | τούτων ἀμετάβλητον. (PS) |

§4 Plato cf. *Tim.* 49b–d, 54b–d

1.18

Ps.-Plut. *Plac.* 1.18 (+ Ps.-Gal. *Hist. phil.* 30); Stob. *Ecl.* 1.18.1abd; Theod. *Cur.* 4.24

ιη΄. Περὶ κενοῦ (PS) |

1. οἱ ἀπὸ Θάλεω φυσικοὶ πάντες μέχρι Πλάτωνος τὸ κενὸν ὡς ὄντως κενὸν | ἀπέγνωσαν.[65] (PS) |
2. Ἐμπεδοκλῆς· "οὐδέ τι τοῦ παντὸς κενὸν πέλει οὐδὲ
5 περιττόν." | (PST) |
3. Λεύκιππος Δημόκριτος Δημήτριος Μητρόδωρος Ἐπίκουρος τὰ μὲν | ἄτομα ἄπειρα τῷ πλήθει, τὸ δὲ κενὸν ἄπειρον τῷ μεγέθει. (PST) |

§1 Thales frs. 153, 350, 488 Wöhrle; physici —
§2 Empedocles B13   §3 Leucippus A15; Democritus fr. 187 Luria; Demetrius Laco test. 3; Metrodorus —; Epicurus fr. 295

[65] ἀπέγνωσαν PS: ἐν τῷ κόσμῳ κενὸν εἶναι λέγουσιν GQ

4. Plato says that the three bodies—for he does not wish them to be or be called elements in the proper sense—are convertible to each other, namely fire, air and water, but that earth cannot be changed to any of these.

1.18

The primary diaphonia or opposition is between rejection of void and various forms of acceptance.

Ps.-Plutarch, *Tenets* (+ Ps.-Galen, *Philosophical History*); Stobaeus, *Anthology*; Theodoret, *Cure of Greek Maladies*

18. On void[51]

1. All physicists from Thales up to and including Plato rejected the void in the real sense of the word.[52]
2. Empedocles: "and of the All nothing is empty or super- 5 fluous."
3. Leucippus, Democritus, Demetrius, Metrodorus, and Epicurus say that the atoms are infinite in number, and the void infinite in size.

---

51 The same theme is treated in a cosmological context in 2.9.
52 It is fortuitous that Ps.-Plutarch and Stobaeus agree here against Ps.-Galen and Quṣṭā.

4. Στράτων ἐξωτέρω τοῦ κόσμου μὴ εἶναι κενόν, ἐνδο-
τέρω δὲ δυνατὸν | γενέσθαι. (ST) |

10 5. Ζήνων καὶ οἱ ἀπ' αὐτοῦ ἐντὸς μὲν τοῦ κόσμου μη-
δὲν εἶναι κενόν, ἔξω δ' | αὐτοῦ ἄπειρον. (PST) |

6. Ἀριστοτέλης τοσοῦτον εἶναι τὸ κενὸν ἐκτὸς τοῦ κό-
σμου, ὥστ' ἀναπνεῖν | εἰς αὐτὸ τὸν οὐρανόν· ἔνδοθεν
γὰρ εἶναι τόπον πύρινον.[66] (P, cf. S)|

§4 Strato fr. 26B   §5 Zeno and Stoics —
§6 Aristotle fr. 201 Rose

1.19

Ps.-Plut. *Plac.* 1.19; Stob. *Ecl.* 1.18.4c, 1b

ιθ'. Περὶ τόπου (PS) |

1. Πλάτων τὸ μεταληπτικὸν τῶν εἰδῶν, ὅπερ εἴρηκε
μεταφορικῶς τὴν | ὕλην, καθάπερ τινὰ "τιθήνην" καὶ
"δεξαμενήν." (PS) |

§1 Plato cf. *Tim.* 49a, 50a–d, 53a

[66] ἔνδοθεν . . . πύρινον G: εἶναι γὰρ αὐτὸν πύρινον PQ

4. Strato says that there is no void outside the cosmos, but that it is possible for it to occur inside.

5. Zeno and his successors say that inside the cosmos there   10
is no void at all, but outside it (sc. the cosmos) it is infinite.

6. Aristotle[53] says that that the void outside the cosmos is exactly large enough for the heaven to breathe into it; for inside there is a fiery place.[54]

1.19

The primary division is between place as adhering to the object on the outside and as its interior distance from side to side.

Ps.-Plutarch, *Tenets*; Stobaeus, *Anthology*

19. On place

1. Plato says place is what partakes of the Forms, like a sort of "wet nurse" and "recipient."[55] By this he has metaphorically denoted matter.[56]

---

53 The name-label here is mistaken (it should be "the Pythagoreans," cf. 2.9.1). The doxa is conflated with the view of Posidonius cited at 2.9.3, creating the same contrast between 1.18.5 and 1.18.6 as is found between 2.9.2 and 2.9.3.

54 The translation of the final clause is based on the text in Ps.-Galen; Ps.-Plutarch reads "for it (sc. the heaven) is fiery."

55 The terms are taken over *verbatim* from *Tim.* 49a6 and 53a3.   56 The phrase "what partakes" and the identification of place with matter are both taken from Aristotle's critique of Plato in *Phys.* 4.2.

2. Ἀριστοτέλης τὸ ἔσχατον τοῦ περιέχοντος συνάπτον
5 τῷ περιεχομένῳ. | (P) |
3. Στράτων τὸ μεταξὺ διάστημα τοῦ περιέχοντος καὶ
τοῦ περιεχομένου. | (S) |

§2 Aristotle cf. *Phys.* 4.4 211b10–12, *Cael.* 4.4 310b7–8
§3 Strato fr. 26B

1.20

Ps.-Plut. *Plac.* 1.20 (+ Ps.-Gal. *Hist. phil.* 31); Stob. *Ecl.*
1.18.1d, 4a

κ'. Περὶ χώρας (PS) |

1. Ζήνων καὶ οἱ ἀπ' αὐτοῦ[67] διαφέρειν κενόν, τόπον,
χώραν· καὶ τὸ μὲν κενὸν | εἶναι ἐρημίαν σώματος, τὸν
δὲ τόπον τὸ ἐπεχόμενον ὑπὸ σώματος, τὴν | δὲ χώραν
τὸ ἐκ μέρους ἐπεχόμενον, ὥσπερ ἐπὶ τῆς τοῦ οἴνου
5 πιθάκνης. | (PS) |
2. Ἐπίκουρος ὀνόμασι πᾶσιν παραλλάττειν κενόν τό-
πον χώραν. (S) |

§1 Zeno and successors 1.95, 2.504
§2 Epicurus fr. 271

[67] Ζήνων καὶ οἱ ἀπ' αὐτοῦ S: οἱ Στωικοὶ καὶ Ἐπίκουρος P

2. Aristotle says it is the outermost of what surrounds that
connects with what is surrounded.　　　　　　　　　　5
3. Strato says it is the interval between what surrounds and
what is surrounded.

1.20

*The division is between positing different meanings for
three related terms or seeing them as equivalent.*

Ps.-Plutarch, *Tenets* (+ Ps.-Galen, *Philosophical History*);
Stobaeus, *Anthology*

20. On space

1. Zeno and his successors say that void, place, and space
differ; thus void is vacancy of body, place what is occupied
by a body, and space what is partially occupied, as in the
case of a jar of wine.　　　　　　　　　　　　　5
2. Epicurus says that all these terms are to be used inter-
changeably: void, place, and space.

1.21

Ps.-Plut. *Plac.* 1.21 (+ Ps.-Gal. *Hist. phil.* 37), Qusṭā 1.21;
Stob. *Ecl.* 1.8.40b, 45

κα΄. Περὶ χρόνου (PS) |

1. Πυθαγόρας τὴν σφαῖραν τοῦ περιέχοντος.[68] (PS) |
2. Πλάτων αἰῶνος εἰκόνα κινητήν, ἢ διάστημα τῆς
τοῦ κόσμου κινήσεως. | (PS) |
5 2α. واما ارسطوطاليس فانه زعم انه عدد حركة الفلك. | (Q) |
3. Ἐρατοσθένης τὴν τοῦ ἡλίου πορείαν. (PS) |

§1 Pythagoras B33   §2 Plato cf. *Tim.* 37d
§2α cf. Arist. *Phys.* 4.11 219b1–2, 4.14 223b21–23, *Cael.* 1.9
279a14–15
§3 Eratosthenes fr. V.6

[68] τὸν χρόνον, εἶναι add. P

1.21

The primary division is between time as corporeal and as (incorporeal) accident.

Ps.-Plutarch, *Tenets* (+ Ps.-Galen, *Philosophical History*), Quṣṭā; Stobaeus, *Anthology*

21. On time[57]

1. Pythagoras says that time is the sphere of that which encompasses.
2. Plato says that time is a moving image of eternity, or the dimension of the motion of the cosmos.
2a. *Aristotle maintained that time is the number of the*   5 *motion of the (celestial) sphere.*[58]
3. Eratosthenes says that time is the course of the sun.

[57] This chapter and the following are the first of three sets of chapters with headings that distinguish between "on x" and "on the substance (*ousia*) of x"; cf. also 1.25–26, on necessity, and 1.27–28, on fate. The distinction that Aëtius has in mind in each case is far from clear.

[58] This lemma has survived in Quṣṭā only. Translation Robert Turnbull.

1.22

Ps.-Plut. *Plac.* 1.22 (+ Ps.-Gal. *Hist. phil.* 38); Stob. *Ecl.*
1.8.40b, 45

κβ′. Περὶ οὐσίας χρόνου (PS) |

1. Πλάτων οὐσίαν χρόνου τὴν τοῦ οὐρανοῦ κίνη-
σιν. (PS) |
2. οἱ Στωικοὶ αὐτὴν τὴν κίνησιν. (PS) |
3. Ξενοκράτης μέτρον τῶν γενητῶν, καὶ κίνησιν ἀί-
διον. (S) |
5 4. Ἑστιαῖος ὁ Περίνθιος φυσικὸς φορὰν ἄστρων πρὸς
ἄλληλα. (S) |
5. Στράτων τὸ ἐν κινήσει καὶ ἠρεμίᾳ ποσόν. (S) |
6. Ἐπίκουρος σύμπτωμα, τοῦτο δ' ἐστὶ παρακολού-
θημα, κινήσεων. (S) |

§1 Plato cf. *Tim.* 37d
§2 Stoics 2.514
§3 Xenocrates fr. 79
§4 Hestiaeus fr. 3
§5 Strato fr. 33
§6 Epicurus fr. 294

1.22

The primary division is between time as motion as accidental yet subsisting in reality and motion as entirely conceptual; there is a secondary one between time as ungenerated or generated.

Ps.-Plutarch, *Tenets* (+ Ps.-Galen, *Philosophical History*); Stobaeus, *Anthology*

22. On the substance of time

1. Plato says that the substance of time is the motion of the heaven.[59]
2. The Stoics say that it is motion itself.
3. Xenocrates says it is a measure of what is generated, and also everlasting motion.
4. Hestiaeus of Perinthus, the natural philosopher, says it 5 is the motion of the heavenly bodies in relation to each other.
5. Strato says it is the quantitative in motion and rest.
6. Epicurus says it is a concomitant, that is an accompaniment, of motions [or changes].

[59] The attribution to Plato, in the previous chapter and here, of a basically Stoic definition of time is also found in contemporary authors such as Philo of Alexandria and the Middle Platonist manual of Alcinous.

7. Ἀντιφῶν[69] καὶ Κριτόλαος νόημα ἢ μέτρον[70] τὸν χρό-
νον, οὐδ᾽ ὑπόστασιν. | (S) |

10 8. καὶ οἱ μὲν πλείους ἀγένητον τὸν χρόνον, (PS) |
9. Πλάτων δὲ γενητὸν κατ᾽ ἐπίνοιαν. (PS) |

§7 Antiphon B9   Critolaus fr. 14   §8 anonymi —
§9 Plato — (cf. Arist. Cael. 1.10 279b32–280a2, Simp. in Cael.
303.33–304.6)

1.23

Ps.-Plut. Plac. 1.23; Stob. Ecl. 1.19.1

κγ΄. Περὶ κινήσεως (S) |

1. Πυθαγόρας Πλάτων· κίνησίς ἐστι διαφορά τις ἢ
ἑτερότης ἐν ὕλῃ, ᾗ ἔστιν | ὕλη. οὗτος πάσης κινήσεως
κοινὸς ὅρος. (PS) |
2. Ἀριστοτέλης· ἐντελέχεια κινητοῦ. (PS) |

§1 Pythagoras —; Plato —
§2 Aristotle cf. Phys. 3.2 202a7–8, 8.1 251a9–10, 8.5 257b8a–9

[69] Ἀντιφάνης varia lectio S
[70] ἢ μέτρον: fort. ἡμέτερον = opinio Boethi ap. Them. Phys.
160.6

7. Antiphon and Critolaus say that time is a concept or measure,[60] and not something that exists on its own.

8. Moreover, the majority of philosophers say that time is 10 ungenerated.[61]

9. But Plato says that it is generated in thought.

1.23

Views on motion are first divided in an ascending series according to number, next as regards existence, and third as to the relation to perception and/or reason.

Ps.-Plutarch, *Tenets*; Stobaeus, *Anthology*

23. On motion

1. Pythagoras Plato: motion is a difference or alteration in matter *qua* matter. This is the shared definition of every form of motion.[62]

2. Aristotle: motion is entelechy of the movable.

---

60 Or "our concept" if the emendation is accepted. But this view is attributed to Boethus the Peripatetic, who does not occur elsewhere in the *Placita*.

61 Cf. the view attributed to Pythagoras and Heraclitus on the generation of the cosmos at 2.4.1.

62 A real, i.e., technical definition that also serves as nominal definition of the meaning of the word *kinêsis* (motion, or change), followed in the next paragraphs by contrasting real definitions.

5 3. Δημόκριτος· ἓν γένος κινήσεως τὸ κατὰ παλ-
μόν.[71] (PS) |

4. Ἐπίκουρος δύο εἴδη κινήσεως, τὸ κατὰ στάθμην
καὶ τὸ κατὰ παρέγκλισιν.[72] | (PS) |

5. εἰσὶ δέ τινες, οἳ καὶ τέταρτον εἶδος εἰσάγουσι, τὸ
κατ᾽ οὐσίαν, ὅπερ ἐστὶ | τὸ κατὰ γένεσιν. (S) |

10 6. ἄλλοι δὲ καὶ τὴν διανοητικὴν προστιθέασι, μέχρι
γὰρ τῶν πέντε προὔβησαν. | (S) |

7. Διόδωρος ὁ Κρόνος κεκινῆσθαι μέν τι, κινεῖσθαι δὲ
μηδέν. (S) |

8. Ἡράκλειτος ἠρεμίαν μὲν καὶ στάσιν ἐκ τῶν ὅλων
ἀνῄρει· ἔστι γὰρ | τοῦτο τῶν νεκρῶν· κίνησιν δ᾽ ἀίδιον

15 μὲν τοῖς ἀιδίοις φθαρτὴν δὲ τοῖς | φθαρτοῖς ἀπεδί-
δου. (PS) |

9. Ἡρόφιλος κινήσεως τὴν μὲν λόγῳ θεωρητήν, τὴν
δ᾽ αἰσθητήν. (PS) |

10. Ἀσκληπιάδης πᾶσαν κίνησιν αἰσθητήν. (S) |

§3 Democritus A47   §4 Epicurus fr. 280
§§5–6 anonymi —   §7 Diodorus Cronus fr. 121
§8 Heraclitus A6   §9 Herophilus fr. 142
§10 Asclepiades p. 726

[71] <ἀπο>παλμόν dub. MR, cf. 1.12.5
[72] lac. susp. MR

3. Democritus: there is one[63] kind of motion, that which occurs through vibration.   5

4. Epicurus says there are two[64] kinds of motion, that which occurs perpendicularly and that which occurs through rebounding.[65]

5. But there are some who introduce a fourth kind, that which occurs substantially, i.e., that which occurs in terms of coming to be.

6. Yet others add intellectual motion as well, so in fact they   10
have advanced up to the number five.

7. Diodorus Cronus says that things have moved to some extent, but that nothing is moving (sc. in actuality).

8. Heraclitus removed rest and standing still from the whole of things, for this belongs to corpses; to everlasting things he assigned everlasting motion and to perishable things he assigned perishable motion.   15

9. Herophilus says that there is motion that is observable by reason and there is motion that is sense perceptible.

10. But Asclepiades says all motion is sense perceptible.

63 The number has been reduced to fit the division.

64 This number has also been reduced to fit the division, cf. 1.12.5, where there are three.

65 A lemma on three kinds of motion seems to have fallen out here.

1.24

Ps.-Plut. *Plac.* 1.24 (+ Ps.-Gal. *Hist. phil.* 39); Stob. *Ecl.* 1.20.1ad

κδ′. Περὶ γενέσεως καὶ φθορᾶς (PS) |

1. Παρμενίδης Μέλισσος Ζήνων ἀνῄρουν γένεσιν καὶ φθορὰν διὰ τὸ | νομίζειν τὸ πᾶν ἀκίνητον. (PS) |
2. Ἐμπεδοκλῆς Ἀναξαγόρας Δημόκριτος Ἐπίκουρος
5 καὶ πάντες, ὅσοι | κατὰ συναθροισμὸν τῶν λεπτομε-
ρῶν σωμάτων κοσμοποιοῦσι, συγκρίσεις | μὲν καὶ
διακρίσεις εἰσάγουσι, γενέσεις δὲ καὶ φθορὰς οὐ κυ-
ρίως· | οὐ γὰρ κατὰ τὸ ποιὸν ἐξ ἀλλοιώσεως, κατὰ δὲ
τὸ ποσὸν ἐκ συναθροισμοῦ | ταύτας γίνεσθαι. (PS) |
3. Πυθαγόρας καὶ πάντες, ὅσοι παθητὴν τὴν ὕλην
10 ὑποτίθενται, κυρίως | γένεσιν καὶ φθορὰν γίνεσθαι·
ἐκ γὰρ ἀλλοιώσεως τῶν στοιχείων καὶ | τροπῆς καὶ
ἀναλύσεως γένεσ<ιν> καὶ φθορ<άν>,[73] παράθεσιν καὶ
μῖξιν, | κρᾶσίν τε καὶ σύγχυσιν γίνεσθαι. (PS) |

§1 Parmenides A29; Melissus A12; Zeno —
§2 Empedocles A44; Anaxagoras A65; Democritus —; Epicurus —
§3 Pythagoras etc. —

1.24

The primary division is between denial and acceptance of coming to be and passing away; there is a secondary one between alterations of continuous matter and combination and separation of discrete particles.

Ps.-Plutarch, *Tenets* (+ Ps.-Galen, *Philosophical History*); Stobaeus, *Anthology*

24. On coming to be and passing away

1. Parmenides, Melissus, and Zeno abolished coming to be and passing away because they held that the All is unmoved.

2. Empedocles, Anaxagoras, Democritus, Epicurus, and all those who make a cosmos through aggregation of bodies composed of fine particles introduce combinations and separations, but not comings to be and perishings in the true sense. For these do not come to be according to quality from alteration, but according to quantity from aggregation.

3. Pythagoras and all those who assume that matter is passive say that coming to be and passing away occur in the true sense. For through qualitative alteration of the elements and their turning and dissolution there takes place coming to be and passing away, juxtaposition and mixing, blending and fusion.

---

73 γένεσ<ιν καὶ φθορ<άν> coni. MR: γενέσεως καὶ φθορᾶς S (secl. edd.)

Ps.-Plut. *Plac.* 1.25 (+ Ps.-Gal. *Hist. phil.* 40); Stob. *Ecl.* 1.4.7ac; Theod. *Cur.* 6.3–4, 13

κε΄. Περὶ ἀνάγκης (PS) |

1. Θαλῆς· ἰσχυρότατον ἀνάγκη, κρατεῖ γὰρ τοῦ παντός. (PS) |

2. Πυθαγόρας ἀνάγκην ἔφη περικεῖσθαι τῷ κόσμῳ. (PST) |

3. Παρμενίδης καὶ Δημόκριτος πάντα κατ᾽ ἀνάγκην,
5 τὴν αὐτὴν δ᾽ εἶναι | εἱμαρμένην καὶ Δαίμονα[74] καὶ Δίκην καὶ πρόνοιαν καὶ κοσμοποιόν. (PST) |

4. Λεύκιππος πάντα κατ᾽ ἀνάγκην, τὴν δ᾽ αὐτὴν ὑπάρχειν εἱμαρμένην· | λέγει γὰρ ἐν τῷ Περὶ νοῦ· "οὐδὲν χρῆμα μάτην γίγνεται, ἀλλὰ πάντα | ἐκ λόγου τε καὶ ὑπ᾽ ἀνάγκης." (S) |

§1 Thales frs. 154, 341, 395 Wöhrle   §2 Pythagoras —
§3 Parmenides A32, B12.3, B8.14; Democritus frs. 23, 589
Luria   §4 Leucippus B2

[74] καὶ Δαίμονα T, cf. 2.7.1[7]: om. PS

1.25

Various nominal definitions explaining the meaning and scope of reference of the word ananke *(necessity), and various views about providence and necessity as the same or different.*

Ps.-Plutarch, *Tenets* (+ Ps.-Galen, *Philosophical History*); Stobaeus, *Anthology*; Theodoret, *Cure of Greek Maladies*

25. On necessity

1. Thales: necessity is the strongest of all things, for it rules over the universe.

2. Pythagoras said that necessity embraces the cosmos.[66]

3. Parmenides and Democritus say that all things happen in accordance with necessity and that it is the same as fate [5] and *daimôn*[67] and justice and providence and that which makes the cosmos.

4. Leucippus says that all things happen in accordance with necessity and that it is the same as fate. For he states in the *On Intellect*, "nothing happens at random, but all things happen both for a reason and by necessity."

[66] This does in vague terms describe what necessity does.

[67] The inclusion in this list of the term *daimôn*, derived from Parmenides' poem, occurs only in Theodoret.

10 5. Πλάτων τὰ μὲν εἰς πρόνοιαν ἀνάγει, τὰ δ᾽ εἰς ἀνά-
γκην. (PS) |

§5 Plato cf. *Tim.* 30b–c, 44c, 47e–48a

1.26

Ps.-Plut. *Plac.* 1.26 (+ Ps.-Gal. *Hist. phil.* 41); Stob. *Ecl.*
1.4.7c

κϛ΄. Περὶ οὐσίας ἀνάγκης (P) |

1. Ἐμπεδοκλῆς οὐσίαν ἀνάγκης αἰτίαν χρηστικὴν
τῶν ἀρχῶν καὶ τῶν | στοιχείων. (PS) |
2. Δημόκριτος τὴν ἀντιτυπίαν καὶ φορὰν καὶ πληγὴν
τῆς ὕλης. (P) |
5 3. Πλάτων ὁτὲ μὲν τὴν ὕλην ὁτὲ δὲ τὴν τοῦ ποιοῦντος
πρὸς τὴν ὕλην | σχέσιν. (PS) |

§1 Empedocles A45
§2 Democritus A66
§3 Plato cf. *Tim.* 47e–48a, 68e–69a

5. Plato ascribes some things to providence, other things   10
to necessity.

1.26

Various real definitions of mostly corporeal realities as the
substance of necessity, and different views of this sub-
stance.

Ps.-Plutarch, *Tenets* (+ Ps.-Galen, *Philosophical History*);
Stobaeus, *Anthology*

26. On the substance of necessity

1. Empedocles says that the substance of necessity is a
cause that is able to make use of the principles and the
elements.
2. Democritus says that the substance of necessity is the
resistance and motion and blow of matter.
3. Plato says that the substance of necessity is sometimes   5
matter and sometimes the disposition of the maker toward
matter.

Ps.-Plut. *Plac.* 1.27; Stob. *Ecl.* 1.5.15; Theod. *Cur.* 6.3–4, 13–14

κζ'. Περὶ εἱμαρμένης (PS) |

1. Ἡράκλειτος πάντα καθ' εἱμαρμένην, τὴν δ' αὐτὴν ὑπάρχειν καὶ ἀνάγκην· | γράφει γοῦν· "ἔστι γὰρ εἱμαρμένη πάντως."[75] (PST) |

2. Πλάτων ἐγκρίνει μὲν τὴν εἱμαρμένην ἐπὶ τῶν ἀν-
5 θρωπίνων ψυχῶν καὶ | βίων, συνεισάγει δὲ καὶ τὴν παρ' ἡμᾶς αἰτίαν. (P) |

3. οἱ Στωικοὶ Πλάτωνι ἐμφερῶς, καὶ τὴν μὲν ἀνάγκην ἀνίκητόν φασιν | αἰτίαν καὶ βιαστικήν, τὴν δ' εἱμαρμένην συμπλοκὴν αἰτιῶν τεταγμένην, | ἐν ᾗ συμπλοκῇ καὶ τὸ παρ' ἡμᾶς, ὥστε τὰ μὲν εἱμάρθαι τὰ δ' ἀνειμάρθαι. | (P) |

10 4. Χρύσιππος[76] μὴ διαφέρειν τοῦ εἱμαρμένου τὸ κατηναγκασμένον, τὴν δὲ | εἱμαρμένην εἶναι κίνησιν

§1 Heraclitus A8, B137   §2 Plato cf. *Leg.* 10.904c
§3 Stoics 2.976   §4 Chrysippus 2.916

[75] γράφει . . . πάντως S: om. PT
[76] Χρύσιππος T: om. S

1.27

The division is between nominal definitions of various absolute and mitigated forms of determinism.

Ps.-Plutarch, *Tenets*; Stobaeus, *Anthology*; Theodoret, *Cure of Greek Maladies*

27. On fate

1. Heraclitus says that all things occur in accordance with fate, and that it (fate) and necessity are the same.[68] Indeed he writes, "for it (sc. necessity) is fate in every respect."

2. Plato recognizes the role of fate in relation to human souls and lives, but along with it he also introduces the cause that relates to us. 5

3. The Stoics, agreeing with Plato, say that necessity is an invincible and compelling cause, while fate is an ordered nexus of causes. In this nexus there is also the element that relates to us, so that some things are fated for us and others not fated.

4. Chrysippus says that what has been necessitated does not differ from what is fated, and that it is an everlasting, 10

---

68 Cf. 1.7.13 (Heraclitus).

ἀΐδιον συνεχῆ καὶ τεταγμένην[77] κατ' ἐπιπλοκὴν | τῶν μερῶν συνηρτημένην. (ST) |

5. Ζήνων ὁ Στωικὸς ἐν τῷ Περὶ φύσεως δύναμιν κινη-τικὴν τῆς ὕλης κατὰ | ταὐτὰ καὶ ὡσαύτως, ἥντινα μὴ
15 διαφέρειν πρόνοιαν καὶ φύσιν καλεῖν. | (ST) |

6. Ἀντίπατρος ὁ Στωικὸς θεὸν ἀπεφαίνετο τὴν εἱμαρ-μένην. (S)

§5 Zeno 1.176   §6 Antipater 3.35

1.28

Ps.-Plut. *Plac.* 1.28 (+ Ps.-Gal. *Hist. phil.* 42); Stob. *Ecl.* 1.5.15; Theod. *Cur.* 6.14

κη΄. Περὶ οὐσίας εἱμαρμένης (P) |

1. Ἡράκλειτος οὐσίαν εἱμαρμένης λόγον τὸν διὰ τῆς οὐσίας τοῦ παντὸς | διήκοντα· αὕτη δ' ἐστὶ τὸ αἰθέριον σῶμα, σπέρμα τῆς τοῦ παντὸς | γενέσεως καὶ περι_όδου μέτρον τεταγμένης. (PS) |

5 2. Πλάτων λόγον ἀΐδιον καὶ νόμον ἀΐδιον τῆς τοῦ παντὸς φύσεως. (PS) |

§1 Heraclitus A8   §2 Plato —

[77] τὴν . . . τεταγμένην T: om. S

120

continuous and ordered movement in accordance with an articulated nexus of its parts.

5. Zeno the Stoic says in *On nature* that fate is a force that moves matter in the same respect and in the same way. It makes no difference to call it providence and nature.   15

6. Antipater the Stoic declared that fate is a god.[69]

1.28

The chapter deals with various real definitions of corporeal as opposed to incorporeal realities as the substance of fate, with an emphasis on strong determinism.

Ps.-Plutarch, *Tenets* (+ Ps.-Galen, *Philosophical History*); Stobaeus, *Anthology*; Theodoret, *Cure of Greek Maladies*

28. On the substance of fate

1. Heraclitus says that the substance of fate is the *logos* that passes through the being of the All. It is the etherial body, seed of the coming-to-be of the All and measure of its ordered revolution.

2. Plato says that it is everlasting *logos* (reason) and ever-   5
lasting law of the nature of the All.

---

69 This differs from "God is fate," which would belong in 1.7.

3. Χρύσιππος δύναμιν πνευματικὴν τάξει τοῦ παντὸς διοικητικήν· καὶ πάλιν ἐν τοῖς Ὅροις· "εἱμαρμένη ἐστὶν ὁ τοῦ κόσμου λόγος· ἢ λόγος τῶν | ἐν τῷ κόσμῳ προνοίᾳ διοικουμένων· ἢ λόγος, καθ' ὃν τὰ μὲν γεγονότα | γέγονε τὰ δὲ γινόμενα γίνεται τὰ δὲ γενησόμενα γενήσεται." (PST) |

10 4. οἱ ἄλλοι[78] Στωικοὶ εἱρμὸν αἰτιῶν, τουτέστι τάξιν καὶ ἐπισύνδεσιν ἀπαράβατον. | (PT) |

5. Ποσειδώνιος τρίτην ἀπὸ Διός· πρῶτον μὲν γὰρ εἶναι τὸν Δία, δεύτερον | δὲ τὴν φύσιν, τρίτην δὲ τὴν εἱμαρμένην. (PS)|

§3 Chrysippus cf. 2.913   §4 Stoics 2.917
§5 Posidonius fr. 103

1.29

Ps.-Plut. *Plac.* 1.29 (+ Ps.-Gal. *Hist. phil.* 43); Stob. *Ecl.* 1.6.17ac, 7.9a; Theod. *Cur.* 6.3–4, 15

κθ′. Περὶ τύχης (PS) |

1. Πλάτων αἰτίαν ἐν προαιρετικοῖς[79] κατὰ συμβεβηκὸς καὶ παρακολούθημα | καὶ σύμπτωμα, καὶ[80] προαι-

§1 Plato —

[78] ἄλλοι G: non hab. PQ

3. Chrysippus says that it is a pneumatic force that is administrative for the ordering of the All. And again in *The definitions*: "fate is the *logos* of the cosmos, or *logos* of what is administered by providence in the cosmos, or *logos* in accordance with which what has happened happened, what is happening happens, and what will happen will happen."

4. The other Stoics say that it is a concatenation of causes, 10 that is an inviolable ordering and linking together.

5. Posidonius says that it is third in line from Zeus; for first he says there is Zeus, second there is nature, third there is fate.

1.29

Chance differs from necessity and fate. The divisions between chance and the spontaneous, or between chance/the spontaneous in relation or not with the voluntary, are not very pronounced.

Ps.-Plutarch, *Tenets* (+ Ps.-Galen, *Philosophical History*); Stobaeus, *Anthology*; Theodoret, *Cure of Greek Maladies*

29. On chance

1. Plato says that chance is an accidental cause in the realm of the voluntary, as well as an adventitious consequence

---

79 προαιρετικοῖς P: ἀπροαιρέτοις S
80 καὶ σύμπτωμα καὶ S: καὶ πάλιν ξύμπτωμα φύσεως ἢ T

ρέσεως κατὰ τὴν πρὸς τὸ τέλος πρόθεσιν | ἐναλλακτι-
κὴν σχέσιν. (PST) |

5 2. Ἀριστοτέλης αἰτίαν κατὰ συμβεβηκός ἐν τοῖς καθ᾽
ὁρμὴν ἕνεκά τινος | γιγνομένοις ἄδηλον καὶ ἄστατον.
διαφέρειν δὲ τῆς τύχης τὸ αὐτόματον· | τὸ μὲν γὰρ
ἀπὸ τύχης καὶ τοῦ αὐτομάτου εἶναι ἐν τοῖς πρακτέοις
| πάντως· τὸ δ᾽ αὐτόματον οὐκ ἀπὸ τύχης, ἐν γὰρ τοῖς
ἔξω πράξεως· καὶ | τὴν μὲν τύχην τῶν λογικῶν, τὸ δ᾽
10 αὐτόματον καὶ τῶν λογικῶν καὶ τῶν | ἀλόγων ζῴων
καὶ ἀψύχων σωμάτων· καὶ τὴν μὲν τύχην προαιρέτως
| συμβαίνειν, τὸ δ᾽ ἀπροαιρέτως· καὶ τὴν μέν τινος
ὑπάρχοντος γίγνεσθαι, | τὸ δὲ ἀλόγως, μηδενὸς ἔξω
βουλευθέντος. (PST) |

3. Ἐπίκουρος[81] ἄστατον αἰτίαν προσώποις χρόνοις
τόποις·[82] <καὶ πάντα> κατ᾽ | ἀνάγκην κατὰ προαίρεσιν
κατὰ τύχην <γίγνεσθαι>.[83] (PS) |

15 4. Ἀναξαγόρας καὶ Δημόκριτος καὶ οἱ Στωικοὶ ἄδηλον
αἰτίαν ἀνθρωπίνῳ | λογισμῷ· ἃ μὲν γὰρ εἶναι κατ᾽
ἀνάγκην, ἃ δὲ καθ᾽ εἱμαρμένην, ἃ δὲ | κατὰ προαίρε-
σιν, ἃ δὲ κατὰ τύχην, ἃ δὲ κατὰ τὸ αὐτόματον. (PST) |

§2 Aristotle cf. *Phys.* 2.5 197a5–10, 2.6 197a33–b32, *Met.* 11.8
1065a30–b4   §3 Epicurus frs. 380, 375
    §4 Anaxagoras A66; Democritus A70; Stoics 2.966

[81] καὶ Δημόκριτος add. T
[82] τόποις PQ: τρόποις S
[83] καὶ <πάντα> . . . <γίγνεσθαι> Usener, MR

and a fortuitous event. It is also a substituted attitude of
the voluntary with regard to the envisaged purpose.

2. Aristotle says that chance is an accidental cause that is   5
unclear and unstable in the realm of what occurs according to an impulse toward some end. There is a difference,
he says, between chance and the spontaneous. For what
occurs by chance and also spontaneously are both certainly in the realm of action, but what is spontaneous
only does not occur by chance, for it is in the realm outside
action. And chance belongs to rational beings only,
whereas the spontaneous occurs in the case of rational and
irrational living beings and also unsouled bodies. In addi-   10
tion, chance occurs through the exercise of will, the spontaneous without it; and the former occurs when there is
somebody who has decided, but the latter occurs without
the intervention of reason, without anything having been
decided externally.

3. Epicurus says that chance is a cause that is unstable in
relation to persons, times and places, <and that all things
occur> by necessity, through choice, and by chance.

4. Anaxagoras, Democritus, and the Stoics say that chance   15
is a cause that is unclear to human reasoning. For there
are things that occur by necessity, that occur by fate, that
occur by chance, and that occur spontaneously.

1.30

Ps.-Plut. *Plac.* 1.30 (+ Ps.-Gal. *Hist. phil.* 20); Stob. *Ecl.* 1.41

λ'. Περὶ φύσεως (P, cf. S) |

1. Ἐμπεδοκλῆς φύσιν μηδεν<ὸς>⁸⁴ εἶναι, μῖξιν δὲ τῶν στοιχείων καὶ διάστασιν. | γράφει γὰρ οὕτως ἐν τῷ πρώτῳ τῶν Φυσικῶν·

> ἄλλο δέ τοι ἐρέω· φύσις οὐδεν<ός>⁸⁵ ἐστιν
> ἁπάντων
> θνητῶν, οὐδέ τις οὐλομένου θανάτοιο τελευτή, |
> ἀλλὰ μόνον μῖξίς τε διάλλαξίς τε μιγέντων
> ἐστί, φύσις δὲ βροτοῖς ὀνομάζεται
> ἀνθρώποισιν. (P) |

2. Ἀναξαγόρας ὁμοίως τὴν φύσιν σύγκρισιν καὶ διά-κρισιν, τουτέστι | γένεσιν καὶ φθοράν. (P) |

§1 Empedocles B8   §2 Anaxagoras cf. B17

⁸⁴ μηδεν<ὸς> coni. Diels Stein sec.
⁸⁵ οὐδεν<ός> coni. Diels Stein sec.

1.30

What people believe to be the nature of individual entities is in reality the result of the combination and separation of elementary substances.

Ps.-Plutarch, *Tenets* (+ Ps.-Galen, *Philosophical History*); Stobaeus, *Anthology*

30. On nature

1. Empedocles[70] says that there is no such thing as origin (*physis*),[71] only mixing and separation of the elements. For in the first book of his *Physics* (i.e., physical poem) he writes as follows:

> But I shall tell you something more: there is no origin
>   (*physis*) of all
> that is human, nor is there an end consisting of
>   wretched death,
> but only mixing and separation of what has been
>   mixed,
> and "nature" is what it is called by human beings.

2. In the same way Anaxagoras[72] says that nature is a combination and separation, which is coming-to-be and passing away.

---

70 Empedocles and Anaxagoras: cf. 1.24.2.

71 The Greek word *physis* may mean "origin" as well as "nature." The heading shows that the chapter forms a bookend with 1.1, "What nature is," but the doxai use *physis* in the sense of "origin."   72 See above, n. 70.

BOOK II

COSMOLOGY

INTRODUCTION

Transmission

Book 2 is the best attested part of the *Placita*. Ps.-Plutarch, whose abridged version best preserves the work's original structure, has thirty-two chapters. It can be shown, however, that, unusually, he almost certainly passed over two small chapters, as indicated by evidence in the other two witnesses.[1] Stobaeus, using the different method of the anthologist, takes up most of the book in his cosmological chapters (21–27). Theodoret in his paraphrasing manner uses material from fourteen of the chapters. The reason that this book is so well attested is that Stobaeus appears to have been very thorough in his excerpting. He omits only eighteen of its 217 doxai, and of these, five have been replaced by excerpts from Arius Didymus, while six others are brief anonymous doxai of little importance to him. Unlike in other parts of the work, the Byzantine editors apparently refrained from reducing the contents. It may

[1] See the notes on 2.2a and 2.5a.

128

be concluded, therefore, that the book is as good as complete.

In this book there are a number of passages in which it is very difficult to reconcile the text as preserved by the two main witnesses, Ps.-Plutarch and Stobaeus. These "irreducible" passages are further briefly discussed in Appendix II, to which the reader is referred at the relevant points in the apparatus criticus. See also General Introduction 2.2.2.

Contents

The subject matter of the book is indicated prospectively in its Procemium and retrospectively in the Procemium to Book 3. Moving from the principles and the elements (i.e., Book 1), it turns to the "products" (*apotelesmata*), beginning with the most comprehensive, that is, the cosmos. Looking back, Aëtius refers to the book as "the account of the things in the heavens." The book thus focuses on cosmology as it relates to the cosmos as a whole and to its heavenly realm. The contents of the book have a clear and straightforward structure. There are five thematic clusters: chapters 1 to 10, on the cosmos as a totality; 11 and 12, on the heaven; 13 to 19, on the heavenly bodies; 20 to 24, on the sun; 25 to 31, on the moon. The final chapter links the clusters together on the subject of the lengths of time of the heavenly bodies' movements. This sequence moves from the whole to the parts, and from the outside of the cosmos to the inside, a process that is germane to the work as a whole. The clusters also follow a recurrent pattern in the way they treat their subjects. They deal with topics related to the question types of substance, followed

129

by those of other categories, such as quantity, relative position, and so on, as well as question types on cause and origin. The subjects treated are generally well indicated in the chapter headings.

Name-Labels

The vast majority of the name-labels, which are a constituent of every doxa, refer to philosophers in physics or natural philosophy, but a limited number of other authors are also mentioned.[2] They amount to an impressive range of fifty-three individuals and groups, ranging from Thales in the sixth century to Posidonius in the first. The most frequently named are Plato, Aristotle, Empedocles, and the Stoics, but closer examination shows a predominance of names from the Presocratic period, when there was a strong diversity of opinions on cosmological subjects. Another feature of the book is the prevalence of multiple name-labels, especially those of three names or more.

Because the book is so well preserved, it is possible to have a high degree of confidence in the completeness and ordering of the individual chapters. The contents of its chapters are for the most part systematically structured through the consistent application of the characteristic dialectical method of the *Placita*, involving extensive use of the techniques of diaphonia and diaeresis (with often a

[2] Scientists (Aristarchus, 2.24.7; Eratosthenes, 2.31.3; Eudoxus, 2.19.3; Seleucus, 2.1.7); a scholar (Apollodorus of Athens, 2.16.7); a poet (Aratus, 2.19.3). No doctors are named in this book.

compromise view in between) or an organized list of differing views.[3] But historiographical considerations also play a role in the ordering of lemmata, notably in the way that the opening doxa very often represents the view of a foundational figure, for example, Pythagoras in chapter 1, Anaximander in chapters 20 and 24. In general, however, the book is far more dialectical than historical in its ordering of doxai. Another feature of the book is the brevity of many of its lemmata, which make heavy use of the technique of ellipsis, that is, the suppression of verbs of saying and the subject of the views that are put forward.

Sources

The Presocratic views, which are so dominant in the book, go back to writings and traditions that are almost entirely lost, rendering this material all the more valuable, but at the same time making it very difficult to determine its accuracy. The main source for the Platonic views is the *Timaeus*, as is to be expected, but its formulation has often passed through a Middle Platonist or Neopythagorean filter, for example, in chapter 6. Aristotle's cosmology in the *De caelo* plays an important role in the structuring of chapters 1 through 19, but the *Placita* differ in the detailed attention that is paid to the sun and the moon in chapters 20 to 31. For Epicurus, the doxographer was able to make use of summaries of his doctrines. At 2.7.3 he may have drawn directly from the *Letter to Pythocles*. The other

---

[3] On these techniques, see further the General Introduction and Glossary.

Hellenistic school to be heavily represented in this book is the Stoa. Extensive parallels with the doxography on physics in Diogenes Laertius *VP* 7.132–46 (and also the fragments of Arius Didymus) suggest that this material was drawn from earlier doxographies rather than from original writings.

There is ample evidence to show that the material that Aëtius has collected in this book stands for the most part in a dialectical-doxographical tradition that ultimately goes back to the Peripatos but underwent considerable development in the intervening centuries. The most valuable witness to this tradition in the period just preceding Aëtius is Philo of Alexandria. In a significant text, Philo poses questions of the heavens (and also of the mind/soul) that bear an uncanny resemblance to doxai in Book 2 (and also Book 4), though lacking all name-labels.[4] Other authors with similar material are Cicero, Arius Didymus, doxographies in Hippolytus and Ps.-Plutarch (*Stromateis*). In Philo, but also Achilles in the introductory manual to Aratus' *Phaenomena*, there are verbal parallels that prove that some of these views go back to a very specific common tradition. It is more difficult, however, to trace the antecedent history of this tradition. On two occasions in this book there are rare secondary references to Theophrastus (2.20.5, 2.29.8). The former cites his *Physics*, which we tend to accept. Some material, for example, in chapter 31, may also be taken from Eudemus. It can be considered certain that much of this often bizarre cosmological material from early Greek philosophy found has been sluiced

---

[4] Philo *Somn.* 1.22–23; for the doxai on the soul/mind, see the Introduction to Book 4.

through the researches of the Peripatos, and that the method of dealing with this material owes much to methods developed by Aristotle and his successors. But precise details on how these processes took place are not available.[5]

5 See further the General Introduction 1.5.

⟨TITLE⟩[1]

ΑΕΤΙΟΥ ΠΕΡΙ ΤΩΝ ΑΡΕΣΚΟΝΤΩΝ
ΤΟ Β′,[2]

ἐν ᾧ κεφάλαια τάδε·

⟨Index⟩

Ps.-Plut. *Plac.*

α′. Περὶ κόσμου
β′. Περὶ σχήματος κόσμου
⟨β⁺′. Περὶ κινήσεως κόσμου⟩[3]
5   γ′. Εἰ ἔμψυχος ὁ κόσμος καὶ προνοίᾳ διοικούμενος
δ′. Εἰ ἄφθαρτος ὁ κόσμος
ε′. Πόθεν τρέφεται ὁ κόσμος
⟨ε⁺′. Ποῦ ἔχει τὸ ἡγεμονικὸν ὁ κόσμος⟩[4]

---

[1] Ps.-Plut. *Plac.* 2; Theod. *Cur.* 4.31, cf. 2.95, 5.16
[2] tit. T: Περὶ τῶν ἀρεσκόντων τοῖς φιλοσόφοις φυσικῶν δογμάτων ἐπιτομῆς τὸ β′
[3] tit. add. MR²
[4] tit. add. MR

AETIUS
ON THE PLACITA

BOOK II

in which the following chapter headings are found:[1]

⟨Index⟩

Ps.-Plutarch, *Tenets*

---

[1] On the title and the list of chapter headings, or pinax, see above on Book 1 and the General Introduction 1.3.

[2] On this chapter, see below, ch. 2.2a n. 10; if it was deleted by Ps.-Plutarch, as we postulate, its title must have been included in the pinax. [3] This chapter was deleted by Ps.-Plutarch, but its title must have been included in the pinax.

ϛ'. Ἀπὸ ποίου πρώτου στοιχείου ἤρξατο ὁ θεὸς κοσμοποιεῖν |

10 ζ'. Περὶ τάξεως τοῦ κόσμου |

η'. Τίς ἡ αἰτία τοῦ τὸν κόσμον ἐγκλιθῆναι |

θ'. Περὶ τοῦ ἐκτὸς τοῦ κόσμου, εἰ ἔστι κενόν |

ι'. Τίνα δεξιὰ τοῦ κόσμου καὶ τίνα ἀριστερά |

ια'. Περὶ οὐρανοῦ, τίς ἡ τούτου οὐσία |

15 ιβ'. Περὶ διαιρέσεως οὐρανοῦ, εἰς πόσους κύκλους διαιρεῖται |

ιγ'. Τίς ἡ οὐσία τῶν ἄστρων πλανητῶν καὶ ἀπλανῶν |

ιδ'. Περὶ σχημάτων ἀστέρων |

ιε'. Περὶ τάξεως ἀστέρων |

ιϛ'. Περὶ τῆς τῶν ἀστέρων φορᾶς καὶ κινήσεως |

20 ιζ'. Πόθεν φωτίζονται οἱ ἀστέρες |

ιη'. Περὶ τῶν ἄστρων τῶν καλουμένων Διοσκούρων |

ιθ'. Περὶ ἐπισημασίας ἀστέρων |

κ'. Περὶ οὐσίας ἡλίου |

κα'. Περὶ μεγέθους ἡλίου |

25 κβ'. Περὶ σχήματος ἡλίου |

κγ'. Περὶ τροπῶν ἡλίου |

κδ'. Περὶ ἐκλείψεως ἡλίου |

κε'. Περὶ οὐσίας σελήνης |

κϛ'. Περὶ μεγέθους σελήνης |

30 κζ'. Περὶ σχήματος σελήνης |

κη'. Περὶ φωτισμῶν σελήνης |

κθ'. Περὶ ἐκλείψεως σελήνης |

λ'. Περὶ ἐμφάσεως σελήνης καὶ διὰ τί γεώδης φαίνεται |

λα΄. Περὶ τῶν ἀποστημάτων τῆς σελήνης |

35 λβ΄. Περὶ ἐνιαυτοῦ, πόσος ἑκάστου τῶν πλανητῶν χρόνος, καὶ τίς ὁ μέγας | ἐνιαυτός (P) |

<Prooemium>

Ps.-Plut. *Plac.* prooem.

τετελεκὼς τοίνυν τὸν περὶ ἀρχῶν καὶ στοιχείων καὶ τῶν συνεδρευόντων αὐτοῖς | λόγον τρέψομαι πρὸς τὸν ἐπὶ τῶν ἀποτελεσμάτων, ἀπὸ τοῦ περιεκτικωτάτου | πάντων ἐνστησάμενος. (P) |

<Procemium>

*Transition from the principles of nature set out in Book 1
to the realia of the cosmos and its contents, starting with
the heavenly region.*

Ps.-Plutarch, *Tenets*

Having thus completed my account of the principles and
elements and what is closely associated with them, I shall
turn to the account concerned with the products, starting
with the most comprehensive of all things.

AETIUS

2.1

After introducing the cosmos by means of a nominal definition, the chapter treats two main questions, whether it is unique or there are infinity many kosmoi, *and whether*

Ps.-Plut. *Plac.* 2.1 (+ Ps.-Gal. *Hist. phil.* 44); Stob. *Ecl.* 1.21.3ab, 6c, 1.22.3b–d; Theod. *Cur.* 4.15

α′. Περὶ κόσμου (PS) |

1. Πυθαγόρας πρῶτος ὠνόμασε τὴν τῶν ὅλων περιοχὴν "κόσμον" ἐκ τῆς ἐν | αὐτῷ τάξεως. (PS) |

2 Θαλῆς Πυθαγόρας Ἐμπεδοκλῆς Ἔκφαντος Παρμενίδης Μέλισσος | Ἡράκλειτος Ἀναξαγόρας Πλάτων Ἀριστοτέλης Ζήνων ἕνα τὸν κόσμον. | (PST) |

3. Ἀναξίμανδρος Ἀναξιμένης Ἀρχέλαος Ξενοφάνης Διογένης Λεύκιππος | Δημόκριτος, Ἐπίκουρος καὶ ὁ τούτου καθηγητὴς Μητρόδωρος ἀπείρους | κόσμους ἐν τῷ ἀπείρῳ κατὰ πᾶσαν περίστασιν.⁵ (PST) |

§1 Pythagoras 14.21   §2 Thales A13b; Pythagoras —; Empedocles —; Ecphantus 51.3; Parmenides A36; Melissus A9; Heraclitus A10; Anaxagoras A63; Plato cf. *Tim.* 31a; Aristotle cf. *Cael.* 1.8; Zeno 1.97

§3 Anaximander A17; Anaximenes 13A10; Archelaus A13; Xenophanes A37; Diogenes A10; Leucippus —; Democritus fr. 352 Luria; Epicurus fr. 301; Metrodorus A7

⁵ περίστασιν P: περιαγωγήν S

BOOK II: COSMOLOGY

2.1

it is limited or unlimited in extent. In both cases there are diametrically opposed views.

Ps.-Plutarch, *Tenets* (+ Ps.-Galen, *Philosophical History*); Stobaeus, *Anthology*; Theodoret, *Cure of Greek Maladies*

1. On the cosmos

1. Pythagoras was the first[4] to call the container of all things "cosmos" on the basis of the order present in it.
2. Thales, Pythagoras, Empedocles, Ecphantus, Parmenides, Melissus, Heraclitus, Anaxagoras, Plato, Aristotle, and Zeno say that the cosmos is unique.
3. Anaximander, Anaximenes, Archelaus, Xenophanes, Diogenes, Leucippus, Democritus, Epicurus, and his teacher Metrodorus say that there are infinite[5] *kosmoi* in the infinite space throughout the entire surrounding area.

[4] An example of the "first discoverer" motif, common in early accounts of the development of Greek philosophy. Other examples in this book are at 2.12.2 (Pythagoras again), and at 2.24.1, 2.28.5 (both Thales).
[5] Sc. infinitely many.

10 4. τῶν ἀπείρους ἀποφηναμένων τοὺς κόσμους Ἀναξί-
μανδρος τὸ ἴσον | αὐτοὺς ἀπέχειν ἀλλήλων, (S) |

5. Ἐπίκουρος ἄνισον εἶναι τὸ μεταξὺ τῶν κόσμων
διάστημα. (S) |

6. Ἐμπεδοκλῆς τὸν τοῦ ἡλίου περίδρομον εἶναι περι-
γραφὴν τοῦ πέρατος | τοῦ κόσμου. (PS) |

15 7. Σέλευκος ὁ Ἐρυθραῖος καὶ Ἡρακλείδης ὁ Ποντικὸς
ἄπειρον τὸν κόσμον. | (PS) |

8. Διογένης καὶ Μέλισσος τὸ μὲν πᾶν ἄπειρον, τὸν δὲ
κόσμον πεπεράνθαι. | (PS) |

9. οἱ Στωικοὶ διαφέρειν τὸ πᾶν καὶ τὸ ὅλον· πᾶν μὲν
20 γὰρ εἶναι τὸ σὺν τῷ | κενῷ τῷ ἀπείρῳ, ὅλον δὲ χωρὶς
τοῦ κενοῦ τὸν κόσμον· ὥστε[6] τὸ αὐτὸ | εἶναι τὸ ὅλον
καὶ τὸν κόσμον.[7] (PS) |

    §4 Anaximander A17
    §5 Epicurus fr. 301a
    §6 Empedocles A50
    §7 Seleucus test. 5; Heraclides fr. 74
    §8 Diogenes A10; Melissus —
    §9 Stoics 2.522

    [6] ὥστε οὐ P
    [7] ὥστε . . . κόσμον om. S

4. Of those that declare there to be infinite *kosmoi*, Anax- 10
imander says that they are at an equal distance from each
other,[6]

5. whereas Epicurus says that the distance between the
kosmoi is unequal.

6. Empedocles says that the revolution of the sun is the
perimeter of the cosmos' limit.

7. Seleucus from the Red Sea[7] and Heraclides from Pon- 15
tus say that the cosmos is infinite.

8. Diogenes and Melissus say that the All is infinite, but
the cosmos is limited.

9. The Stoics say that the All and the whole differ,[8] for the
All is the cosmos together with the infinite void, whereas 20
the whole is the cosmos apart from the void; as a result the
whole and the cosmos amount to the same.

[6] This surprising view was probably suggested by the distances between the various cosmic rings and the earth; cf. 2.20.1,
2.21.1, 2.25.1.

[7] Perhaps better, "from the Persian gulf," since that is closer
to the city of Babylon, with which Seleucus is associated.

[8] Cf. 1.5.1.

2.2

Ps.-Plut. *Plac.* 2.2 (+ Ps.-Gal. *Hist. phil.* 45); Stob. *Ecl.* 1.15.6b; Theod. *Cur.* 4.16

β΄. Περὶ σχήματος κόσμου (PS) |

1. οἱ μὲν Στωικοὶ σφαιροειδῆ τὸν κόσμον, (PST) |
2. ἄλλοι δὲ κωνοειδῆ, (P, cf. T) |
3. οἱ δ᾽ ᾠοειδῆ.[8] (P, cf. T) |
5   4. Λεύκιππος καὶ Δημόκριτος σφαιροειδῆ τὸν κόσμον, | (S, cf. T) |
5. Ἐπίκουρος δ᾽ ἐνδέχεσθαι μὲν εἶναι σφαιροειδεῖς τοὺς κόσμους, ἐνδέχεσθαι | δὲ καὶ ἑτέροις σχήμασι κεχρῆσθαι. (P) |

§1 Stoics 2.547
§4 Leucippus A22; Democritus fr. 385 Luria
§5 Epicurus fr. 302

[8] ᾠοειδῆ PT: κυκλοειδῆ G

2.2

A list of differing views, opposed to the view that various shapes are possible.

Ps.-Plutarch, *Tenets* (+ Ps.-Galen, *Philosophical History*); Stobaeus, *Anthology*; Theodoret, *Cure of Greek Maladies*

2. On the shape of the cosmos

1. The Stoics say that the cosmos is like a ball[9] (i.e., spherical),
2. but others say that it is like a cone,
3. while yet others say that it is like an egg (i.e., ovoid).
4. Leucippus and Democritus say that the cosmos is like a ball.   5
5. Epicurus, however, says that it is possible that the *kosmoi* are like a ball, but that it is possible that they make use of other shapes as well.

---

9 On the translation in adjectives ending in -*eidês*, see General Introduction 3.3(8).

Stob. *Ecl*. 1.21.3b; Theod. *Cur.* 4.16

⟨β⁺′. Περὶ κινήσεως κόσμου⟩[10] |

1. οἱ μὲν μυλοειδῶς, (T) |
2. οἱ δὲ τρόχου δίκην περιδινεῖσθαι ⟨τὸν κό-
σμον⟩.[11] (T) |
3. ⟨οἱ Στωικοὶ⟩[12] μήτε αὔξεσθαι δὲ μήτε μειοῦσθαι τὸν
5 κόσμον, | τοῖς δὲ μέρεσιν ὁτὲ μὲν παρεκτείνεσθαι
πρὸς πλείονα τόπον, | ὁτὲ δὲ συστέλλεσθαι. (S) |

§1 —
§2 Anaximenes A12
§3 Stoics 2.597

[9] cap. deest in MR
[10] tit. coni. MR² ex T: non hab. P
[11] add. MR²
[12] add. MR²

2.2a

Three kinds of motion are set out in two diaereses. The first two circular motions are opposed, the one in a vertical, the other in a horizontal plane. The third kind is opposed to the first two, involving expansion and contraction.

Stobaeus, *Anthology*; Theodoret, *Cure of Greek Maladies*

⟨2a. On the motion of the cosmos⟩[10]

1. Some say that the cosmos moves like a millstone,
2. while others say that it whirls in the manner of a wheel.
3. ⟨The Stoics⟩ say that the cosmos neither increases or diminishes, but with its parts it sometimes extends to a   5 more ample location, while on other occasions, it contracts.

[10] Because the first two lemmata are found in an enclave of Aëtian doxai in Theodoret, they should be inserted here, though not included in the other witnesses. Indeed, most unusually, here and in 2.5a, Ps.-Plutarch deletes the entire chapter. Compare other chapters on motion: 1.23 (principle), 2.16 (stars), 2.23–24 (sun), 2.27–28 (moon), 3.13 (earth), 4.6 (soul). The doxa in Stobaeus is better located in this chapter rather than in 2.4, where Diels placed it.

2.3

Ps.-Plut. *Plac.* 2.3 (+ Ps.-Gal. *Hist. phil.* 46); Stob. *Ecl.*
1.21.3c, 6ab; Theod. *Cur.* 4.16

γ΄. Εἰ ἔμψυχος ὁ κόσμος καὶ
προνοίᾳ διοικούμενος (PS) |

1. οἱ μὲν ἄλλοι πάντες ἔμψυχον τὸν κόσμον καὶ προνοίᾳ
διοικούμενον. | (PST) |

2. Λεύκιππος δὲ καὶ Δημόκριτος καὶ Ἐπίκουρος οὐδέ-
5 τερα τούτων, φύσει | δὲ ἀλόγῳ ἐκ τῶν ἀτόμων συν-
εστῶτα.[13] (PST) |

3. Ἔκφαντος ἐκ μὲν τῶν ἀτόμων συνεστάναι τὸν
κόσμον, διοικεῖσθαι δὲ | ὑπὸ προνοίας. (S) |

4. Ἀριστοτέλης οὔτ᾽ ἔμψυχον ὅλον δι᾽ ὅλου, οὔτε μὴν
αἰσθητικὸν οὔτε | λογικὸν οὔτε νοερὸν οὔτε προνοίᾳ
10 διοικούμενον· τὰ μὲν γὰρ οὐράνια | τούτων πάντων
κοινωνεῖν, σφαίρας γὰρ περιέχειν ἐμψύχους καὶ ζωτι-
κάς, | τὰ δὲ περίγεια μηδενὸς αὐτῶν, τῆς δ᾽ εὐταξίας
κατὰ συμβεβηκὸς | οὐ προηγουμένως μετέχειν. (PS) |

§1 anonymi —   §2 Leucippus A22; Democritus fr. 23,
589 Luria; Epicurus fr. 382   §3 Ecphantus fr. 4   §4 Aristotle cf. *Cael.* 2.3 285a29, 286a9–12; Arius Didymus fr. 9

2.3

Two questions are again combined, whether the cosmos is a living being or not and whether it is administered by providence, followed by two compromise views.

Ps.-Plutarch, *Tenets* (+ Ps.-Galen, *Philosophical History*); Stobaeus, *Anthology*; Theodoret, *Cure of Greek Maladies*

3. Whether the cosmos is ensouled and administered by providence

1. All other philosophers say that the cosmos is ensouled and administered by providence.
2. But Leucippus, Democritus and Epicurus say that it is constituted out of atoms by an unreasoning natural force. 5
3. Ecphantus says that the cosmos is constituted out of atoms, but is nevertheless administered by providence.
4. Aristotle says that the cosmos is neither ensouled through and through, nor is it endowed with sense perception, or rational or intellective, or administered by providence. In fact, the heavenly realm shares in all these 10
characteristics, as it contains ensouled spheres that are endowed with life. The earthly realm, however, shares in none of them, but shares in its well-ordered state contingently, not primarily.

---

13 4–5 vid. app. sec.

2.4

Ps.-Plut. *Plac.* 2.4 (+ Ps.-Gal. *Hist. phil.* 47); Stob. *Ecl.* 1.20cf, 1.21.6c; Theod. *Cur.* 4.16

δ΄. Εἰ ἄφθαρτος ὁ κόσμος (P) |

1. Πυθαγόρας Ἡράκλειτος γενητὸν κατ᾽ ἐπίνοιαν τὸν κόσμον, οὐ κατὰ[14] | χρόνον.[15] (ST) |

2. οἱ Στωικοὶ ὑπὸ θεοῦ ‹γεγενῆσθαι τὸν κόσμον›.[16] (P) |

5 3. Ἐπίδικος ὑπὸ φύσεως γεγενῆσθαι τὸν κόσμον. (S) |

4. Ἀρχέλαος ὑπὸ θερμοῦ καὶ ψύχους[17] συστῆναι τὸν κόσμον. (S) |

5. Ξενοφάνης Παρμενίδης Μέλισσος ἀγένητον καὶ ἀίδιον καὶ ἄφθαρτον | τὸν κόσμον. (PS, cf. T) |

§1 Pythagoras —; Heraclitus A10   §2 Stoics 2.575
§3 Epidicus —   §4 Archelaus A14
§5 Xenophanes A37; Parmenides A36; Melissus A9

[14] coni. MR
[15] 2–3 vid. app. sec.
[16] fort. post κόσμον add. κατὰ χρόνον
[17] θερμοῦ: θεοῦ S corr. edd.   ψύχους coni. MR², ἐμψυχρίας coni. Meineke prob. Diels, ἐμψυχίας S MR

2.4

Despite its heading, the chapter treats the two questions of the cosmos' generation and its destructibility, moving from the former to the latter, with the view of its eternity providing the transition between them.

Ps.-Plutarch, *Tenets* (+ Ps.-Galen, *Philosophical History*); Stobaeus, *Anthology*; Theodoret, *Cure of Greek Maladies*

4. Whether the cosmos is indestructible

1. Pythagoras and Heraclitus say that the cosmos is generated in thought, but not in time.
2. The Stoics say that through the agency of God <it has come into being>.[11]
3. Epidicus says that the cosmos has come into being 5
through the agency of nature.
4. Archelaus says that the cosmos was constituted through the agency of warmth and cold.
5. Xenophanes, Parmenides, and Melissus say that the cosmos is ungenerated, everlasting and indestructible.[12]

[11] Possibly add <in time>. See Appendix II, Book 2.
[12] These characteristics are transferred from Eleatic Being to the cosmos.

6. οἱ φάμενοι δὲ τὴν διακόσμησιν αἰώνιον ὑπάρχειν
10 περιοδευτικοὺς εἶναί | φασι χρόνους, καθ᾽ οὓς κατὰ
ταὐτὰ καὶ ὡσαύτως γίγνεσθαι πάντα καὶ | τὴν αὐτὴν
διασῴζεσθαι τοῦ κόσμου διάταξίν τε καὶ διακόσμη-
σιν. (S) |

7. Ἀναξίμανδρος Ἀναξιμένης Ἀναξαγόρας Ἀρχέλαος
Διογένης Λεύκιππος | φθαρτὸν τὸν κόσμον. (ST) |

8. καὶ οἱ Στωικοὶ φθαρτὸν τὸν κόσμον, κατ᾽ ἐκπύρω-
σιν δέ. (S, cf. P) |

15 9. Πλάτων φθαρτὸν μὲν τόν κόσμον, ὅσον ἐπὶ τῇ φύ-
σει, αἰσθητὸν γὰρ εἶναι, | διότι καὶ σωματικόν, οὐ
μὴν φθαρησόμενόν γε προνοίᾳ καὶ συνοχῇ θεοῦ.
| (PS) |

10. Ἀριστοτέλης τὸ ὑπὸ τὴν σελήνην μέρος τοῦ
κόσμου παθητικόν, ἐν ᾧ καὶ | τὰ περίγεια κηραίνε-
ται. (PS) |

20 11. Ἐμπεδοκλῆς τὸν κόσμον φθείρεσθαι κατὰ τὴν
ἀντεπικράτειαν τοῦ | Νείκους καὶ τῆς Φιλίας. (S) |

12. Δημόκριτος φθείρεσθαι τὸν κόσμον τοῦ μείζονος
τὸν μικρότερον νικῶντος. | (S) |

§6 anonymi cf. SVF 2.597
§7 Anaximander A17; Anaximenes fr. 121 Wöhrle; Anaxagoras
A65; Archelaus A14; Diogenes A10; Leucippus A22
§8 Stoics 2.585
§9 Plato cf. Tim. 28b–c, 41a–b
§10 Aristotle cf. Ps.-Arist. Mu. 2 392a32–35
§11 Empedocles A52
§12 Democritus A84

6. But there are those who say that its ordering is eternal, yet also say that there are periodic times in accordance with which all things come into being in exactly the same way and preserve the same disposition and ordering of the cosmos.

7. Anaximander, Anaximenes, Anaxagoras, Archelaus, Diogenes, and Leucippus say that the cosmos is destructible.

8. The Stoics too say that the cosmos is destructible, but this occurs in the conflagration.

9. Plato says the cosmos is destructible as far as its nature is concerned, for it is sense perceptible—since it is also corporeal—, but that through the providence and supervision of God it will certainly not be destroyed.

10. Aristotle says that the part of the cosmos below the moon is passible, the part in which also the things on earth perish.

11. Empedocles says that the cosmos is destroyed in accordance with the successive dominance of Strife and Love.

12. Democritus says that the cosmos is destroyed when the larger one overcomes the smaller one.

13. Ἐπίκουρος πλείστοις τρόποις τὸν κόσμον φθείρε-
25 σθαι· καὶ γὰρ ὡς ζῷον[18] | καὶ ὡς φυτὸν καὶ πολλα-
χῶς. (PS) |

§13 Epicurus fr. 305

2.5

Ps.-Plut. *Plac.* 2.5 (+ Ps.-Gal. *Hist. phil.* 48); Stob. *Ecl.*
1.20.1g, 1.21.6bd

ε΄. Πόθεν τρέφεται ὁ κόσμος (PS) |

1. Ἀριστοτέλης· εἰ τρέφεται ὁ κόσμος, καὶ φθαρήσε-
ται· ἀλλὰ μὴν οὐδεμιᾶς |ἐπιδεῖται τροφῆς· διὰ τοῦτο
καὶ ἀίδιος. (PS) |
2. Πλάτων αὐτὸν αὑτῷ τὸν κόσμον ἐκ τοῦ φθίνοντος
5 κατὰ μεταβολὴν τὸ | τρέφον παρέχεσθαι. (P) |
3. Φιλόλαος διττὴν εἶναι τὴν φθοράν, τὸ μὲν ἐξ οὐρα-

§1 Aristotle —
§2 Plato cf. *Tim.* 33c–d
§3 Philolaus A18

[18] 24–25 vid. app. sec.

13. Epicurus says that the cosmos is destroyed in a multitude of ways, for example as an animal and as a plant and in numerous other ways.

25

2.5

Division into the views that there is no nourishment for the cosmos and that it does occur, the latter being further divided into two kinds of internal nourishment.

Ps.-Plutarch, *Tenets* (+ Ps.-Galen, *Philosophical History*); Stobaeus, *Anthology*

5. Where does the cosmos obtain its nourishment from[13]

1. Aristotle: if the cosmos obtains nourishment, it will also be subject to destruction; but it is certainly not in need of any nourishment; for this reason it is everlasting as well.
2. Plato says that the cosmos itself provides nourishment for itself from that which perishes through transformation.
3 . Philolaus says that this destruction (i.e., transforma-

5

[13] Cf. note on 2.17.

νίου[19] πυρὸς ῥυέντος, τὸ | δ᾽ ἐξ ὕδατος σεληνιακοῦ
περιστροφῇ τοῦ ἀστέρος[20] ἀποχυθέντος· καὶ | τούτων
εἶναι τὰς ἀναθυμιάσεις τροφὰς τοῦ κόσμου. (PS) |

2.5a[21]

Stob. *Ecl.* 1.21.1, 6de

⟨ε⁺′. Ποῦ ἔχει τὸ ἡγεμονικὸν ὁ κόσμος⟩[22] (S) |

1. Πλάτων τὸ ἡγεμονικὸν τοῦ κόσμου ἐν οὐρανῷ.[23] (S) |
2. Κλεάνθης ὁ Στωικὸς ἐν ἡλίῳ. (S) |
3. Ἀρχέδημος ἐν γῇ. (S) |
5 4. Φιλόλαος ἐν τῷ μεσαιτάτῳ πυρί, ὅπερ τρόπεως
δίκην προυπεβάλλετο | τῆς τοῦ παντὸς ⟨σφαίρας⟩[24] ὁ
δημιουργὸς θεός. (S) |

§1 Plato *Tim.* 36e–37c
§2 Cleanthes 1.499
§3 Archedemus fr. 15
§4 Philolaus A17

[19] φθοράν] τροφήν G   τὸ μὲν . . . τὸ δὲ vid. app. sec.
οὐρανίου coni. Corsinus, οὐρανοῦ PS², ὑγροῦ S¹
[20] ἀστέρος P²S¹, ἀέρος P¹S²
[21] cap. abest in P
[22] tit. add. MR ex S, ὁ κόσμος add. Diels
[23] lemma coni. MR ex S
[24] ⟨σφαίρας⟩ coni. Diels

tion) is twofold, on the one hand from heavenly fire that has rushed down, on the other hand from moon water that has been poured forth by the conversion of the air; and the exhalations of these are nourishment for the cosmos.[14]

2.5a

A list of four views on where the hegemonikon *of the cosmos is located.*

Stobaeus, *Anthology*

⟨5a. Where does the cosmos have its ruling part⟩[15]

1. Plato says the ruling part of the cosmos is in the heaven.
2. Cleanthes the Stoic says it is in the sun.
3. Archedemus says it is in the earth.
4. Philolaus says it is in the innermost fire, which the craftsman god first set under the sphere of the universe like a keel. 5

---

[14] Most exceptionally Stobaeus records this lemma twice (indicated by S^1 and S^2 in the apparatus to the text).

[15] This chapter was omitted by Ps.-Plutarch in his *Epitome*; cf. 2.2a n. 10.

2.6

Ps.-Plut. *Plac.* 2.6 (+ Ps.-Gal. *Hist. phil.* 49); Stob. *Ecl.* 1.21.3b, 6c, 1.22.1f

ς′. Ἀπὸ ποίου πρώτου²⁵ στοιχείου
ἤρξατο ὁ θεός κοσμοποιεῖν (P) |

1. οἱ φυσικοὶ καὶ οἱ Στωικοὶ²⁶ ἀπὸ γῆς ἄρξασθαί φασι τὴν γένεσιν τοῦ | κόσμου καθάπερ ἀπὸ κέντρου· ἀρχὴ δὲ σφαίρας τὸ κέντρον. (PS) |
2. Πυθαγόρας ἀπὸ πυρὸς καὶ τοῦ πέμπτου στοιχείου. (PS) |
5   3. Ἐμπεδοκλῆς τὸν μὲν αἰθέρα πρῶτον διακριθῆναι, δεύτερον δὲ τὸ πῦρ | ἐφ᾽ ᾧ τὴν γῆν, ἐξ ἧς ἄγαν περισφιγγομένης τῇ ῥύμῃ τῆς περιφορᾶς | ἀναβλύσαι τὸ ὕδωρ· ἐξ οὗ ἀναθυμιαθῆναι τὸν ἀέρα καὶ γενέσθαι τὸν μὲν | οὐρανὸν ἐκ τοῦ αἰθέρος τὸν δ᾽ ἥλιον ἐκ τοῦ πυρός, πιληθῆναι δ᾽ ἐκ τῶν | ἄλλων τὰ περίγεια. (P) |

§1 physicists —; Stoics 2.581   §2 Pythagoras —
§3 Empedocles A49

²⁵ πρώτου om. G   ²⁶ nom. coni. MR, οἱ φυσικοὶ P Diels, οἱ Στωικοὶ S, cf. 1.9.2, Ach 17.14

2.6

Five different answers are given to the question raised, organized by means of a division between a physical and a nonphysical starting point.

Ps.-Plutarch, *Tenets* (+ Ps.-Galen, *Philosophical History*); Stobaeus, *Anthology*

6. From what kind of first element did the god begin to make the cosmos[16]

1. The physicists and the Stoics say that the genesis of the cosmos started from the earth as from a center; the starting point of a sphere is its center.
2. Pythagoras says that the genesis of the cosmos started from fire and the fifth element.[17]
3. Empedocles says that first the ether was separated out, 5
second fire, and after it the earth. When the earth was excessively constricted by the rush of the revolution (sc. of the cosmos), water spouted forth. From it the air was exhaled and the heaven came into being from the ether, the sun from fire, while the earthly regions were condensed from the other elements.

[16] Note that there is no reference to a creating god in the body of the chapter, only in its heading (but cf. above, 2.4.2, 2.5.4). It may have been added later, e.g., under the influence of early Middle Platonism. For a parallel chapter on the generation of human beings, see 5.17.
[17] Cf. 1.7.23 and n. 34.

10 4. Πλάτων τὸν ὁρατὸν κόσμον γεγονέναι πρὸς[27] παρά-
δειγμα τοῦ νοητοῦ | κόσμου· τοῦ δ' ὁρατοῦ κόσμου
προτέραν μὲν τὴν ψυχήν, μετὰ δὲ ταύτην | τὸ σωμα-
τοειδὲς τὸ ἐκ πυρὸς μὲν καὶ γῆς πρῶτον, ὕδατος δὲ
καὶ ἀέρος | δεύτερον. (PS) |

5. Πυθαγόρας πέντε σχημάτων ὄντων στερεῶν, ἅπερ
15 καλεῖται καὶ "μαθηματικά," | ἐκ μὲν τοῦ κύβου φησὶ
γεγονέναι τὴν γῆν, ἐκ δὲ τῆς πυραμίδος | τὸ πῦρ, ἐκ
δὲ τοῦ ὀκταέδρου τὸν ἀέρα, ἐκ δὲ τοῦ εἰκοσαέδρου
τὸ ὕδωρ, | ἐκ δὲ τοῦ δωδεκαέδρου τὴν τοῦ παντὸς
σφαῖραν. (PS) |

6. Πλάτων δὲ καὶ ἐν τούτοις πυθαγορίζει. (P) |

§4 Plato cf. *Tim.* 28a–b, 31b–32c, 34b–c   §5 Pythagoras,
cf. Philolaus A15   §6 Plato cf. *Tim.* 53e–55c

2.7

Ps.-Plut. *Plac.* 2.7 (+ Ps.-Gal. *Hist. phil.* 50); Stob. *Ecl.*
1.22.1abde, 1.15.6d

ζ'. Περὶ τάξεως τοῦ κόσμου (PS) |

1. Παρμενίδης στεφάνας εἶναι περιπεπλεγμένας ἐπαλ-
λήλους, τὴν μὲν ἐκ | τοῦ ἀραιοῦ τὴν δ' ἐκ τοῦ πυκνοῦ,

§1 Parmenides A37, cf. B11–12

[27] πρὸς P: om. S

4. Plato says that the visible cosmos came into being in   10
respect of the model of the intelligible cosmos. But of the
visible cosmos the soul is prior, and after it there is the
corporeal part, consisting of fire and earth first, of water
and air second.

5. Pythagoras says that, since there are five solid shapes,
which are also called "mathematical," the earth came into   15
being from the cube, fire from the pyramid, air from the
octahedron, water from the icosahedron, and the sphere
of the universe from the dodecahedron.

6. Plato in these matters too pythagorizes.[18]

2.7

The main division is between cosmologies in which the
elements have a fixed location in various concentric con-
figurations and the opposed view that they are not fixed.

Ps.-Plutarch, *Tenets* (+ Ps.-Galen, *Philosophical History*);
Stobaeus, *Anthology*

7. On the order of the cosmos

1. Parmenides says there are bands interwoven one around
another, the one made up of the rare, the other of the

---

[18] In fact, the elemental shapes attributed in the previous
lemma to Pythagoras derive from Plato's *Timaeus*.

μικτὰς δ' ἄλλας ἐκ φωτὸς καὶ σκότους | μεταξὺ τού-
των· καὶ τὸ περιέχον δὲ πάσας τείχους δίκην στερεὸν
5 | ὑπάρχειν, ὑφ' ᾧ πυρώδης στεφάνη· καὶ τὸ μεσαίτα-
τον πασῶν[28] περὶ ὃ | πάλιν πυρώδης· τῶν δε συμ-
μιγῶν τὴν μεσαιτάτην ἁπάσαις ⟨ἀρχήν⟩ τε | καὶ
⟨αἰτίαν⟩[29] πάσης κινήσεως καὶ γενέσεως ὑπάρχειν,
ἥντινα καὶ | δαίμονα κυβερνῆτιν καὶ κληροῦχον ἐπο-
νομάζει, δίκην τε καὶ ἀνάγκην. | καὶ τῆς μὲν γῆς
ἀπόκρισιν εἶναι τὸν ἀέρα, διὰ τὴν βιαιοτέραν αὐτῆς |
10 ἐξατμισθέντα πίλησιν, τοῦ δὲ πυρὸς ἀναπνοὴν τὸν
ἥλιον καὶ τὸν | γαλαξίαν κύκλον· συμμιγῆ δ' ἐξ ἀμ-
φοῖν εἶναι τὴν σελήνην, τοῦ τ' ἀέρος | καὶ τοῦ πυρός.

περιστάντος δ' ἀνωτάτω πάντων τοῦ αἰθέρος ὑπ'
αὐτῷ | τὸ πυρῶδες ὑποταγῆναι τοῦθ' ὅπερ κεκλήκαμεν
οὐρανόν, ὑφ' ᾧ ἤδη τὰ | περίγεια. (PS) |
15 2. Λεύκιππος καὶ Δημόκριτος χιτῶνα κύκλῳ καὶ ὑμένα
περιτείνουσι τῷ κόσμῳ, διὰ τῶν ἀγκιστροειδῶν ἀτό-
μων συμπεπλεγμένον. (PS) |
3. Ἐπίκουρος ἐνίων μὲν κόσμων ἀραιὸν τὸ πέρας
ἐνίων δὲ πυκνόν, καὶ | τούτων τὰ μέν τινα κινούμενα
τὰ δ' ἀκίνητα. (PS) |

§2 Leucippus–Democritus 67A23, fr. 386 Luria
§3 Epicurus fr. 303

28 post πασῶν add. στερεὸν Diels
29 ⟨ἀρχήν⟩ τε καὶ ⟨αἰτίαν⟩ coni. Diels VS ex Simp.: τε καὶ
S, τοκέα coni. Diels Davis sec.

dense, while others between these are mixed from light
and darkness. And that which surrounds them all is solid
in the manner of a wall, below which there is a fiery band.   5
And also solid is that which is right in the middle of all the
bands, around which again there is a fiery band. But of the
mixed bands the most central is both the ⟨origin⟩ and
the ⟨cause⟩ of all motion and coming into being for all the
others, which he also calls governing *daimôn*, holder of
the lots, Justice and Necessity. And air is a secretion from
the earth which is vaporized through the earth's stronger   10
condensation. The sun and the Milky way are the exhalation of fire. The moon is a mixture of both air and fire.

The ether encircles above everything else, below which
the fiery part that we call heaven is disposed, and below it
again the earthly regions have their place.[19]

2. Leucippus and Democritus stretch around the cosmos   15
in a circle a cloak and a membrane woven together by
means of hook-shaped atoms.

3. Epicurus says that of some *kosmoi* the limit is rare but
of others it is dense, and of these limits some are in motion, while others are unmoved.[20]

[19] The lengthy doxa on the structure of the cosmos, details of
which go back to Parmenides' poem (esp. B11–12), falls into two
parts. Lines 1–12a are protological, i.e., describing what happened when the cosmos originated; lines 12b–14 describe the
current structure of the cosmos.

[20] The information for this doxa may have been derived from
Epicurus' *Letter to Pythocles*, Diog. Laert. 10.88.

4. Πλάτων πῦρ πρῶτον εἶτ᾽ αἰθέρα μεθ᾽ ὃν ἀέρα ἐφ᾽ ᾧ
20 ὕδωρ, τελευταίαν | δὲ γῆν· ἐνίοτε δὲ τὸν αἰθέρα τῷ
πυρὶ συνάπτει. (P) |

5. Ἀριστοτέλης πρῶτον μὲν αἰθέρα ἀπαθῆ, πέμπτον
δή τι σῶμα· μεθ᾽ ὃν | παθητὰ πῦρ ἀέρα ὕδωρ· τελευ-
ταίαν δὲ γῆν. τούτων δὲ τοῖς μὲν | οὐρανίοις ἀποδεδό-
σθαι τὴν κυκλικὴν κίνησιν, τῶν δ᾽ ὑπ᾽ ἐκεῖνα τεταγμέ-
νων | τοῖς μὲν κούφοις τὴν ἄνω τοῖς δὲ βαρέσι τὴν
κάτω. (PS) |

25 6. Φιλόλαος πῦρ ἐν μέσῳ περὶ τὸ κέντρον, ὅπερ
"ἑστίαν" τοῦ παντὸς καλεῖ | καὶ "Διὸς οἶκον" καὶ "μη-
τέρα θεῶν," "βωμόν" τε καὶ "συνοχὴν" καὶ "μέτρον |
φύσεως"· καὶ πάλιν πῦρ ἕτερον ἀνωτάτω, τὸ περιέχον.
πρῶτον δ᾽ εἶναι | φύσει τὸ μέσον, περὶ δὲ τοῦτο δέκα
σώματα θεῖα χορεύειν, οὐρανόν, | <πέν>τε[30] πλανήτας,
μεθ᾽ οὓς ἥλιον, ὑφ᾽ ᾧ σελήνην, ὑφ᾽ ᾗ τὴν γῆν, ὑφ᾽ ᾗ
30 | τὴν ἀντίχθονα, μεθ᾽ ἃ σύμπαντα τὸ πῦρ ἑστίας περὶ
τὰ κέντρα τάξιν | ἐπέχον.

τὸ μὲν οὖν ἀνωτάτω μέρος τοῦ περιέχοντος, ἐν ᾧ
τὴν εἰλικρίνειαν | εἶναι τῶν στοιχείων, "Ὄλυμπον" κα-
λεῖ· τὰ δὲ ὑπὸ τὴν τοῦ | Ὀλύμπου φοράν, ἐν ᾧ τοὺς
πέντε πλανήτας μεθ᾽ ἡλίου καὶ σελήνης | τετάχθαι,
"Κόσμον." τὸ δ᾽ ὑπὸ τούτοις ὑποσέληνόν τε καὶ περί-

§4 Plato —   §5 cf. Aristotle *Cael.* 1.3 270b22, Ps.-Arist.
Mu. 2 392a5–b17   §6 Philolaus A16

30 <πέν>τε coni. MR: τε S, τ<οὺς >έ´ dub. Diels

4. Plato says that there is first fire, then ether, followed by air, after which there is water, and earth is last. But some- 20
times he connects ether with fire.

5. Aristotle says that impassible ether is first, which is in-deed a fifth body. After it follow the passible elements fire, air, water, and earth is last. And of these circular motion is given to the heavenly regions, whereas in the case of the elements below them upward motion is given to the light ones and downward motion to the heavy ones.

6. Philolaus says that there is fire in the middle around the 25
center, which he calls the universe's "hearth" and "Zeus' house" and the "gods' mother," "altar" and "continuity," and "measure of nature." And again there is another high-est fire, that which surrounds the universe. The center is first by nature, and around this ten divine bodies dance: the heaven, the ⟨five⟩ planets, after them the sun, under it the moon, under it the earth, under it the counterearth, 30
and after all of them there is fire, which has the position of the hearth in relation to the centers.

Moreover, he calls the highest part of the surrounding region "Olympus," in which he says the purity of the ele-ments exists, while the region under the orbit of Olympus, in which the five planets together with the sun and the moon are positioned, he calls "Cosmos." The sublunary

35 γειον μέρος, | ἐν ᾧ τὰ τῆς φιλομεταβόλου γενέσεως,
"Οὐρανόν." καὶ περὶ μὲν τὰ | τεταγμένα τῶν μετεώρων
γίνεσθαι τὴν σοφίαν, περὶ δὲ τῶν γινομένων | τὴν
ἀταξίαν τὴν ἀρετήν, τελείαν μὲν ἐκείνην, ἀτελῆ δὲ
ταύτην. (S)

7. Ἐμπεδοκλῆς μὴ διὰ παντὸς ἑστῶτας εἶναι μηδ'
ὡρισμένους τοὺς τόπους | τῶν στοιχείων, ἀλλὰ πάντα
τοὺς ἀλλήλων μεταλαμβάνειν. (PS) |

§7 Empedocles A35

2.8

Ps.-Plut. *Plac.* 2.8 (+ Ps.-Gal. *Hist. phil.* 51); Stob. *Ecl.*
1.15.6cd

η΄. Τίς ἡ αἰτία τοῦ τὸν κόσμον ἐγκλιθῆναι (P) |

1. Διογένης Ἀναξαγόρας μετὰ τὸ συστῆναι τὸν κό-
σμον καὶ τὰ ζῷα ἐκ τῆς | γῆς ἐξαγαγεῖν ἐγκλιθῆναί
πως τὸν κόσμον ἐκ τοῦ αὐτομάτου εἰς τὸ | μεσημη-

§1 Diogenes A11; Anaxagoras A67

and earthly part below these, in which the realm of   35
change-loving generation is located, he calls "Heaven." In
addition he says that wisdom arises concerning what is
ordered in the regions on high, whereas virtue arises concerning the disorder of what comes into being, the former
being complete, but the latter incomplete.[21]
7. Empedocles says that the locations of the elements are
not completely fixed or determined, but all share in the
locations of each other.

2.8

*Opposition between two causes of the cosmos' tilt in early
cosmologies, the former nonphysical, the latter purely me-
chanical.*

Ps.-Plutarch, *Tenets* (+ Ps.-Galen, *Philosophical History*);
Stobaeus, *Anthology*

8. What is the cause of the cosmos having been tilted[22]

1. Diogenes and Anaxagoras say that after the cosmos had
been formed and had produced the animals from the
earth, the cosmos somehow of its own accord was tilted

---

[21] This long lemma also falls into two parts. The first gives a
Pythagorean cosmology as reported by Aristotle in *Cael.* 2.13.
The second part contradicts the first and is regarded by scholars
as likely to be inauthentic.

[22] Cf. 3.12, on the tilting of the earth.

βρινὸν αὐτοῦ μέρος· ἴσως ὑπὸ προνοίας, ἵν' ἃ μὲν
5 ἀοίκητα | γένηται ἃ δ' οἰκητὰ μέρη τοῦ κόσμου κατὰ
ψῦξιν καὶ ἐκπύρωσιν καὶ | εὐκρασίαν. (PS) |
2. Ἐμπεδοκλῆς τοῦ ἀέρος εἴξαντος τῇ τοῦ ἡλίου ὁρμῇ,
ἐπικλιθῆναι τὰς | ἄρκτους, καὶ τὰ μὲν βόρεια ὑψωθῆ-
ναι τὰ δὲ νότια ταπεινωθῆναι, καθ' ὃ | καὶ τὸν ὅλον
κόσμον. (PS) |

§2 Empedocles A58

2.9

Ps.-Plut. *Plac.* 2.9 (+ Ps.-Gal. *Hist. phil.* 52); Stob. *Ecl.*
1.18.4bc

θ'. Περὶ τοῦ ἐκτὸς τοῦ κόσμου,
εἰ ἔστι κενόν[31] (P) |

1. οἱ μὲν ἀπὸ Πυθαγόρου ἐκτὸς εἶναι τοῦ κόσμου
κενόν, εἰς ὃ ἀναπνεῖ ὁ | κόσμος καὶ ἐξ οὗ. (PS) |

§1 Pythagoreans —
[31] tit. P: εἰ ἔστι κενόν om. EG

toward its midday region; this occurred perhaps through the agency of providence,[23] so that some of the cosmos' parts are uninhabitable but others are habitable in virtue 5 of chilling and excessive heating and a temperate climate.[24]

2. Empedocles says that, when the air gave way through the onrush of the sun, the north and south poles were tilted, and the northern parts were lifted up but the southern parts were lowered, in accordance with which the entire cosmos was tilted as well.

2.9

The main division is between three different views on an extracosmic void and rejection of any kind of void.

Ps.-Plutarch, *Tenets* (+ Ps.-Galen, *Philosophical History*); Stobaeus, *Anthology*

9. On what is outside the cosmos, whether there is a void[25]

1. Pythagoras and his successors say that there exists a void outside the cosmos, into which and from which the cosmos breathes.

[23] Very likely a Stoic reinterpretation.

[24] In this final phrase, the first two nouns explain "uninhabitable," the third "habitable," in both cases relating to parts of the earth rather than to the cosmos as a whole.

[25] This subject was already discussed in 1.18, with which there is considerable overlap.

2. οἱ δὲ Στωικοὶ εἶναι κενόν, εἰς ὃ κατὰ τὴν ἐκπύρωσιν
5 ἀναλύεται, ἄπειρον.³² | (PS) |

3. Ποσειδώνιος οὐκ ἄπειρον, ἀλλ᾽ ὅσον αὔταρκες εἰς
τὴν διάλυσιν. (PS) |

4. Πλάτων Ἀριστοτέλης³³ μήτ᾽ ἐκτὸς τοῦ κόσμου μήτ᾽
ἐντὸς μηδὲν εἶναι | κενόν.³⁴ (PS) |

§2 Stoics 2.609   §3 Posidonius F84, 97   §4 Plato
cf. *Tim.* 33c, 58a; Aristotle *Cael.* 1.9 278b23–24, 279a6–7

2.10

Ps.-Plut. *Plac.* 2.10 (+ Ps.-Gal. *Hist. phil.* 53); Stob. *Ecl.*
1.15.6de

ιʹ. Τίνα δεξιὰ τοῦ κόσμου
καὶ τίνα ἀριστερά (P) |

1. Πυθαγόρας Πλάτων Ἀριστοτέλης δεξιὰ τοῦ κό-
σμου τὰ ἀνατολικὰ μέρη, | ἀφ᾽ ὧν ἡ ἀρχὴ τῆς κινή-
σεως, ἀριστερὰ δὲ τὰ δυτικά. {οὔθ᾽ ὕψος δέ | φασιν
οὔτε βάθος ἔχειν τὸν κόσμον, καθ᾽ ὃν λόγον ὕψος μὲν

§1 Pythagoras —; Plato —; Aristotle cf. *Cael.* 2.2

³² ἄπειρον EG: τὸ ἄπειρον P, ὁ κόσμος ἄπειρος ὢν S
³³ Πλάτων Ἀριστοτέλης EQ: om. Ἀριστοτέλης GS

2. But the Stoics say that there exists a void, into which the
cosmos dissolves at the conflagration, and it is infinite.   5
3. Posidonius says that it is not infinite, but only to the
extent that is sufficient for the cosmos' dissolution.
4. Plato and Aristotle say that there is no void either outside the cosmos or inside it.

2.10

*On the assumption that the cosmos is a living being with
its own motion, two views are opposed, though the exact
nature of the contrast is not very clear.*

Ps.-Plutarch, *Tenets* (+ Ps.-Galen, *Philosophical History*);
Stobaeus, *Anthology*

10. What are the right parts of the cosmos
and what are the left

1. Pythagoras, Plato, and Aristotle say that the right parts
of the cosmos are the eastern regions, from which the
movement has its origin, while the western regions are its
left parts. {But they say that the cosmos has neither height
nor depth in the sense that height is said to be the dimen-

---

³⁴ 6–8 leg. P ἐν τῷ πρώτῳ Περὶ κενοῦ (id est 1.18.6, aut
glossa ad §3). Ἀριστοτέλης ἔλεγεν εἶναι κενόν. Πλάτων μητ'
ἐκτὸς κτλ.

5 λέγεται τὸ | κάτωθεν ἄνω διάστημα, βάθος δὲ τὸ ἄνω-
θεν κάτω. μηδὲν γὰρ εἶναι τῶν | οὕτως διαστημάτων
λεγομένων περὶ τὸν κόσμον διὰ τὸ περὶ τὸ ἑαυτοῦ |
μέσον αὐτὸν συνεστάναι, ἀφ' οὗ πρὸς ἅπαν ἐστι καὶ
πρὸς ὃ πανταχόθεν | ταὐτό.}[35] (PS) |

2. Ἐμπεδοκλῆς δεξιὰ μὲν τὰ κατὰ τὸν θερινὸν τροπι-
10 κόν, ἀριστερὰ δὲ τὰ | κατὰ τὸν χειμερινόν. (PS) |

§2 Empedocles A50

2.11

Ps.-Plut. *Plac.* 2.11 (+ Ps.-Gal. *Hist. phil.* 54); Stob. *Ecl.*
1.23.1–2

ια'. Περὶ οὐρανοῦ, τίς ἡ τούτου οὐσία[36] (PS) |

1. Ἀναξιμένης καὶ Παρμενίδης[37] τὴν περιφορὰν τὴν
ἐξωτάτω γῆς εἶναι. | (PS) |

§1 Anaximenes A13; cf. Parmenides A38

[35] οὔθ' ὕψος . . . ταὐτό S, dubium an Aëtiana sint
[36] tit. P: Περὶ οὐρανοῦ EG, Περὶ τῆς οὐρανοῦ οὐσίας S,
cf. Q
[37] καὶ Παρμενίδης om. PEGQ   γῆς εἶναι Diels DG: τῆς
γῆς εἶναι S, γηίνην P

sion upward from below and depth is the dimension 5
downward from above. For, they say, none of the dimen-
sions understood in this way are relevant to the cosmos
because it is established around its own center, from which
it is the same distance to every part and toward which it is
the same from every part.}[26]

2. Empedocles says that the regions at the summer solstice
are the right parts of the cosmos, whereas the regions at 10
the winter solstice are the left parts.

2.11

*A series of views, with the first two and the last two pairs
forming an opposition between heavy/cold and light/hot
substance and the middle view representing a compromise
between them.*

Ps.-Plutarch, *Tenets* (+ Ps.-Galen, *Philosophical History*);
Stobaeus, *Anthology*

11. On heaven, what is its substance[27]

1. Anaximenes and Parmenides[28] say that the outermost
periphery is of earth.

---

[26] It must be considered uncertain whether the latter part of
the doxa, only found in Stobaeus, derives from Aëtius' compendium.   [27] The treatment of cosmological topics now moves
from the cosmos (or the universe) as a whole to the heaven (*oura-
nos*) as its uppermost part.   [28] The name-label of Parmenides
is found only in Stobaeus; it is not included in the tradition of
Ps.-Plutarch. It recurs in §4. It happens quite often in the compendium, however, that a philosopher appears more than once in
the same chapter.

2. Ἐμπεδοκλῆς στερέμνιον εἶναι τὸν οὐρανὸν ἐξ ἀέρος
5 συμπαγέντος ὑπὸ | πυρὸς κρυσταλλοειδῶς, τὸ πυρῶ-
δες καὶ τὸ ἀερῶδες ἐν ἑκατέρῳ τῶν | ἡμισφαιρίων
περιέχοντα. (PS) |
3. Ἀναξίμανδρος ἐκ θερμοῦ καὶ ψυχροῦ μίγματος.
(PS) |
4. Παρμενίδης Ἡράκλειτος Στράτων Ζήνων πύρινον
εἶναι τὸν οὐρανόν. | (PS) |
10 5. Ἀριστοτέλης ἐκ πέμπτου σώματος.[38] (PS) |

§2 Empedocles A51   §3 Anaximander A17a
§4 Parmenides A38; Heraclitus A10; Strato fr. 42; Zeno the
Stoic 1.116   §5 Aristotle cf. *Cael*. 1.2 269a31

2.12

Ps.-Plut. *Plac*. 2.12 (+ Ps.-Gal. *Hist. phil*. 55); Stob. *Ecl*.
1.23.3

ιβʹ. Περὶ διαιρέσεως οὐρανοῦ,
εἰς πόσους κύκλους διαιρεῖται[39] (PS) |

1. Θαλῆς Πυθαγόρας οἱ ἀπ' αὐτοῦ μεμερίσθαι τὴν τοῦ
παντὸς οὐρανοῦ | σφαῖραν εἰς κύκλους πέντε, οὕστι-
νας προσαγορεύουσι "ζώνας"· καλεῖται | δ' αὐτῶν ὁ

§1 Thales A13c; Pythagoras —

38 7–10 S: text. P non sanus
39 tit. P: εἰς πόσους κύκλους διαιρεῖται om. GQ, cf. S

2. Empedocles says that the heaven is solid, consisting of air that has been compacted together by fire in crystalline 5 fashion, containing the fiery element and the airy element in each of the hemispheres.

3. Anaximander says that the heaven consists of a hot and cold mixture.

4. Parmenides, Heraclitus, Strato, and Zeno say that the heaven is fiery.

5. Aristotle says that the heaven consists of a fifth body. 10

2.12

A single doxa representing the standard view on the question, to which an additional comment is added.

Ps.-Plutarch, *Tenets* (+ Ps.-Galen, *Philosophical History*); Stobaeus, *Anthology*

12. On the division of heaven,
into how many zones it is divided[29]

1. Thales, Pythagoras, and his successors say that the sphere of the entire heaven has been divided into five circles, to which they give the name "zones." Of these the

---

[29] The topic here differs from the division of the cosmos into elemental spheres in 2.7. Cf. also 3.14, on zones in relation to the earth.

μὲν ἀρκτικός τε καὶ ἀειφανής, ὁ δὲ θερινὸς τροπικός,
5 ὁ δ' | ἰσημερινός, ὁ δὲ χειμερινὸς τροπικός, ὁ δ'
ἀνταρκτικός τε καὶ ἀφανής· | λοξὸς δὲ τοῖς τρισὶ μέ-
σοις ὁ καλούμενος ζῳδιακὸς ὑποβέβληται, | παρεπι-
ψαύων τῶν μέσων τριῶν· πάντας δ' αὐτοὺς ὁ μεσημ-
βρινὸς πρὸς | ὀρθὰς ἀπὸ τῶν ἄρκτων ἐπὶ τὸ ἀντίξουν⁴⁰
τέμνει. (PS) |

2. Πυθαγόρας πρῶτος ἐπινενοηκέναι λέγεται τὴν λό-
10 ξωσιν τοῦ ζῳδιακοῦ | κύκλου, ἥντινα Οἰνοπίδης ὁ
Χῖος ὡς ἰδίαν ἐπίνοιαν σφετερίζεται. (PS) |

§2 Pythagoras —; Oenopides fr. 7

2.13

*A long series of doxai, basically structured by a division
between the view that the stars consist of a rock-like substance and the view that they are fiery or ethereal. There*

Ps.-Plut. *Plac.* 2.13 (+ Ps.-Gal. *Hist. phil.* 56); Stob. *Ecl.*
1.24.1a–n, 1.24.10; Theod. *Cur.* 4.17

ιγ'. Τίς ἡ οὐσία τῶν ἄστρων
πλανητῶν καὶ ἀπλανῶν⁴¹ (PS) |

1. Θαλῆς γεώδη μὲν, ἔμπυρα δὲ τὰ ἄστρα. (PST) |

§1 Thales A17a

⁴⁰ ἀντίξουν P: ἀντικρύ S
⁴¹ tit. E: add. καὶ πῶς συνέστη P, Τίς ἡ οὐσία τῶν ἀστέρων
QPs (cf. Ach), Περὶ οὐσία ἄστρων S

first is called the arctic and always appearing, the second
the summer tropic, the third the equatorial, the fourth the   5
winter tropic, and the last the antarctic and invisible. In
relation to the three middle circles, the so-called zodiac
circle has been placed diagonally, touching the three middle circles. But the meridian cuts all of them at right an-
gles from the arctic regions to its opposite.

2. Pythagoras is said to have been the first[30] to have recognized the tilting of the zodiac circle, which Oenopides   10
of Chios appropriates as his own idea.

2.13

is a general movement from the first to the second pole of
division, with some additional themes included as well.

Ps.-Plutarch, *Tenets* (+ Ps.-Galen, *Philosophical History*);
Stobaeus, *Anthology*; Theodoret, *Cure of Greek Maladies*

13. What is the substance of the heavenly bodies,
both planets and fixed stars

1. Thales says that the heavenly bodies are earthy but inflamed.

---

[30] On the "discoverer" motif, see n. 4 on 2.1. Here the accusa-
tion of subsequent theft is added, incorrectly if the account of
Eudemus fr. 145 Wehrli is to be believed.

2. Ἐμπεδοκλῆς πύρινα ἐκ τοῦ πυρώδους, ὅπερ ὁ ἀὴρ
ἐν ἑαυτῷ περιέχων | ἐξανέθλιψε κατὰ τὴν πρώτην διά-
κρισιν. (PS) |

5 3. Ἀναξαγόρας τὸν περικείμενον αἰθέρα[42] πύρινον μὲν
εἶναι κατὰ τὴν | οὐσίαν, τῇ δ᾽ εὐτονίᾳ τῆς περιδινή-
σεως ἀναρπάσαντα πέτρους ἀπὸ τῆς | γῆς καὶ κατα-
φλέξαντα τούτους ἠστερικέναι. (PST) |

4. Διογένης κισηρώδη τὰ ἄστρα, διαπνοὰς δ᾽ αὐτὰ
νομίζει τοῦ κόσμου· εἶναι δὲ διάπυρα.[43] (PST) |

10 5. Δημόκριτος πέτρους. (ST) |

6. Ἀρχέλαος μύδρους, διαπύρους δέ. (S) |

7. Ἀναξίμανδρος πιλήματα ἀέρος τροχοειδῆ, πυρὸς
ἔμπλεα, κατά τι μέρος | ἀπὸ στομίων ἐκπνέοντα φλό-
γας. (ST) |

8. Παρμενίδης καὶ Ἡράκλειτος πιλήματα πυρὸς. (S) |

15 9. Ἀναξιμένης πυρίνην μὲν τὴν φύσιν τῶν ἄστρων,
περιέχειν δέ τινα καὶ | γεώδη σώματα συμπεριφερό-
μενα τούτοις ἀόρατα. (S) |

10. Διογένης δὲ συμπεριφέρεσθαι τοῖς φανεροῖς
ἄστροις ἀφανεῖς λίθους καὶ | παρ᾽ αὐτὸ τοῦτ᾽ ἀνωνύ-

§2 Empedocles A53   §3 Anaxagoras A71
§4 Diogenes A12   §5 Democritus A85
§6 Archelaus A15   §7 Anaximander A18
§8 Parmenides A39; Heraclitus A11
§9 Anaximenes A14   §10 Diogenes A12

[42] αἰθέρα PS: ἀέρα E, αἰθέρα ἀέρα G
[43] εἶναι δὲ διάπυρα om. P

2. Empedocles says that they are fiery, made from fire-like material, which the air enfolded within itself and squeezed out in the first separation.

3. Anaxagoras says that the surrounding ether [31] is fiery in substance, but through the vigor of the whirling movement it snatched up rocks from the earth, ignited these and made them into heavenly bodies [or: arranged them in constellations].

4. Diogenes says that the heavenly bodies are sponge-like, and he considers them to be the respiratory vents of the cosmos; they are also inflamed.

5. Democritus says that they are rocks.

6. Archelaus says that they are clumps of iron, but inflamed.

7. Anaximander says that they are wheel-like condensations of air, filled with fire, partly expelling flames from vents.

8. Parmenides and Heraclitus says that they are condensations of fire.

9. Anaximenes says that the nature of the heavenly bodies is fiery, but that it also includes some earthy bodies that are borne around with these and are invisible.

10. Diogenes, however, says that stones that are invisible and in addition nameless are borne around together with

---

[31] As is evident in the app. crit., both here and in §15 there is much confusion in the witnesses between air (*aêr*) and ether (*aithêr*).

μους, πίπτοντας[44] δὲ πολλάκις ἐπὶ τὴν γῆν | σβέν-
νυσθαι, καθάπερ τὸν ἐν Αἰγὸς ποταμοῖς πυροειδῶς
20 κατενεχθέντα | ἀστέρα πέτρινον. (PST) |

11. Ἐμπεδοκλῆς τοὺς μὲν ἀπλανεῖς ἀστέρας συνδε-
δέσθαι τῷ κρυστάλλῳ, | τοὺς δὲ πλανήτας ἀνεῖ-
σθαι. (PS) |

12. Πλάτων ἐκ μὲν τοῦ πλείστου μέρους πυρίνους,
μετέχοντας δὲ καὶ τῶν | ἄλλων στοιχείων κόλλης
δίκην. (PST) |

25 13. Ἀριστοτέλης ἐκ τοῦ πέμπτου σώματος. (ST) |

14. Ξενοφάνης ἐκ νεφῶν μὲν πεπυρωμένων, σβεννυμέ-
νους δὲ καθ' ἑκάστην | ἡμέραν ἀναζωπυρεῖν νύκτωρ,
καθάπερ τοὺς ἄνθρακας· τὰς γὰρ ἀνατολὰς | καὶ τὰς
δύσεις ἐξάψεις εἶναι καὶ σβέσεις. (PST) |

15. Ἡρακλείδης καὶ οἱ Πυθαγόρειοι ἕκαστον τῶν
30 ἀστέρων κόσμον ὑπάρχειν, | γῆν περιέχοντα ἀέρα τε
καὶ αἰθέρα[45] ἐν τῷ ἀπείρῳ αἰθέρι· ταῦτα δὲ τὰ δόγματα ἐν τοῖς Ὀρφικοῖς φέρεται· κοσμοποιοῦσι γὰρ
ἕκαστον τῶν | ἀστέρων. (PST) |

16. Ἐπίκουρος οὐδὲν ἀπογινώσκει τούτων, ἐχόμενος
τοῦ ἐνδεχομένου. (PS) |

§11 Empedocles A54   §12 Plato cf. *Tim.* 40a
§13 Aristotle cf. *Cael.* 1.2 269a31   §14 Xenophanes
21A38   §15 Heraclides fr. 75; Pythagoreans cf. note at
58A18 DK; Orphici fr. 30F   §16 Epicurus cf. note at
p. 382.13 Usener

[44] πίπτοντας P: πίπτοντα S prob. Laks-Most (coniunx.
cum §4)   [45] ἀέρα τε καὶ om. E, τε καὶ αἰθέρα om. ST

the visible heavenly bodies, but that often they fall to the
earth and are quenched, just as in the case of the heavenly
body in the form of a rock (i.e., meteorite) that descended   20
in a fire-like manner at Aegospotami.

11. Empedocles says that the fixed heavenly bodies were
stuck to the crystalline heaven, but the planets were released.

12. Plato says that the heavenly bodies are for the most
part fiery, but also partake in the other elements in the
manner of glue.

13. Aristotle says that they are made from the fifth body.   25

14. Xenophanes says that they consist of incandescent
clouds, and that every day they are extinguished and then
flare up again at night, just like coals; for the risings and
settings of the heavenly bodies are in fact kindlings and
quenchings.

15. Heraclides and the Pythagoreans say that each of the
heavenly bodies exists as a separate cosmos which includes
an earth, air and ether in the unlimited ether.[32] These   30
doctrines are reported in the Orphic writings, for they too
make each of the heavenly bodies into a cosmos.

16. Epicurus does not reject any of these views, holding
fast to what is possible.

[32] Cf. 2.7.6 and note.

2.14

Ps.-Plut. *Plac.* 2.14 (+ Ps.-Gal. *Hist. phil.* 56a); Stob. *Ecl.* 1.24.1k, 2d; Theod. *Cur.* 4.20

ιδ΄. Περὶ σχημάτων[46] ἀστέρων (PS) |

1. οἱ Στωικοὶ σφαιρικοὺς τοὺς ἀστέρας, καθάπερ τὸν κόσμον καὶ ἥλιον καὶ | σελήνην,[47] (PST) |
2. Κλεάνθης κωνοειδεῖς. (PST) |
5   3. Ἀναξιμένης ἥλων δίκην καταπεπηγέναι τῷ κρυσταλλοειδεῖ. (PS) |
4. ἔνιοι δὲ πέταλα εἶναι πύρινα, ὥσπερ ζωγραφήματα. (P) |

§1 Stoics 2.681
§2 Cleanthes 1.508
§3 Anaximenes A14,B2a
§4 anonymi cf. Anaximenes A14

[46] σχήματος E (cf. Ach)
[47] οἱ Στωικοί: οἱ μὲν ἄλλοι S, οἱ μὲν T   καθάπερ . . . σελήνην om. S (καὶ σελήνην E)

2.14

A division between two views in which the stars' shape is three-dimensional and two views in which it is basically two-dimensional.

Ps.-Plutarch, *Tenets* (+ Ps.-Galen, *Philosophical History*); Stobaeus, *Anthology*; Theodoret, *Cure of Greek Maladies*

14. On the shapes of the stars[33]

1. The Stoics say that the stars are spherical, just like the cosmos, the sun and the moon.
2. Cleanthes says that they are like a cone.
3. Anaximenes says that they have been affixed to the crys- 5
talline heaven in the manner of studs.
4. But some say that they are fiery leaves, like pictures.

---

[33] Chapters on shape follow those on substance (*ousia*) for the cosmos (2.2) and the earth (3.10). In the case of the sun and the moon, there are also chapters on shape (2.22, 2.27), but chapters on size (2.21, 2.26) are interposed first. This chapter is the only one that in the title according to most witnesses speaks of "shapes" in the plural.

2.15

Ps.-Plut. *Plac.* 2.15 (+ Ps.-Gal. *Hist. phil.* 57); Stob. *Ecl.*
1.24.1eghl, 1.24.2abe, 5

ιε΄. Περὶ τάξεως ἀστέρων (P) |

1. Ξενοκράτης[48] κατὰ μιᾶς ἐπιφανείας οἴεται κεῖσθαι
τοὺς ἀστέρας. (PS) |
2. οἱ δ᾽ ἄλλοι Στωικοὶ πρὸ τῶν ἑτέρων τοὺς ἑτέρους ἐν
ὕψει καὶ βάθει. | (PS) |
5 3. Δημόκριτος τὰ μὲν ἀπλανῆ πρῶτον, μετὰ δὲ ταῦτα
τοὺς πλανήτας, ἐφ᾽ | οἷς ἥλιον φωσφόρον σελή-
νην. (PS) |
4. Πλάτων μετὰ τὴν τῶν ἀπλανῶν θέσιν πρῶτον φαί-
νωνα λεγόμενον τὸν | τοῦ Κρόνου, δεύτερον φαέθοντα
τὸν τοῦ Διός, τρίτον πυρόεντα τὸν τοῦ | Ἄρεος, τέταρ-
τον ἑωσφόρον[49] τὸν τῆς Ἀφροδίτης, πέμπτον στίλ-
10 βοντα τὸν | τοῦ Ἑρμοῦ, ἕκτον ἥλιον, ἕβδομον σε-
λήνην. (PS) |

§1 Xenocrates fr. F82   §2 Stoics 2.689
§3 Democritus A86   §4 Plato cf. *Tim.* 38c–d

[48] Ξενοκράτης PS: Ξενοφάνης G κεῖσθαι S: κινεῖσθαι PEG
[49] ἑωσφόρον PES: φωσφόρον GQ

2.15

The first two doxai continue the opposition from the previous chapter. The remaining five are based on the distinction between the fixed stars and the planets as ordered in various sequences.

Ps.-Plutarch, *Tenets* (+ Ps.-Galen, *Philosophical History*); Stobaeus, *Anthology*

15. On the order of the heavenly bodies

1. Xenocrates thinks that the stars lie on a single plane.
2. But the others, the Stoics, say that the ones are placed in front of the others in height and depth.
3. Democritus orders the fixed stars first, then after them   5
the planets, followed by the sun, the light-bringer (i.e., Venus) and the moon.
4. Plato after the positioning of the fixed stars arranges first the star of Cronus called the Shining one, second the star of Zeus called the Radiant one, third the star of Ares called the Fiery one, fourth the star of Aphrodite called Dawn-bringer, fifth the star of Hermes called the Gleamer, sixth   10
the sun, and seventh the moon.[34]

---

[34] This and the following doxa set out the classic opposition between the Pythagorean-Platonic and the Chaldean order of the planets. The term *mathêmatikoi*, here translated "astronomers," can also be rendered as "mathematicians" or "scientists," depending on the context. See also note to 4.14. Of the names, the only ones actually used by Plato in his account in the *Timaeus* are "Dawn-bringer" and "of Hermes."

5. τῶν μαθηματικῶν τινὲς μὲν ὡς Πλάτων, τινὲς δὲ μέσον πάντων τὸν | ἥλιον. (PS) |

6. Ἀναξίμανδρος καὶ Μητρόδωρος ὁ Χῖος καὶ Κράτης ἀνωτάτω μὲν | πάντων τὸν ἥλιον τετάχθαι, μετ᾽ αὐτὸν
15 δὲ τὴν σελήνην, ὑπὸ δ᾽ αὐτοὺς | τὰ ἀπλανῆ τῶν ἄστρων καὶ τοὺς πλανήτας. (PS) |

7. Παρμενίδης πρῶτον μὲν τάττει τὸν ἑῷον, τὸν αὐτὸν δὲ νομιζόμενον ὑπ᾽ | αὐτοῦ καὶ ἕσπερον, ἐν τῷ αἰθέρι· μεθ᾽ ὃν τὸν ἥλιον, ὑφ᾽ ᾧ τοὺς ἐν τῷ | πυρώδει ἀστέρας, ὅπερ "οὐρανὸν" καλεῖ. (S) |

8. Ἀπολλόδωρος ἐν τῷ δευτέρῳ Περὶ θεῶν Πυθαγο-
20 ρείαν εἶναι τὴν περὶ | τοῦ τὸν αὐτὸν εἶναι φωσφόρον τε καὶ ἕσπερον δόξαν.[50] (S) |

§5 astronomers — §6 Anaximander A18; Metrodorus cf. A9; Crates Mallotes fr. F5a §7 Parmenides A40
§8 Apollodorus F91

2.16

Ps.-Plut. *Plac.* 2.16 (+ Ps.-Gal. *Hist. phil.* 58); Stob. *Ecl.* 1.24.1ck, 2bc

ιϛ΄. Περὶ τῆς τῶν ἀστέρων φορᾶς καὶ κινήσεως
(PS) |

1. Ἀναξαγόρας Δημόκριτος Κλεάνθης ἀπ᾽ ἀνατολῶν ἐπὶ δυσμὰς φέρεσθαι | πάντας τοὺς ἀστέρας. (PS) |

§1 Anaxagoras A78; Democritus fr. 387; Cleanthes 1.507
[50] 19–20 = 2.16.7 MR

5. Of the astronomers some order the heavenly bodies as Plato does, others place the sun in the middle of all the planets.

6. Anaximander, Metrodorus of Chios, and Crates say that the sun has been ordered highest of all the heavenly bodies, but after it the moon, and below them the fixed stars and the planets.

7. Parmenides places the Dawn-star, which is considered by him to be identical with the Evening-star, as first in the ether; after it the sun, beneath which he places the heavenly bodies (i.e., stars) in the fiery region, which he calls "heaven."

8. Apollodorus in the second book of his *On gods* says that the view that the light-bringer and the evening star are the same heavenly body is Pythagorean.[35]

2.16

A somewhat messy chapter with various opposed kinds of movement and additional comments.

Ps.-Plutarch, *Tenets* (+ Ps.-Galen, *Philosophical History*); Stobaeus, *Anthology*

16. On the conveyance and movement of the heavenly bodies

1. Anaxagoras, Democritus, and Cleanthes say that all the heavenly bodies are borne from east to west.

---

[35] This doxa could also be placed at the end of the next chapter (where it has been placed in MR). Here it forms an antithetical note to the previous Parmenidean view.

2. Ἀλκμαίων καὶ οἱ μαθηματικοὶ τοὺς πλανήτας τοῖς
5 ἀπλανέσιν ἀπὸ δυσμῶν | ἐπ' ἀνατολὰς ἀντιφέρε-
σθαι. (PS) |

3. Ἀριστοτέλης ὑπὸ τῶν σφαιρῶν, ἐφ' ὧν[51] ἕκαστα
συμβέβηκε, (S) |

4. Ἀναξίμανδρος ὑπὸ τῶν κύκλων καὶ τῶν σφαιρῶν,
ἐφ' ὧν ἕκαστος | βέβηκε, φέρεσθαι. (PS) |

5. Ἀναξιμένης οὐχ[52] ὑπὸ τὴν γῆν περὶ αὐτὴν δὲ στρέ-
10 φεσθαι τοὺς ἀστέρας. | (PS) |

6. Πλάτων καὶ οἱ μαθηματικοὶ[53] ταὐτὸν πεπονθέναι τῷ
ἑωσφόρῳ τὸν στίλβωνα, | ἰσοδραμεῖν δὲ αὐτοὺς τῷ
ἡλίῳ καὶ συμπεριφέρεσθαι αὐτῷ· | καὶ τότε μὲν προ-
ανατέλλοντα ἑωσφόρον φαίνεσθαι, τότε δὲ ἐπικαταδυ-
όμενον | "ἕσπερον" καλεῖσθαι.[54] (PS) |

§2 Alcmaeon A4; astronomers —
§3 Aristotle cf. *Cael.* 2.8 289b30–34, *Met.* 12.8
§4 Anaximander A18
§5 Anaximenes A14
§6 Plato cf. *Tim.* 38c–d; astronomers —

[51] ἐφ' ὧν MR, cf. Diels *DG*: ὑφ' ὧν S
[52] οὐχ ES: ὁμοίως P   περὶ αὐτὴν δὲ S, cf. E: καὶ περὶ
αὐτὴν P
[53] v.l. S τῶν μαθηματικῶν τινες μὲν ὡς Πλάτων, et vid.
app. sec.
[54] post lemma pos. MR lemma Apollodori, nunc 2.15.8

2. Alcmaeon and the astronomers[36] say that the planets are borne in an opposite direction to the fixed stars from west 5 to east.

3. Aristotle says that the heavenly bodies are borne by the spheres on which each of them is situated.

4. Anaximander says that the heavenly bodies are borne by the circles and the spheres on which each of them has mounted.

5. Anaximenes says that the heavenly bodies whirl not beneath the earth but around it. 10

6. Plato and the astronomers say that the Gleamer (Mercury) experiences the same as the Dawn-bringer (Venus),[37] and that they run a course equal to the sun and revolve together with it; and at one time it (i.e., Venus) appears when rising as the dawn-bringer, while at another time when setting it is called the "evening star."

[36] On the term *mathêmatikoi* here and in l. 11, see the note to the previous chapter.

[37] The Platonic names for the two planets were already introduced in the previous chapter (2.15.4).

2.17

Ps.-Plut. *Plac.* 2.17 (+ Ps.-Gal. *Hist. phil.* 59); Stob. *Ecl.* 1.24.1ilm, 3

ιζ΄. Πόθεν φωτίζονται οἱ ἀστέρες (P) |

1. Μητρόδωρος ἅπαντας τοὺς ἀπλανεῖς ἀστέρας ὑπὸ τοῦ ἡλίου προσλάμπεσθαι. | (PS) |
2. Στράτων καὶ αὐτὸς τὰ ἄστρα ὑπὸ τοῦ ἡλίου φωτίζεσθαι. (S) |
5   3. Διότιμος Τύριος ὁ Δημοκρίτειος τὴν αὐτὴν τούτοις εἰσηνέγκατο γνώμην. | (S) |
4. Ἡράκλειτος καὶ οἱ Στωικοὶ τρέφεσθαι τοὺς ἀστέρας ἐκ τῆς ἐπιγείου | ἀναθυμιάσεως. (PS) |
5. Ἀριστοτέλης μὴ δεῖσθαι τὰ οὐράνια τροφῆς· οὐ
10 γὰρ φθαρτὰ ἀλλ᾽ ἀίδια. | (PS) |
6. Πλάτων κοινῶς[55] ὅλον τὸν κόσμον καὶ τὰ ἄστρα ἐξ αὐτῶν τρέφεσθαι. | (PS) |

§1 Metrodorus A9   §2 Strato fr. 43
§3 Diotimus Tyrius fr. 1   §4 Heraclitus A11; Stoics 2.690
§5 Aristotle cf. *Cael.* 1.3 270b1–5, *Met.* 12.8 1073a34
§6 Plato cf. *Tim.* 33c–d

55 Πλάτων κοινῶς ES: Πλάτων οἱ Στωικοί P

2.17

The chapter combines two topics: the first three doxai discuss the illumination of the heavenly bodies, the final three the source of their nourishment.

Ps.-Plutarch, *Tenets* (+ Ps.-Galen, *Philosophical History*); Stobaeus, *Anthology*

17. From where do the heavenly bodies obtain their illumination[38]

1. Metrodorus says that all the fixed stars are shone upon by the sun.

2. Strato too says that the stars are illuminated by the sun.

3. Diotimus of Tyre, the follower of Democritus, introduced the same opinion as these men. 5

4. Heraclitus and the Stoics say that the heavenly bodies are nourished from the earthly exhalation.

5. Aristotle says that the heavenly beings have no need of nourishment, for they are not perishable but everlasting. 10

6. Plato says that the whole cosmos and the stars jointly obtain their nourishment from themselves.

---

[38] This chapter has probably joined together two separate chapters in earlier versions of the *Placita* that Aëtius has drawn upon. The topic of the final three doxai has already been discussed for the cosmos as a whole in 2.5.

2.18

Ps.-Plut. *Plac.* 2.18 (+ Ps.-Gal. *Hist. phil.* 60); Stob. *Ecl.* 1.24.1n

ιη'. Περὶ τῶν ἄστρων τῶν καλουμένων
Διοσκούρων (P) |

1. Ξενοφάνης τοὺς ἐπὶ τῶν πλοίων φαινομένους οἷον ἀστέρας νεφέλια εἶναι | κατὰ τὴν ποιὰν κίνησιν παραλάμποντα. (PS) |

2. Μητρόδωρος τῶν ὁρώντων ὀφθαλμῶν μετὰ δέους
5 καὶ καταπλήξεως | εἶναι στιλβηδόνας. (P) |

§1 Xenophanes A39   §2 Metrodorus A10

2.19

Ps.-Plut. *Plac.* 2.19 (+ Ps.-Gal. *Hist. phil.* 61); Stob. *Ecl.* 1.24.1kl, 4

ιθ'. Περὶ ἐπισημασίας ἀστέρων[56] (PS) |

1. Πλάτων τὰς ἐπισημασίας τάς τε χειμερινάς καὶ τὰς θερινὰς κατὰ τὰς | τῶν ἀστέρων ἐπιτολάς τε καὶ

§1 Plato *Tim.* 40c–d

[56] καὶ πῶς γίνεται χειμὼν καὶ θέρος add. P, cf. Q

2.18

A clear opposition between two kinds of explanation, phys-
ical in the case of the first view, from the viewpoint of the
observer for the second.

Ps.-Plutarch, *Tenets* (+ Ps.-Galen, *Philosophical History*);
Stobaeus, *Anthology*

18. On the stars called the Dioscuri[39]

1. Xenophanes says that that the star-like appearances on
ships are cloudlets that light up in accordance with the
kind of movement that they have.
2. Metrodorus says that they (i.e., the Dioscuri) are the
flashing of eyes that gaze with fear and consternation.   5

2.19

An opposition between two views, with a third doxa il-
lustrating the first of these with a poetic quote.

Ps.-Plutarch, *Tenets* (+ Ps.-Galen, *Philosophical History*);
Stobaeus, *Anthology*

19. On signs of the seasons produced by
the heavenly bodies

1. Plato says that the signs relating to winter and summer
occur in accordance with the risings and settings of the

---

39 This chapter discusses the phenomenon called St. Elmo's
fire.

δυσμὰς γίνεσθαι, ἡλίου τε καὶ σελήνης καὶ | τῶν ἄλ-
λων πλανητῶν καὶ ἀπλανῶν.[57] (PS) |

5 2. Ἀναξιμένης δὲ διὰ μὲν ταῦτα μηδὲν τούτων, διὰ δὲ
τὸν ἥλιον μόνον. (PS) |

3. Εὔδοξος Ἄρατος κοινῶς διὰ πάντας τοὺς ἀστέρας,
ἐν οἷς φησιν·

αὐτὸς γὰρ τά γε σήματ᾿ ἐν οὐρανῷ ἐστήριξεν,
ἄστρα διακρίνας· ἐσκέψατο δ᾿ εἰς ἐνιαυτὸν
ἀστέρας,
οἵ κε μάλιστα τετυγμένα σημαίνοιεν. (PS) |

§2 Anaximenes A14   §3 Eudoxus F142; Aratus *Phaen.* 10–12

2.20

*The main division is determined by the antithesis between
the sun as fire and the view that it is an inflamed earthy
rock. In between are views relating it to the intermediate*

Ps.-Plut. *Plac.* 2.20 (+ Ps.-Gal. *Hist. phil.* 62); Stob. *Ecl.*
1.25.1a–h, 3a–i; Theod. *Cur.* 4.21

κ'. Περὶ οὐσίας ἡλίου[58] (PS) |

1. Ἀναξίμανδρος κύκλον εἶναι ὀκτωκαιεικοσαπλα-
σίονα τῆς γῆς, ἁρματείῳ | τροχῷ παραπλήσιον τὴν

§1 Anaximander A21

[57] ἡλίου . . . ἀπλανῶν non hab. S, del. Diels
[58] add. καὶ ὅτι δύο καὶ τρεῖς εἰσίν P

heavenly bodies, namely the sun and the moon and the other planets and fixed stars.

2. Anaximenes, however, says that through these other 5 heavenly bodies none of these signs occur, but through the sun only.

3. Eudoxus and Aratus say that they occur jointly through all the heavenly bodies, in the verses in which he (i.e., Aratus) says:[40]

> For he himself (i.e., Zeus) fixed the signs in heaven,
> distinguishing the constellations; and for the year he devised
> heavenly bodies to give especially well-constructed signs.

2.20

elements air and water. The final five doxai explore unusual views.

Ps.-Plutarch, *Tenets* (+ Ps.-Galen, *Philosophical History*); Stobaeus, *Anthology*; Theodoret, *Cure of Greek Maladies*

20. On the substance of the sun

1. Anaximander says there is a circle twenty-eight times the earth, similar to a chariot wheel with a hollow rim,

---

40 Poetic quotes are rare in the *Placita* outside 1.1–7, 1.30, and 4.12. These lines from Aratus' famous astronomical poem are the only example of a poetic quote in Book 2.

ἀψῖδα ἔχοντα κοίλην, πλήρη πυρός, κατά τι | μέρος
ἐκφαίνουσαν διὰ στομίου τὸ πῦρ ὥσπερ διὰ πρηστῆ-
5 ρος αὐλοῦ· | καὶ τοῦτ᾽ εἶναι τὸν ἥλιον. (PS) |

2. Ξενοφάνης ἐκ νεφῶν πεπυρωμένων εἶναι τὸν
ἥλιον. (ST, cf. P) |

3. Ἀναξιμένης Παρμενίδης πύρινον ὑπάρχειν τὸν
ἥλιον. (S) |

4. Ἀντιφῶν πῦρ ἐπινεμόμενον μὲν τὸν περὶ τὴν γῆν
ὑγρὸν ἀέρα, ἀνατολὰς | δὲ καὶ δύσεις ποιούμενον τῷ
10 τὸν μὲν ἐπικαιόμενον αἰεὶ προλείπειν, τοῦ | δ᾽ ὑπο-
νοτιζομένου πάλιν ἀντέχεσθαι. (S) |

5. Ξενοφάνης, ⟨ὡς⟩[59] Θεόφραστος ἐν τοῖς Φυσικοῖς
γέγραφεν, ἐκ πυριδίων | τῶν συναθροιζομένων μὲν ἐκ
τῆς ὑγρᾶς ἀναθυμιάσεως συναθροιζόντων | δὲ τὸν
ἥλιον. (PS) |

6. Ἡράκλειτος Ἑκαταῖος Κλεάνθης[60] ἄναμμα νοερὸν
15 ἐκ θαλάττης. (PS) |

7. Πλάτων ἐκ πλείστου πυρός, μετέχειν δὲ καὶ τῶν
ἄλλων σωμάτων. | (PT) |

8. Ἀναξαγόρας Δημόκριτος Μητρόδωρος μύδρον ἢ
πέτρον διάπυρον. | (PST) |

§2 Xenophanes A40   §3 Anaximenes A15; Parmenides
A41   §4 Antiphon B26   §5 Xenophanes A40; Theophrastus fr. 232   §6 Heraclitus A12; Hecataeus B9; Cleanthes 1.501   §7 Plato cf. *Tim.* 40a   §8 Anaxagoras A72;
Democritus A87; Metrodorus A11

59 ⟨ὡς⟩ coni. MR   60 οἱ Στωικοί P

filled with fire, revealing the fire in a particular part through an opening as through a blowtorch, and this is the 5 sun.

2. Xenophanes says that the sun is formed from incandescent clouds.

3. Anaximenes and Parmenides say that the substance of the sun is fiery.

4. Antiphon says that it is fire encroaching on the moist air around the earth, and producing sunrises and sunsets by continually leaving the burning air behind it and in turn clamping onto the slightly dampened air before it. 10

5. Xenophanes, ⟨as⟩ Theophrastus has written in his *Physics*,[41] says that it is formed from firelets that are gathered together out of the moist exhalation and so gather together the sun.

6. Heraclitus, Hecataeus, and Cleanthes say that the sun is an intelligent ignited mass formed from the sea. 15

7. Plato says that it consists of fire for the most part, but also has a share of the other elements.

8. Anaxagoras, Democritus, and Metrodorus say that it is a fiery clump or rock.

---

[41] A rare reference to a secondary source of the doxa. It will refer to a cosmological discussion in Theophrastus' *Physics*, not to the *Physikôn doxai* (or rather *Physikai doxai*), as Diels postulated.

20 9. Θαλῆς γεώδη. (ST) |

10. Διογένης κισηροειδῆ τὸν ἥλιον, εἰς ὃν ἀπὸ τοῦ
αἰθέρος ἀκτῖνες ἐναποστηρίζονται. | (ST) |

11. Ἀριστοτέλης σφαῖραν ἐκ τοῦ πέμπτου σώμα-
τος. (PT) |

12. Φιλόλαος ὁ Πυθαγόρειος ὑαλοειδῆ, δεχόμενον μὲν
25 τοῦ ἐν τῷ κόσμῳ | πυρὸς τὴν ἀνταύγειαν, διηθοῦντα
δὲ πρὸς ἡμᾶς τό τε φῶς καὶ τὴν | ἀλέαν, ὥστε τρόπον
τινὰ διττοὺς ἡλίους γίγνεσθαι, τό τε ἐν τῷ οὐρανῷ |
πυρῶδες καὶ τὸ ἀπ' αὐτοῦ πυροειδὲς κατὰ τὸ ἐσοπτρο-
ειδές, εἰ μή τις | καὶ τρίτον λέξει,[61] τὴν ἀπὸ τοῦ ἐν-
όπτρου κατ' ἀνάκλασιν διασπειρομένην | πρὸς ἡμᾶς
αὐγήν· καὶ γὰρ ταύτην προσονομάζομεν ἥλιον οἱονεὶ
30 εἴδωλον | εἰδώλου. (PST) |

13. Ἐμπεδοκλῆς δύο ἡλίους, τὸν μὲν ἀρχέτυπον, πῦρ
ἐν τῷ ἑτέρῳ | ἡμισφαιρίῳ τοῦ κόσμου πεπληρωκὸς τὸ
ἡμισφαίριον, ἀεὶ κατ' ἀντικρὺ | τῇ ἀνταυγείᾳ ἑαυτοῦ
τεταγμένον· τὸν δὲ φαινόμενον ἀνταύγειαν ἐν τῷ |
ἑτέρῳ ἡμισφαιρίῳ τῷ τοῦ ἀέρος τοῦ θερμομιγοῦς πε-
35 πληρωμένῳ, ἀπὸ | κυκλοτεροῦς τῆς γῆς κατ' ἀνάκλα-
σιν ἐγγιγνομένην εἰς τὸν Ὄλυμπον[62] | τὸν κρυσταλ-
λοειδῆ, συμπεριελκομένην δὲ τῇ κινήσει τοῦ πυρίνου·

§9 Thales A17a   §10 Diogenes A13
§11 Aristotle cf. *Cael.* 1.2 269a31   §12 Philolaus A19
§13 Empedocles A56, cf. B44

61 ὥστε . . . λέξει vid. app. sec.
62 Ὄλυμπον Q: ἥλιον PES

9. Thales says that it is earthy. 20

10. Diogenes says that it is pumice-like, and that rays from the ether fix themselves into it.

11. Aristotle says that it is a sphere made up of the fifth body.

12. Philolaus the Pythagorean says that it is glass-like, on the one hand receiving the reflection of the fire in the 25 cosmos, on the other hand pushing the light and the heat through toward us, so that in a way there are two suns, both the fiery one in the heaven and the one derived from it which is fire-like through being mirror-like, unless someone will say that there is also a third, the beam spread out toward us from the mirror through reflection; for it is this that we call the sun, like an image of an image. 30

13. Empedocles says that there are two suns: one the original, which is fire in the one hemisphere of the cosmos and fills the hemisphere, always stationed opposite its own reflection; the other the visible sun, which is its reflection in the other hemisphere, namely the one filled with air mixed with heat, arising from the circular earth through a 35 reflection onto the crystal-like Olympus (i.e., heaven),[42] and revolving together with the motion of the fiery ele-

---

[42] This is a rare example of a passage where the Arabic translation is the only witness to preserve the original reading, as proven by fr. B44 preserved by Plutarch.

ὡς δὲ | βραχέως εἰρῆσθαι {συντεμόντα},[63] ἀνταύγειαν
εἶναι τοῦ περὶ τὴν γῆν | πυρὸς τὸν ἥλιον. (PS) |

14. Ἐπίκουρος. γήινον πύκνωμα κισηροειδὲς καὶ
40 σπογγοειδὲς ταῖς κατάτρήσεσιν | ὑπὸ τοῦ πυρὸς
ἀνημμένον. (PS) |

15. Ἡράκλειτος ἄναμμα, ἐν μὲν ταῖς ἀνατολαῖς τὴν
ἔξαψιν ἔχοντα, τὴν δὲ | σβέσιν ἐν ταῖς δυσμαῖς. (G) |

16. Παρμενίδης τὸν ἥλιον καὶ τὴν σελήνην ἐκ τοῦ γα-
λαξίου κύκλου ἀποκριθῆναι, | τὸν μὲν ἀπὸ τοῦ ἀραιο-
45 τέρου μίγματος, ὃ δὴ θερμόν, τὴν δὲ ἀπὸ | τοῦ πυκνο-
τέρου, ὅπερ ψυχρόν. (S) |

§14 Epicurus fr. 343   §15 Heraclitus T437, 595 Mouraviev
§16 Parmenides A43

2.21

Ps.-Plut. *Plac.* 2.21 (+ Ps.-Gal. *Hist. phil.* 63); Stob. *Ecl.*
1.25.1cg, 3ef; Theod. *Cur.* 1.97, 4.22

κα΄. Περὶ μεγέθους ἡλίου (PST) |

1. Ἀναξίμανδρος[64] τὸν μὲν ἥλιον ἴσον εἶναι τῇ γῇ, τὸν
δὲ κύκλον, ἀφ᾽ οὗ τὴν | ἐκπνοὴν ἔχει καὶ ὑφ᾽ οὗ φέρε-
ται, ἑπτακαιεικοσαπλασίονα τῆς γῆς. | (PST) |

§1 Anaximander A21

[63] συντεμόντα secl. Diels VS
[64] καὶ Ἀναξιμένης add. T 1.97

ment; to sum up briefly, the sun is a reflection of the fire around the earth.

14. Epicurus says that it is an earthy concentration inflamed by the fire in its cavities in the manner of a pumice stone or sponge.   40

15. Heraclitus says that it is an ignited mass, which is kindled in the east and extinguished in the west.[43]

16. Parmenides says that the sun and the moon have been separated off from the circle of the Milky Way, the former from the more rarefied mixture that is hot, the latter from the denser mixture that is cold.   45

2.21

A list of views basically descending from large to small.

Ps.-Plutarch, *Tenets* (+ Ps.-Galen, *Philosophical History*); Stobaeus, *Anthology*; Theodoret, *Cure of Greek Maladies*

21. On the size of the sun

1. Anaximander says that the sun is equal to the earth in size, and that the circle from which it has its vent and by which it is moved, is twenty-seven times the earth.

[43] Here Ps.-Galen alone preserves a doxa that, though basically a doublet of §6, is likely to go back to Aëtius.

5 2. Ἐμπεδοκλῆς δὲ ἴσον τῇ γῇ τὸν κατὰ τὴν ἀνταύ-
γειαν. (ST) |
3. Ἀναξαγόρας πολλαπλασίονα Πελοποννήσου. (PT) |
4. Ἡράκλειτος εὖρος ποδὸς ἀνθρωπείου. (PST) |
5. Ἐπίκουρος⁶⁵ τηλικοῦτον ἡλίκος φαίνεται, ἢ μικρῷ
τινι μείζω ἢ ἐλάττω. | (PS) |

§2 Empedocles A56	§3 Anaxagoras A72
§4 Heraclitus B3	§5 Epicurus fr. 345

2.22

Ps.-Plut. *Plac.* 2.22 (+ Ps.-Gal. *Hist. phil.* 64); Stob. *Ecl.*
1.25.1dghi; Theod. *Cur.* 4.22

κβ′. Περὶ σχήματος ἡλίου (PST) |

1. Ἀναξιμένης Ἀλκμαίων πλατὺν ὡς πέταλον τὸν
ἥλιον. (PS) |
2. Ἡράκλειτος σκαφοειδῆ, ὑπόκυρτον. (PST) |
3. οἱ Πυθαγόρειοι <καὶ>⁶⁶ οἱ Στωικοὶ σφαιροειδῆ, ὡς
5 τὸν κόσμον καὶ τὰ | ἄστρα. (PST) |
4. Ἐπίκουρος ἐνδέχεσθαι τὰ προειρημένα πάντα. (P) |

§1 Anaximenes A15; Alcmaeon A4	§2 Heraclitus A12
§3 Pythagoreans —; Stoics 2.654	§4 Epicurus fr. 344

⁶⁵ post nom. add. P πάλιν φησὶν ἐνδέχεσθαι τὰ προειρη-
μένα πάντα ἢ   ⁶⁶ <καὶ> coni. MR, cf. 2.13.15

2. But Empedocles says that it, namely the Sun that ap- 5
pears in virtue of the reflection, is equal to the earth in
size.
3. Anaxagoras says that it is many times the size of the
Peloponnese.
4. Heraclitus says that it is the breadth of a human foot.
5. Epicurus says that it is the size that it appears, or a just
little larger or smaller.

2.22

*A sequence of three shapes, to which is opposed a "modal"
view that they are all possible.*

Ps.-Plutarch, *Tenets* (+ Ps.-Galen, *Philosophical History*);
Stobaeus, *Anthology*; Theodoret, *Cure of Greek Maladies*

22. On the shape of the sun

1. Anaximenes and Alcmaeon say that the sun is flat, like
a leaf.
2. Heraclitus says that it is bowl-like,[44] somewhat convex.
3. The Pythagoreans ⟨and⟩ the Stoics say that it is like a
ball, just like the cosmos and the stars. 5
4. Epicurus says that all the above-mentioned shapes are
possible.

[44] On our translations of adjectives ending in *-eidês*, see the
note to 2.2.

Ps.-Plut. *Plac.* 2.23 (+ Ps.-Gal. *Hist. phil.* 65); Stob. *Ecl.* 1.25.1d, 3acehi

κγ΄. Περὶ τροπῶν ἡλίου (PS) |

1. Ἀναξιμένης ὑπὸ πεπυκνωμένου ἀέρος καὶ ἀντιτύπου ἐξωθεῖσθαι τὰ | ἄστρα. (PS) |

2. Ἀναξαγόρας ἀνταπώσει τοῦ πρὸς ταῖς ἄρκτοις
5   ἀέρος, ὃν αὐτὸς συνωθῶν | ἐκ τῆς πυκνώσεως ἰσχυρο-
ποιεῖ. (PS) |

3. Διογένης ὑπὸ τοῦ ἀντιπίπτοντος τῇ θερμότητι ψύ-
χους σβέννυσθαι τὸν | ἥλιον. (PS) |

4. Ἐμπεδοκλῆς ὑπὸ τῆς περιεχούσης αὐτὸν σφαίρας κωλυομενον ἄχρι | παντὸς εὐθυπορεῖν καὶ ὑπὸ τῶν τροπικῶν κύκλων. (PS) |

10 5. Δημόκριτος ἐκ τῆς περιφερούσης αὐτὸν δινή-
σεως. (S) |

6. οἱ Στωικοὶ κατὰ τὸ διάστημα τῆς ὑποκειμένης τρο-

§1 Anaximenes A15   §2 Anaxagoras A72
§3 Diogenes A13   §4 Empedocles A58
§5 Democritus A89   §6 Stoics 1.508, 2.658

2.23

Loosely structured sequence of doxai, moving from early and rather obscure views to the final, more sophisticated theory of the standard cosmological model.

Ps.-Plutarch, *Tenets* (+ Ps.-Galen, *Philosophical History*); Stobaeus, *Anthology*

23. On the turnings of the sun[45]

1. Anaximenes says that the heavenly bodies are pushed off course by condensed and resistant air.

2. Anaxagoras says that the turnings are caused by the repulsion of the northern air, which it (i.e., the sun) by pushing makes strong as the result of the condensation 5 that occurs.

3. Diogenes says that the sun is quenched by the cold that collides with the heat.

4. Empedocles says that the turnings are caused by the sphere that surrounds it (i.e., the sun) and prevents it from continuing its course in a straight line, and by the solstitial circles.

5. Democritus says that they are caused as the result of the 10 whirling that carries it (i.e., the sun) around.

6. The Stoics say that the sun's course is determined by the

---

[45] This is the first chapter of which, in the form of Ps.-Plutarch's *Epitome*, a papyrus snippet has been found in Antinoopolis in Egypt. See the General Introduction 2.1.2.

φῆς διέρχεσθαι τὸν | ἥλιον· ὠκεανὸς δ᾽ ἐστὶν ἢ γῆ,[67]
ἧς τὴν ἀναθυμίασιν ἐπινέμεται· συγκαταφέρεσθαι |
δὲ τὸν ἥλιον κινούμενον ἕλικα ἐν τῇ σφαίρᾳ, ἀπὸ
τοῦ ἰσημερινοῦ | ἐπί τε ἄρκτου καὶ νότου, ἅπερ ἐστὶ
πέρατα τῆς ἕλικος. (PS) |

15 7. ἄλλοι δὲ ἐπ᾽ εὐθείας αὐτὸν κινεῖσθαι τὴν ἕλικα οὐ
περὶ σφαῖραν | ποιοῦντα, περὶ δὲ κύλινδρον. (S) |

8. Πλάτων Πυθαγόρας Ἀριστοτέλης παρὰ τὴν λόξω-
σιν τοῦ ζωδιακοῦ | κύκλου, δι᾽ οὗ φέρεται λοξοπορῶν
ὁ ἥλιος, καὶ κατὰ δορυφορίαν τῶν | τροπικῶν κύκλων·
ταῦτα δὲ πάντα καὶ ἡ σφαῖρα δείκνυσιν. (P) |

§7 anonymi —   §8 Plato cf. *Tim.* 38e–39a; Pythagoras —;
Aristotle cf. Arius Didymus fr. 32

2.24

Ps.-Plut. *Plac.* 2.24 (+ Ps.-Gal. *Hist. phil.* 66); Stob. *Ecl.*
1.25.1acgi, 3bek

κδ΄. Περὶ ἐκλείψεως ἡλίου (PS) |

1. Θαλῆς πρῶτος ἔφη ἐκλείπειν τὸν ἥλιον τῆς σελήνης
αὐτὸν ὑπερχομένης | κατὰ κάθετον, οὔσης φύσει γεώ-

§1 Thales A17a

[67] γῆ P: non hab. S (lac. susp. Wachsmuth, qui coni. ἡ μεγάλη
θάλασσα vel sim.)

distance covered in accordance with the food available to it. This is the ocean or the earth,[46] from which it consumes the exhalation. And they say the sun as it moves produces a concomitant spiral on the sphere, from the equinoctial circle to both the northern and the southern tropics, which are the limits of the spiral.

7. But others say that its movement makes a spiral in a straight line by doing this not on a sphere, but on a cylinder.

8. Plato, Pythagoras, and Aristotle say that they result from the tilting of the zodiac circle, through which the sun moves in an oblique course, and in accordance with the guardianship of the solstitial circles. All these matters the sphere also demonstrates.[47]

15

2.24

Loosely structured series of explanations, beginning this time with the standard view, and continuing with mostly antiquated and sometimes quite odd theories.

Ps.-Plutarch, *Tenets* (+ Ps.-Galen, *Philosophical History*); Stobaeus, *Anthology*

24. On the eclipse of the sun

1. Thales was the first to say[48] that the sun undergoes an eclipse when the moon with its earthy nature proceeds

---

[46] Alternatively, "or the great sea," if Wachsmuth's conjecture is accepted.

[47] "Sphere" here refers to a teaching model of the universe, as depicted on the famous Naples mosaic of the school of Plato.

[48] On the "discoverer" motif, see n. 4 on 2.1.

δους· βλέπεσθαι δὲ τοῦτο | κατοπτρικῶς ὑποτιθεμένῳ τῷ δίσκῳ. (PS) |

5   2. οἱ Πυθαγόρειοι Ἐμπεδοκλῆς <ὁμοίως>.[68] (S) |

3. Ἀναξίμανδρος τοῦ στομίου τῆς τοῦ πυρὸς διεκπνοῆς ἀποκλειομένου. | (PS) |

4. Ἡράκλειτος κατὰ τὴν τοῦ σκαφοειδοῦς στροφήν, ὥστε τὸ μὲν κοῖλον | ἄνω γίνεσθαι τὸ δὲ κυρτὸν κάτω πρὸς τὴν ἡμετέραν ὄψιν. (PS) |

10 5. Ξενοφάνης κατὰ σβέσιν· ἕτερον δὲ πάλιν πρὸς ταῖς ἀνατολαῖς γίνεσθαι· | παριστόρηκε δὲ καὶ ἔκλειψιν ἡλίου ἐφ᾽ ὅλον μῆνα καὶ πάλιν ἔκλειψιν | ἐντελῆ, ὥστε τὴν ἡμέραν νύκτα φανῆναι. (PS) |

6. ἔνιοι πύκνωμα τῶν ἀοράτως ἐπερχομένων τῷ δίσκῳ νεφῶν. (P) |

7. Ἀρίσταρχος τὸν ἥλιον ἵστησι μετὰ τῶν ἀπλανῶν,
15 τὴν δὲ γῆν κινεῖ περὶ | τὸν ἡλιακὸν κύκλον καὶ κατὰ τὰς ταύτης ἐγκλίσεις σκιάζεσθαι. (PS) |

8. Ξενοφάνης πολλοὺς εἶναι ἡλίους καὶ σελήνας κατὰ τὰ κλίματα τῆς γῆς | καὶ ἀποτομὰς καὶ ζώνας· κατά

---

§2 Pythagoreans —; Empedocles A59
§3 Anaximander A21
§4 Heraclitus A12
§5 Xenophanes A41
§6 anonymi —
§7 Aristarchus cf. p. 305 Heath
§8 Xenophanes 21A41a

[68] coni. MR, cf. 2.28.6

perpendicularly in between it and the earth; this is visible by means of reflection when the disk (i.e., of a mirror)[49] is placed underneath.

2. The Pythagoreans and Empedocles ‹hold a similar view›.

3. Anaximander says that the sun is eclipsed when the mouth through which the outpouring of fire occurs is blocked.

4. Heraclitus says that it undergoes an eclipse in accordance with the turning of its bowl-like shape, so that the hollow aspect faces upward and the convex aspect faces downward in the direction of our vision.

5. Xenophanes says that it undergoes an eclipse through quenching. And another sun occurs in the east. He has also recounted that there was an eclipse (i.e., failure) of the sun for an entire month, and moreover that a total eclipse took place, so that the day appeared as night.

6. Some thinkers say that it is a concentration of clouds invisibly passing in front of the sun's disk.

7. Aristarchus makes the sun stand still together with the fixed stars, while he moves the earth in the circle of the sun and says that it (i.e., the sun) is cast in shadow in accordance with the tiltings of this body (i.e., the earth).[50]

8. Xenophanes says that there are many suns and moons in accordance with the latitudes of the earth and its sec-

[49] The word "disk" here must refer to a mirror, whereas below in lines 13 and 17 it refers to the sun's shape as it appears to an observer on earth.

[50] The only reference to Aristarchus' cosmological theories (he is also mentioned in 1.15 and 4.13). The doxa here would have been better placed in the previous chapter.

τινα δὲ καιρὸν ἐμπίπτειν τὸν δίσκον εἴς | τινα ἀποτο-
μὴν τῆς γῆς οὐκ οἰκουμένην ὑφ' ἡμῶν, καὶ οὕτως
ὥσπερ | κενεμβατοῦντα ἔκλειψιν ὑποφαίνειν. ὁ δ'
20 αὐτὸς τὸν ἥλιον εἰς ἄπειρον | μὲν προιέναι, δοκεῖν δὲ
κυκλεῖσθαι διὰ τὴν ἀπόστασιν. (PS) |

2.25

Ps.-Plut. *Plac.* 2.25 (+ Ps.-Gal. *Hist. phil.* 67); Stob. *Ecl.*
1.26.1a–hk; Theod. *Cur.* 4.21, 23

κε΄. Περὶ οὐσίας σελήνης (PS) |

1. Ἀναξίμανδρος κύκλον εἶναι ἐννεακαιδεκαπλάσιον
τῆς γῆς, ὅμοιον ἁρματείῳ ‹τροχῷ› κοίλην ἔχοντα τὴν
ἁψῖδα καὶ πυρὸς πλήρη, καθάπερ ‹τὸν› | τοῦ ἡλίου,
κείμενον λοξόν, ὡς κἀκεῖνον, ἔχοντα μίαν ἐκπνοήν,
5 οἷον πρηστῆρος | αὐλόν· ἐκλείπειν δὲ κατὰ τὰς ἐπι-
στροφὰς τοῦ τροχοῦ.[69] (PS) |
2. Ἀναξιμένης Παρμενίδης Ἡράκλειτος πυρίνην. (ST) |

§1 Anaximander A22   §2 Anaximenes A16; Parmenides
A42; Heraclitus T446 Mouraviev

[69] ὅμοιον . . . τροχοῦ vid. app sec.

tions and zones. But at a certain moment the sun's disk falls into a section of the earth that is not inhabited by us, and in this way, as if treading on emptiness, discloses an eclipse. The same thinker says that the sun advances indefinitely, but seems to go in a circle because of the re-   20
move away from us.

2.25

The main division is between the view that the moon is basically fiery and the view that it is primarily made of earth (each represented by the two first Milesian philosophers). The theme is further discussed in 2.30.

Ps.-Plutarch, *Tenets* (+ Ps.-Galen, *Philosophical History*); Stobaeus, *Anthology*; Theodoret, *Cure of Greek Maladies*

25. On the substance of the moon

1. Anaximander says that the moon is a circle nineteen times the earth, resembling a chariot wheel, having a rim that is hollow and full of fire, like the circle of the sun, lying tilted, as that circle does too, with a single blowhole, like a blowtorch; and it undergoes eclipse in accordance   5
with the turnings of the wheel.
2. Anaximenes, Parmenides, and Heraclitus say that the moon is fiery.

3. Ξενοφάνης νέφος εἶναι πεπυρωμένον πεπιλημέ-
νον,[70] (PST) |

4. Κλεάνθης δὲ πυροειδῆ. (S) |

5. Ποσειδώνιος δὲ καὶ οἱ πλεῖστοι τῶν Στωικῶν[71]
10 μικτὴν ἐκ πυρὸς καὶ ἀέρος. | (PS) |

6. Ἐμπεδοκλῆς ἀέρα συνεστραμμένον νεφοειδῆ, πε-
πηγότα ὑπὸ πυρός, | ὥστε σύμμικτον. (S) |

7. Πλάτων ἐκ πλείονος τοῦ πυρώδους. (PS) |

8. Ἀριστοτέλης <ἐκ τοῦ πέμπτου σώματος>.[72] (cf. S) |

15 9. Θαλῆς γεώδη. (ST) |

10. Ἀναξαγόρας Δημόκριτος στερέωμα διάπυρον,
ἔχον ἐν ἑαυτῷ πεδία καὶ | ὄρη καὶ φάραγγας. (PST) |

11. Διογένης κισηροειδὲς ἄναμμα. (S) |

12. Ἴων σῶμα τῇ μὲν ὑελοειδές, διαυγές, τῇ δὲ ἀφεγ-
γές. (S) |

20 13. Βήρωσος ἡμιπύρωτον σφαῖραν. (S) |

14. Ἡρακλείδης καὶ Ὄκελλος γῆν ὀμίχλῃ περιεχο-
μένην. (PST) |

15. Πυθαγόρας κατοπτροειδὲς σῶμα. (PST) |

---

§3 Xenophanes A43   §4 Cleanthes —   §5 Posidonius
F122; Stoics 2.671, 506   §6 Empedocles A60   §7 Plato cf.
Tim. 40a   §8 Aristotle cf. *Cael.* 1.2 269a31   §9 Thales fr.
356 Wöhrle   §10 Anaxagoras A77; Democritus A90
  §11 Diogenes A14   §12 Ion A7   §13 Berossus F19a
  §14 Heraclides fr. 76; Ocellus T9   §15 Pythagoras —

[70] vid. app. sec.   [71] οἱ Στωικοί P
[72] coni. MR, cf. 2.13.8, 2.20.11

3. Xenophanes says that it is an incandescent compressed cloud,

4. but Cleanthes says that it is fire-like.

5. Posidonius, however, and most of the Stoics say that it is mixed out of fire and air.   10

6. Empedocles says that it is cloud-like compacted air, fixed by fire so that it forms a compound.

7. Plato says that it is formed for the most part from the fiery material.

8. Aristotle says that it is formed ‹from the fifth body›.

9. Thales says that it is earthy.   15

10. Anaxagoras and Democritus say that it is an inflamed solid mass, which has in it plains and mountains and ravines.

11. Diogenes says that it is a sponge-like ignited mass.

12. Ion says that it is a body that is partly glass-like and transparent, partly opaque.

13. Berossus says that it is a half-inflamed sphere.   20

14. Heraclides and Ocellus say that it is earth surrounded by mist.

15. Pythagoras says that it is a mirror-like body.

Ps.-Plut. *Plac.* 2.26 (+ Ps.-Gal. *Hist. phil.* 67a); Stob. *Ecl.* 1.26.1bhk; Theod. *Cur.* 4.23

κϛ΄. Περὶ μεγέθους σελήνης (PS) |

1. οἱ Στωικοὶ μείζονα τῆς γῆς ἀποφαίνονται ὡς καὶ τὸν ἥλιον. (PST) |

2. Παρμενίδης ἴσην τῷ ἡλίῳ, καὶ γὰρ ἀπ᾿ αὐτοῦ φωτίζεσθαι. (PST) |

3. Ἀριστοτέλης ἐλάττονα τῆς γῆς, (ST) |

5 4. ἄλλοι δὲ σπιθαμῆς ἔχειν διάμετρον. (T) |

§1 Stoics 2.666
§2 Parmenides A42
§3 Aristotle —
§4 anonymi —

2.26

A sequence of views from large to small, similar to 2.21, on the sun, but disrupted by the anomalous second lemma.

Ps.-Plutarch, *Tenets* (+ Ps.-Galen, *Philosophical History*); Stobaeus, *Anthology*; Theodoret, *Cure of Greek Maladies*

26. On the size of the moon

1. The Stoics say that the moon is larger than the earth, as the sun is also.
2. Parmenides says that it is equal to the sun in size, and that it is in fact illuminated by it.[51]
3. Aristotle says that it is smaller in size than the earth,
4. But others say that it has the diameter of a span.[52]   5

[51] The additional comment anticipates 2.28 (and esp. §6).
[52] This doxa, found only in Theodoret, neatly parallels the Heraclitan view on the sun at 2.21.4, but there is no evidence linking it to Heraclitus (or anyone else).

2.27

Ps.-Plut. *Plac.* 2.27 (+ Ps.-Gal. *Hist. phil.* 68); Stob. *Ecl.* 1.26.1cfik; Theod. *Cur.* 4.24

κζ'. Περὶ σχήματος σελήνης (PS) |

1. οἱ Στωικοὶ σφαιροειδῆ εἶναι ὡς τὸν ἥλιον· (PS) |
2. σχηματίζεσθαι δὲ αὐτὴν πολλαχῶς, καὶ γὰρ πανσέληνον γινομένην καὶ | διχότομον καὶ ἀμφίκυρτον καὶ μηνοειδῆ. (S) |
5 3. Ἡράκλειτος σκαφοειδῆ, (PS) |
4. Κλεάνθης πιλοειδῆ, (S) |
5. Ἐμπεδοκλῆς δισκοειδῆ, (PS) |
6. ἄλλοι κυλινδροειδῆ. (PS) |

§§1–2 Stoics 2.667
§3 Heraclitus A12
§4 Cleanthes 1.506
§5 Empedocles A60
§6 anonymi —

2.27

Division between the standard spherical view (followed by the shapes of the phases of the moon), as opposed to a number of nonspherical shapes.

Ps.-Plutarch, *Tenets* (+ Ps.-Galen, *Philosophical History*); Stobaeus, *Anthology*; Theodoret, *Cure of Greek Maladies*

27. On the shape of the moon

1. The Stoics say that the moon is like a ball, just as the sun is.
2. And, they say, it is shaped in many different ways, for it becomes full moon and half moon and gibbous and moon-like (i.e., crescent shaped).
3. Heraclitus says that it is bowl-like. 5
4. Cleanthes says that it is hat-like.
5. Empedocles says that it is disk-like.
6. But others say that it is cylinder-like.

Ps.-Plut. *Plac.* 2.28 (+ Ps.-Gal. *Hist. phil.* 69); Stob. *Ecl.* 1.26.2

κη′. Περὶ φωτισμῶν σελήνης (PS) |

1. Ἀναξίμανδρος Ξενοφάνης Βήρωσος ἴδιον αὐτὴν ἔχειν φῶς. (PS) |
2. Ἀριστοτέλης ἴδιον μέν, ἀραιότερον δέ πως. (S) |
3. οἱ Στωικοὶ ἀμαυροφανές, ἀεροειδὲς γάρ. (S) |
5 4. Ἀντιφῶν ἰδιοφέγγη τὴν σελήνην, τὸ δ᾽ ἀποκρυπτό-
μενον περὶ αὐτὴν ὑπὸ | τῆς προσβολῆς τοῦ ἡλίου
ἀμαυροῦσθαι, πεφυκότος τοῦ ἰσχυροτέρου | πυρὸς τὸ
ἀσθενέστερον ἀμαυροῦν· ὃ δὴ συμβαίνειν καὶ περὶ τὰ
ἄλλα | ἄστρα. (PS) |
5. Θαλῆς πρῶτος ἔφη ὑπὸ τοῦ ἡλίου[73] φωτίζε-
σθαι. (PS) |

§1 Anaximander A22; Xenophanes A43; Berossus F19b
§2 Aristotle —   §3 Stoics 2.670
§4 Antiphon B27   §5 Thales fr. 159, 357 Wöhrle

[73] Θαλῆς πρῶτος . . . ἡλίου S: Θαλῆς καὶ οἱ ἀπ᾽ αὐτοῦ ὑπὸ τοῦ ἡλίου PEQ, Θαλῆς δὲ ἀπὸ τοῦ ἡλίου G

2.28

Division between views in which the moon has its own light and the view that it is illuminated by the sun. The final doxa belongs to the former group, but it is left to the end because it compares the moon with the sun.

Ps.-Plutarch, *Tenets* (+ Ps.-Galen, *Philosophical History*); Stobaeus, *Anthology*

28. On the illuminations of the moon

1. Anaximander, Xenophanes, and Berossus say that the moon has its own light.
2. Aristotle says that it has its own light, but it is somewhat thinner.
3. The Stoics say that its light is dim in appearance, for it is air-like.
4. Antiphon says that the moon has its own gleam, and the   5
gleam that is hidden around it[53] is dimmed by the approach of the sun, since it is natural for the stronger fire to make the weaker one dim, which indeed also occurs in the case of the other heavenly bodies.
5. Thales was the first to say that it is illuminated by the sun.[54]

[53] Or, "the part of it that is hidden away."
[54] On the "discoverer" motif, see n. 4 on 2.1.

10 6. Πυθαγόρας Παρμενίδης Ἐμπεδοκλῆς Ἀναξαγόρας
Μητρόδωρος | ὁμοίως. (S) |

7. Ἡράκλειτος τὸ αὐτὸ πεπονθέναι τὸν ἥλιον καὶ τὴν
σελήνην· σκαφοειδεῖς | γὰρ ὄντας τοῖς σχήμασι τοὺς
ἀστέρας, δεχομένους τὰς ἀπὸ τῆς | ὑγρᾶς ἀναθυμιά-
σεως αὐγάς, φωτίζεσθαι πρὸς τὴν φαντασίαν, λα-
15 μπρότερως | μὲν τὸν ἥλιον, ἐν καθαρωτέρῳ γὰρ ἀέρι
φέρεσθαι, τὴν δὲ σελήνην | ἐν θολωτέρῳ καὶ διὰ τοῦτο
ἀμαυροτέραν φαίνεσθαι. (PS) |

§6 Pythagoras —; Parmenides A42, cf. B14; Empedocles A60;
Anaxagoras A77; Metrodorus A12   §7 Heraclitus A12

2.29

Ps.-Plut. *Plac.* 2.29 (+ Ps.-Gal. *Hist. phil.* 70); Stob. *Ecl.*
1.26.3; Theod. *Cur.* 4.24

κθ′. Περὶ ἐκλείψεως σελήνης (PST) |

1. Ἀναξίμανδρος τοῦ στομίου τοῦ περὶ τὸν τροχὸν
ἐπιφραττομένου. (PS) |

§1 Anaximander A22

220

6. Pythagoras, Parmenides, Empedocles, Anaxagoras, and   10
Metrodorus say likewise.

7. Heraclitus says that the sun and the moon undergo the
same experience: since they are heavenly bodies that are
bowl-like in their shapes and receive their radiance from
the moist exhalation, they are illuminated in their appearance, the sun doing so more brightly because it moves in   15
air that is purer, whereas the moon moves in murkier air
and for this reason appears dimmer.

2.29

*Awkwardly combines explanations of irregular lunar
eclipses with views relating to its regular phases. The final
two doxai distinguish more clearly between these two phenomena.*

Ps.-Plutarch, *Tenets* (+ Ps.-Galen, *Philosophical History*);
Stobaeus, *Anthology*; Theodoret, *Cure of Greek Maladies*

29. On the eclipse of the moon

1. Anaximander says that the moon is eclipsed when the
orifice on the wheel of fire is obstructed.

2. Βήρωσος κατὰ τὴν πρὸς ἡμᾶς ἐπιστροφὴν τοῦ
ἀπυρώτου μέρους. | (PS) |

5 3. Ἀλκμαίων Ἡράκλειτος Ἀντιφῶν κατὰ τὴν τοῦ σκα-
φοειδοῦς στροφὴν | καὶ τὰς περικλίσεις. (PS) |

4. τῶν Πυθαγορείων τινὲς κατὰ τὴν Ἀριστοτέλειον
ἱστορίαν καὶ τὴν | Φιλίππου τοῦ Ὀπουντίου ἀπόφασιν
ἀνταυγείᾳ καὶ ἀντιφράξει[74] τοτὲ μὲν | τῆς γῆς τοτὲ δὲ
τῆς ἀντίχθονος. (PS) |

10 5. τῶν δὲ νεωτέρων εἰσί τινες οἷς ἔδοξε κατ᾽ ἐπινέμη-
σιν φλογὸς κατὰ | μικρὸν ἐξαπτομένης τεταγμένως,
ἕως ἂν τὴν τελείαν πανσέληνον | ἀποδῷ, καὶ πάλιν
ἀναλόγως μειουμένης μέχρι τῆς συνόδου, καθ᾽ ἣν |
τελείως σβέννυται. (PS) |

6. Ξενοφάνης καὶ τὴν μηνιαίαν ἀπόκρυψιν κατὰ σβέ-
σιν. (S) |

15 7. Θαλῆς Ἀναξαγόρας Πλάτων Ἀριστοτέλης οἱ Στω-
ικοὶ οἱ μαθηματικοὶ[75] | συμφώνως τὰς μὲν μηνιαίους
ἀποκρύψεις συνοδεύουσαν αὐτὴν ἡλίῳ καὶ | περιλαμ-

§2 Berossus F19c   §3 Alcmaeon A4; Heraclitus A12;
Antiphon B28   §§4–5 Pythagoreans 58B36, cf. Arist. *de
Pythag.* fr. 16 Ross; Philip of Opus fr. 10   §6 Xenophanes
A43   §7 Thales fr. 159, 357 Wöhrle; Anaxagoras A77;
Plato —; Aristotle cf. *Cael.* 2.14 297b29, fr. 210 Rose; Stoics
2.676; astronomers —

[74] ἀντιφράξει S (sed om. ἀνταυγείᾳ καὶ): ἐπιφράξει P
[75] Θαλῆς Ἀναξαγόρας S, om. PEG   Ἀριστοτέλης PEG,
om. S   οἱ μαθηματικοὶ PE: τοῖς μαθηματικοῖς S

2. Berossus says that it is eclipsed in accordance with the turning of the uninflamed part of the moon toward us.

3. Alcmaeon, Heraclitus, and Antiphon say that it is eclipsed in accordance with the turning of the bowl-like shape of the moon and its lateral motions.

4. Some of the Pythagoreans according to the research of Aristotle and the assertion of Philip of Opus say that it is eclipsed through reflection and obstruction, sometimes of the earth and sometimes of the counterearth.

5. But among more recent thinkers there are some, who are of the opinion that an eclipse takes place in accordance with the dissemination of a flame that slowly catches alight in an orderly manner, until it produces the complete full moon, and then analogously diminishes again until the conjunction with the sun, when it is completely extinguished.

6. Xenophanes says that the monthly concealment too takes place by quenching.

7. Thales, Anaxagoras, Plato, Aristotle, the Stoics, and the astronomers agree in unison that it the moon produces the monthly concealments by traveling together with the sun

πομένην ποιεῖσθαι, τὰς δ' ἐκλείψεις εἰς τὸ σκίασμα
τῆς γῆς | ἐμπίπτουσαν, μεταξὺ μὲν ἀμφοτέρων τῶν
ἀστέρων γινομένης, μᾶλλον | δὲ τῆς σελήνης ἀντι-
φραττομένης. (PS) |

20   8. Ἀναξαγόρας, ὥς φησι Θεόφραστος, καὶ τῶν ὑπο-
κάτω τῆς σελήνης ἔσθ' | ὅτε σωμάτων ἐπιπροσθούν-
των. (S) |

§8 Anaxagoras A77; Theophrastus fr. 236

2.30

*Not very systematically structured, but the main division
in 2.25 continues to exert influence. The first four doxai
relate to the earthy view, the second group of four assume*

Ps.-Plut. *Plac.* 2.30 (+ Ps.-Gal. *Hist. phil.* 71); Stob. *Ecl.*
1.26.4

λ'. Περὶ ἐμφάσεως σελήνης καὶ διὰ τί γεώδης
φαίνεται[76] (PS) |

1. τῶν Πυθαγορείων τινὲς μέν, ὧν ἐστι Φιλόλαος, τὸ
γεωφανὲς αὐτῆς εἶναι[77] | διὰ τὸ περιοικεῖσθαι τὴν

§1 Pythagoreans A20; Philolaus test. A20

[76] tit. PE (sed αὐτῆς pro σελήνης): Περὶ ἐμφάσεως αὐτῆς
S   [77] τῶν . . . εἶναι S: οἱ Πυθαγόρειοι γεώδη φαίνεσθαι
τὴν σελήνην PE

and being illuminated by it, whereas it produces the eclipses by descending into the shadow of the earth that interposes itself between the two heavenly bodies, or rather when the moon is obstructed by the earth.

8. Anaxagoras, as Theophrastus says,[55] says that it is   20
eclipsed also when it happens that bodies in the space below the moon interpose themselves.

2.30

an ethereal nature, while the final lemma again compares the sun and moon (cf. 2.28.7).

Ps.-Plutarch, *Tenets* (+ Ps.-Galen, *Philosophical History*); Stobaeus, *Anthology*

30. On its appearance and why it appears to be earthy

1. Some of the Pythagoreans, of whom Philolaus is one, say that its earthy appearance is caused by the fact that the

---

[55] As at 2.20.5, the doxographer takes the unusual step of indicating Theophrastus as the source of the report (whether direct or, as is more likely, indirect). But unlike in the other passage, he does not specify a particular work. See further the General Introduction 1.6 and the Introduction to Book 2.

σελήνην καθάπερ τὴν παρ' ἡμῖν γῆν μείζοσι | ζώοις
καὶ φυτοῖς μείζοσι καὶ καλλίοσιν· εἶναι γὰρ πεντεκαι-
5 δεκαπλάσια | τὰ ἐπ' αὐτῆς ζῷα τῇ δυνάμει μηδὲν
περιττωματικὸν ἀποκρίνοντα, καὶ | τὴν ἡμέραν τοσ-
αύτην τῷ μήκει. (PS) |

2. ἄλλοι δὲ τὴν ἐν τῇ σελήνῃ ἔμφασιν ἀνάκλασιν εἶ-
ναι τῆς πέραν τοῦ διακεκαυμένου | κύκλου τῆς οἰκου-
μένης ὑφ' ἡμῶν θαλάττης. (S) |

3. Ἀναξαγόρας ἀνωμαλότητα τοῦ συγκρίματος διὰ τὸ
10 ψυχρομιγὲς ἅμα καὶ | γεῶδες, τὰ μὲν ἐχούσης ὑψηλά,
τὰ δὲ ταπεινά, τὰ δὲ κοῖλα· {καὶ | παραμεμῖχθαι τῷ
πυροειδεῖ τὸ ζοφῶδες, ὧν τὸ πάθος ὑποφαίνει τὸ σκι-
ερόν· | ὅθεν "ψευδοφανῆ" λέγεσθαι τὸν ἀστέρα.}[78] (PS) |

4. Δημόκριτος ἀποσκιάσματα τῶν ὑψηλῶν ἐν αὐτῇ
μερῶν· ἄγκη γὰρ αὐτὴν | ἔχειν καὶ νάπας. (S) |

15 5. Παρμενίδης διὰ τὸ παραμεμῖχθαι τῷ περὶ αὐτὴν
πυρώδει τὸ ζοφῶδες, | ‹ὧν τὸ πάθος ὑποφαίνει τὸ σκι-
ερόν·› ὅθεν "ψευδοφανῆ" λέγεσθαι τὸν | ἀστέρα.[79] (S) |

6. οἱ Στωικοὶ διὰ τὸ ἀερομιγὲς τῆς οὐσίας μὴ εἶναι
αὐτῆς ἀκήρατον τὸ | σύγκριμα. (PS) |

20 7. Ἀριστοτέλης μὴ εἶναι αὐτῆς ἀκήρατον τὸ σύγκριμα

§2 anonymi —   §3 Anaxagoras A77
§4 Democritus A90   §5 Parmenides B21 ("Falsches")
§6 Stoics 2.669   §7 Aristotle cf. GA 3.11 761b23

[78] 10–12 καὶ . . . ἀστέρα secl. MR (cf. 15–16)
[79] ὧν . . . σκιερόν transp. MR ex l. 11   ψευδοφανῆ S,
etiam in l. 12, sed illic leg. P ψευδοφαῆ

moon is inhabited, just like our earth, but with animals and plants that are larger and more beautiful. For they say that the animals on it are fifteen-fold in power and do not 5 discharge any excrement, and that the day is the same in length (i.e., fifteen-fold).

2. But others say that the appearance in the moon is a reflection of the sea beyond the circle of the Torrid zone of the world inhabited by us.

3. Anaxagoras says that it is caused by unevenness of its composition on account of cold being mixed in together with the earthy component, the moon having some parts 10 that are high, others that are low, and others that are hollow. {Moreover, he says that the dark component has been mixed in with the fire-like component, the effect of which causes the shadowy coloring to appear; for this reason the heavenly body is called "falsely appearing."}[56]

4. Democritus says that it is caused by the shadow effects of the high areas in it; for it has glens and vales.

5. Parmenides says that it occurs on account of the dark 15 component having been mixed in with the fire-like component in it, ⟨the effect of which causes the shadowy coloring to appear⟩; for this reason the heavenly body is called "falsely appearing."

6. The Stoics say that on account of the air mixed in the substance its composition is not unblemished.

7. Aristotle says that its composition is not unblemished 20

[56] The bracketed passage is most likely a doublet from the doxa of Parmenides (ll. 15–17), to which the missing words in angle brackets have to be restored.

διὰ τὰ πρόσγεια | ἀερώματα τοῦ αἰθέρος, ὃν προσα-
γορεύει σῶμα πέμπτον. (S) |

8. οἱ ἀπὸ τῶν μαθηματικῶν τὸ ἀνώμαλον συγκριτικὸν
αἰτιῶνται. καθάπερ | οὖν τῶν προσαυγαζομένων ὑπὸ
τοῦ ἡλίου νεφῶν τὰ μὲν ἀραιότερα μέρη | λαμπρότερα
φαίνεσθαι, τὰ δὲ πυκνότερα ἀμαυρότερα, οὕτως καὶ
25 τῆς | σελήνης ἐοικυίας μὲν νεφελοειδεῖ πιλήματι,
προσαυγαζομένης δ᾽ ὑπὸ τοῦ ἡλίου. (S) |

9. Ξενοφάνης τὸν μὲν ἥλιον χρήσιμον εἶναι πρὸς τὴν
τοῦ κόσμου καὶ τὴν | τῶν ἐν αὐτῷ ζῴων γένεσίν τε καὶ
διοίκησιν, τὴν δὲ σελήνην παρέλκειν. | (S) |

§8 astronomers —   §9 Xenophanes A42

2.31

Ps.-Plut. *Plac.* 2.30 (+ Ps.-Gal. *Hist. phil.* 72); Stob. *Ecl.*
1.26.5; Theod. *Cur.* 4.24

λα΄. Περὶ τῶν ἀποστημάτων τῆς σελήνης[80] (PST) |

1. Ἐμπεδοκλῆς διπλάσιον ἀπέχειν τὴν σελήνην ἀπὸ
τοῦ ἡλίου ἤπερ ἀπὸ | τῆς γῆς.[81] (PST) |

§1 Empedocles A61

80 tit. MR (cf. GQ): Περὶ τῶν ἀποστημάτων S, cf. E qui add.
αὐτῆς (sc. σελήνης), Περὶ τῶν ἀποστημάτων τῆς σελήνης
πόσον ἀφέστηκε τοῦ ἡλίου P   81 P: διπλάσιον ἀπέχειν (sc.
τὸ διάστημα) τῆς σελήνης ἀπὸ γῆς ἤπερ ἀπὸ τοῦ ἡλίου S

because the ether, which he calls the fifth body, becomes aerated close to the earth.

8. The successors of the astronomers[57] regard its compositional unevenness as the cause. Just as in the case of clouds illuminated by the sun the thinner parts are brighter and the thicker parts are darker, so it happens in the case of the moon, which resembles a cloud-like compressed 25 body and is illuminated by the sun.

9. Xenophanes says that the sun is useful for the generation and administration of the cosmos and the living beings in it, but the moon is redundant.

2.31

Two separate diaereses. The former moves from simple to complex answers, the latter introduces a different subject not covered by the chapter's heading.

Ps.-Plutarch, *Tenets* (+ Ps.-Galen, *Philosophical History* 72); Stobaeus, *Anthology*; Theodoret, *Cure of Greek Maladies*

31. On the distances of the moon

1. Empedocles says that the moon is double the distance from the sun that it is from the earth.

----

[57] On this term (also used in the next chapter), see the notes above, on 2.15–16.

2. οἱ ἀπὸ τῶν μαθηματικῶν ὀκτωκαιδεκαπλάσιον. (PS) |

5   3. Ἐρατοσθένης τὸν ἥλιον ἀπέχειν τῆς γῆς σταδίων μυριάδας τετρακοσίας | καὶ ὀκτάκις μυρίας, τὴν δὲ σελήνην ἀπέχειν τῆς γῆς μυριάδας | ἑβδομήκοντα ὀκτὼ σταδίων. (PST) |

4. Ἐμπεδοκλῆς τοῦ ὕψους τοῦ ἀπὸ τῆς γῆς εἰς ⟨τὸν⟩ οὐρανόν, ἥτις ἐστὶν | ἀφ' ἡμῶν ἀνάτασις, πλείονα εἶ-
10 ναι τὴν κατὰ τὸ πλάτος διάστασιν, κατὰ | τοῦτο τοῦ οὐρανοῦ μᾶλλον ἀναπεπταμένου διὰ τὸ ᾠῷ παραπλη- σίως τὸν | κόσμον κεῖσθαι. (S) |

5. Βόηθος δὲ πρὸς τὴν φαντασίαν δέχεται τὸ ἀνα- πεπταμένον, οὐ κατὰ τὴν | ὑπόστασιν. (S) |

§2 anonymi, cf. Aristarchus *Magn.* p. 352 Heath
§3 Eratosthenes fr. I.40
§4 Empedocles A50
§5 Boethus the Stoic fr.9

2. But the successors of the astronomers say that it is eighteen times.

3. Eratosthenes says that the sun is distant four hundred and eight myriads[58] of stades from the earth, and that the moon is distant seventy-eight myriads of stades from the earth.

4. Empedocles says that the distension of the heaven in its breadth is greater than the height from the earth to heaven, which is its extension from us, the increased extent of the heaven having occurred for the reason that the cosmos is lying on its side in the manner similar to an egg.

5. But Boethus understands the extent as a matter of appearance, not of reality.[59]

[58] There is much confusion in the manuscripts regarding this first number. The likely correct figure of 4,080,000 stades—a myriad is ten thousand—is found in Eusebius and Lydus, and supported by Theodoret, who abridges to the round figure of four million. The "stade" is a distance of 600 feet, i.e., ca. 180 meters.

[59] Here too, as in 2.28, the doxographer appears to have combined two separate subjects in his sources. The distinction between reality and appearance in the final two doxai has previously occurred in 2.19, and will be important when discussing meteorological phenomena in Book 3.

2.32

Ps.-Plut. *Plac.* 2.32 (+ Ps.-Gal. *Hist. phil.* 73); Stob. *Ecl.*
1.8.42

λβ′. Περὶ ἐνιαυτοῦ, | πόσος ἑκάστου τῶν πλανητῶν
χρόνος, καὶ τίς ὁ μέγας ἐνιαυτός[82] (P) |

1. ἐνιαυτός ἐστι Κρόνου μὲν ἐνιαυτῶν περίοδος τρι-
άκοντα, Διὸς δώδεκα, | Ἄρεος δυεῖν, Ἡλίου δώδεκα
5 μῆνες· οἱ δ' αὐτοὶ Ἑρμοῦ καὶ Ἀφροδίτης, | ἰσόδρομοι
γάρ· σελήνης ἡμέραι τριάκοντα· οὗτος γὰρ ὁ τέλειος
μὴν ἀπὸ | φάσεως εἰς σύνοδον. (PS) |
2. γίγνεσθαι δὲ τὸν λεγόμενον μέγαν ἐνιαυτόν, ὅταν
ἐπὶ τοὺς ⟨αὐτοὺς⟩ ἀφ' | ὧν ἤρξαντο τῆς κινήσεως
ἀφίκωνται τόπους. (S) |
3. τὸν δέ γε μέγαν ἐνιαυτὸν οἱ μὲν ἐν τῇ ὀκταετηρίδι
τίθενται, (PS) |
10 4. οἱ δ' ἐν τῇ ἐννεακαιδεκαετηρίδι, (PS) |

82 tit. PQ: πόσος . . . ἐνιαυτός om. EG

2.32

There are again two main diaereses: the first between planetary years and the Great year; the second between two kinds of Great year, the one shorter, the other maximal.

Ps.-Plutarch, *Tenets* (+ Ps.-Galen, *Philosophical History*); Stobaeus, *Anthology*

32. On the year, how great the time of the revolution of each of the planets is, and what the Great year is

1. A year for Saturn is a period of thirty years, for Jupiter it is twelve years, for Mars two years, for the Sun twelve months; and the same months are the period for Mercury and Venus, for they move at the same speed. The period 5 of the moon is thirty days, for this is the complete month from its appearance to the conjunction with the sun.
2. But they say that the so-called Great year occurs whenever the planets reach the same locations from which they commenced their motion.[60]
3. But as far as the Great year is concerned, some thinkers place it in the eighth year,
4. others in the nineteenth year, 10

[60] The nominal definition of "Great year" does not distinguish between (1) the shorter luni-solar Great year (doxai 3–6), involving the solar and lunar cycles only, and (2) the maximal Great year, bringing all the planets back to the same point (doxai 8–10). The expression "starting point (literally, 'head') of time" in the additional explanation at l. 14 is obscure.

5. οἱ δ' ἐν τοῖς τετραπλασίοις ἔτεσιν, (S) |

6. οἱ δ' ἐν τοῖς ἑξήκοντα ἑνὸς δέουσιν, ἐν οἷς Οἰνοπίδης καὶ Πυθαγόρας· | (PS) |

7. οἱ δ' ἐν τῇ λεγομένῃ κεφαλῇ τοῦ χρόνου,[83] αὕτη δ'
15 ἐστὶ τῶν ἑπτὰ πλανητῶν | ἐπὶ ταύτῃ ἡμέρᾳ τῆς ἐξ
ἀρχῆς[84] φορᾶς ἐπάνοδος. (S) |

8. Ἡράκλειτος ἐκ μυρίων ὀκτακισχιλίων ἡλιακῶν. (PS) |

9. Διογένης ὁ Στωικὸς ἐκ πέντε καὶ ἑξήκοντα καὶ τριακοσίων ἐνιαυτῶν | τοσούτων ὅσος ἦν ὁ καθ' Ἡράκλειτον ἐνιαυτός. (PS) |

10. ἄλλοι δὲ δι' ἑπτακισχιλίων ἑπτακοσίων ἑβδομήκοντα ἑπτά. (P) |

§6 Oenopides fr. 9; Pythagoras —
§8 Heraclitus A13
§9 Diogenes of Babylon fr. 28

[83] χρόνου coni. Taylor: Κρόνου S Diels *DG*, κόσμου Diels *VS DK*
[84] ἀρχῆς Taylor: ἄρκτου S

234

5. others in the years that are a fourfold (i.e., in the seventy-sixth year),

6. yet others in the sixtieth year minus one (i.e., fifty-nine), among whom are Oenopides and Pythagoras.

7. But there are others who place it in the so-called starting point of time, and this is the return of the seven planets on the same day of their movement from the beginning. 15

8. Heraclitus says that the Great year consists of 18,000 solar years.[61]

9. Diogenes the Stoic says that the Great year consists of 365 years times what the Great year was according to Heraclitus.

10. But others say that the Great year occurs every 7,777 years.

[61] From the parallel account in Censorinus and other considerations, it is likely that the correct number is 10,800. But it is more probable that the mistake was taken over from earlier accounts than that it is the result of scribal error, so it should not be emended.

BOOK III

METEOROLOGY AND THE EARTH

INTRODUCTION

Transmission

Of the five books in Aëtius' compendium, Book 3 is by far the shortest in terms of chapters (18), doxai (109), and absolute length. Like Book 5, it is seriously incomplete. This is the direct result of the manner of its transmission. In carrying out his abridgment, Ps.-Plutarch does not appear to have deviated from his method elsewhere. But regrettably, the evidence that Stobaeus could have provided suffered at the hands of Byzantine epitomators: his excerpts are available only for chapters 1 through 8 and 17 (with a single Platonic doxa from 15). For the remaining chapters, they are entirely missing. As a result, Ps.-Plutarch contributes ninety-one lemmata, but Stobaeus only sixty. To make matters worse, Theodoret ignores this book entirely. Chapters 9 through 16, for which basically only Ps.-Plutarch and his tradition are available, have thus been considerably truncated. At best, we can only speculate on how Ps.-Plutarch might have abridged the material that he found in the original work.

Contents

Book 3 is unique in having two introductory statements on its contents.[1] The first of these divides it from Book 2. It states that in the preceding book the "things in the heavens" (*ta ourania*) have been treated, and that it is now the turn of "the things on high" (*ta metarsia*) in the third (book). By mentioning both the *ourania* and the *metarsia*, it emphasizes the unity and coherence of the compendium as a whole. Chapter 1, on the Milky Way, can be regarded as having a transitional function, since it was considered to be the first and highest of the *metarsia*, and so closest to the *ourania*. The prooemium also draws attention to the book's unity, by referring to the "position of the earth," which is discussed in chapter 11 and can be taken to be representative of all the chapters relating to the earth in the second half of the book. In the second introductory passage, which we have not set out separately but attached to chapter 8, these two parts of the sublunary world, *metarsia* and *prosgeia*, are again mentioned, the former as having been treated, the latter as to be treated in what follows, that is, in chapters 9 to 17.

A special problem is caused by the chapter "On the halo." In Ps.-Plutarch it is placed last, and so is numbered as chapter 18. As Diels already saw, it most likely has been displaced from its original position after chapter 5, on the rainbow. Stobaeus' excerpts do not include it, but the evi-

---

[1] In Book 1, the first lemma of chapter 8 could be taken as such, making two for the book, but it really relates only to the two preceding chapters on theology.

dence of Photius' index supports the hypothesis of its displacement. It could be argued that a location at the end of the book brings about a return to the *metarsia* and thus would underline its unity. We consider this, however, to be less likely. Moreover, moving it to an earlier position has the pleasing result that the book is divided into two equal halves of nine chapters each.

A subsidiary argument in favor of this decision is that the division between Books 3 and 4 is less clear-cut than that between Books 2 and 3. The two chapters dealing with the sea (16–17) are followed beyond the book division by the remaining chapter on terrestrial waters (4.1), on the Nile. In the final position accorded it by Ps.-Plutarch, the chapter on the halo gets in the way. Moreover, it is not found in Ps.-Galen, whose abridged version of 4.1 follows on directly after that of 3.17. Finally, both 3.17 and 4.1, as we shall soon see, present *recherché* name-labels not, or very rarely, found elsewhere in the *Placita*.

A further feature that needs to be noted is that an important contrast is introduced at the beginning of chapter 5, on the rainbow, which has the effect of introducing another subdivision, this time in the chapters on the *metarsia*. It is between meteorological phenomena that are real (*kath' hypostasin*) and those that are merely optical (*kat' emphasin*). The postponement of this preliminary consideration might give rise to puzzlement. But in fact it faithfully echoes the procedure of Aristotle's *Meteorology*, where this is made an important thematic issue as late as, and only in, Book 3, in which the rainbow and similar phenomena are treated. There is certainly no need to link this contrast with the name of Posidonius, as used to be the *opinio communis*.

From a macrostructural perspective, from Book 2 onward Aëtius is bent on following an order that goes from the periphery to the center, not only in the treatise as a whole but also in the present book: from the highest atmospheric phenomenon of the Milky Way via comets (ch. 2), thunder and lightning (3), clouds (4), rainbow (5), rods (6), winds (7), and summer and winter (8) to a cluster of chapters dealing with the earth and the sea. Because of this arrangement, all the issues concerned with the earth, even those regarding its position and behavior as a cosmic body, are treated in Book 3 after those in the atmosphere. Here Aëtius differs from the treatment of these topics by Aristotle. In Aristotle's *On the Heavens*, the earth (*Cael.* 2.13) is part of the cosmic system, like the sun and the moon. In the *Placita* the issues raised by Aristotle regarding the earth have been interposed between the treatment of winds and of earthquakes, both subjects treated at length in Aristotle's *Meteorology*. The macrostructure of Book 3 is thus the outcome of a rearrangement of the Aristotelian template, or templates. That this did not have to be the case is clear from Seneca's different approach in the *Naturales quaestiones* and from other parallels. We note further that the section on the earth (chs. 9–15) presents topics following the succession of the Aristotelian categories (compare the parallel sections on the stars, sun, and moon in Book 2 and on the soul in Book 4), namely, quantity and substance (9, note the inverted order), quality (10), place (11), position (12), action/passion (13), quantity again (14), and action/passion again (15).

Name-Labels

The name-labels in Book 3 differ in several respects from what is found elsewhere. For chapters 1 to 15 they denote philosophers exclusively, but chapter 16 includes the Sophist Antiphon (who dabbled in natural philosophy), and in chapter 17, on the tides, we encounter no less than five nonphilosophers: Pytheas, Timaeus, Crates, Apollodorus, and Seleucus.[2] It is also worth pointing out that in this book there are a number of philosophers whose views are proportionately more frequently included than elsewhere: Metrodorus (nine doxai), Anaxagoras (eight), Anaximenes (six), Anaximander (four), and Heraclides (three). Conversely, other philosophers are underrepresented: Plato (only two), Empedocles (three), Pythagoras (one), and Heraclitus (one). The number of multiple name-labels is also the lowest of all the books.

When the ordering of the sequence of name-labels in each chapter is examined, it emerges that Book 3 is the most historical of all the books. Not surprisingly, it also appears to be the least dialectical, so contrasts strongly with Book 2, where these two positions are reversed.[3] Nevertheless, it would be a mistake to think that dialectical considerations do not play an important role, as can be

[2] A comparable lineup of nonphilosophers is found only in 4.1, which likewise treats a subject not dealt with by Aristotle. See further the Introduction to Book 4. For these philosophers, see the Index of Names.

[3] For the relevant statistics underlying these conclusions, see Jeremiah, "Statistical Explorations," 301, 314–25, and 335.

seen from our introductory notices for each chapter in the translation. Successions play a minor role but are evident in the placement of Thales first in chapters 9, 10, 11, and 15, while Pythagoras or Pythagoreans obtain first position in 1, 2, and 14.

Comparative Material

For most of the book, but not for chapters 8, 9, and 12, there is plentiful comparative material to be found in the proximate and the wider doxographical traditions.[4] Among the more valuable texts are Lucretius' *De rerum natura*, Books 5–6; Seneca's *Naturales quaestiones*; Strabo; Manilius; Ps.-Aristotle's *De mundo*; Pliny the Elder; the physical fragments of Arrian; Diogenes Laertius; the Aratean scholia; and Achilles (only chs. 32–34). The similarities in macrostructure between Lucretius and Aëtius cannot be coincidental. However, whether his master Epicurus himself, in enumerating possible causes of meteorological phenomena, made use of an early form of the *Placita* cannot be proven but is certainly not impossible.[5]

Ultimate Sources

For the ultimate sources of much of the material contained in the book, we must go back to the Peripatos and think of the otherwise lost sources used and cited by Aristotle, Theophrastus, and their predecessors. The highly influential *Meteorology* of Aristotle together with chapter

[4] On these traditions, see further the General Introduction 1.5.
[5] On the question, see Runia, "Epicurus," 409–11.

2.13 of the *De caelo* have already been mentioned. Some material may go back directly to these works, but use may also have been made of later epitomai. Important parallels for the meteorological section and on earthquakes are found in the *Metarsiology* of Theophrastus, though its attribution has been questioned.[6] This work uses the method of diaeresis and question types extensively, but it is strikingly devoid of any name-labels. Later Hellenistic sources are used only sparsely, except for chapter 17, on tides, which treats a subject that emerged only after Aristotle. In general, updating is rather rare. It is telling that the name-label of Posidonius is only found twice, in chapters 1 and 17.

[6] German version of the Arabic translation in Daiber, "The *Meteorology* of Theophrastus." Doubts regarding the attribution to Theophrastus are voiced by Bakker, *Epicurean Meteorology*, but not shared by us.

⟨TITLE⟩[1]

ΑΕΤΙΟΥ ΠΕΡΙ ΤΩΝ ΑΡΕΣΚΟΝΤΩΝ
ΤΟ Γ´,[2] |

ἐν ᾧ κεφάλαια τάδε· |

⟨Index⟩

Ps.-Plut. *Plac.*

¹ Ps.-Plut. *Plac.* 3; Theod. *Cur.* 4.31, cf. 2.95, 5.16

² tit. T: Περὶ τῶν ἀρεσκόντων φιλοσόφοις φυσικῶν δογμάτων ἐν ἐπιτομῇ τὸ γ´ P

³ hic transpos. de loco ultimo MR (= 3.18 in ed. Diels)

AETIUS
ON THE PLACITA

BOOK III

in which the following chapter headings are found:[1]

[1] On the title and the list of chapter headings, or pinax, see above on Book 1 and the General Introduction 1.3.

[2] In Ps.-Plutarch this chapter has been misplaced as 3.18.

<Procemium>

Ps.-Plut. *Plac.*

περιοδευκὼς ἐν τοῖς προτέροις ἐν ἐπιτομῇ τὸν περὶ
τῶν οὐρανίων | λόγον, σελήνη δ᾽ αὐτῶν τὸ μεθόριον,
τρέψομαι ἐν τῷ τρίτῳ πρὸς τὰ | μετάρσια· ταῦτα δ᾽
ἐστὶ τὰ ἀπὸ τοῦ κύκλου τῆς σελήνης καθήκοντα | μέ-
χρι πρὸς τὴν θέσιν τῆς γῆς, ἥντινα κέντρου τάξιν
5 ἐπέχειν τῇ περιοχῇ | τῆς σφαίρας νενομίκασιν. ἄρξο-
μαι δ᾽ ἐντεῦθεν. (P) |

246

BOOK III: METEOROLOGY AND THE EARTH

⟨Proœmium⟩

Transition from the ourania *set out in Book 2 to the* metarsia *and* prosgeia, *starting with the Milky Way.*

Ps.-Plutarch, *Tenets*

Having in the previous books systematically and by way of an epitome gone through the account of the things in the heavens—of which the moon is the boundary—, I shall turn in the third book to the things on high. These are situated from the orbit of the moon down to the position of the earth, which they (sc. the natural philosophers) believe to occupy the place of the center in the circumference of the sphere. I shall begin from there.   5

3.1

Ps.-Plut. *Plac.* 3.1 (+ Ps.-Gal. *Hist. phil.* 74); Stob. *Ecl.* 1.27.1–8

α΄. Περὶ τοῦ γαλαξίου κύκλου (PS) |

1. κύκλος ἐστὶ νεφελοειδὴς ἐν μὲν τῷ ἀέρι διὰ παντὸς φαινόμενος, διὰ δὲ | τὴν λευκόχροιαν γαλαξίας ὀνομαζόμενος. (PS) |

2. τῶν Πυθαγορείων οἱ μὲν ἔφασαν ἀστέρος εἶναι διά-
5 καυσιν, ἐκπεσόντος | μὲν ἀπὸ τῆς ἰδίας ἕδρας, δι᾽ οὗ δὲ ἐπέδραμε χωρίου κυκλοτερῶς αὐτὸ | καταφλέξαντος ἐπὶ τοῦ κατὰ Φαέθοντα ἐμπρησμοῦ· (PS) |

3. οἱ δὲ τὸν ἡλιακὸν ταύτῃ φασὶ κατ᾽ ἀρχὰς γεγονέναι δρόμον. (S) |

4. τινὲς δὲ κατοπτρικὴν εἶναι φαντασίαν τοῦ ἡλίου τὰς αὐγὰς πρὸς τὸν | οὐρανὸν ἀνακλῶντος, ὅπερ καὶ
10 ἐπὶ τῆς ἴριδος καὶ ἐπὶ τῶν νεφῶν | συμβαίνει. (S) |

5. Μητρόδωρος διὰ τὴν πάροδον τοῦ ἡλίου· τοῦτον γὰρ εἶναι τὸν ἡλιακὸν | κύκλον. (PS) |

§1 — §§2–4 Pythagoreans B.37c §3 cf. Oenopides
41.10 §4 cf. Hippocrates 42.6 §5 Metrodorus A13

3.1

A nominal definition is placed at the beginning. The principal diaphonia pertains to the Milky Way qua physical phenomenon, as opposed to the view that it is an optical illusion.

Ps.-Plutarch, *Tenets* (+ Ps.-Galen, *Philosophical History*); Stobaeus, *Anthology*

1. On the circle of the Milky Way

1. It is a cloud-like circle in the air, continually visible, called Milky Way because of its white color.

2. Some of the Pythagoreans said that it is the result of the scorching by a heavenly body that departed from its proper 5 setting and set alight the region through which it moved in a circle at the time of the conflagration caused by Phaethon.[3]

3. But other Pythagoreans said that originally the sun's orbit followed this route.

4. Some say,[4] however, that it is an appearance, as in a mirror, of the sun, which bends back [i.e., reflects] its rays against the heaven, just as what happens both in the case of the rainbow and of the clouds. 10

5. Metrodorus says that it occurred through the passage of the sun, for this is the circle that the sun makes.

---

[3] A rare mythical reference is included among the scientific explanations.

[4] That is, the mathematician Hippocrates of Chios, believed to be a Pythagorean.

6. Παρμενίδης τὸ τοῦ πυκνοῦ καὶ ἀραιοῦ μῖγμα γα-
λακτοειδὲς ἀποτελέσαι ǀ χρῶμα. (PS) ǀ

15 7. Ἀναξαγόρας τὴν σκιὰν τῆς γῆς κατὰ τοῦτο τὸ
μέρος ἵστασθαι τοῦ ǀ οὐρανοῦ, ὅταν ὑπὸ τὴν γῆν ὁ
ἥλιος γινόμενος μὴ πάντα φωτίζῃ. (PS) ǀ

8. Δημόκριτος πολλῶν καὶ μικρῶν καὶ συνεχῶν ἀστέρων συμφωτιζομένων ǀ ἀλλήλοις συναυγασμὸν διὰ
τὴν πύκνωσιν. (PS) ǀ

9. Ἀριστοτέλης ἀναθυμιάσεως ξηρᾶς ἔξαψιν πολλῆς
20 τε καὶ συνεχοῦς· καὶ ǀ οὕτω κόμην πυρὸς ὑπὸ τὸν
αἰθέρα κατωτέρω τῶν πλανητῶν. (PS) ǀ

10. οἱ Στωικοὶ τοῦ αἰθερίου πυρὸς ἀραιότητα ἀνώτε-
ρον τῶν πλανητῶν. ǀ (G) ǀ

11. Ποσειδώνιος πυρὸς σύστασιν, ἄστρου μὲν μανώτεραν,[4] αὐγῆς δὲ ǀ πυκνοτέραν.[5] (PS) ǀ

§6 Parmenides A43a
§7 Anaxagoras A80
§8 Democritus A91
§9 Aristotle cf. *Mete*. 1.8 345b31–346b6
§10 Stoics —
§11 Posidonius F129

[4] μανώτεραν S: μανώτερον MR, λαμπρότερον P
[5] πυκνότεραν S: πυκνότερον P, MR

6. Parmenides says that the whitish color is the result of the mixture of the dense and the rare element.

7. Anaxagoras says that the shadow of the earth rests upon   15
this section of the heaven [i.e., where the Milky Way is visible], when the sun, having arrived under the earth, no longer illuminates everything.

8. Democritus says it is the combined illumination of numerous and small and contiguous stars giving off light together because of their density.

9. Aristotle says it is an ignition of a large and continuous portion of the dry exhalation; thus we have a head of hair   20
[i.e., the tail of a comet] consisting of fire, underneath the ether and lower than the planets.

10. The Stoics say it is a loose-textured form of the etherial fire, higher than the planets.[5]

11. Posidonius says it is a solid structure, consisting of a fire, that is rarer than a star but denser than a bright light.

[5] Unusually, this lemma is preserved only in Ps-Galen.

3.2

§§1–9 are about comets, §§10–11 about shooting stars.
The principal diaphonia of §§1–9 is between comets, as
real and as phenomenal or illusory. §§10–11 apply this to

Ps.-Plut. *Plac.* 3.2 (+ Ps.-Gal. *Hist. phil.* 75); Stob. *Ecl.*
1.28.1a

β′. Περὶ κομητῶν καὶ διᾳττόντων καὶ δοκίδων (PS) |

1. τῶν ἀπὸ Πυθαγόρου τινὲς μὲν ἀστέρα φασὶν εἶναι
τὸν κομήτην τῶν οὐκ | ἀεὶ φαινομένων, διά τινος δ᾽
ὡρισμένου χρόνου περιοδικῶς ἀνατελλόντων. | (PS) |

5 2. ἄλλοι δ᾽ ἀνάκλασιν τῆς ἡμετέρας ὄψεως πρὸς
τὸν ἥλιον, παραπλησίαν | ταῖς κατοπτρικαῖς ἐμφάσε-
σιν. (PS) |

3. Ἀναξαγόρας Δημόκριτος σύνοδον ἀστέρων δυοῖν ἢ
καὶ πλειόνων κατὰ | συναυγασμόν. (PS) |

4. Ἀριστοτέλης τῆς ξηρᾶς ἐκ γῆς ἀναθυμιάσεως διά-
10 πυρον σύστασιν. | (PS) |

5. Στράτων ἄστρου φῶς περιληφθὲν νέφει πυκνῷ,
καθάπερ ἐπὶ τῶν | λαμπτήρων γίνεται. (PS) |

§§1–2 Pythagoreans —
§3 Anaxagoras A81; Democritus —
§4 Aristotle cf. *Mete.* 1.7 344a8–15
§5 Strato fr. 51

3.2

shooting stars; §§5–6 present compromise views; §12 is
about all these phenomena together as real.

Ps.-Plutarch, *Tenets* (+ Ps.-Galen, *Philosophical History*);
Stobaeus, *Anthology*

2. On comets and shooting stars and beams

1. Some of the successors of Pythagoras say that the comet
is one of those stars that are not always visible, but at a
certain time they periodically appear above the horizon.
2. But other successors of Pythagoras say that it is the re-   5
flection of our vision upon the sun, similar to the images
that are reflected in mirrors.
3. Anaxagoras and Democritus say that it is a conjunction
of two or even more stars through their giving off light
together.
4. Aristotle says that it is a fiery structure consisting of the
dry exhalation from the earth.   10
5. Strato says that it is the light of a star enclosed in a
compact cloud, as is the case with fire in lanterns.

6. Ἡρακλείδης ὁ Ποντικὸς νέφος μετάρσιον ὑπὸ μετ-
αρσίου φωτὸς καταυγαζόμενον. | ὁμοίως δ' αἰτιολογεῖ
15 πωγωνίαν ἅλω δοκίδα κίονα καὶ τὰ | συγγενῆ τούτοις,
καθάπερ ἀμέλει πάντες οἱ Περιπατητικοί, παρὰ τοὺς
| τοῦ νέφους ταυτὶ γίνεσθαι σχηματισμούς. (PS) |
7. Ἐπιγένης πνεύματος ἀναφορὰν γεωμιγοῦς πεπυρω-
μένου. (PS) |
8. Βόηθος ἀέρος ἀνημμένου φαντασίαν. (PS) |
9. Διογένης ἀστέρας εἶναι τοὺς κομήτας. (PS) |
20 10. Ἀναξαγόρας τοὺς καλουμένους διάττοντας καὶ
ἅπτοντας ἀπὸ τοῦ | αἰθέρος σπινθήρων δίκην κατα-
φέρεσθαι· διὸ καὶ παραυτίκα σβέννυσθαι. | (PS) |
11. Μητρόδωρος τὴν εἰς τὰ νέφη τοῦ ἡλίου βιαίαν
ἔμπτωσιν ὡς βέλος | πολλάκις σπινθηρίζειν. (PS) |
25 12. Ξενοφάνης πάντα τὰ τοιαῦτα νεφῶν πεπυρωμένων
συστήματα ἢ | κινήματα. (PS) |

§6 Heraclides fr. 77
§7 Epigenes —
§8 Boethus fr. 9
§9 Diogenes T30 Laks
§10 Anaxagoras A82
§11 Metrodorus A14
§12 Xenophanes A44

6. Heraclides of Pontus says that it is a cloud high in the sky illuminated by a light high in the sky. He provides the same causal explanation for bearded star, halo, beam, pillar, and their ilk, just as of course all the Peripatetics do, 15 namely that these phenomena arise in accordance with the configurations of the clouds.

7. Epigenes says that it is the ascent of inflamed *pneuma* mixed with earth.

8. Boethus says that it is an appearance of ignited air.

9. Diogenes says that the comets are stars.

10. Anaxagoras says that the phenomena called shooting 20 stars fall down from the ether and are kindled like sparks, which is why they are also immediately extinguished.

11. Metrodorus says that a violent immission into the clouds of the light of the sun in the manner of a projectile often causes the emission of sparks.

12. Xenophanes says that all these phenomena are combi- 25 nations or movements of ignited clouds.

3.3

*The chapter utilizes the question type of cause and the
category of substance. Thunder is mentioned nine times,
with lightning as an epiphenomenon; the thunderbolt and
prestêr (firewind) seven times; and the typhoon three*

Ps.-Plut. *Plac.* 3.3 (+ Ps.-Gal. *Hist. phil.* 76); Stob. *Ecl.*
1.29

γ΄. Περὶ βροντῶν ἀστραπῶν κεραυνῶν πρηστήρων
τε καὶ τυφώνων | (PS) |

1. Ἀναξίμανδρος ἐκ τοῦ πνεύματος ταυτὶ πάντα συμ-
βαίνειν· ὅταν γὰρ | περιληφθὲν νέφει παχεῖ βιασάμε-
5 νον ἐκπέσῃ τῇ λεπτομερείᾳ καὶ | κουφότητι, τόθ᾽ ἡ μὲν
ῥῆξις τὸν ψόφον, ἡ δὲ διαστολὴ παρὰ τὴν | μελανείαν
τοῦ νέφους τὸν διαυγασμὸν ἀποτελεῖ. (PS) |
2. Ἀναξιμένης ταὐτὰ τούτῳ παρατιθεὶς τὸ ἐπὶ τῆς
θαλάσσης, ἥτις | σχιζομένη ταῖς κώπαις παραστίλ-
βει. (S) |
3. Μητρόδωρος ὅταν εἰς νέφος πεπηγὸς ὑπὸ πυκνότη-
10 τος ἐμπέσῃ πνεῦμα, | τῇ μὲν συνθραύσει τὸν κτύπον
ἀποτελεῖ, τῇ δὲ πληγῇ καὶ τῷ σχισμῷ | διαυγάζει, τῇ
δ᾽ ὀξύτητι τῆς φορᾶς προσλαμβάνον τὴν ἀπὸ τοῦ

§1 Anaximander A23
§2 Anaximenes A17
§3 Metrodorus A15

256

times. The division on a gliding scale in §§1–12 mostly explains thunder by the interaction of external factors and clouds, while §13–§14 offer other though similar explanations.

Ps.-Plutarch, *Tenets* (+ Ps.-Galen, *Philosophical History*); Stobaeus, *Anthology*

3. On thunders, lightnings, thunderbolts, firewinds, and typhoons

1. Anaximander says that all these (sc. five) result from the *pneuma*. For when air surrounded by a thick cloud bursts out, having forced its way owing to its being constituted of small particles and to its lightness, then the breaking forth 5 produces the noise, and the contrast with the blackness of the cloud the piercing brightness.

2. Anaximenes agrees with him, citing in addition what occurs in the case of the sea, which flashes when split by the oars.[6]

3. Metrodorus says that when *pneuma* falls upon a cloud that has become frozen through its density, it produces the 10 noise by breaking it up, flashes through the impact and the splitting, and throws off a thunderbolt through the velocity

---

[6] §2 and §5: such appeals to common experience are a feature of meteorological theorizing, as also often found in Aristotle's *Meteorology*.

ἡλίου | θερμότητα κεραυνοβολεῖ· τοῦ δὲ κεραυνοῦ τὴν
ἀσθένειαν εἰς πρηστῆρα | περιίστησιν. (PS) |

4. Ἀναξαγόρας, ὅταν τὸ θερμὸν εἰς τὸ ψυχρὸν ἐμ-
15 πέσῃ (τοῦτο δ᾽ ἐστὶν | αἰθέριον μέρος εἰς ἀερῶδες) τῷ
μὲν ψόφῳ τὴν βροντὴν ἀποτελεῖ, τῷ δὲ | παρὰ τὴν
μελανείαν τοῦ νέφους χρώματι τὴν ἀστραπήν· τῷ δὲ
πλήθει | καὶ μεγέθει τοῦ φωτὸς τὸν κεραυνόν· τῷ δὲ
πολυσωματωτέρῳ πυρὶ τὸν | τυφῶνα· τῷ δὲ νεφελομι-
γεῖ τὸν πρηστῆρα. (PS) |

5. Ἀρχέλαος ταὐτὸ[6] λέγει παρατιθεὶς τὸ τῶν διαπύρων
20 λίθων καθιεμένων | εἰς ψυχρὸν ὕδωρ πάθος. (S) |

6. Ξενοφάνης ἀστραπὰς γίνεσθαι λαμπρυνομένων
τῶν νεφῶν κατὰ τὴν | κίνησιν. (S) |

7. Ἐμπεδοκλῆς ἔμπτωσιν φωτὸς εἰς νέφος ἐξείργον-
τος τὸν ἀνθεστῶτα | ἀέρα, οὗ τὴν μὲν σβέσιν καὶ
25 τὴν θραῦσιν κτύπον ἀπεργάζεσθαι, τὴν δὲ | λάμψιν
ἀστραπήν, κεραυνὸν δὲ τὸν τῆς ἀστραπῆς τόνον. (S) |

8. Διογένης ἔμπτωσιν[7] πυρὸς εἰς νέφος ὑγρόν βρον-
τὴν μὲν τῇ σβέσει | ποιοῦντος,[8] τῇ δὲ λαμπηδόνι τὴν
ἀστραπήν. συναιτιᾶται δὲ καὶ τὸ πνεῦμα. | (S) |

9. Ἡράκλειτος βροντὴν μὲν κατὰ συστροφὰς ἀνέμων

§4 Anaxagoras A84   §5 Archelaus A16
§6 Xenophanes A45   §7 Empedocles A63
§8 Diogenes A16   §9 Heraclitus A14

[6] ταὐτὸ corr. Meineke: τοῦτο S
[7] ἔμπτωσιν corr. Canter: ἐμπύρωσιν S
[8] ποιοῦντος Natorp: ποιοῦν S

of its movement, also making use of the sun's heat. But if the resultant thunderbolt is weak, it converts it into a firewind (*prêstêr*).[7]

4. Anaxagoras says that when the hot falls onto the cold (that is, an etherial portion onto an air-like one), it produces thunder by its noise and lightning by its color as set off against the blackness of the cloud; by the mass and size of its light it produces the thunderbolt; by fire containing a greater multitude of corpuscles the *typhôn*;[8] by fire mingled with a cloud the firewind.

5. Archelaus says the same, citing the effect of inflamed stones being submerged in cold water.

6. Xenophanes says that lightning arises when clouds start to shine forth because of their movement.

7. Empedocles says there is light falling upon a cloud, which shuts out the resisting air. Its quenching and destruction produce the crash and its flash the lightning. The thunderbolt is the lightning's intensity.

8. Diogenes says there is fire falling upon a wet cloud. By its quenching it produces thunder, by its flashing lightning. He also adduces the *pneuma* as an accessory cause.

9. Heraclitus says that thunder results from gatherings of

---

[7] It is not clear what the phenomena are that are indicated by the terms *prêstêr* and *typhôn*; possible renderings are firewind, whirlwind, hurricane, waterspout.

[8] See previous note.

AETIUS

30 καὶ νεφῶν καὶ | ἐμπτώσεις πνευμάτων εἰς τὰ νέφη,
ἀστραπὰς δὲ κατὰ τὰς τῶν ⟨ἀνα⟩θυμιωμένων⁹ | ἐξ-
άψεις, πρηστῆρας δὲ κατὰ νεφῶν ἐμπρήσεις καὶ σβέ-
σεις. | (S) |

10. Λεύκιππος πυρὸς ἐναποληφθέντος¹⁰ νέφεσι παχυ-
τάτοις ἔκπτωσιν | ἰσχυρὰν βροντὴν ἀποτελεῖν ἀπο-
φαίνεται. (S) |

35 11. Δημόκριτος βροντὴν μὲν ἐκ συγκρίματος ἀνω-
μάλου, τὸ περιειληφὸς | αὐτὸ νέφος πρὸς τὴν κάτω
φορὰν ἐκβιαζομένου· ἀστραπὴν δὲ σύγκρουσιν¹¹ | νε-
φῶν, ὑφ᾽ ἧς τὰ γεννητικὰ τοῦ πυρὸς διὰ τῶν πολυ-
κένων | ἀραιωμάτων ταῖς παρατρίψεσιν εἰς τὸ αὐτὸ
συναλιζόμενα διηθεῖται· | κεραυνὸν δὲ ὅταν ἐκ καθα-
40 ρωτέρων καὶ λεπτοτέρων, ὁμαλωτέρων τε καὶ | "πυκ-
ναρμόνων," καθάπερ αὐτὸς γράφει, γεννητικῶν τοῦ
πυρὸς ἡ φορὰ | βιάσηται·¹² πρηστῆρα δ᾽, ὅταν πολυ-
κενώτερα συγκρίματα πυρὸς ἐν | πολυκένοις κατασχε-
θέντα χώραις καὶ περιοχαῖς ὑμένων ἰδίων | σωματο-
ποιούμενα τῷ πολυμιγεῖ τὴν ἐπὶ τὸ βάρος ὁρμὴν
λάβῃ. (S) |

12. Χρύσιππος ἀστραπὴν ἔξαψιν νεφῶν ἐκτριβομένων
45 ἢ ῥηγνυμένων ὑπὸ | πνεύματος, βροντὴν δ᾽ εἶναι τὸν
τούτων ψόφον· ἅμα δὲ γίνεσθαι ἐν τῷ | ἀέρι βροντήν
τε καὶ ἀστραπήν, πρότερον δὲ τῆς ἀστραπῆς ἀντι-
λαμβάνεσθαι | ἡμᾶς διὰ τὸ τῆς ἀκοῆς ὀξυτέραν εἶναι

§10 Leucippus A25   §11 Democritus A93
§12 Chrysippus 2.703

260

winds and clouds and from impacts of *pneumata* upon the   30
clouds, lightnings when what is evaporated catches fire,
and firewinds through the burnings and quenchings of
clouds.

10. Leucippus says that the powerful emission of fire cut
off inside very dense clouds produces thunder.

11. Democritus says that thunder results from a com-   35
pound of uneven composition, which forces its way out
of the cloud containing it in a downward motion. Lightning is a collision of clouds because of which the fire-
engendering particles are filtered through their quite
empty interstices and are pushed through together while
rubbing against each other. A thunderbolt arises occurs
whenever there is a forcing of the motion of fire-
engendering particles that are purer and finer, more even
and "close-fitted," as he himself writes. A firewind arises   40
whenever compounds of fire containing much void, de-
tained in quite empty places, assume a bodily form in the
envelopes of their own membranes, and being composed
of many ingredients acquire an impulse toward heaviness.

12. Chrysippus says lightning is the ignition of clouds being rubbed and ruptured by *pneuma*, and thunder is the   45
sound of these. Thunder and lightning both arise in the air
at the same time, but we apprehend the lightning sooner
on account of vision being sharper than hearing. When-

---

9 ⟨ἀνα⟩θυμιωμένων corr. Schuster
10 ἐναποληφθέντος corr. Canter, -λειφθέντος S
11 σύγκρουσιν corr. Diels: σύγκρασιν S
12 βιάσηται corr. Gaisford: βιώσηται S

τὴν ὅρασιν· ὅταν δ' ἡ τοῦ | πνεύματος φορὰ σφοδρο-
τέρα γένηται καὶ πυρώδης, κεραυνὸν ἀποτελεῖσθαι· |
ὅταν δὲ ἄθρουν ἐκπέσῃ τὸ πνεῦμα καὶ ἧττον πεπυρω-
50 μένον, πρηστῆρα | γίγνεσθαι, ὅταν δ' ἔτι ἧττον ᾖ πε-
πυρωμένον τὸ πνεῦμα, τυφῶνα. | (S) |

13. Ἀριστοτέλης ἐξ ἀναθυμιάσεως καὶ τὰ τοιαῦτα γί-
νεσθαι τῆς ξηρᾶς· ὅταν | οὖν ἐντύχῃ μὲν τῇ ὑγρᾷ,
παραβιάζηται δὲ τὴν ἔξοδον, τῇ μὲν | παρατρίψει καὶ
τῇ ῥήξει τὸν ψόφον τῆς βροντῆς γίνεσθαι, τῇ δ' ἐξ-
55 άψει | τῆς ξηρότητος τὴν ἀστραπὴν παρίστησι. (PS) |

14. Στράτων θερμοῦ ψυχρῷ παρείξαντος, ὅταν ἐκβια-
σθὲν τύχῃ, τὰ τοιαῦτα | γίνεσθαι, βροντὴν μὲν ἀπορ-
ρήξει, φάει δ' ἀστραπήν, τάχει δὲ κεραυνόν,[13] | πρη-
στῆρας δὲ καὶ τυφῶνας τῷ πλεονασμῷ τῷ τῆς ὕλης,
ἣν ἑκάτερος | αὐτῶν ἐφέλκεται, θερμοτέραν μὲν ὁ πρη-
60 στήρ, παχυτέραν δὲ ὁ τυφών. | (PS) |

15. οἱ Στωικοὶ βροντὴν μὲν προσκρουσμὸν νεφῶν,
ἀστραπὴν δὲ ἔξαψιν ἐκ | παρατρίψεως, κεραυνὸν δὲ
σφοδροτέραν ἔκλαμψιν, πρηστῆρα δὲ | νωθεστέ-
ραν. (PS) |

§13 Aristotle cf. *Mete.* 2.9 369a10–b11
§14 Strato fr. 52
§15 Stoics 2.705

13 Στράτων . . . κεραυνόν S: om. P qui add. ll. 58–59 πρηστῆρας . . . τυφών post l. 55 nomine Stratonis omisso

262

ever the *pneuma*'s motion becomes stronger and fiery, a thunderbolt is produced; whenever the *pneuma* escapes all together and is less inflamed, a firewind arises; and 50 whenever the *pneuma* is even less inflamed, a *typhôn*.

13. Aristotle says that such things too result from the dry exhalation. When it encounters the moist exhalation, it forces its way out, and the noise of the thunder is produced by the friction and the bursting, while the ignition of the 55 dry ingredient brings about the lightning flash.

14. Strato says that such things occur whenever hot yields to cold, when it happens that it is forced out: thunder occurs through the bursting out, the lightning flash through the light, the thunderbolt through the speed, and firewinds and *typhônes* through the excessive quantity of matter that each of them draws to itself, hotter matter in the case of the firewind, denser in that of the *typhôn*. 60

15. The Stoics say that thunder is a collision of clouds, lightning an ignition through friction, thunderbolt a stronger flash, and firewind a slower one.

Ps.-Plut. *Plac.* 3.4 (+ Ps.-Gal. *Hist. phil.* 77); Stob. *Ecl.* 1.31.1–5

δ′. Περὶ νεφῶν ὁμίχλης ὑετῶν δρόσου χιόνος πάχνης χαλάζης (PS) |

1. Ἀναξιμένης νέφη μὲν γίνεσθαι παχυνθέντος ἐπὶ πλεῖον τοῦ ἀέρος, | μᾶλλον δ᾽ ἐπισυναχθέντος ἐκθλί-βεσθαι τοὺς ὄμβρους, χιόνα δέ, | ἐπειδὰν τὸ κατα-φερόμενον ὕδωρ παγῇ, χάλαζαν δ᾽ ὅταν συμπερι-
5 ληφθῇ | τι τῷ ὑγρῷ πνευματικόν. (PS) |
2. Ἀναξαγόρας νέφη μὲν καὶ χιόνα παραπλησίως, χάλαζαν δ᾽ ὅταν ἀπὸ | τῶν παγέντων νεφῶν προωσθῇ τινα πρὸς τὴν γῆν, ἃ δὴ ταῖς καταφοραῖς | ἀποψυχό-μενα[14] στρογγυλοῦται. (S) |
3. Μητρόδωρος ἀπὸ τῆς ὑδατώδους ἀναφορᾶς ὑπὸ τοῦ
10 ἀέρος συνίστασθαι | τὰ νέφη. (PS) |

§1 Anaximenes A17   §2 Anaxagoras A85
§3 Metrodorus A16

14 ἀποψυχόμενα coni. MR² (-ούμενα MR per errorem): ἀπο-ψυχρούμενα S

3.4

The chapter utilizes the question type of cause and the category of substance, cf. 3.3. The key term is clouds, the diaeretic structure depends on the matter from which they are formed.

Ps.-Plutarch, *Tenets* (+ Ps.-Galen, *Philosophical History*); Stobaeus, *Anthology*

4. On clouds, mist, rains, dew, snow, hoar frost, hail

1. Anaximenes says that clouds occur when air becomes more condensed, and that the rains are squeezed out when it becomes even more compacted; and hail occurs when water freezes during its downward course, and snow when a pneumatic ingredient is amalgamated with the moisture.[9] 5

2. Anaxagoras says that clouds and snow occur similarly (sc. as according to Anaximenes), but that hail is formed whenever some particles are ejected from the frozen clouds toward the earth, which form into balls as they become cold in their downward movement.

3. Metrodorus says that clouds are formed by the air from the watery updraft. 10

---

[9] As Diels saw, "snow" and "hail" have been swapped around in the text. But since the witnesses agree, the mistake must have been present in Aëtius' text, so it should be retained.

4. Ξενοφάνης ἀπὸ τῆς τοῦ ἡλίου θερμότητος ὡς ‹προ-
κατ›αρκτικῆς[15] αἰτίας | τὰν τοῖς μεταρσίοις συμβαί-
νειν· ἀνελκομένου γὰρ ἐκ τῆς θαλάττης τοῦ | ὑγροῦ τὸ
γλυκὺ διὰ τὴν λεπτομέρειαν διακρινόμενον νέφη τε
συνιστάνειν | ὁμιχλούμενον καὶ καταστάζειν ὄμβρους
15 ὑπὸ πιλήσεως καὶ | διατμίζειν τὰ πνεύματα. γράφει
γὰρ διαρρήδην "πηγὴ δ᾽ ἐστὶ θάλασσ᾽ | ὕδατος." (S) |
5. Ἐπίκουρος ἀπὸ τῶν ἀτόμων· στρογγυλαίνεσθαι δὲ
τὴν χάλαζαν καὶ τὸν | ὑετὸν ἀπὸ τῆς μακρᾶς κατα-
φορᾶς ὑποπεπλασμένον. (PS) |
6. *** καὶ πνεῦμα μὲν ἀποτελεῖν παρῶσαν τὰ νέφη,
20 ὄμβρους δὲ διαχέαν, | χάλαζαν δὲ πιλῆσαν, χιόνα δὲ
συμπεριλαβόμενόν τι τοῦ ἀερώδους. (S) |

§4 Xenophanes A46, B30.1
§5 Epicurus fr. 349
§6 —

15 ‹προκατ›αρκτικῆς coni. MR

4. Xenophanes says that atmospheric phenomena result from the heat of the sun as the preliminary cause. For when moisture is drawn up from the sea and its fresh part is separated off because of its fine-grained consistency, clouds accumulate as it becomes misty, rain is shed owing to condensation, and winds arise owing to evaporation. For he writes explicitly that "source of water is the sea."

5. Epicurus says that they accumulate from atoms; and that hail is formed in round shapes and rain gradually acquires its form in its lengthy descent.

6. *** and that it (?) produces a *pneuma* by pushing the clouds to one side, rain by liquefying them, hail by compressing them, and snow by incorporating a bit of airy substance.[10]

[10] This mutilated doxa cannot be plausibly attributed.

3.5

§§1–6 form a minitreatise, with (Aristotle's) doctrine remaining anonymous; §§7–9 are standard placita. *There is a clear diaphonia between (Aristotle's) view that the visual*

Ps.-Plut. *Plac.* 3.5 (+ Ps.-Gal. *Hist. phil.* 78); Stob. *Ecl.* 1.30.1a

ε'. Περὶ ἴριδος (PS) |

1. Τῶν μεταρσίων παθῶν τὰ μὲν καθ' ὑπόστασιν γίνεται οἷον ὄμβρος | χάλαζα, τὰ δὲ κατ' ἔμφασιν ἰδίαν οὐκ ἔχοντα ὑπόστασιν· αὐτίκα γοῦν | πλεόντων ἡμῶν ἡ ἤπειρος κινεῖσθαι δοκεῖ· ἔστιν οὖν κατ' ἔμφασιν ἡ
5 ἶρις. | (PS) |
2. Πλάτων φησὶ Θαύμαντος αὐτὴν γενεαλογῆσαι τοὺς ἀνθρώπους διὰ τὸ | θαυμάσαι ταύτην. Ὅμηρος "ἠύτε πορφυρέην ἶριν θνητοῖσι τανύσσει." διὸ | καὶ ἐμυθεύσαντό τινες αὐτὴν ταύρου κεφαλὴν ἔχουσαν ἀναρροφεῖν τοὺς | ποταμούς. (PS) |
10 3. πῶς οὖν γίνεται ἶρις; ὁρῶμεν δὴ κατὰ γραμμὰς ἢ κατ' εὐθείας ἢ κατὰ | καμπύλας ἢ κατ' ἀνακλωμένας, γραμμὰς ἀδήλους λόγῳ θεωρητὰς καὶ | ἀσωμάτους. κατὰ μὲν οὖν εὐθείας ὁρῶμεν τὰ ἐν ἀέρι καὶ τὰ διὰ τῶν | λίθων τῶν διαυγῶν καὶ κεράτων· λεπτομερῆ γὰρ

§1 —   §2 Plato *Tht.* 155d; Homer *Il.* 17.547
§3 —

3.5

rays are reflected from the droplets to the sun and §§7–8
that the light of the sun is reflected to our eyes via a cloud.
§9 is an additional (or stray) comment and so is placed last.

Ps.-Plutarch, *Tenets* (+ Ps.-Galen, *Philosophical History*);
Stobaeus, *Anthology*

5. On the rainbow

1. Meteorological phenomena are of two sorts. Some, such
as rain and hail, have a real subsistence, others exist only
in appearance and do not have a separate subsistence. To
give an example: when we are sailing, the land appears to
be in motion. Well then, the rainbow exists in appearance
only.   5
2. Plato says that human beings provided the rainbow with
a descent from Thaumas, because they admired (*thauma-
sai*) it. Homer: "as he extends for mortals a lurid rainbow."
For this reason some also told the story that it has a head
like a bull, by which it swallows up rivers.
3. How, then, does the rainbow occur? We in fact look   10
along lines that are straight or that are bent or that are
refracted, lines that are hidden and only visible to reason
and incorporeal. Looking along straight lines we see what
is in the air and what can be seen through transparent
stones and horn, for all these bodies have very fine parti-

ταῦτα πάντα. | καμπύλας δὲ γραμμὰς καθ᾽ ὕδατος
15 βλέπομεν γινομένας· κάμπτεται | γὰρ ἡ ὄψις βίᾳ διὰ
τὴν πυκνοτέραν τοῦ ὕδατος ὕλην· διὸ καὶ τὴν κώπην
| ἐν τῇ θαλάσσῃ μακρόθεν καμπτομένην ὁρῶμεν. τρί-
τος τρόπος τοῦ | βλέπειν τὰ ἀνακλώμενα ὡς τὰ κατ-
οπτρικά. (PS) |

4. ἔστιν οὖν τὸ τῆς ἴριδος πάθος τοιοῦτον. δεῖ γὰρ
ἐπινοῆσαι τὴν ὑγρὰν | ἀναθυμίασιν εἰς νέφος μετα-
20 βάλλουσαν, εἶτ᾽ ἐκ τούτου κατὰ βραχὺ εἰς | μικρὰς
ρανίδας νοτιζούσας· ὅταν οὖν ὁ ἥλιος γένηται ἐν δυ-
σμαῖς, | ἀνάγκη πᾶσα ἶριν ἄντικρυς ἡλίου φαίνεσθαι,
ὅτε ἡ ὄψις προσπεσοῦσα | ταῖς ρανίσιν ἀνακλᾶται,
ὥστε γίνεσθαι τὴν ἶριν. (PS) |

5. εἰσὶ δ᾽ αἱ ρανίδες οὐ σχήματος μορφαί, ἀλλὰ
χρώματος· καὶ ἔχειτὸ μὲν | πρῶτον φοινικοῦν, τὸ δὲ
25 δεύτερον ἁλουργὲς καὶ πορφυροῦν, τὸ δὲ | τρίτον κυά-
νεον καὶ πράσινον· μήποτε τὸ μὲν φοινικοῦν, ὅτι ἡ
λαμπρότης | τοῦ ἡλίου προσπεσοῦσα καὶ ἡ ἀκραι-
φνὴς λαμπηδὼν ἀνακλωμένη | ἐρυθρὸν ποιεῖ καὶ φοι-
νικοῦν τὸ χρῶμα· τὸ δὲ δεύτερον μέρος | ἐπιθολούμε-
νον καὶ ἐκλυόμενον μᾶλλον τῆς λαμπηδόνος διὰ τὰς
ρανίδας | ἁλουργές· ἄνεσις γὰρ τοῦ ἐρυθροῦ τοῦτο. ἔτι
30 δὲ μᾶλλον ἐπιθολούμενον | τὸ διορίζον εἰς τὸ πράσι-
νον μεταβάλλει. (PS) |

§§4–6 anonymous excerpts from Aristotle Mete. 3.4
§4 cf. Mete. 3.2 372a32–b6, 3.4 373b32–34
§5 cf. Mete. 3.4 373b17–24, 374a3–b10

cles. Bent lines we see occurring in water, for the visual 15
ray is bent because the matter of water is denser. This is
of course why from afar we see the oar bending in the sea.
The third way of seeing involves what is reflected, such as
images in mirrors.[11]

4. Well then, the condition of the rainbow is of the last-
mentioned sort. We should assume that the moist exhalation changes into a cloud, and in a short time from this
cloud into small and moist droplets. So when the sun is in 20
the west, it will necessarily follow that the rainbow appears
opposite to the sun, when the visual ray, impacting upon
the droplets, is reflected, so that the rainbow occurs.[12]

5. The droplets are forms not of shape but of color. The
first part has a dark red, the second a sea-violet and purple,
the third a dark blue and light green color. Possibly this 25
dark red color comes about because the splendor of the
sun, falling upon these droplets, and the sudden refraction
of its brilliance produce the color red and dark red. The
second part, becoming turbid and more loosened from the
brilliance because of the droplets, becomes sea-violet, for
this is a looser form of the color red. The outer part, be- 30
coming even more turbid, changes into the color green.

[11] General optics (direct vision), dioptrics (refraction), catop-
trics (reflection), according to contemporary theoretical optics.

[12] Aristotle's theory of the visual ray in *Meteorology* Book 3
contradicts his view of visual perception in the *On the Soul* and
On Sensation, as was already seen by ancient commentators.

6. ἔστιν οὖν τοῦτο δοκιμάσαι δι' ἔργων· εἰ γάρ τις
ἄντικρυς στὰς τοῦ ἡλίου | λάβῃ ὕδωρ καὶ πυτίσῃ, αἱ
δὲ ῥανίδες ἀνάκλασιν πρὸς τὸν ἥλιον λάβωσιν, |
εὑρήσει γινομένην ἶριν· καὶ οἱ ὀφθαλμιῶντες δὲ τοῦτο
πάσχουσιν, ὅταν | εἰς τὸν λύχνον ἀποβλέψωσιν. (PS) |

35   7. Ἀναξιμένης ἶριν γίνεσθαι κατ' αὐγασμὸν ἡλίου
πρὸς νέφει πυκνῷ καὶ | παχεῖ καὶ μέλανι παρὰ τὸ μὴ
δύνασθαι τὰς ἀκτῖνας εἰς τὸ πέραν διακόπτειν | ἐπι-
συνισταμένας αὐτῷ. (P) |

8. Ἀναξαγόρας ἀνάκλασιν ἀπὸ νέφους πυκνοῦ τῆς
ἡλιακῆς περιφεγγείας, | καταντικρὺ δὲ τοῦ κατοπτρί-
40   ζοντος αὐτὴν ἀστέρος διὰ παντὸς ἵστασθαι. | παρα-
πλησίως δὲ αἰτιολογεῖται τὰ καλούμενα παρήλια,
γινόμενα δὲ | κατὰ τὸν Πόντον. (P) |

9. Μητρόδωρος ὅταν διὰ νεφῶν ἥλιος διαλάμψῃ τὸ
μὲν νέφος κυανίζειν, | τὴν δ' αὐγὴν ἐρυθραίνε-
σθαι. (P) |

§6 cf. *Mete*. 3.4 374a35–b5, 373b2–10, 374a19–23
§7 Anaximenes A18
§8 Anaxagoras A86
§9 Metrodorus A17

6. Now this can be tested by experiment. If one, standing opposite the sun, takes water in one's mouth and spits it out, and the droplets take on a reflection toward the sun, he will find that a rainbow occurs. Patients suffering from ophthalmitis have the same experience when they look into the lamplight.

7. Anaximenes says that the rainbow occurs through the   35
mirroring of the sun's light upon a dense, thick, and black cloud, on account of the inability of the rays to collect together and penetrate to the other side.

8. Anaxagoras says that the rainbow is a reflection of the sun's radiance from a dense cloud, and that it is situated directly opposite to the heavenly body that shows itself as in a mirror. He gives a similar causal explanation of the   40
so-called mock suns (*parhêlia*),[13] which occur around the Black Sea.

9. Metrodorus says that when the sun shines through the clouds the cloud becomes bluish-gray and the beams turn red.

[13] There is no separate chapter on mock suns, but they are subsumed under the subject of rods in 3.6, where the term "countersuns" (*anthêlia*) is used.

3.5a[16]

Ps.-Plut. *Plac*. 3.18; Stob. *Ecl*. ap. Phot. *Bibl*. 167

ε[+']. Περὶ ἄλω (PS) |

1. ἡ δ' ἄλως οὑτωσὶ ἀποτελεῖται· μεταξὺ τῆς σελήνης
ἤ τινος ἄλλου | ἄστρου καὶ τῆς ὄψεως ἀὴρ παχὺς καὶ
ὀμιχλώδης ἵσταται· εἶτ' ἐν τούτῳ | τῆς ὄψεως κατα-
κλωμένης καὶ εὐρυνομένης κᾆθ' οὕτω τῷ κύκλῳ τοῦ |
5 ἄστρου προσπιπτούσης κατὰ τὴν ἔξω περιφέρειαν,
κύκλος δοκεῖ περὶ | τὸ ἄστρον φαίνεσθαι (ὃς κύκλος
φαινόμενος ἄλως καλεῖται, ὅτι ἐστὶν | ἄλῳ προσεοι-
κώς), ἐκεῖ δοκοῦντος τοῦ φάσματος γίνεσθαι, ἔνθα
συνέπεσε | τὸ πάθος[17] τῆς ὄψεως. (P) |

§1 cf. Aristotle *Mete*. 3.2 371b18, 22–24, 3.3 373a21–22

16 cap. hic mov. MR, post 3.17 pos. P
17 συνέπεσε τὸ πάθος coni. Reiske: νῦν ἔπεσε τὸ πάχος P

3.5a

The view that the halo is an optical phenomenon follows on from the previous chapter. The opposite view that it is real phenomenon may have fallen out.

Ps.-Plutarch, *Tenets*; Stobaeus, *Anthology* in Photius, *Library*

5a. On the halo[14]

1. The halo is produced in the following way: between the moon or another heavenly body and our organ of vision there is situated a thick and misty mass of air. Then, when our vision is refracted and broadened in this air and next in this condition falls upon the orb of the heavenly body at its outer circumference, a circle seems to appear around the heavenly body this apparent circle is called halo because it resembles a *halô* (round threshing floor); the apparition seems to come to be in the place where the modification of our vision happened to occur.

5

[14] This chapter is displaced at the end of the book in Ps.-Plutarch. As in 3.5.3–6, the explanation derives from Aristotle, but there is no name-label.

3.6

Ps.-Plut. *Plac*. 3.6 (+ Ps.-Gal. *Hist. phil.*); Stob. *Ecl.* ap. Phot. *Bibl.* 167

ϛ΄. Περὶ ῥάβδων (PS) |

1. τὰ κατὰ τὰς ῥάβδους καὶ ἀνθηλίους συμβαίνοντα μίξει τῆς ὑποστάσεως | καὶ ἐμφάσεως ὑπάρχει, τῶν μὲν νεφῶν ὁρωμένων, οὐ κατ᾽ οἰκεῖον δὲ | χρῶμα, ἀλλ᾽ ἕτερον ὅπερ κατ᾽ ἔμφασιν φαίνεται. ἐν δὲ τούτοις
5 πᾶσι τά | τε κατὰ φύσιν καὶ τὰ ἐπίκτητα ὅμοια συμβαίνει πάθη. (P) |

§1 cf. Aristotle *Mete*. 3.2 372a12

3.6

The compromise blend of semblance and reality relates to the foundational diaphonia of views on meteorological phenomena already introduced at the beginning of 3.5.

Ps.-Plutarch, *Tenets* (+ Ps.-Galen, *Philosophical History*); Stobaeus, *Anthology* in Photius, *Library*

6. On rods

1. The phenomena that happen in the case of rods[15] and countersuns[16] exist through a mixture of real subsistence and mere appearance, because what is seen are really clouds, not however with their own color but with another one that shines forth through reflection. With all phenomena of this kind the properties are similar, both those that   5
are according to nature and those that are acquired.

[15] Another kind of meteor, also known as streaks. These too are mentioned by Aristotle (cf. ch. 3.5a)
[16] See n. 13 on ch. 3.5.

3.7

Ps.-Plut. *Plac.* 3.7 (+ Ps.-Gal. *Hist. phil.* 79); Stob. *Ecl.* 1.32

ζ'. Περὶ ἀνέμων (PS) |

1. Ἀναξίμανδρος ἄνεμον εἶναι ῥύσιν ἀέρος, τῶν λεπτοτάτων ἐν αὐτῷ καὶ | ὑγροτάτων ὑπὸ τοῦ ἡλίου κινουμένων ἢ τηκομένων. (P) |

2. οἱ Στωικοὶ πᾶν πνεῦμα ἀέρος εἶναι ῥύσιν, ταῖς τῶν
5 τόπων δὲ παραλλαγαῖς | τὰς ἐπωνυμίας παραλλάττουσαν· οἷον τὸν ἀπὸ τοῦ ζόφου καὶ τῆς | δύσεως ζέφυρον ὠνόμαζον, τὸν δ'[18] ἀπὸ τῆς ἀνατολῆς καὶ τοῦ ἡλίου | ἀπηλιώτην, τὸν δ' ἀπὸ τῶν ἄρκτων βορέαν, τὸν δ' ἀπὸ τῶν νοτίων λίβα. | (P) |

3. Μητρόδωρος ἐξ ὑδατώδους ἀναθυμιάσεως διὰ τὴν
10 ἡλιακὴν ἔκκαυσιν | γίνεσθαι ὁρμὴν πνευμάτων

§1 Anaximander A24
§2 Stoics 2.697
§3 Metrodorus A18

18 5–6 τὸν, τὸν δ' G: om P

3.7

The chapter utilizes the question type of cause and the categories of substance and place. The principal diaphonia is between §§1–2, wind as a flow of air, and §§3–4, wind as deriving from evaporation.

Ps.-Plutarch, *Tenets* (+ Ps.-Galen, *Philosophical History*); Stobaeus, *Anthology*

7. On winds

1. Anaximander says that wind is a flow of air, the sun putting into motion or melting its subtlest and moistest parts.
2. The Stoics say that each draft (*pneuma*) is a flow of air, which however changes its appellation according to the 5 differences of the places from which it blows. Thus the *Zephyr* is named from the darkness and the west, the *Apêliotês* from the east and the sun, the *Boreas* from the north, and the *Lips* from the southern regions.
3. Metrodorus says that from a moist exhalation heated by the sun an onset of summer winds[17] occurs. And the Ete- 10

[17] "Summer winds": the corrupt Greek text has "divine winds."

θε‹ρ›ι‹ν›ῶν·[19] τοὺς δ' ἐτησίας πνεῖν τοῦ πρὸς | ταῖς
ἄρκτοις παχυνθέντος ἀέρος, ὑποχωροῦντι τῷ ἡλίῳ
κατὰ τὴν | θερινὴν τροπὴν ἐπισυρρέοντος. (P) |
4. Ἀριστοτέλης τῆς ξηρᾶς ἀναθυμιάσεως τὴν πρώτην
ἀναφοράν· γίνεσθαι | δέ ποτε τῇ ξηρᾷ πρὸς τὴν ὑγρὰν
μῖξιν. (S) |

§4 Aristotle cf. *Mete.* 2.4 360a12–13, 361b1

3.8

Ps.-Plut. *Plac.* 3.8 (+ Ps.-Gal. *Hist. phil.* 80); Stob. *Ecl.*
1.8.42b

η′. Περὶ χειμῶνος καὶ θέρους (P) |

1. Ἐμπεδοκλῆς καὶ οἱ Στωικοὶ χειμῶνα μὲν γίνεσθαι
τοῦ ἀέρος ἐπικρατοῦντος | τῇ πυκνώσει καὶ εἰς τὸ ἀνω-
τέρω βιαζομένου, θερείαν δὲ τοῦ | πυρός, ὅταν εἰς τὸ
κατωτέρω βιάζηται. (PS) |
5 2. περιγεγραμμένων δέ μοι τῶν μεταρσίων, ἐφοδευθή-
σεται καὶ τὰ πρόσγεια. | (P) |

§1 Empedocles A65; Stoics 2.696

[19] θε‹ρ›ι‹ν›ῶν coni. MR: †θείων P

sian winds blow when the air that is more compacted in the north flows together with the sun when it recedes at the summer solstice.

4. Aristotle says that wind is the first updraught of the dry exhalation. There sometimes occurs a mixing of the dry exhalation with the wet.

3.8

The single doxa is followed by an authorial note.

Ps.-Plutarch, *Tenets* (+ Ps.-Galen, *Philosophical History*); Stobaeus, *Anthology*

8. On winter and summer

1. Empedocles and the Stoics say that winter occurs when the air prevails by its thickness and presses the sun upward; and summertime because fire prevails, when it presses the sun downward.

2. Now I have described the things on high, the account will proceed to the things on earth.[18]   5

---

[18] The authorial note adverts again to the distinction made in the proœmium and effectively divides the book into its two parts. See further the Introduction to Book 3.

3.9

The chapter coalesces three themes in the categories of
quantity and substance: §2 opposed to §1 and §§3–5, dia-
phonia of number; §§3–4a, diaphonia of size; and §§4b–5,

Ps.-Plut. *Plac*. 3.9 (+ Ps.-Gal. *Hist. phil.* 81); Stob. *Ecl.*
1.33

θ΄. Περὶ γῆς καὶ τίς ἡ ταύτης οὐσία καὶ πόσαι
(PS) |

1. Θαλῆς καὶ οἱ ἀπ᾽ αὐτοῦ μίαν εἶναι τὴν γῆν. (P) |
2. Ἱκέτης ὁ Πυθαγόρειος δύο, ταύτην καὶ τὴν ἀντί-
χθονα. (P) |
3. οἱ Στωικοὶ τὴν γῆν μίαν καὶ πεπερασμένην. (P) |
5 4. Ξενοφάνης ἐκ τοῦ κατωτέρω μέρους εἰς ἄπειρον²⁰
ἐρριζῶσθαι, ἐξ ἀέρος | δὲ καὶ πυρὸς συμπαγῆναι. (P) |
5. Μητρόδωρος τὴν μὲν γῆν ὑπόστασιν εἶναι καὶ
τρύγα τοῦ ὕδατος, τὸν δ᾽ | ἥλιον τοῦ ἀέρος. (P) |

§1 Thales fr. 160 Wöhrle
§2 Hicetas 50.2
§3 Stoics 2.647
§4 Xenophanes A47
§5 Metrodorus A20

20 post ἄπειρον hab. μέρος aut βάθος aut πάθος P

3.9

diaeresis of substance (the reference to the sun in §5 is a maverick fossil). The number of earths (single or multiple) also plays a part in the next seven chapters.

Ps.-Plutarch, *Tenets* (+ Ps.-Galen, *Philosophical History*); Stobaeus, *Anthology*

9. On the earth, and what is its substance and how many there are[19]

1. Thales and his successors say there is only one earth.
2. Hicetas the Pythagorean says that there are two, this one and the counterearth.[20]
3. The Stoics say that there is one earth, and that it is finite.
4. Xenophanes says that it is rooted toward infinity on its nether part; and that it has been compounded from air and fire.
5. Metrodorus says that the earth is a sediment and dregs of the water, but the sun is the same of the air.[21]

[19] On the sequence of chapters (3.9–15) presenting topics on the earth according to the (Aristotelian) categories, see further the Introduction to Book 3.

[20] Cf. Philolaus at 3.11.3.

[21] Cf. Metrodorus at 3.15.6.

3.10

Ps.-Plut. *Plac*. 3.10 (+ Ps.-Gal. *Hist. phil.* 82); Stob. *Ecl.*
1.34

ι΄. Περὶ σχήματος γῆς (PS) |

1. Θαλῆς καὶ οἱ Στωικοὶ²¹ σφαιροειδῆ τὴν γῆν. (P) |
2. Ἀναξίμανδρος λίθῳ κίονι τὴν γῆν προσφερῆ, τῶν
ἐπιπέδων <δὲ αὐτῆς | γυρῶν>.²² (P) |
5 3. Ἀναξιμένης τραπεζοειδῆ. (P) |
4. Λεύκιππος τυμπανοειδῆ. (P) |
5. Δημόκριτος δισκοειδῆ μὲν τῷ πλάτει, κοίλην δὲ τῷ
μέσῳ.²³ (P) |

§1 Thales fr. 161 Wöhrle; Stoics 2.648
§2 Anaximander A25
§3 Anaximenes A20
§4 Leucippus A26
§5 Democritus A94

²¹ Στωικοὶ EQ: ἀπ᾽ αὐτοῦ G
²² <δὲ αὐτῆς γυρῶν> coni. MR ex Q
²³ τῷ μέσῳ E, τὸ μέσον PQ

3.10

The chapter utilizes the category of quality to give a neat diaeresis of shapes, basically in chronological order.

Ps.-Plutarch, *Tenets* (+ Ps.-Galen, *Philosophical History*); Stobaeus, *Anthology*

10. On the shape of the earth

1. Thales and the Stoics[22] say that the earth is like a ball.[23]
2. Anaximander says that the earth resembles a column drum, ⟨with curved surfaces⟩.[24]
3. Anaximenes says that it is like a slab.   5
4. Leucippus says that it is like a kettledrum.
5. Democritus says that it is like a disk in breadth, but hollow at the center.

---

[22] The Stoics are added to Thales to indicate the dominant view, cf. 2.2, 2.14, 2.22, 2.27.

[23] On the translation of adjectives ending in *-eidês* prominent in this chapter, see General Introduction 3.3(8).

[24] The additional text is furnished by Quṣṭā and confirmed by Hippolytus.

3.11

Ps.-Plut. *Plac*. 3.11 (+ Ps.-Gal. *Hist. phil.* 83); Stob. *Ecl.* 1.33

ιαʹ. Περὶ θέσεως γῆς (PS) |

1. οἱ ἀπὸ Θάλεω τὴν γῆν μέσην. (P) |
2. Ξενοφάνης πρώτην, εἰς ἄπειρον γὰρ ἐρριζῶ-
σθαι. (P) |
3. Φιλόλαος ὁ Πυθαγόρειος τὸ μὲν πῦρ μέσον (τοῦτο
5   γὰρ εἶναι τοῦ παντὸς | Ἑστίαν), δευτέραν δὲ τὴν ἀντί-
χθονα, τρίτην δ᾽ ἣν οἰκοῦμεν γῆν, ἐξ | ἐναντίας κει-
μένην τε καὶ περιφερομένην τῇ ἀντίχθονι· παρ᾽ ὃ καὶ
μὴ | ὁρᾶσθαι ὑπὸ τῶν ἐν τῇδε τοὺς ἐν ἐκείνῃ. (P) |

§1 Thales A15
§2 Xenophanes A47
§3 Philolaus A17

3.11

Diaeresis of positions in the category of place, in rough chronological order.

Ps.-Plutarch, *Tenets* (+ Ps.-Galen, *Philosophical History*); Stobaeus, *Anthology*

11. On the location of the earth

1. The successors of Thales say the earth is in the middle.
2. Xenophanes says it is first, for it is rooted in infinity.
3. Philolaus the Pythagorean says that the fire is in the middle (for this is the Hearth of the universe), that the counterearth is second, and third the earth we inhabit, situated opposite the counterearth and circling along with it, which is why those in that one are not seen by those in this one.[25]

---

[25] Cf. Hicetas at 3.9.2, Ecphantus at 3.13.3.

Ps.-Plut. *Plac*. 3.12

ιβ΄. Περὶ ἐγκλίσεως γῆς (P) |

1. Λεύκιππος παρεκπεσεῖν τὴν γῆν εἰς τὰ μεσημβρινὰ μέρη διὰ τὴν ἐν τοῖς | μεσημβρινοῖς ἀραιότητα, ἅτε δὴ πεπηγότων τῶν βορείων διὰ τὸ κατεψῦχθαι | τοῖς κρυμοῖς, τῶν δ᾿ ἀντιθέτων πεπυρωμένων. (P) |

5   2. Δημόκριτος διὰ τὸ ἀσθενέστερον εἶναι τὸ μεσημ-βρινὸν τοῦ περιέχοντος | αὐξομένην τὴν γῆν κατὰ τοῦτο ἐγκλιθῆναι· τὰ γὰρ βόρεια ἄκρατα τὰ δὲ | με-σημβρινὰ κέκραται· ὅθεν κατὰ τοῦτο βεβάρηται, ὅπου περισσή ἐστι | τοῖς καρποῖς καὶ τῇ αὔξῃ. (P) |

§1 Leucippus A27
§2 Democritus A96

3.12

Diaeresis of atomist doxai in the category of position and in chronological order.

Ps.-Plutarch, *Tenets*

12. On the inclination of the earth[26]

1. Leucippus says that the earth slopes down toward the southern parts because of the loose texture in its southern parts, since the northern parts are congealed because refrigerated by the frost, whereas the opposite parts have been ignited.

2. Democritus says that because the southern part of what is around it is weaker the earth becomes larger and is tilted in that direction; for the north is unmixed while the south is mixed; for this reason the earth has become heavy in that direction, where there is more of it because of the fruits of the earth and their increase.

[26] A comparable division of the heavens was given above in 2.8.

3.13

Ps.-Plut. *Plac*. 3.13 (+ Ps.-Gal. *Hist. phil*. 84); Stob. *Ecl*. 1.35

ιγ΄. Πότερα μένει ἡ γῆ ἢ κινεῖται[24] (PS) |

1. οἱ μὲν ἄλλοι μένειν τὴν γῆν. (P) |

2. Φιλόλαος δ᾽ ὁ Πυθαγόρειος κύκλῳ περιφέρεσθαι περὶ τὸ πῦρ κατὰ | κύκλον λοξὸν[25] ὁμοιοτρόπως ἡλίῳ καὶ σελήνῃ. (P) |

5   3. Ἡρακλείδης ὁ Ποντικὸς καὶ Ἔκφαντος ὁ Πυθαγόρειος κινοῦσι μὲν τὴν | γῆν, οὐ μήν γε μεταβατικῶς, ἀλλὰ τρεπτικῶς, τροχοῦ δίκην ἐνηξονισμένην | ἀπὸ δυσμῶν ἐπ᾽ ἀνατολὰς περὶ τὸ ἴδιον αὐτῆς κέντρον. (P) |

4. Δημόκριτος κατ᾽ ἀρχὰς μὲν πλάζεσθαι τὴν γῆν διά τε μικρότητα καὶ | κουφότητα, πυκνωθεῖσαν δὲ τῷ 10 χρόνῳ καὶ βαρυνθεῖσαν καταστῆναι. | (P) |

§1 anonymi cf. 44A21   §2 Philolaus A21   §3 Heraclides fr. 65B; Ecphantus 51.5   §4 Democritus A95

[24] tit. S: Περὶ κινήσεως γῆς PGQ
[25] κύκλον λοξὸν corr. Reiske: κύκλου λοξοῦ P

3.13

The primary diaphonia of rest and motion in the category of place is between the Ionic majority and the Italian succession, with a subsidiary diaphonia of two kinds of motion and a compromise position at the end.

Ps.-Plutarch, *Tenets* (+ Ps.-Galen, *Philosophical History*); Stobaeus, *Anthology*

13. Whether the earth is at rest or moves[27]

1. The others say that the earth is at rest.
2. But Philolaus the Pythagorean says that it moves about the fire in an oblique circle in the same [or: a similar] way as sun and moon.
3. Heraclides of Pontus and Ecphantus the Pythagorean cause the earth to move, though not from one place to another, but by revolution in the manner of a wheel upon an axle, from west to east about its own center.
4. Democritus says that the earth originally wandered around because of its small size and lightness, but having become denser and heavier in time it came to a halt.[28]

5

10

27 The chapter heading in Photius' index of Stobaeus (it is missing in the mss.) is to be preferred to the title with *peri* (on the motion of the earth) in the tradition of Ps.-Plutarch because it gives a more precise description of its contents. Moreover, that latter title is ambiguous and could refer to earthquakes, which are not discussed until 3.17.

28 Cf. Democritus at 3.15.7, Seleucus at 3.17.9.

3.14

Ps.-Plut. *Plac*. 3.14 (+ Ps.-Gal. *Hist. phil.* 85)

ιδ΄. Περὶ διαιρέσεως γῆς,
πόσαι εἰσὶ ζῶναι αὐτῆς (P) |

1. Πυθαγόρας τὴν γῆν ἀναλόγως τῇ τοῦ {παντὸς}[26]
οὐρανοῦ σφαίρᾳ διῃρῆσθαι | εἰς πέντε ζώνας, ἀρκτι-
κὴν ἀνταρκτικὴν θερινὴν χειμερινὴν ἰσημερινήν, ὧν |
ἡ μέση ‹τῆς θερινῆς καὶ χειμερινῆς›[27] τὸ μέσον τῆς
5   γῆς ὁρίζει, παρ' αὐτὸ | τοῦτο διακεκαυμένη καλουμένη·
ἡ δ' οἰκητή ἐστιν ἡ {μέση τῆς θερινῆς | καὶ χειμερι-
νῆς}[28] ‹θερινή›,[29] εὔκρατός τις οὖσα. (P) |
2. Παρμενίδης πρῶτος ἀφώρισε τῆς γῆς τοὺς οἰκου-
μένους τόπους ὑπὸ ταῖς | δυσὶ ζώναις ταῖς τροπι-
καῖς.[30] (P) |

§1 Pythagoras —   §2 Parmenides A44a

[26] παντὸς PG: om. Q, secl. MR[2]
[27] ‹τῆς θερινῆς καὶ χειμερινῆς› suppl. MR ex ll. 5–6
[28] {μέση τῆς θερινῆς καὶ χειμερινῆς} damn. MR
[29] ‹θερινή› suppl. MR ex l. 3
[30] lemma trad. ap. P 3.11.4 hic transp. Beck

3.14

The category of quantity (number) again, now applied to the single earth.

Ps.-Plutarch, *Tenets* (+ Ps.-Galen, *Philosophical History*)

14. On the division of the earth, how many its zones are[29]

1. Pythagoras says that the earth, in analogy to the sphere of the {whole}[30] heaven, is divided into five zones: arctic, antarctic, summer tropic, winter tropic, equatorial, of which that in between the summer and winter zone delimits the middle part of the earth,[31] which for that reason (sc. because it occupies the middle section) is called   5
scorched. But the inhabitable zone is ‹the summer tropic›, which is one that is temperate.
2. Parmenides was the first to define the inhabited zones of the earth under the two tropic zones.[32]

---

[29] A comparable division of the heavens was given above in 2.12.

[30] The word *pantos* (whole) is superfluous and may be omitted.

[31] The text in Ps.-Plutarch is corrupt, but can be rescued with a simple transposition.

[32] Another example of the "first discoverer" motif; cf. the note on 2.1.1.

3.15

There is a distinction as well as an association between the earth's local motion in earthquakes and its cosmic motion (or lack thereof) around its axis or around another center of the cosmos. An irregular diaeresis relating to physical

Ps.-Plut. *Plac.* 3.15 (+ Ps.-Gal. *Hist. phil.* 86); Stob. *Ecl.* 1.36.1

ιε΄. Περὶ σεισμῶν γῆς (PS) |

1. Θαλῆς μὲν καὶ Δημόκριτος ὕδατι τὴν αἰτίαν τῶν σεισμῶν προσάπτουσιν, | (P) |

2. οἱ δὲ Στωικοὶ σεισμὸν εἶναι λέγουσι τὸ ἐν τῇ γῇ
5 ὑγρὸν εἰς ἀέρα διακρινόμενον | καὶ ἐκπῖπτον. (P) |

3. Ἀναξιμένης ξηρότητα καὶ ὑγρότητα[31] τῆς γῆς αἰ-
τίαν τῶν σεισμῶν, ὧν τὴν | μὲν αὐχμοὶ γεννῶσι τὴν
δ᾽ ἐπομβρίαι. (P) |

4. Ἀναξαγόρας ἀέρος ὑποδύσει τῇ μὲν πυκνότητι τῆς
ἐπιφανείας προσπίπτοντος, | τῷ δ᾽ ἔκκρισιν λαβεῖν μὴ
10 δύνασθαι τρόμῳ τὸ περιέχον | κραδαίνοντος. (P) |

§1 Thales fr. 163 Wöhrle; Democritus —
§2 Stoics 2.707
§3 Anaximenes cf. A21
§4 Anaxagoras A89

[31] ὑγρότητα G: ἀραιότητα P

3.15

substances and/or forces explains local motions. §§6–10
are explicit about the earth's rest (cf. 3.13.1), presumably
presupposed in §§1–5.

Ps.-Plutarch, *Tenets* (+ Ps.-Galen, *Philosophical History*);
Stobaeus, *Anthology*

15. On earthquakes

1. Thales and Democritus assign the cause of earthquakes
to water,
2. whereas the Stoics say an earthquake is the moisture in
the earth that is separated and bursts out into the air.   5
3. Anaximenes says that the dryness and wetness of the
earth are the cause of earthquakes, the former of which is
produced by droughts, the latter by heavy rains.
4. Anaxagoras says that they are caused by the striving of
the air to get out, which when it hits the compactness of
the surface is not able find a way through and so shakes
what surrounds it with a tremor.   10

5. Ἀριστοτέλης διὰ τὴν τοῦ ψυχροῦ ⟨τῷ θερμῷ⟩[32] πανταχόθεν ἀντιπερίστασιν, | κάτωθεν καὶ ἄνωθεν αὐτῷ[33] περιστάντος· τὸ γὰρ θερμὸν ἀνωτέρω | γενέσθαι σπεύδει ἅτε δὴ κοῦφον ὄν· διὰ τοῦτο ἐν ἀπολήψει γινομένης | τῆς ξηρᾶς ἀναθυμιάσεως τῇ σφηνώ-
15 σει καὶ τοῖς ἀνθελιγμοῖς διαταράττεσθαι. | (P) |

6. Μητρόδωρος μηδὲν ἐν τῷ οἰκείῳ τόπῳ σῶμα κινεῖσθαι, εἰ μή τις προώσειεν[34] | ἢ καθελκύσειε κατ' ἐνέργειαν· διὸ μηδὲ τὴν γῆν, ἅτε δὴ κειμένην | φυσικῶς, κινεῖσθαι, τόπους δέ τινας αὐτῆς ⟨ὑπο⟩νοστεῖν τ⟨ῷ⟩ σάλ⟨ῳ⟩.[35] | (P) |

20 7. Παρμενίδης Δημόκριτος διὰ τὸ πανταχόθεν ἴσον ἀφεστῶσαν μένειν ἐπὶ | τῆς ἰσορροπίας, οὐκ ἔχουσαν αἰτίαν δι' ἣν δεῦρο μᾶλλον ἢ ἐκεῖσε | ῥέψειεν ἄν· διὰ τοῦτο μόνον μὲν κραδαίνεσθαι μὴ κινεῖσθαι δέ. (P) |

8. Ἀναξιμένης διὰ τὸ πλάτος ἐποχεῖσθαι τῷ ἀέρι. (P) |

9. οἱ δέ φασιν ἐφ' ὕδατος, καθάπερ τὰ πλαταμώδη καὶ
25 σανιδώδη ἐπὶ τῶν | ὑδάτων· διὰ τοῦτο κινεῖσθαι. (P) |

§5 Aristotle cf. *Mete.* 2.8 365b21–29
§6 Metrodorus A21
§7 Parmenides A44; Democritus A98, frs. 4, 379, 403 Luria
§8 Anaximenes A20
§9 anonymi —

32 ⟨τῷ θερμῷ⟩ add. Reiske
33 αὐτῷ corr. Reiske: αὐτῇ P, αὐτοῦ G
34 προώσειεν corr. Dübner: προσώσειεν P
35 ⟨ὑπο⟩νοστεῖν τ⟨ῷ⟩ σάλ⟨ῳ⟩ coni. Diels: †νοστεῖν τοῖς ἄλλοις P

5. Aristotle says that they are caused by the enclosing from all sides ‹of the hot› by the cold, which presses on it from below and from above; for the hot strives to get higher up, as it is light. For this reason the dry exhalation, having become imprisoned, is agitated because of the obstruction and the convolutions. 15

6. Metrodorus says that no body that is in its proper place moves, unless one were actually to push it forward or drag it down; therefore, the earth does not move either, as it is located in its natural place, though some places collapse because of the trembling.

7. Parmenides and Democritus[33] say that the earth re- 20 mains in equilibrium because it is equidistant on all sides (sc. from the surrounding heavens); it has no ground for moving this way rather than that; for this reason it is merely shaken, but it does not move.

8. Anaximenes says it does not move because of its broad surface being carried upon the air.

9. But others believe that it is carried upon the water, as boards and broad planks on waters (i.e., watery surfaces), 25 and for this reason it moves.

[33] Cf. Democritus at 3.13.4.

10. Πλάτων πάσης μὲν κινήσεως ἐξ εἶναι περιστά-
σεις, ἄνω καὶ κάτω, ἐπὶ τὰ | δεξιὰ καὶ θάτερα, ἔμπρο-
σθεν καὶ ὄπισθεν· κατ᾽ οὐδεμίαν δὲ τούτων | ἐνδέχε-
σθαι τὴν γῆν κινεῖσθαι, ἐν τῷ πανταχόθεν ἰσωτάτῳ[36]
κειμένην· | μένειν μὲν ἀκίνητον, μηδὲν ἔχουσαν ἐξαί-
30 ρετον εἰς τὸ ῥέψαι μᾶλλον, | τόπους δ᾽ αὐτῆς κατ᾽
ἀραιότητα σαλεύεσθαι. (PS) |

11. Ἐπίκουρος ἐνδέχεσθαι μὲν ὑπὸ πάχους ἀέρος τοῦ
ὑποκειμένου ὑδατώδους | ὄντος ἀνακρουομένην αὐτὴν
καὶ οἷον ὑποτυπτομένην κινεῖσθαι· | ἐνδέχεσθαι δὲ καὶ
σηραγγώδη τοῖς κατωτέρω μέρεσι καθεστῶσαν ὑπὸ |
τοῦ διασπειρομένου πνεύματος εἰς τὰς ἀντροειδεῖς
35 κοιλότητας ἐμπίπτοντος | σαλεύεσθαι. (P) |

§10 Plato cf. *Phd.* 109a, 111d–e, *Tim.* 34a, 40b–d
§11 Epicurus fr. 350

36 ἰσωτάτῳ SQ: κατωτάτην P, κατωτάτῳ edd.

10. Plato says that there are six directions of motion in all: up and down, to the right and to the left, forward and backward;[34] it is not possible that the earth should be moved in any of these modes, for it is located at the most equal distance (sc. from the surrounding heavens); it remains immobile, since it does not have any preference causing it to incline in any particular direction; but it does   30
have places that shake because of its thinness.

11. Epicurus says that it is possible that the earth moves when it is thrown upward and as it were struck from beneath by thick and humid air that lies beneath it; but it is also possible that, as it is full of holes in its nether parts, it is shaken by the wind that is dispersed through its cavern-   35
ous hollows.

[34] This doctrine of the six species of locomotion (the seventh in a circle is omitted) might have been expected in 1.23.

3.16

The chapter utilizes the question type of cause and the category of substance; the doxai are in both systematic and chronological order. Salinity is explained in different ways, with §6 also including the production of sweet

Ps.-Plut. *Plac.* 3.16 (+ Ps.-Gal. *Hist. phil.* 87); Stob. *Ecl.* 1.37

ιϛ΄. Περὶ θαλάσσης, πῶς συνέστη καὶ
πῶς ἐστι πικρά (PS) |

1. Ἀναξίμανδρος τὴν θάλασσάν φησιν εἶναι τῆς πρώ-
της ὑγρασίας λείψανον, | ἧς τὸ μὲν πλεῖον μέρος ἀ-
εξήρανε τὸ πῦρ, τὸ δὲ ὑπολειφθὲν διὰ | τὴν ἔκκαυσιν
μετέβαλεν. (P) |

5 2. Ἀναξαγόρας τοῦ κατ᾽ ἀρχὴν λιμνάζοντος ὑγροῦ
περικαέντος ὑπὸ τῆς | ἡλιακῆς περιφορᾶς καὶ τοῦ λι-
παροῦ ἐξατμισθέντος εἰς ἀλυκίδα καὶ | πικρίαν τὸ
λοιπὸν ὑποστῆναι. (P) |

3. Ἐμπεδοκλῆς "ἱδρῶτα τῆς γῆς" ἐκκαιομένης ὑπὸ τοῦ
ἡλίου διὰ τὴν ἐπὶ τὸ | πλεῖον πίλησιν.[37] (P) |

§1 Anaximander A27   §2 Anaxagoras A90
§3 Empedocles A66, B55

[37] ἐπὶ τὸ πλεῖον πίλησιν E: ἐπιπόλαιον πλῆσιν aut πλύ-
σιν P

3.16

water. The primary diaphonia obtains between §§1–5,
which relate to the origin of the sea, and §6, implying that
the process involved is continuous.

Ps.-Plutarch, *Tenets* (+ Ps.-Galen, *Philosophical History*);
Stobaeus, *Anthology*

16. On the sea, how it came to be and how it is bitter[35]

1. Anaximander says that the sea is the remainder of the primal moisture. The greatest part of this the fire dried up, but what remained altered its quality (i.e., became bitter) because of the great heat.

2. Anaxagoras says that, when in the beginning water existed as a standing pool, it was scorched by the movement of the sun about it [or: the revolution of the sun] and the fattish part of the water was exhaled,[36] so what was left turned to saltiness and bitterness.

3. Empedocles says that the sea is "sweat of the earth" heated by the sun because of the greater compression.

[35] The papyrus does not appear to have space for this extended title, but it should be retained because it clearly echoes Aristotle's introduction of the subject at *Mete.* 2.1 353a32.

[36] Salt was believed to contain fat.

10 4. Ἀντιφῶν ἱδρῶτα τοῦ θερμοῦ, ἐξ οὗ τὸ περιληφθὲν
ὑγρὸν ἀπεκρίθη, τῷ | καθεψηθῆναι παραλυκίσασα,
ὅπερ ἐπὶ παντὸς ἱδρῶτος συμβαίνει. (P) |
5. Μητρόδωρος διὰ τὸ διηθεῖσθαι διὰ τῆς γῆς μετει-
ληφέναι τοῦ περὶ αὐτὴν | πάχους, καθάπερ τὰ διὰ τῆς
τέφρας ὑλιζόμενα. (P) |
6. οἱ ἀπὸ Πλάτωνος τοῦ στοιχειώδους ὕδατος τὸ μὲν
15 ἐξ ἀέρος κατὰ περίψυξιν | συνιστάμενον γλυκὺ γίνε-
σθαι, τὸ δ᾽ ἀπὸ γῆς κατὰ περίκαυσιν | καὶ ἐκπύρωσιν
ἀναθυμιώμενον ἁλμυρόν. (P) |

§4 Antiphon B32   §5 Metrodorus A19
§6 Plato's successors —

3.17

*The chapter utilizes the question type of cause and the
categories of place and' substance. There is an opposition
between §§1–4, celestial bodies, and §§5–8, watery causes,*

Ps.-Plut. *Plac.* 3.17 (+ Ps.-Gal. *Hist. phil.* 88); Stob. *Ecl.*
1.38

ιζ΄. Πῶς ἀμπώτιδες γίνονται καὶ πλήμμυραι (PS) |

1. Ἀριστοτέλης Ἡρακλείδης ὑπὸ τοῦ ἡλίου τὰ πλεῖ-
στα τῶν πνευμάτων | κινοῦντος καὶ συμπεριφέροντος·

chapter Posidonius fr. 317 Theiler   §1 Aristotle cf. *Mete.*
2.1 354a5–8, 2.8 366a18–20, *GA* 4.10 777b17–778a2; Heraclides
fr. 78

4. Antiphon says that the sea is sweat of the hot, from 10
which the moist remainder was separated, becoming salty
by drying out, as happens with all sweat.
5. Metrodorus says that the sea by being strained through
the earth acquired some part of its density, just as is the
case with what is filtered through ashes.
6. The successors of Plato say that of the elemental water
the part that comes together by cooling from air becomes 15
sweet, but the part that is exhaled from the earth through
heating and burning becomes salty.

3.17

*while the compromise §9 mentions both moon and sea, and
like §§1 and 4, adds wind as a subsidiary cause.*

Ps.-Plutarch, *Tenets* (+ Ps.-Galen, *Philosophical History*);
Stobaeus, *Anthology*

17. How low and high tides occur

1. Aristotle and Heraclides say the tides are caused by the
sun, which moves the majority of the winds and whirls

ὑφ᾽ ὧν ἐμβαλλόντων μὲν προωθουμένην | ἀνοιδεῖν τὴν
5 Ἀτλαντικὴν θάλασσαν καὶ κατασκευάζειν τὴν | πλήμ-
μυραν, καταληγόντων δ᾽ ἀντιπερισπωμένην ὑποβαί-
νειν, ὅπερ εἶναι | τὴν ἄμπωτιν. (PS) |

2. <Δικαίαρχος ὁ>[38] Μεσ<σ>ήνιος ἡλίῳ καὐτὸς τὴν
αἰτίαν ἀνατίθησι, καθ᾽ οὓς | μὲν ἂν τόπους γένηται
τῆς γῆς πλημμύροντι τὰ πελάγη, ἐξ ὧν δ᾽ ἂν | τύχῃ
παραποστὰς ὑποσυνέλκοντι· ταῦτα δὲ συμβαίνειν
10 περὶ τὰς ἑῴας | καὶ τὰς μεσημβρινὰς ἐκκλίσεις. (S) |

3. Πυθέας ὁ Μασσαλιώτης τῇ πληρώσει τῆς σελήνης
τὰς πλημμύρας | γίνεσθαι τῇ δὲ μειώσει τὰς ἀμπώτι-
δας. (PS) |

4. Ποσειδώνιος ὑπὸ μὲν τῆς σελήνης κινεῖσθαι τοὺς
ἀνέμους, ὑπὸ δὲ | τούτων τὰ πελάγη, ἐν οἷς τὰ προει-
ρημένα γίνεσθαι πάθη. (S) |

15 5. Πλάτων ἐπὶ τὴν αἰώραν φέρεται τῶν ὑδάτων· εἶναι
γάρ τινα φυσικὴν | αἰώραν διά τινος ἐγγείου[39] τρήμα-
τος περιφέρουσαν τὴν παλίρροιαν, ὑφ᾽ | ἧς ἀντικυμαί-
νεσθαι τὰ πελάγη. (PS) |

6. Τίμαιος ὁ Ταυρομενίτης τοὺς ἐμβάλλοντας ποτα-
μοὺς εἰς τὴν Ἀτλαντικὴν | διὰ τῆς Κελτικῆς ὀρεινῆς

§2 Dicaearchus fr. 127   §3 Pytheas fr. 2
§4 Posidonius F138   §5 Plato cf. *Phd.* 111e–112a
§6 Timaeus F73

[38] <Δικαίαρχος ὁ> Μεσ<σ>ήνιος Meineke: ***ηνιος Με-
σήνιος S, <Εὐή>νιος Elter ex ind. Phot.
[39] ἐγγείου S: στομίου P

them about; as these throw themselves upon the Atlantic
sea, this is thrust forward and swells and produces the high   5
tide; when they are ceasing the sea pulls back and sub-
sides, which is the low tide.

2. ‹Dicaearchus› of Messene,[37] too, attributes the cause
to the sun, which instigates flooding in whatever regions
of the earth it reaches, but gradually draws them away with
itself in whatever regions it happens to recede from. These
events take place in relation to the morning and afternoon   10
displacements.

3. Pytheas of Marseille says that the high tides occur
through the waxing of the moon, the low tides through its
waning.

4. Posidonius says the winds are moved by the moon, and
the seas in turn by these winds, in which (i.e., the seas) the
aforesaid effects (i.e., the tides) take place.

5. Plato attributes them to the oscillation of the waters.   15
For there is a sort of natural oscillation that through a
tunnel in the earth moves the reflux hither and thither;
and by this reflux the seas surge back.

6. Timaeus of Taormina gives as the cause those rivers that
fall from the mountains of Celtic Gaul into the Atlantic.

---

[37] The name-label is probable but not certain. Photius in his
index of names records the otherwise unknown Euenius.

20 αἰτιᾶται προωθοῦντας μὲν ταῖς ἐφόδοις | καὶ πλήμμυ-
ραν ποιοῦντας, ὑφέλκοντας δὲ ταῖς ἀναπαύλαις καὶ
ἀμπώτιδας κατασκευάζοντας. (PS) |

7. Κράτης ὁ γραμματικὸς τὸν ἀντισπασμὸν τῆς θα-
λάσσης αἰτιᾶται. (S) |

8. Ἀπολλόδωρος ὁ Κερκυραῖος τὰς ἐκ τοῦ Ὠκεανοῦ
παλιρροίας. (S) |

9. Σέλευκος ὁ μαθηματικὸς ἀντιγεγραφὼς Κράτητι,
25 κινῶν καὐτὸς τὴν γῆν, | ἀντικόπτειν αὐτῆς τῷ δίνῳ
φησὶ {καὶ τῇ κινήσει}[40] τὴν περιστροφὴν τῆς σελήνης·
τοῦ δὲ | μεταξὺ ἀμφοτέρων τῶν σωμάτων ἀντιπερι-
σπωμένου πνεύματος καὶ | ἐμπίπτοντος εἰς τὸ Ἀτλαν-
τικὸν πέλαγος κατὰ λόγον οὕτω συγκυμαίνεσθαι | τὴν
θάλασσαν. (PS) |

§7 Crates fr.7
§8 Apollodorus of Corcyra —
§9 Seleucus fr. 6a–b

[40] post φησὶ add. καὶ . . . κινήσει P, prob. edd. damn. MR
ut glossa

306

Upon their entering upon that sea, they violently press upon it, and so cause the high tide; but when they with- 20
draw by their resting, they produce the low tides as well.
7. Crates the grammarian gives as the cause the reciprocal push and pull of the sea.
8. Apollodorus of Corcyra gives as the cause the refluxes from the Ocean.
9. Seleucus the astronomer,[38] who wrote against Crates and who, too, moves the earth,[39] says that the revolution 25
of the moon hinders its rotation (sc. of the earth); as the wind between these two bodies (sc. the earth and the moon) withdraws from and falls upon the Atlantic Ocean, correspondingly the sea produces its waves.

[38] On the term *mathêmatikos* here, see above at 2.15.4.
[39] That is, by axial rotation; cf. Heraclides and Ecphantus at 3.13.3.

BOOK IV

PSYCHOLOGY

INTRODUCTION

Transmission

In terms of length, Book 4 is the second longest of the work (only Book 1 is longer). This is perhaps a little surprising, since it has only twenty-four chapters, but is caused by some very long doxai, notably in chapters 11, 12, 20, 21, and 22. The book is reasonably well attested in the witnesses. To the twenty-three chapters in Ps.-Plutarch must be added chapter 7a, preserved only in Stobaeus,[1] who however appears not to have included chapter 1, on the Nile, for it is not even mentioned in Photius' index. The process of reduction carried out by Byzantine redactors has also left its mark: chapters 4, 5, 10, 12, 14, 18, 20, 21, 22, and 23 are wholly or mostly lacking, though we know from the index that, with the exception of chapter 5, the anthologist did excerpt these chapters. Theodoret very

---

[1] Its absence in Ps.-Plutarch is quite exceptional (the only other missing chapters appear to be 2.2a and 2.5a), but its presence in the original compendium is confirmed by Theodoret.

usefully utilizes the section of chapters 2 to 7, providing four lemmata not present in the two other witnesses. But thereafter he finds no use for the compendium. Because of this patchy state of transmission, we must assume that a fair number of lemmata are missing in chapters lacking in Stobaeus and not utilized by Theodoret.

Contents

The main focus of the book is on the doctrine of the soul, and if it stood alone it would no doubt be entitled *Peri psychês*. But in fact there is overlap between it and what precedes and follows it. Chapter 1, on the Nile, apparently forming a transition from Book 3 and its final chapters on the sea and the tides, stands on its own. But taking note of the introductory statement at the beginning of the book, we might also regard it as representing an isolated case of "particular phenomena" (*ta kata meros*), as compared to the general phenomena of Book 3.

However this may be, the main body of the book is formed by chapters 2 through 21, which divide rather neatly into two parts: (1) 2 to 7a, on the soul, per se, that is, its substance, parts, leading part, movement, and indestructibility; these chapters are very clearly organized in terms of categories and question types, as elsewhere in the compendium; (2) 8 to 21, on epistemology, that is, the senses in general and particular, sense perception and its reliability, concept formation, voice, etc. The presence of two lengthy and exclusively Stoic chapters (11–12), on the origin of sense perception and on meanings of "impression" and cognate terms, interrupts the systematic ordering of the book and is clear evidence of later Hellenistic updating. The same applies to another Stoic chapter (21), on how the soul comes to be sentient. The final two chapters (22–23) may be regarded as addenda, the former introducing an important psychosomatic topic and the latter a question on psychosomatic relations in general. They clearly form a transition to Book 5, on the physiology of the body.

Name-Labels

The name-labels used in Book 4 show some interesting and distinctive features. The number of individual names, sixty-one in total, is high compared with the other books, resulting in a wide and diverse coverage. Apart from the usual bevy of philosophers, there are three scientists, four doctors, and even two historians.[2] The number of group name-labels is definitely higher than the average, notably, Academics four times, Peripatetics five times, and the Stoics as high as seventeen times. Hellenistic name-labels are especially prominent in chapters 1 through 10. The presence of very late names—Posidonius, Asclepiades, and latest of all, Xenarchus—is striking and may be taken as clear evidence of updating closer to Aëtius' own time.[3] Lastly, there are multiple labels that are quite prominent, with some very long lists at 4.7.1 (six names), 4.7a.1 (five)

[2] Admittedly, three of these are found in the exceptional first chapter, on the Nile. Chapter 3.17, on tides, also has a number of unusual name-labels. On these name-labels, see further the Index of Names.

[3] For details on the names and the location of their doxai, see the Index of Names.

and, most remarkably, 4.9.1 (eleven, on the falsity of the sensations). Successions play a subordinate role: Thales occurs first only twice, Pythagoras more often (five times), but always in combination with Plato and Aristotle, never on his own. As for the relative contributions of dialectic and historiography, Book 4 takes an intermediate position between Book 2, which is the most dialectical, and Book 3, which is the most historical.[4]

Comparative Material

In order to place the contents of this book in a historical context, there is much material available. The proximate tradition is very rich. Diogenes Laertius' Stoic doxography provides numerous parallels (*VP* 7.156–59). The parallels in Lucretius are of particular interest because they antedate Aëtius by a century. It is possible that his master Epicurus provided a template, as witnessed by the scholion at Diogenes Laertius *VP* 10.66, but this Lucretius would then have updated. There is also copious material parallel to chapters in Books 4 and 5 of the *De anima* of Tertullian, which is generally accepted as dependent on the second-century AD doctor Soranus, who in turn was indebted to the earlier doxographical tradition. Other authors who provide insight into the wider doxographical tradition on the soul are Cicero (in the *Lucullus* and *Tusculan Disputations*), Philo of Alexandria, Galen, Ps.-Alexander (*Mantissa*), and later authors such as Porphyry, Iamblichus, Macrobius, and Nemesius.

[4] For more details, see Jeremiah "Statistical Explorations," 310–19.

Sources

In terms of organization, the account of the soul, per se, is mostly based on Aristotle's *On the Soul*, and that of sense perception on the same work and its appendix, the *Parva Naturalia*. It is important to recognize that Aristotle regarded the subject of sense perception, including the epistemological issue of its trustworthiness, as belonging to the domain of physics (this applies also to Theophrastus' treatment of the same issues in his *De sensibus*), which is a primary explanation for its inclusion in Aëtius' *physikos logos*. But Aristotle's discussion of concept formation is dispersed in various works, and he moreover excluded the study of the *nous* (intellect) as related to the objects of thought from physics. So it is not surprising that for these subjects the *Placita* give preference to Stoic accounts. As already noted, a number of chapters are entirely Stoic, with no other name-labels used, while much further Stoic material is also included elsewhere. Such placement of epistemological issues in a psychological context appears to agree with the practice of Chrysippus and Diogenes of Babylon. Because the *Placita* is an account of physics, it could not begin with logical or epistemological subjects, unlike the compendium of Ps.-Galen, *Historia philosopha*, which treats these first, before turning to Ps.-Plutarch and producing an epitome of his epitome.

Ultimate Sources

As for the ultimate sources of much of the material in the book, especially as related to Presocratic authors, we must go back to the Peripatos and postulate otherwise lost sources used by Aristotle, Theophrastus, and their predecessors. Chapter 1, on the Nile, depends on accounts in Herodotus and Ps.-Aristotle's *De inundacione Nili*. For the twelve doxai attributed to Plato, the *Timaeus* and *Philebus* were used. Chapters on the individual senses show some convergences with Theophrastus' *De sensibus*. But for the general approach, the titles, and some of the lemmata, the ultimate debt to Aristotle's psychological writings is without doubt the greatest.

⟨TITLE⟩[1]

ΑΕΤΙΟΥ ΠΕΡΙ ΤΩΝ ΑΡΕΣΚΟΝΤΩΝ
ΤΟ Δ΄,[2] |

ἐν ᾧ κεφάλαια τάδε· |

⟨Index⟩

Ps.-Plut. *Plac.*

1 Ps.-Plut. *Plac.* 4; Theod. *Cur.* 4.31, cf. 2.95, 5.16
2 tit. T: Περὶ ἀρεσκόντων φιλοσόφοις φυσικῶν δογμάτων
τὸ δ΄ P   3 tit. ex S: abest in P

314

AETIUS
ON THE PLACITA

BOOK IV

in which the following headings are found:[1]

<Index>

Ps.-Plutarch, *Tenets*

---

[1] On the list of chapter headings, or pinax, see above on Book 1 and the General Introduction 1.3.

θ′. Εἰ ἀληθεῖς αἱ αἰσθήσεις καὶ φαντασίαι |

ι′. Πόσαι εἰσὶν αἱ αἰσθήσεις |

ια′. Πῶς γίνεται ἡ αἴσθησις καὶ ἡ ἔννοια καὶ ὁ κατὰ <ἐν>διάθεσιν λόγος |

15 ιβ′. Τίνι διαφέρει φαντασία φανταστὸν φανταστικὸν φάντασμα |

ιγ′. Περὶ ὁράσεως, πῶς ὁρῶμεν |

ιδ′. Περὶ κατοπτρικῶν ἐμφάσεων |

ιε′. Εἰ ὁρατὸν τὸ σκότος |

ιϛ′. Περὶ ἀκοῆς |

20 ιζ′. Περὶ ὀσφρήσεως |

ιη′. Περὶ γεύσεως |

ιθ′. Περὶ φωνῆς |

κ′. Εἰ ἀσώματος ἡ φωνὴ καὶ πῶς ἠχὼ γίνεται |

κα′. Πόθεν αἰσθητικὴ γίνεται ἡ ψυχὴ καὶ τί αὐτῆς τὸ ἡγεμονικόν |

25 κβ′. Περὶ ἀναπνοῆς |

κγ′. Περὶ παθῶν σωματικῶν καὶ εἰ συναλγεῖ τούτοις ἡ ψυχή |

⟨Procemium⟩

Ps.-Plut. *Plac.*

Περιωδευμένων δὲ τῶν τοῦ κόσμου μερῶν διαβήσομαι πρὸς τὰ | κατὰ μέρος. (P)

4.1

Ps.-Plut. *Plac.* 4.1 (+ Ps.-Gal. *Hist. phil.* 89)

α΄. Περὶ Νείλου ἀναβάσεως (P) |

1. Θαλῆς τοὺς ἐτησίας ἀνέμους οἴεται πνέοντας τῇ Αἰγύπτῳ ἀντιπροσώπους | ἐπαίρειν τοῦ Νείλου τὸν ὄγκον διὰ τὸ τὰς ἐκροὰς αὐτοῦ τῇ | παροιδήσει τοῦ ἀντιπαρήκοντος πελάγους ἀνακόπτεσθαι. (P) |

5 2. Εὐθυμένης ὁ Μασσαλιώτης ἐκ τοῦ Ὠκεανοῦ καὶ τῆς ἔξω θαλάσσης | γλυκείας κατ᾽ αὐτὸν οὔσης νομίζει πληροῦσθαι τὸν ποταμόν. (P) |

§1 Thales A16
§2 Euthymenes F2

318

BOOK IV: PSYCHOLOGY

⟨Proœmium⟩

Transition from Books 2 and 3 and forward to the contents of Books 4 and 5.

Ps.-Plutarch, *Tenets*

The parts of the cosmos having now been treated systematically, I shall continue in the direction of the particular phenomena.

4.1

The chapter deals in chronological order with various proposed causes of this unusual and much disputed phenomenon.

Ps.-Plutarch, *Tenets* (+ Ps.-Galen, *Philosophical History*)

1. On the rising of the Nile

1. Thales believes that the Etesian (i.e., northwest) winds blowing opposite Egypt raise up the volume of the Nile because its outflows are beaten back by the swelling of the sea that has advanced opposite it.

2. Euthymenes of Massilia is of the opinion that the river 5
is filled from the Ocean and from the outer sea, which according to him is sweet.

3. Ἀναξαγόρας ἐκ τῆς χιόνος τῆς ἐν τῇ Αἰθιοπίᾳ, τη-
κομένης μὲν ἐν τῷ | θέρει, ψυχομένης δὲ τῷ χει-
μῶνι. (P) |

4. Δημόκριτος τῆς χιόνος τῆς ἐν τοῖς πρὸς ἄρκτον
10 μέρεσιν ὑπὸ θερινὰς | τροπὰς ἀναλυομένης τε καὶ
διαχεομένης νέφη μὲν ἐκ τῶν ἀτμῶν πιλοῦσθαι· |
τούτων δ' ἀνελαυνομένων πρὸς μεσημβρίαν καὶ τὴν
†Αἴγυπτον†[4] | ὑπὸ τῶν ἐτησίων ἀνέμων, ἀποτελεῖσθαι
ῥαγδαίους ὄμβρους, ὑφ' ὧν | ἀναπίμπλασθαι τάς τε
λίμνας καὶ τὸν Νεῖλον ποταμόν. (P) |

5. Ἡρόδοτος ὁ συγγραφεὺς ἴσον μὲν ἐκ τῶν πηγῶν
15 φέρεσθαι χειμῶνος καὶ | θέρους, φαίνεσθαι δ' ἐλάτ-
τονα τοῦ χειμῶνος διὰ τὸ ἐν τούτῳ τῷ καιρῷ | πλη-
σίον ἰόντα τὸν ἥλιον τῆς Αἰγύπτου ἐξατμίζειν τὰ
νάματα. (P) |

6. Ἔφορος ὁ ἱστοριογράφος κατὰ θέρος φησὶν ἀνα-
χαλᾶσθαι τὴν ὅλην | Αἴγυπτον καὶ οἱονεὶ ἐξιδροῦν τὸ
πολὺ νᾶμα· συνδίδωσι δ' αὐτῇ καὶ ἡ | Ἀραβία καὶ ἡ
Λιβύη παρὰ τὸ ἀραιὸν καὶ ὑπόψαμμον. (P) |

20 7. Εὔδοξος τοὺς ἱερεῖς φησι λέγειν τὰ ὄμβρια τῶν
ὑδάτων κατὰ[5] τὴν | ἀντιπερίστασιν τῶν ὡρῶν· ὅταν
γὰρ ἡμῖν ᾖ θέρος τοῖς ὑπὸ τὸν θερινὸν | τροπικὸν

§3 Anaxagoras A91   §4 Democritus A99
§5 cf. Herodotus *Hist.* 2.24–25   §6 Ephorus F65c
§7 Eudoxus F288

4 †Αἴγυπτον† expect. Αἰθιοπίαν Diels edd.
5 κατὰ corr. Diels Roeper sec.: καὶ P.

3. Anaxagoras believes it is filled from the snow in Ethiopia, which melts in summer but cools in winter.

4. Democritus believes that, when the snow in the northern parts melts and dissolves at the times of the summer solstice, clouds are formed by compression from the vapors; and that these, when driven toward the south and †Egypt†[2] by the Etesian winds, produce torrential rains, by which the pools and the river Nile are filled.

5. Herodotus the prose writer says that the river is borne from its springs in equal measure in winter and in summer, but seems to be less in winter because in that season the sun comes closer to Egypt and draws the streams up as vapor.

6. Ephorus the historian says that in the summer the whole of Egypt grows slack and, as it were, is sweating out the large stream. Arabia and Libya also contribute because of their loose-textured and rather sandy nature.

7. Eudoxus says that the priests state that the cause of the flood is rainwater corresponding to the reciprocal change of the seasons. For when it is summer for us who live under the summer solstice, then it is winter for those who

---

[2] A mistake on the part of Aëtius. He should have written Ethiopia.

οἰκοῦσιν, τότε τοῖς ὑπὸ τὸν χειμερινὸν τροπικὸν
ἀντοίκοις | χειμών ἐστιν, ἐξ ὧν τὸ πλημμῦρον ὕδωρ
καταρρήγνυται. (P) |

4.2

Ps.-Plut. *Plac*. 4.2; Stob. *Ecl*. 1.49.1a; Theod. *Cur*. 5.17–18

β΄. Περὶ ψυχῆς (PST) |

1. Θαλῆς ἀπεφήνατο πρῶτος τὴν ψυχὴν φύσιν ἀει-
κίνητον ἢ αὐτοκίνητον. | (PST) |
2. Ἀλκμαίων φύσιν αὐτοκίνητον κατὰ ἀίδιον κίνησιν,
5 καὶ διὰ τοῦτο | ἀθάνατον αὐτὴν καὶ προσεμφερῆ τοῖς
θείοις[6] ὑπολαμβάνει. (ST) |
3. Πυθαγόρας ἀριθμὸν ἑαυτὸν κινοῦντα, τὸν δὲ ἀριθ-
μὸν ἀντὶ τοῦ νοῦ παραλαμβάνει, | (PST) |
4. ὁμοίως δὲ καὶ Ξενοκράτης. (ST) |
5. Πλάτων οὐσίαν νοητὴν ἐξ ἑαυτῆς κινητὴν κατ᾽
10 ἀριθμὸν ἐναρμόνιον | κινουμένην. (PT) |

§1 Thales A22a   §2 Alcmaeon A12   §3 Pythagoras —
§4 Xenocrates fr. 90   §5 Plato cf. *Phdr*. 245c, *Tim*.
35a–36b, 41d, Ps.-Plato *Def*. 411c

[6] θείοις S: θεοῖς coni. Diels sed cf. Arist. *de An*. 1.2 405a32

live on the other side of the meridian under the winter solstice, which is from where the floodwater rushes down.

4.2

The contents are summarized in 4.3.1. This and the follow-ing chapter present an exclusive diaphonia: the soul is either incorporeal or corporeal.

Ps.-Plutarch, *Tenets*; Stobaeus, *Anthology*; Theodoret, *Cure of Greek Maladies*

2. On the soul

1. Thales was the first to declare that the soul is a nature that is ever-moving, or rather self-moved.
2. Alcmaeon says that it is a nature that is self-moved with everlasting motion, and for this reason he assumes that it   5
is immortal and resembles the divine beings.
3. Pythagoras says that it is a number moving itself; he takes number as denoting Intellect.
4. And similarly Xenocrates says this as well.
5. Plato says that it is an intelligible substance, moved of itself, in motion according to a numerical harmony.   10

6. Ἀριστοτέλης ἐντελέχειαν πρώτην σώματος φυσικοῦ, ὀργανικοῦ, | δυνάμει ζωὴν ἔχοντος· τὴν δ' "ἐντελέχειαν"⁷ ἀκουστέον ἀντὶ τοῦ εἴδους καὶ | τῆς ἐνεργείας. (PST) |

7. Δικαίαρχος ἁρμονίαν τῶν τεσσάρων στοιχείων. (PST) |

15 8. Ἀσκληπιάδης ὁ ἰατρὸς συγγυμνασίαν τῶν αἰσθήσεων. (PS) |

§6 Aristotle cf. *de An.* 2.1 412a27–b1   §7 Dicaearchus
fr. 21A   §8 Asclepiades pp. 724, 726

4.3

Ps.-Plut. *Plac.* 4.3; Stob. *Ecl.* 1.49.1b; Theod. *Cur.* 5.18

γʹ. Εἰ σῶμα ἡ ψυχὴ καὶ τίς ἡ οὐσία αὐτῆς (P) |

1. οὗτοι πάντες οἱ προτεταγμένοι ἀσώματον τὴν ψυχὴν ὑποτίθενται, | φύσιν λέγοντες αὐτοκίνητον καὶ οὐσίαν νοητὴν καὶ τοῦ φυσικοῦ | ὀργανικοῦ ζωὴν ἔχοντος ἐντελέχειαν. (P) |

⁷ ἐντελέχειαν PT: ἐνδελέχειαν S

6. Aristotle says that it is the first entelechy (i.e., actuality) of a body that is natural, organic, and potentially possessing life; and this "entelechy" must be understood to denote form and activity.

7. Dicaearchus says that it is a harmony of the four elements.

8. Asclepiades the doctor says that it is a common exercising of the senses. 15

4.3

Division according to number (and arranged according to the elements) of corporealist views of soul between monists, §§2–10, and pluralists, §§11–13, concluding with a compromise view.

Ps.-Plutarch, *Tenets*; Stobaeus, *Anthology*; Theodoret, *Cure of Greek Maladies*

3. Whether the soul is a body and what its substance is

1. All those arrayed previously assume that the soul is incorporeal, saying that it is self-moved, an intelligible substance, and the entelechy (i.e., actuality) of the natural organic entity that has life.

5 2. Ἀναξιμένης Ἀναξίμανδρος[8] Ἀναξαγόρας Ἀρχέλαος
Διογένης ἀεροειδῆ | ἔλεγόν τε καὶ σῶμα. (PST) |
3. οἱ Στωικοὶ πνεῦμα νοερὸν θερμόν. (PST) |
4. Παρμενίδης δὲ καὶ Ἵππασος καὶ Ἡράκλειτος[9] πυ-
ρώδη. (ST) |
5. Δημόκριτος πυρῶδες σύγκριμα ἐκ τῶν λόγῳ θεω-
10 ρητῶν, σφαιρικὰς | μὲν ἐχόντων τὰς ἰδέας, πυρίνην δὲ
τὴν δύναμιν, ὅπερ σῶμα εἶναι. | (PS) |
6. Ἡρακλείδης φωτοειδῆ τὴν ψυχὴν ὡρίσατο. (ST) |
7. Λεύκιππος ἐκ πυρὸς εἶναι τὴν ψυχήν. (S) |
8. Διογένης ὁ Ἀπολλωνιάτης ἐξ ἀέρος τὴν ψυχήν. (S) |
15 9. Ἵππων ἐξ ὕδατος τὴν ψυχήν. (S) |
10. Ξέναρχος ὁ Περιπατητικὸς καί τινες ἕτεροι τῆς
αὐτῆς αἱρέσεως | τὴν κατὰ τὸ εἶδος τελειότητα καὶ
ἐντελέχειαν, καθ᾽ ἑαυτὴν οὖσαν | ἅμα καὶ μετὰ τοῦ
σώματος συντεταγμένην. (S) |
11. Ἐπίκουρος κρᾶμα ἐκ τεττάρων, ἐκ ποιοῦ πυρώ-
20 δους, ἐκ ποιοῦ | ἀερώδους, ἐκ ποιοῦ πνευματικοῦ, ἐκ
τετάρτου τινὸς ἀκατονομάστου, τοῦτο δ᾽ ἦν αὐτῷ τὸ
αἰσθητικόν· ὧν τὸ μὲν πνεῦμα | κίνησιν, τὸν δὲ ἀέρα

§2 Anaximenes A23; Anaximander A29; Anaxagoras A93;
Archelaus A17; Diogenes T5b   §3 Stoics 2.779
    §4 Parmenides A45; Hippasus 18.9; Heraclitus T460 Mou-
raviev   §5 Democritus A102   §6 Heraclides fr. 46a,d
    §7 Leucippus A28   §8 Diogenes T5b
    §9 Hippo A10   §10 Xenarchus —
    §11 Epicurus fr. 315

8 Ἀναξίμανδρος om. S   9 καὶ Ἡράκλειτος T: om. S

326

2. Anaximenes, Anaximander, Anaxagoras, Archelaus, and   5
Diogenes said that it is air-like[3] and a body.

3. The Stoics say that it is an intelligent warm *pneuma*.

4. Parmenides, Hippasus and Heraclitus say that that it is
fire-like.

5. Democritus says that it is a fiery compound of things
that are observable by reason, having forms that are spher-   10
ical but with the potency of fire, which is a body.

6. Heraclides defined the soul as light-like.

7. Leucippus says that the soul consists of fire.

8. Diogenes of Apollonia says that the soul consists of air.

9. Hippo says that the soul consists of water.   15

10. Xenarchus the Peripatetic and certain others of the
same School say that it is the completion and entelechy
(i.e., actuality) with respect to the form, existing *per se*
while simultaneously being conjoined with the body.

11. Epicurus says that it is a mixture of four ingredients,
namely of a fiery quality, an aerial quality, a pneumatic   20
quality, and of a fourth quality that is nameless; this last,
for him, is the perceptive part. Of these the *pneuma* brings

---

[3] On the translation of adjectives ending in *-eidês*, see the note
to 2.2.

ἠρεμίαν, τὸ δὲ θερμὸν τὴν φαινομένην | θερμότητα
τοῦ σώματος, τὸ δ' ἀκατονόμαστον τὴν ἐν ἡμῖν ἐμποι-
εῖν[10] | αἴσθησιν, ἐν οὐδενὶ γὰρ τῶν ὀνομαζομένων
25 στοιχείων εἶναι | αἴσθησιν. (PST) |

12. Ἐμπεδοκλῆς μῖγμα ἐξ αἰθερώδους καὶ ἀερώδους
⟨καὶ ὑδατώδους | καὶ γεώδους⟩ οὐσίας.(T) |

13. Κριτίας ἐξ αἵματος εἶπε καὶ ἐξ ὑγροῦ. (T) |

14. Ἡράκλειτος τὴν μὲν τοῦ κόσμου ψυχὴν ἀναθυμία-
30 σιν ἐκ τῶν ἐν | αὐτῷ ὑγρῶν, τὴν δ' ἐν τοῖς ζῴοις ἀπὸ
τῆς ἐκτὸς καὶ τῆς ἐν αὐτοῖς | ἀναθυμιάσεως, ὁμο-
γενῆ. (P) |

§12 Empedocles —   §13 Critias —
§14 Heraclitus A15

4.4

Ps.-Plut. *Plac.* 4.4; Stob. *Ecl.* 1.49.7a, 50.35; Theod. *Cur.*
5.19–21

δ'. Περὶ μερῶν ψυχῆς (PS) |

1. Πυθαγόρας Πλάτων κατὰ μὲν τὸν ἀνωτάτω λόγον
διμερῆ τὴν ψυχήν, τὸ | μὲν γὰρ ἔχειν λογικὸν τὸ δ'
ἄλογον· κατὰ δὲ τὸ προσεχὲς καὶ ἀκριβὲς | τριμερῆ,

§1 Pythagoras Plato cf. *Resp.* 4.439d–e

[10] ἐμποιεῖν Heeren Diels ex cod. Vat.: ἐμποιεῖ S

about movement, the air rest, the warm component the perceptible warmth of the body, while the anonymous component brings about the perception in us humans, for perception is not present in any of the elements that have names.   25

12. Empedocles says that it is a blend of an ethereal and an aerial ⟨and a watery and an earthy⟩ substance.[4]

13. Critias said that it is a blend of blood and [or: i.e.,] of moisture.

14. Heraclitus says that the Soul of the cosmos is an exhalation from the moistures that are in it (sc. the cosmos),   30
and that the soul in living beings derives from the exterior exhalation as well as from that which is within them (sc. the living beings) and is of the same kind.

4.4

Division of the parts of soul according to number and function in ascending order, §§1–5, followed by one in descending order, §§6–8.

Ps.-Plutarch, *Tenets*; Stobaeus, *Anthology*; Theodoret, *Cure of Greek Maladies*

4. On the parts of soul

1. Pythagoras and Plato according to their most general definition say that the soul is bipartite, for it has a rational part on the one hand and an irrational on the other. But

---

[4] For the conjecture, cf. 5.25.4. At *de An.* 1.2 404b11–12 Aristotle says that for Empedocles the soul is composed "of all the elements."

τὸ γὰρ ἄλογον διαιροῦσιν εἴς τε τὸ θυμικὸν καὶ τὸ
5 ἐπιθυμητικόν. | (PT) |

2. Ξενοκράτης τὸ μὲν αἰσθητικόν, τὸ δὲ λογικόν. (T) |

3. Ἀριστοτέλης[11] πέντε ἐνεργείας, τὴν ὀρεκτικήν, τὴν
θρεπτικήν, τὴν | αἰσθητικήν, τὴν μεταβατικήν, τὴν
διανοητικήν. (T) |

4. οἱ Στωικοὶ ἐξ ὀκτὼ μερῶν φασι συνεστάναι, πέντε
10 μὲν τῶν αἰσθητικῶν, | ὁρατικοῦ ἀκουστικοῦ ὀσφρητι-
κοῦ γευστικοῦ ἁπτικοῦ, ἕκτου δὲ φωνητικοῦ, ἑβδόμου
δὲ σπερματικοῦ, ὀγδόου δ' αὐτοῦ τοῦ ἡγεμονικοῦ,
ἀφ' οὗ | ταῦτα πάντα ἐπιτέταται[12] διὰ τῶν οἰκείων
ὀργάνων, προσφερῶς ταῖς τοῦ | πολύποδος πλεκτά-
ναις. (PT) |

5. Ἀπολλοφάνης <ἐξ ἐννέα μερῶν φησι τὴν ψυχὴν
συνεστάναι>.[13] (S) |

15 6. οἱ δέ γε Πυθαγόρου διάδοχοι ἐκ πέντε στοιχείων τὸ
σῶμα κραθῆναι | φάντες—τοῖς γὰρ τέτταρσι ξυνέτα-
ξαν τὸ αἰθέριον—ἰσαρίθμους εἶναι | ἔφασαν ταύτῃ καὶ
τῆς ψυχῆς τὰς δυνάμεις· καὶ ταύτας ὠνομάκασι νοῦν
| καὶ φρόνησιν καὶ ἐπιστήμην καὶ δόξαν καὶ αἴσθη-
σιν. (T) |

§2 Xenocrates fr. 126   §3 Aristotle cf. *de An.* 2.2
413b11–13, 2.3 414a31–32   §4 Stoics 2.827
§5 Apollophanes cf. *SVF* 1.405
§6 Pythagoreans cf. Arist. *de An.* 1.2 404b21–24

11 Ἀριστοτέλης coni. MR: ὁ δὲ Νικομάχου T
12 ἐπιτέταται corr. Zeller Diels: (ἐπι)τέτακται P
13 <ἐξ ἐννέα . . . συνεστάναι> suppl. Elter

according to what is proximate and precise it is tripartite, for they divide the irrational into the spirited and the con- 5 cupiscible.

2. Xenocrates says that one part of the soul is perceiving, and the other rational.

3. Aristotle said there are five activities of soul, the appetitive, the nurturing, the perceiving, the locomotive, the cogitating.

4. The Stoics say the soul consists of eight parts: five perceiving parts, viz. seeing, hearing, smelling, tasting, touch- 10 ing; as sixth the speaking part; as seventh the seminal part; as eighth the regent part itself, from which all these other parts are extended through their own organs, similarly to the tentacles of an octopus.

5. Apollophanes ‹says that the soul consists of nine parts›.[5]

6. The successors of Pythagoras, positing that the body is 15 a blend of five elements—for to the four they added the ethereal element—said the powers of the soul too are in respect of this division equal in number, and these they called intelligence and understanding and knowledge and opinion and sensation.

[5] From the inclusion of Apollophanes' name-label in Photius' index of names, when combined with the doxa preserved by Tertullian in a similar context, Elter deduced that in all likelihood the same doxa was originally present here.

7. Δημόκριτος Ἐπίκουρος διμερῆ τὴν ψυχήν, τὸ μὲν λογικὸν ἔχουσαν ἐν | τῷ θώρακι καθιδρυμένον, τὸ δὲ
20 ἄλογον καθ' ὅλην τὴν σύγκρισιν τοῦ | σώματος διεσπαρμένον. (P) |

8. ὁ δὲ Δημόκριτος πάντα μετέχειν φησὶ ψυχῆς ποιᾶς, καὶ τὰ νεκρὰ τῶν | σωμάτων, διότι ἀεὶ διαφανῶς τινος θερμοῦ καὶ αἰσθητικοῦ μετέχει, τοῦ | πλείονος διαπνεομένου.[14] (PS) |

§7 Democritus A105; Epicurus fr. 312
§8 Democritus A117

4.5

Ps.-Plut. *Plac.* 4.5; Theod. *Cur.* 5.22

ε΄. Τί τὸ τῆς ψυχῆς ἡγεμονικὸν καὶ ἐν τίνι ἐστίν (PT) |

1. Πλάτων Δημόκριτος ἐν ὅλῃ τῇ κεφαλῇ. (PT) |
2. Ἱπποκράτης ἐν ἐγκεφάλῳ. (T) |
3. Στράτων ἐν μεσοφρύῳ. (PT) |

§1 Democritus A105; Plato cf. *Tht.* 184d, *Tim.* 44d–e
§2 Hippocrates of Cos cf. *Morb. sacr.* 14, 17
§3 Strato fr. 57

7. Democritus and Epicurus say that the soul is bipartite, having the rational part established in the breast, and the irrational part diffused through the whole compound of   20 the body.

8. But Democritus says that all things participate in a sort of soul, even dead bodies, because they patently continue to participate in something warm and perceptive, though most of this is expired out of them.

4.5

Definitions of the regent part in accordance with top-down division between head and chest (or brain and heart) and subsidiary top-down divisions of locations in head or chest, concluding with the compromise doxai of §§13–14.

Ps.-Plutarch, *Tenets*; Theodoret, *Cure of Greek Maladies*

5. What the regent part is, and in which part[6] it is found

1. Plato and Democritus say it is in the whole head.
2. Hippocrates says it is in the brain.
3. Strato says it is in the part of the forehead between the eyebrows.

---

[6] Sc. of the body

---

[14] ὁ δὲ . . . διαπνεομένου P: Δημόκριτος τὰ νεκρὰ τῶν σωμάτων αἰσθάνεσθαι S

5 4. Ἐρασίστρατος δὲ ὁ ἰατρὸς περὶ τὴν τοῦ ἐγκεφάλου
μήνιγγα, ἣν "ἐπικρανίδα" | λέγει. (PT) |

5. Ἡρόφιλος ἐν τῇ τοῦ ἐγκεφάλου κοιλίᾳ, ἥτις ἐστὶ
καὶ βάσις. (PT) |

6. Παρμενίδης ἐν ὅλῳ τῷ θώρακι καὶ Ἐπίκουρος. (PT) |

7. Ἀριστο<τέ>λης[15] οἱ Στωικοὶ πάντες ἐν ὅλῃ τῇ καρ-
10 δίᾳ ἢ τῷ περὶ τὴν | καρδίαν πνεύματι. (PT) |

8. Διογένης ἐν τῇ ἀρτηριακῇ κοιλίᾳ τῆς καρδίας, ἥτις
ἐστὶ πνευματική. | (PT) |

9. Ἐμπεδοκλῆς ἐν τῇ τοῦ αἵματος[16] συστάσει. (PT) |

10. οἱ δ' ἐν τῷ τραχήλῳ τῆς καρδίας, (P) |

15 11. οἱ δ' ἐν τῷ περικαρδίῳ ὑμένι, (PT) |

12. οἱ δ' ἐν τῷ διαφράγματι. (PT) |

13. τῶν νεωτέρων τινὲς διήκειν ἀπὸ κεφαλῆς μέχρι
τοῦ διαφράγματος. | (P) |

14. Πυθαγόρας τὸ μὲν ζωτικὸν περὶ τὴν καρδίαν, τὸ
20 δὲ λογικὸν καὶ νοερὸν | περὶ τὴν κεφαλήν. (P) |

---

§4 Erasistratus fr. 40 §5 Herophilus fr. 137a

§6 Parmenides A45; Epicurus fr. 312 §7 Aristotle cf.
Iuv. 3 469a4–7, 469a33–b1, *PA* 3.4 665b18–23; Stoics 2.838

§8 Diogenes of Apollonia A20; more likely Diogenes the
Stoic, cf. *SVF* 3.30 §9 Empedocles A97

§§10–13 anonymi — §14 Pythagoras —

15 Ἀριστο<τέ>λης coni. MR: Ἀριστοκλῆς T
16 fort. <περικαρδίου> post αἵματος, cf. Emped. B105.3

4. Erasistratus says it is in the membrane enveloping the 5
brain, which he calls "on the skull" (*epikranis*).

5. Herophilus says it is in the ventricle of the brain, which
is also its base.

6. Parmenides says it is in the whole chest; as also does
Epicurus.

7. Aristotle and all the Stoics[7] say it is in the whole heart,
or in the *pneuma* about the heart. 10

8. Diogenes says it is in the arterial ventricle of the heart,
which is pneumatic.

9. Empedocles says it is in the compound of the blood.

10. Some people say it is in the neck of the heart,

11. But others in the pericardium, 15

12. And yet others in the midriff.

13. Some of the later thinkers say that it extends from the
head to the midriff.

14. Pythagoras says that the life-sustaining part is in the
region of the heart, the rational and intelligent in the re- 20
gion of the head.

[7] This is not accurate; cf. 4.21.1[20–21].

4.6

Ps.-Plut. *Plac*.4.6; Stob. *Ecl*. 1.49.7bc

ϛ′. Περὶ κινήσεως ψυχῆς (PS) |

1. Πλάτων ἀεικίνητον μὲν τὴν ψυχήν, τὸν δὲ νοῦν ἀκίνητον τῆς μεταβατικῆς | κινήσεως. (PS) |

2. Ἀριστοτέλης ἀκίνητον τὴν ψυχὴν πάσης κινήσεως
5 προηγουμένην, τῆς | δὲ κατὰ συμβεβηκὸς μετέχειν, καθάπερ τὰ σχήματα καὶ τὰ πέρατα καὶ | καθάπαξ τὰ περὶ τοῖς σώμασιν εἴδη.[17] (PS) |

§1 Plato cf. *Phdr*. 245b–c   §2 Aristotle cf. *de An*. 1.3 405b32–406a2, 406a17–20, 1.4 408b30–31

4.7

Ps.-Plut. *Plac*. 4.7; Stob. *Ecl*. 1.49.7c; Theod. *Cur*. 1.63, 5.23–24

ζ′. Περὶ ἀφθαρσίας ψυχῆς (PS) |

1. Πυθαγόρας Ἀναξαγόρας Διογένης Πλάτων Ἐμπεδοκλῆς Ξενοκράτης | ἄφθαρτον εἶναι τὴν ψυχήν. (PST) |

§1 Pythagoras —; Anaxagoras A93; Diogenes A20; Plato cf. *Phdr*. 245c; Empedocles —; Xenocrates fr. 130b

4.6

Two diaphonically opposed views, each of which sports an internal exception.

Ps.-Plutarch, *Tenets*; Stobaeus, *Anthology*

6. On the motion of soul

1. Plato says that the soul is ever-moving, but that the intellect is unmoved as regards locomotion.
2. Aristotle says that the soul is unmoved because it is prior to all motion, but it does partake of accidental motion, just 5 as do the shapes and boundaries and in general all the formal aspects that relate to bodies.

4.7

Diaphonic opposition between the extreme views in §1 and §4, and division of views including compromise ones on a gliding scale.

Ps.-Plutarch, *Tenets*; Stobaeus, *Anthology*; Theodoret, *Cure of Greek Maladies*

7. On the indestructibility of soul

1. Pythagoras, Anaxagoras, Diogenes, Plato, Empedocles, and Xenocrates say that the soul is indestructible.

---

17 τὰ περὶ . . . εἴδη S: τὰ εἴδη τῶν σωμάτων P

AETIUS

2. Ἡράκλειτος ἐξιοῦσαν[18] τοῦ σώματος εἰς τὴν τοῦ
5 παντὸς ἀναχωρεῖν | ψυχὴν πρὸς τὸ ὁμογενές. (PT) |

3. οἱ Στωικοὶ ἐξιοῦσαν ἐκ τῶν σωμάτων οὔπω φθείρε-
σθαι·[19] τὴν μὲν | ἀσθενεστέραν ἅμα τοῖς συγκρίμασι
{γίνεσθαι},[20] ταύτην δ᾽ εἶναι τῶν | ἀπαιδεύτων· τὴν δ᾽
ἰσχυροτέραν, οἵα ἐστὶ περὶ τοὺς σοφούς, καὶ μέχρι |
τῆς τοῦ παντὸς ἐκπυρώσεως ‹ἐπιδιαμένειν›.[21] (PT) |

10 4. Δημόκριτος Ἐπίκουρος Ἀριστοτέλης φθαρτὴν τῷ
σώματι συνδιαφθειρομένην. | (PT) |

5. Πυθαγόρας Πλάτων τὸ μὲν λογικὸν ἄφθαρτον· καὶ
γὰρ τὴν ψυχὴν οὐ | θεὸν ἀλλ᾽ ἔργον τοῦ ἀιδίου θεοῦ
ὑπάρχειν· τὸ δ᾽ ἄλογον φθαρτόν. | (PT) |

§2 Heraclitus A17 §3 Stoics 2.810
§4 Democritus A109; Epicurus fr. 336
§5 Pythagoras —; Plato cf. *Tim.* 30b, 69c–e

18 ψυχήν. Ἡράκλειτος ἐξιοῦσαν coni. MR: τὴν ψυχήν . . .
ὁ δὲ Ἡράκλειτος T: τὴν ψυχὴν *** ἐξιοῦσαν P
19 οὔπω φθείρεσθαι coni. Diels: ὑποφέρεσθαι P
20 ἅμα . . . γίνεσθαι PQ, secl. Diels {γίνεσθαι} secl.
MR
21 ‹ἐπιδιαμένειν› coni. MR

338

2. Heraclitus says that on departing from the body it re-
turns to the Soul of the universe, i.e., to what is of the same   5
kind.
3. The Stoics say that on departing from the bodies it is
not yet destroyed; the weaker soul, that is, that of the
uneducated, is destroyed together with the compounds;
but the stronger, such as the one attributable to the wise,
lasts[8] right up to the total conflagration of the universe.
4. Epicurus, Democritus, and Aristotle say that the soul is   10
mortal, perishing together with the body.
5. Plato and Pythagoras say that the rational part is indestructible; for though the soul is not a god, it is the product
of the everlasting God; but the irrational part is destructible.

[8] An infinitive is required at the end of the sentence and must
have fallen out. The conjecture is based on parallel passages
in Diogenes of Oenoanda, Diogenes Laertius, Hippolytus, and
Origen.

4.7a

Stob. *Ecl.* 1.48.7; Theod. *Cur.* 5.28

ζ᾽. Περὶ νοῦ (S) |

1. Πυθαγόρας Ἀναξαγόρας Πλάτων Ξενοκράτης Κλεάνθης θύραθεν εἰσκρίνεσθαι | τὸν νοῦν. (ST) |

2. Παρμενίδης καὶ Ἐμπεδοκλῆς καὶ Δημόκριτος ταὐ-
5 τὸν νοῦν καὶ ψυχήν, | καθ᾽ οὓς οὐδὲν ἂν εἴη ζῷον ἄλογον κυρίως. (S) |

§1 Pythagoras —; Anaxagoras A93; Plato —; Xenocrates fr. 125; Cleanthes 1.523   §2 Parmenides A45; Empedocles A96, cf. B110.10; Democritus —

4.7a

Diaphonic division of the relation between intellect and soul.

Stobaeus, *Anthology*; Theodoret, *Cure of Greek Maladies*

7a. On intellect[9]

1. Pythagoras, Anaxagoras, Plato, Xenocrates, and Cleanthes say that the intellect enters from outside (sc. as a separate component).

2. Parmenides, Empedocles, and Democritus say that intellect and soul are the same thing. According to them no 5 living being could be without reason in the true sense of the word.

[9] Unusually, Ps.-Plutarch omitted this chapter, but it is preserved in Stobaeus and partly utilized by Theodoret.

4.8

*The Stoic and other definitions of sensation and sense
object(s) include those of the sense organ(s) and involve
various, even diaphonically opposed, explanations of the
sensory process. Related issues treated are questions such*

Ps.-Plut. *Plac.* 4.8 (+ Ps.-Gal. *Hist. phil.* 90); Stob. *Ecl.*
4.232.7–15 Meineke + 1.50.1–2a, 1.51.3–6, 1.50.10–16
Wachsmuth

η′. Περὶ αἰσθήσεως καὶ αἰσθητῶν (PS) |

1. οἱ Στωικοὶ ὁρίζονται οὕτως τὴν αἴσθησιν· "αἴσθη-
σίς ἐστιν ἀντίληψις δι᾽ | αἰσθητηρίου ἢ κατάληψις."
πολλαχῶς δὲ λέγεται ἡ αἴσθησις, ἥ τε γὰρ | ἕξις καὶ
ἡ δύναμις καὶ ἡ ἐνέργεια. καὶ ἡ φαντασία ἡ καταλη-
5 πτικὴ δι᾽ | αἰσθητηρίου γίνεται κατὰ τὸ ἡγεμονικόν
{ἀφ᾽ οὗ συνίσταται}.[22] πάλιν δ᾽ | αἰσθητήρια λέγεται
πνεύματα νοερά, ἀπὸ τοῦ ἡγεμονικοῦ ⟨ἀφ᾽ οὗ συν-
ίσταται⟩[23] | ἐπὶ τὰ ὄργανα τεταμένα. (PS)[24] |
2. Ἐπίκουρος· "τὸ μόριόν ἐστιν ἡ αἴσθησις, ἥτις
ἐστὶν ἡ δύναμις, καὶ τὸ | ἐπαίσθημα, ὅπερ ἐστὶ τὸ
10 ἐνέργημα"· ὥστε διχῶς παρ᾽ αὐτῷ λέγεσθαι | αἴσθη-
σιν μὲν τὴν δύναμιν, αἰσθητὸν δὲ τὸ ἐνέργημα. (PS) |

§1 Stoics 2.850   §2 Epicurus fr. 249

[22] {ἀφ᾽ οὗ συνίσταται} hic damn. MR: om. Q
[23] ⟨ἀφ᾽ οὗ συνίσταται⟩ ex l. 5 hic transp. MR
[24] 1–7 S ex ms. L, non hab. Wachsmuth, ret. Meineke

4.8

as to what extent soul, or body, or both are concerned; whether sensations are of bodies or incorporeals; and the extent to which, according to various schools, sensation amounts to cognition.

Ps.-Plutarch, *Tenets* (+ Ps.-Galen, *Philosophical History*); Stobaeus, *Anthology*

8. On sensation and sense objects

1. The Stoics define sensation as follows: "sensation is perception or cognition via a sensor (i.e., sense organ)." Sensation is spoken of in several senses, for it is a condition as well as a faculty and an activity. Also the cognitive impression occurs via a sensor in the regent part. Moreover, sensors denote intellectual breaths, extended from the regent part from which they arise to the organs.[10] 5

2. Epicurus: "sense/sensation is the bodily part that is the faculty, and the sensory recognition that is the activity";[11] so it is spoken of by him in two ways: sense as the faculty, sensory recognition as the activity. 10

[10] This lemma in Stobaeus was wrongly excised by Wachsmuth. It is still present in Diels *DG*, but he later changed his mind.

[11] Unusually, the first two doxai contain verbatim quotations instead of the standard *oratio obliqua*.

3. Πλάτων τὴν αἴσθησιν ἀποφαίνεται ψυχῆς καὶ σώ-
ματος κοινωνίαν πρὸς | τὰ ἐκτός· ἡ μὲν γὰρ δύναμις
ψυχῆς, τὸ δ' ὄργανον σώματος· ἄμφω δὲ | διὰ φαντα-
σίας²⁵ ἀντιληπτικὰ τῶν ἔξωθεν. (PS) |

4. κατὰ τοὺς Περιπατητικοὺς τετραχῶς· ἐξ οὗ τὸ ἡγε-
15   μονικόν, δι' οὗ τὸ | ὄργανον καὶ αἰσθητήριον, καθ' ὃ
ἡ ἐνέργεια, καὶ ⟨οὗ⟩²⁶ ἕνεκα τὸ αἰσθητόν. | (S) |

5. Λεύκιππος Δημόκριτος τὰς αἰσθήσεις καὶ τὰς νοή-
σεις ἑτεροιώσεις εἶναι | τοῦ σώματος. (S) |

6. Ἀριστοτέλης τὴν αἴσθησιν ἑτεροίωσιν αἰσθητ⟨ι-
20   κ⟩οῦ²⁷ καὶ μεσότητα | ⟨αἰσθητοῦ⟩·²⁸ κοινὴν δὲ αἴσθη-
σιν τὴν τῶν συνθέτων²⁹ εἰδῶν κριτικήν, εἰς ἣν | πᾶ-
σαι³⁰ συμβάλλουσιν αἱ ἁπλαῖ τὰς ἰδίας ἑκάστη
⟨φαντασίας⟩,³¹ ἐν ᾗ τὸ | μεταβατικὸν ἀφ' ἑτέρου εἰς
ἕτερον οἷον σχήματος ⟨καὶ⟩³² κινήσεως σώματος, | ἐν
μεθορίῳ τοῦ λογικοῦ καὶ τοῦ ἀλόγου, μνήμης καὶ νοῦ
μετέχουσα, | διατείνουσα καὶ ἐπὶ τὰ ἄλογα τῶν ζῴων,
25   καθὸ ποσὴν διανοίας ἀναλογίαν | ἔχει· κοινὰ δ' ἐστὶν
ὄψεως μὲν καὶ ἁφῆς σχῆμα, ὄψεως δὲ καὶ | ἀκοῆς
διάστημα, πασῶν δὲ κίνησις καὶ μέγεθος καὶ ἀριθ-
μός. (S) |

§3 Plato cf. *Phlb*. 34a, *Tim*. 43c, 46c, Ps.-Plato *Def*. 414c
§4 Peripatetics —   §5 Leucippus A30; Democritus frs.
68, 436 Luria   §6 Aristotle cf. *de An*. 2.4 415b24, 2.11
424a4–5, 3.1 425a13–15

25 [φαν]τασιας Ant: φαντασίαν PS, φαντασίας iam coni.
Reiske   26 ⟨οὗ⟩ add. Meineke   27 αἰσθητ⟨ικ⟩οῦ coni.
MR: αἰσθητοῦ S   28 ⟨αἰσθητοῦ⟩ add. MR

3. Plato declares that sensation is the commonality of soul and body with regard to what is outside; for the faculty belongs to the soul, the organ to the body; together they are capable of apprehending what is outside via impression.

4. According to the Peripatetics, sensation occurs in four ways: from which is the regent part, through which the organ, that is, sense organ, according to which the activity, and because of which the sense object.

5. Leucippus and Democritus say that the sensations and the thought processes are alterations of the body.

6. Aristotle says that sensation is an alteration of the sensing part of the soul, and a mean between the extreme properties ⟨of the sense object⟩; the *sensus communis* is the judge of the compounded forms. Toward it all the simple senses each on its own contribute their particular ⟨impressions⟩ and in it (sc. the *sensus communis*) is located the changeover from one form to the other, such as of shape and movement of a body. It lies in between the rational and the nonrational, partaking of memory and intellect, extending even toward the nonrational animals insofar as these possess a certain amount of what is analogous to understanding. Common to sight and touch are: form, to sight and hearing: distance, and to all: motion and size and number.

---

29 συνθέτων Diels ex 4.10.2: συνθέντων S

30 πᾶσαι Diels ex 4.10.2: πάλαι S

31 ⟨φαντασίας⟩ add. Diels ex 4.10.2

32 ⟨καί⟩ add. Diels ex 4.10.2

7. ⟨οἱ⟩ Στωικοὶ τήνδε τὴν κοινὴν αἴσθησιν "ἐντὸς ἀφὴν" προσαγορεύουσι, | καθ᾽ ἣν καὶ ἡμῶν αὐτῶν ἀντιλαμβανόμεθα. (S) |

8. οἱ Στωικοὶ σωμάτων τὰς αἰσθήσεις. (S) |

30 9. οἱ ἀπὸ τῶν ἀρχαίων τῶν περὶ τὰ σώματα ἀσωμά- των λόγων, ἅπερ ἤδη σχήματα | προσαγορεύουσι. (S) |

10. Λεύκιππος Δημόκριτος Ἐπίκουρος τὴν αἴσθησιν καὶ τὴν νόησιν | γίνεσθαι εἰδώλων ἔξωθεν προσιόν- των· μηδενὶ γὰρ ἐπιβάλλειν μηδετέραν | χωρὶς τοῦ προσπίπτοντος εἰδώλου. (PS) |

35 11. οἱ ἄλλοι εἰδῶν ἢ σχημάτων ἑτεροιώσει ἐν ψυχῇ ⟨ἢ⟩[33] τυπώσει, ἀπορροίαις | πάντως μᾶλλον ἢ εἰδώ- λοις. (S) |

12. οἱ Στωικοὶ πᾶσαν αἴσθησιν εἶναι συγκατάθεσιν καὶ κατάληψιν. (S) |

13. ⟨οἱ⟩ Ἀκαδημαικοὶ μὴ εἶναι τὰς αἰσθήσεις μήτε καταλήψεις μήτε συγκαταθέσεις. | (S) |

40 14. οἱ Περιπατητικοὶ οὐκ ἄνευ μὲν συγκαταθέσεως τὰς αἰσθήσεις, οὐ μέντοι | συγκαταθέσεις. (S) |

§7 Stoics 2.852   §8 Stoics 2.851
§9 anonymi —   §10 Leucippus A30; Democritus frs. 68,
436 Luria; Epicurus —   §11 anonymi, i.e., Stoics —
§12 Stoics 2.72   §13 Academics —
§14 Peripatetics —

[33] ⟨ἢ⟩ post ψυχῇ add. MR, post ἑτεροιώσει Wachsmuth

346

7. ⟨The⟩ Stoics call this *sensus communis* "inner touch,"
according to which we also perceive ourselves.

8. The Stoics say that sensations are of bodies.

9. The successors of the ancients say that sensations are of   30
the incorporeal *logoi* relating to the bodies, which they at
the same time describe as shapes.

10. Leucippus, Democritus, and Epicurus say that sensation and thought arise in the soul from images that approach from outside, for neither of these can occur to
anyone without the image falling upon him.

11. Others say that sensation and thought arise in the soul   35
through alteration of forms or shapes or through imprint-
ing; in any case through effluences rather than through
images.

12. The Stoics say that each sensation is an assent and a
cognition.

13. ⟨The⟩ Academics say that the sensations are neither
cognitions nor assents.

14. The Peripatetics say that the sensations are not without   40
assent, but are themselves not assents.

4.9

Variously opposed views concerned with the truth value of sensation(s), the ways of perceiving sense-data, the question whether they exist in reality or are a matter of convention, are pure or compounded, and whether pleasures and

Ps.-Plut. *Plac.* 4.9 (+ Ps.-Gal. *Hist. phil.* 91); Stob. *Ecl.* 1.50.17–35

θ'. Εἰ ἀληθεῖς αἱ αἰσθήσεις καὶ φαντασίαι (PS) |

1. Πυθαγόρας Ἐμπεδοκλῆς Ξενοφάνης Παρμενίδης Ζήνων Μέλισσος | Ἀναξαγόρας Δημόκριτος Μητρόδωρος Πρωταγόρας Πλάτων ψευδεῖς | εἶναι τὰς αἰσθήσεις. (S) |

5   2. οἱ ἀπὸ τῆς Ἀκαδημίας ὑγιεῖς μέν, ὅτι δι' αὐτῶν οἴονται λαβεῖν ἀληθινὰς | φαντασίας, οὐ μὴν ἀκριβεῖς. (S) |

3. Ἀριστοτέλης τὴν αἴσθησιν μὴ πλανᾶσθαι περὶ τὸ ἴδιον, περὶ δὲ τὸ | συμβεβηκός. (S) |

4. οἱ Στωικοὶ τὰς μὲν αἰσθήσεις ἀληθεῖς, τῶν δὲ φαν-
10   τασιῶν τὰς μὲν | ἀληθεῖς τὰς δὲ ψευδεῖς. (PS) |

§1 Pythagoras —; Empedocles —; Xenophanes A49; Parmenides A49; Zeno of Elea cf. A23; Melissus cf. A14; Anaxagoras A96; Democritus fr. 54 Luria; Metrodorus A22; Protagoras —; Plato —   §2 Academics —   §3 Aristotle cf. *de An.* 2.6 418a11–12   §4 Stoics 2.78

*pains are sensory or mental. §§18–20 treat the subsidiary
question whether a wise man can be identified by sensation
or thought, or only by an equally wise man.*

Ps.-Plutarch, *Tenets* (+ Ps.-Galen, *Philosophical History*);
Stobaeus, *Anthology*

9. Whether sensations and impressions are true

1. Pythagoras, Empedocles, Xenophanes, Parmenides,
Zeno, Melissus, Anaxagoras, Democritus, Metrodorus,
Protagoras, and Plato say that sensations are false.
2. The successors of the Academy say that sensations are   5
sound, because they believe that by means of them they
grasp true impressions, though these are not precise.
3. Aristotle says that sensation does not err with regard to
its proper object, but it does err with regard to what is
incidental.
4. The Stoics say that sensations are true, but that of impressions some are true and some false.   10

5. Ἐπίκουρος πᾶσαν αἴσθησιν καὶ πᾶσαν φαντασίαν
ἀληθῆ, τῶν δὲ δοξῶν | τὰς μὲν ἀληθεῖς τὰς δὲ ψευδεῖς.
καὶ ἡ μὲν αἴσθησις μοναχῶς ψευδοποιεῖται | τὰ κατὰ
τὰ³⁴ νοητά, ἡ δὲ φαντασία διχῶς· καὶ γὰρ αἰσθητῶν
| ἐστι φαντασία καὶ νοητῶν.³⁵ (PS) |

15 6. Παρμενίδης Ἐμπεδοκλῆς Ἀναξαγόρας Δημόκριτος
Ἐπίκουρος Ἡρακλείδης | παρὰ τὰς συμμετρίας τῶν
πόρων τὰς κατὰ μέρος αἰσθήσεις | γίνεσθαι τοῦ
οἰκείου, τῶν αἰσθητῶν ἑκάστου ἑκάστῃ ἐναρμόττο-
ντος.³⁶ | (PS) |

7. οἱ Περιπατητικοὶ παρὰ³⁷ τὰς δυνάμεις τῶν αἰσθη-
τηρίων. (S) |

20 8. οἱ μὲν ἄλλοι φύσει τὰ αἰσθητά, (S) |

9. Λεύκιππος δὲ Δημόκριτος³⁸ Διογένης νόμῳ, τοῦτο δ'
ἐστὶ δόξῃ καὶ πάθεσι | τοῖς ἡμετέροις· μηδὲν δ' εἶναι
ἀληθὲς μηδὲ καταληπτὸν ἐκτὸς τῶν | πρώτων στοι-
χείων, ἀτόμων καὶ κενοῦ· ταῦτα γὰρ εἶναι μόνα φύσει,

25 τὰ δ' | ἐκ τούτων, θέσει καὶ τάξει καὶ σχήματι δια-
φέροντα ἀλλήλων, συμβεβηκότα. | (S)|

---

§5 Epicurus fr. 248   §6 Parmenides A47; Empedocles
A90; Anaxagoras —; Democritus fr. 437 Luria; Epicurus cf.
Ep.Hdt. at Diog. Laert. 10.49; Heraclides of Pontus fr. 63A, B
§7 Peripatetics —   §8 anonymi —   §9 Leucippus
A32; Democritus frs. 95, 243 Luria; Diogenes A23

³⁴ κατὰ τὰ corr. Meineke: τὰ om. PS
³⁵ 12–14 καὶ . . . νοητῶν Stoicis attrib. Usener
³⁶ ἐναρμόττοντος corr. Diels ex 1.15.3: ἀναρμόττοντος S,
ἁρμόζοντος P   ³⁷ παρὰ corr. Meineke: περὶ S
³⁸ post Δημόκριτος add. S καὶ, del. MR

5. Epicurus says that every sensation and every impression is true, but of the opinions some are true and some false; and sensation gives us a false picture in one respect only, namely with regard to objects of thought; but the impression does so in two respects, for there is impression of both sense objects and objects of thought.

6. Parmenides, Empedocles, Anaxagoras, Democritus, Epicurus, and Heraclides say that the particular sensations of their own object occur in accordance with the matching sizes of the pores, each of the sense objects corresponding to each sense.

7. The Peripatetics say that the particular sensations of their own objects come about in relation to the faculties of the sense organs.

8. The others say that sense objects exist by nature,

9. But Leucippus, Democritus, and Diogenes say that they exist by convention, that is, because of our opinion and conditions, and that nothing is real/true or cognitive apart from the primary elements, i.e., the atoms and the void; for only these exist by nature, and those things that derive from them, differing from each other in position and order and shape, are incidental.[12]

---

[12] Cf. 1.15.8, on colors.

10. οἱ τὰ ἄτομα καὶ οἱ τὰ ὁμοιομερῆ καὶ οἱ τὰ ἀμερῆ καὶ τὰ ἐλάχιστα πάντ᾽ | ἐν πᾶσι τὰ αἰσθητὰ ἀναμε-μῖχθαι καὶ μηδὲν αὐτῶν εἰλικρινὲς ὑπάρχειν, | παρὰ δὲ τὰς ἐπικρατείας ὀνομάζεσθαι τοῖον ἢ τοῖον καὶ παρὰ τὴν | πολυαύγειαν. (S) |

30   11. Πυθαγόρας Πλάτων καθαρὸν ἕκαστον εἶναι τῶν αἰσθητῶν ἐξ ἑκάστου | στοιχείου προσερχόμενον. πρὸς μὲν οὖν τὴν ὅρασιν τὸ αἰθερῶδες | πεφυκέναι, πρὸς δὲ τὴν ἀκοὴν τὸ πνευματικόν, πρὸς δὲ τὴν ὄσφρησιν τὸ | πυρῶδες, πρὸς δὲ τὴν γεῦσιν τὸ ὑγρόν, πρὸς δὲ τὴν ἀφὴν τὸ γεῶδες. (S) |

35   12. Ἐπίκουρος τῶν αἰσθητῶν ⟨τὰς⟩ ἡδονὰς ἤδη καὶ τὰς λύπας. (S) |

13. οἱ Περιπατητικοὶ τῶν νοητῶν· οὐ γὰρ πᾶσι φαίνε-ται τὰ αὐτὰ ἡδέα τε | καὶ λυπηρὰ καθάπερ λευκά τε καὶ μέλανα. (S) |

14. Χρύσιππος τὸ μὲν γενικὸν ἡδὺ νοητόν, τὸ δὲ εἰδι-κὸν καὶ προσπῖπτον | ἤδη αἰσθητόν. (S) |

40   15. Ἐμπεδοκλῆς τὰς ἡδονὰς γίνεσθαι τοῖς μὲν ὁμοί-οις ⟨ἐκ⟩ τῶν ὁμοίων | κατὰ δὲ τὸ ἐλλεῖπον πρὸς τὴν ἀναπλήρωσιν, ὥστε τῷ ἐλλείποντι ἡ | ὄρεξις τοῦ ὁμοίου· τὰς δ᾽ ἀλγηδόνας τοῖς ἐναντίοις, ἠλλοτριῶ-σθαι γὰρ | πρὸς ἄλληλα ὅσα διαφέρει κατά τε τὴν σύγκρισιν καὶ τὴν τῶν | στοιχείων κρᾶσιν. (S) |

§10 Atomists —; Homoeomerists —; Amerists —; Ela-chists —   §11 Pythagoras —; Plato cf. *Tim.* 45b–c, 65c–d, 66d, 67b   §12 Epicurus fr. 261   §13 Peripatetics — §14 Chrysippus 2.81   §15 Empedocles A95

10. Those who posit the atoms and those who posit the *homoiomerê* (things with like parts) and those who posit the things without parts and those who posit the infinitesimals say that all sense objects are mixed in all others, and that none of these objects exists in a pure state, and that they are named such or such in relation to what predominates and to the varieties of glittering.

11. Pythagoras and Plato say that each of the sense objects 30 proceeding to us from each element is pure (i.e., unmixed). The aetherial is attuned to sight, the pneumatic to hearing, the fiery to smell, the wet to taste, and the earthy to touch.

12. Epicurus says that the pleasures and pains actually 35 belong with the sense objects.

13. The Peripatetics say that they belong with the objects of thought; for the same things do not appear pleasant or painful to all people the way that white and black things do.

14. Chrysippus says that the generic pleasant is an object of thought, but what is individual and experienced is in fact a sense object.

15. Empedocles says that pleasures come about for what 40 is similar from what is similar, but in accordance with what is lacking for the fulfillment, so that the desire for the similar comes about through what is lacking; but pains come about through what is dissimilar, for what are different as to composition and the blend of the elements are foreign to each other.

45 16. Ἀναξαγόρας πᾶσαν αἴσθησιν μετὰ πόνου. (S) |

17. <οἱ>[39] ἄλλοι ἐπιγίγνεσθαι ἤτοι ἡδονὴν ἢ πόνον οὐδὲ συμπεφυκέναι. (S) |

18. οἱ Στωικοὶ τὸν σοφὸν αἰσθήσει καταληπτὸν ἀπὸ τοῦ εἴδους τεκμηριωδῶς· (S) |

19. οἱ Ἀκαδημαικοὶ λόγῳ γνώριμον· (S) |

50 20. Ἐπίκουρος σοφῷ μόνῳ τὸν σοφόν. (S) |

§16 Anaxagoras A94   §17 anonymi —   §18 Stoics
1.204, 3.568   §19 Academics —   §20 Epicurus —

4.10

Ps.-Plut. *Plac*. 4.10; Stob. *Ecl*. 1.51.2–4, 1.50.7–9

ιʹ. Πόσαι εἰσὶν αἱ αἰσθήσεις (PS) |

1. οἱ Στωικοὶ πέντε τὰς εἰδικὰς αἰσθήσεις, ὅρασιν ἀκοὴν ὄσφρησιν γεῦσιν | ἁφήν. (PS) |

2. Ἀριστοτέλης ἕκτην μὲν οὐ λέγει, κοινὴν δ' αἴσθη-
5 σιν τὴν τῶν συνθέτων | εἰδῶν κριτικήν, εἰς ἣν πᾶσαι συμβάλλουσιν αἱ ἁπλαῖ τὰς ἰδίας ἑκάστη | φαντα-

§1 Stoici 2.853
§2 Aristotle cf. *de An*. 3.1 424b22–23, 425a14–16

[39] οἱ add. Wachsmuth

354

16. Anaxagoras says that each sensation is accompanied by   45
stress.
17. ⟨The⟩ others say that pleasure, or stress, are superve-
nient and do not come about together with the sensation.
18. The Stoics say the wise man can be grasped by sensation from his individual appearance by way of inference
from a sign,
19. The Academics that he is knowable by reason,
20. And Epicurus that the wise man is knowable only to   50
another wise man.[13]

4.10

*Diaeresis according to number, i.e., the canonical five or
more than these five, and their relation to the number of
sense objects.*

Ps.-Plutarch, *Tenets*; Stobaeus, *Anthology*

10. How many senses there are

1. The Stoics say that there are five individual senses:
sight, hearing, smell, taste, touch.
2. Aristotle does not speak of a sixth sense, but mentions
the *sensus communis*, which is the judge of the com-   5
pounded forms. This is the sense toward which all the

---

[13] Based on the well-known maxim "like to like" or "like knows
like."

σίας· ἐν ᾗ τὸ μεταβατικὸν ἀφ' ἑτέρου πρὸς ἕτερον, οἱονεὶ | σχήματος καὶ κινήσεως.[40] (PS) |

3. † Πελλῆς πλείους αἰσθήσεις εἶναι περὶ τὰ ἄλογα ζῷα †. (S) |

4. Δημόκριτος πλείους εἶναι αἰσθήσεις, περὶ τὰ ἄλογα
10 ζῷα καὶ περὶ τοὺς | σοφοὺς καὶ περὶ τοὺς θεούς. (PS) |

5. Δημόκριτος πλείους μὲν εἶναι τὰς αἰσθήσεις τῶν αἰσθητῶν, τῷ δὲ μὴ | ἀναλογίζειν τὰ αἰσθητὰ τῷ πλήθει λανθάνειν. (S) |

6. οἱ δ' ἄλλοι παρίσους. (S) |

§3 —
§4 Democritus A116
§5 Democritus A115
§6 anonymi —

[40] κοινὴν . . . κινήσεως: cf. supra 4.8.6[20–23]

simple sensations each assemble their particular impressions, and in it the act of moving from one to the other, as with shape and motion, occurs.

3. †Pelles[14] says that there are more (sc. than five senses) among the nonrational animals.†

4. Democritus says that there are more (sc. than five) senses among the nonrational animals and among the wise   10
and among the gods.

5. Democritus says that there are more senses than kinds of sense objects, but that this is hidden because the number of the sense objects fails to correspond with the greater number of the senses.

6. But the others[15] say that the senses are equally balanced in number to the sense objects.

[14] The name-label in the Laurentianus manuscript of S does not make sense, and the lemma appears to be partly a doublet of the following doxa attributed to Democritus.

[15] Presumably others than Democritus.

4.11

Ps.-Plut. *Plac.* 4.11 (+ Ps.-Gal. *Hist. phil.* 92)

ια΄. Πῶς γίνεται ἡ αἴσθησις καὶ ἡ ἔννοια καὶ ὁ κατὰ
<ἐν>διάθεσιν[41] | λόγος (P) |

1. οἱ Στωικοί φασιν· ὅταν γεννηθῇ ὁ ἄνθρωπος, ἔχει
τὸ ἡγεμονικὸν μέρος | τῆς ψυχῆς ὥσπερ χαρτίον εὐερ-
5 γὸν εἰς ἀπογραφήν· εἰς τοῦτο μίαν | ἑκάστην τῶν ἐν-
νοιῶν ἐναπογράφεται. |

πρῶτος δὲ ὁ τῆς ἀναγραφῆς τρόπος ὁ διὰ τῶν
αἰσθήσεων· αἰσθανόμενοι | γάρ τινος οἷον λευκοῦ
ἀπελθόντος αὐτοῦ μνήμην ἔχουσιν· |

ὅταν δ᾽ ὁμοειδεῖς πολλαὶ μνῆμαι γένωνται, τότε
φαμὲν ἔχειν ἐμπειρίαν· | ἐμπειρία γάρ ἐστι τὸ τῶν
ὁμοειδῶν φαντασιῶν[42] πλῆθος. |

10 τῶν δ᾽ ἐννοιῶν αἱ μὲν φυσικῶς γίνονται κατὰ τοὺς
εἰρημένους | τρόπους καὶ ἀνεπιτεχνήτως, αἱ δ᾽ ἤδη δι᾽

§1 1–24 Stoics 2.83; 14–15 Stoics 1.149

41 <ἐν>διάθεσιν corr. Wyttenbach
42 φαντασιῶν G: om. PQ

4.11

The general Stoic theory (only, so no other views, cf. 4.21)
of sensation, natural and cultural concept formation, the
constitution of reason, and the distinction between ratio-
nal and nonrational apparitions; supplementing 4.8–10.

Ps.-Plutarch, *Tenets* (+ Ps.-Galen, *Philosophical History*)

11. How sensation and conception and reason [or:
speech] that is located internally occurs

1. The Stoics say: when a human being is born he has the
regent part of his soul like a sheet of papyrus well-prepared
for making a transcript. On this he transcribes for himself
each single one of his conceptions.   5

The first [or: primary] manner of registration[16] is
through the senses. Suppose it is of something white;
when it has gone away, they have a memory of it.

But when many memories of the same sort have occurred, then we say that they have an experience. For an
experience is nothing but the multitude of impressions of
the same sort.

Some of these conceptions arise naturally in the afore-   10
said ways, and without technical elaboration; others are

---

[16] Sc. of external objects; the other, i.e., inner manner of registration (cf. 4.8.7), has been abridged out.

ἡμετέρας διδασκαλίας καὶ | ἐπιμελείας· αὗται μὲν οὖν
"ἔννοιαι" καλοῦνται μόνον, ἐκεῖναι δὲ καὶ | "προλή-
ψεις." |

ὁ δὲ λόγος, καθ᾽ ὃν προσαγορευόμεθα λογικοί, ἐκ
15 τῶν προλήψεων | συμπληροῦσθαι λέγεται κατὰ τὴν
πρώτην ἑβδομάδα. |

ἔστι δ᾽ ἐννόημα[43] φάντασμα διανοίας λογικοῦ
ζῴου· τὸ γὰρ φάντασμα, | ἐπειδὰν λογικῇ προσπίπτῃ
ψυχῇ, τότε "ἐννόημα" καλεῖται, εἰληφὸς | τοὔνομα
παρὰ τοῦ νοῦ. |

διόπερ τοῖς ἀλόγοις ζῴοις ὅσα προσπίπτει φαν-
20 τάσματα, | φαντάσματα μόνον ἐστίν.[44] ὅσα δὲ καὶ
τοῖς θεοῖς καὶ ἡμῖν γε, ταῦτα | {φαντάσματα μόνον
ἐστίν· ὅσα δὲ ἡμῖν, ταῦτα}[45] καὶ φαντάσματα κατὰ |
γένος καὶ ἐννοήματα κατ᾽ εἶδος· ὥσπερ τὰ δηνάρια
καὶ οἱ στατῆρες | αὐτὰ μὲν καθ᾽ αὑτὰ ὑπάρχει δηνά-
ρια <καὶ>[46] στατῆρες, ἐὰν δ᾽ εἰς πλοίων | δοθῇ μίσθω-
σιν, τηνικαῦτα πρὸς τῷ δηνάρια εἶναι καὶ "ναῦλα"
25 λέγεται. (P) |

[43] δ᾽ ἐννόημα Diels: δὲ νόημα PQ
[44] φαντάσματα[2] . . . ἐστίν G: om. P qui verba ad l. 21 transp.
[45] {φαντάσματα . . . ταῦτα} P: del. Diels
[46] <καὶ> add. Diels

produced concurrently with our teaching and instruction. The latter are just called "conceptions," the former also "preconceptions."

And (sc. interior) reason [*logos*, or: speech, thought], which entitles us to be called rational, is said to be completed on the basis of preconceptions at the age of seven years.[17]

A conception is an apparition (*phantasma*) in the thinking faculty of a rational animal; for the apparition is only then called a "conception" (*ennoêma*) when it occurs in a rational soul, deriving its name from the intellect (*nous*).

Accordingly, all the apparitions that occur to nonrational animals are merely apparitions. But those that occur to the gods and to us are both apparitions as to genus and conceptions as to species.[18] Just as denarii and staters,[19] if you consider them in themselves, are simply denarii and staters. But if you use them to pay for a boat trip they are not only called denarii, but a "boat fare" as well.

[17] See also 5.23.1 for the final completion of *logos* at the age of fourteen.

[18] Apparitions and conceptions occurring to the gods: cf. 1.3.20[46].

[19] Roman and Greek coins.

4.12

Ps.-Plut. *Plac.* 4.12 (+ Ps.-Gal. *Hist. phil.* 93); Stob. *Ecl.* 1.58

ιβ′. Τίνι διαφέρει φαντασία φανταστὸν φανταστικὸν
φάντασμα | (P, cf. S) |

1. Χρύσιππος διαφέρειν ἀλλήλων φησὶ τέτταρα
ταῦτα. φαντασία μὲν οὖν | ἐστι πάθος ἐν τῇ ψυχῇ
5 γινόμενον, ἐνδεικνύμενον ἐν αὑτῷ καὶ τὸ | πεποιηκός·
οἷον ἐπειδὰν δι᾽ ὄψεως θεωρῶμέν τι λευκόν,[47] ἔστι
πάθος τὸ | ἐγγεγενημένον διὰ τῆς ὁράσεως ἐν τῇ
ψυχῇ· καὶ <κατὰ>[48] τοῦτο τὸ πάθος | εἰπεῖν ἔχομεν, ὅτι
ὑπόκειται λευκὸν κινοῦν ἡμᾶς· ὁμοίως καὶ διὰ τῆς |
ἁφῆς καὶ τῆς ὀσφρήσεως. |

εἴρηται δ᾽ ἡ φαντασία ἀπὸ τοῦ "φωτός·" καθάπερ
10 γὰρ τὸ φῶς αὐτὸ δείκνυσι | καὶ τὰ ἄλλα τὰ ἐν αὐτῷ
περιεχόμενα, καὶ ἡ φαντασία δείκνυσιν ἑαυτὴν καὶ τὸ
πεποιηκὸς αὐτήν. |

§1 1–28 Chrysippus 2.54; 21–27 Euripides *Or.* 255–57, 258–
59; 28 Homer cf. *Od.* 20.350–58

[47] τι λευκὸν coni. Reiske: τὸ λευκὸν P
[48] <κατὰ> add. Wyttenbach

4.12

Appendix to 4.11: Chryippus' distinctions between various terms relating to sensation.

Ps.-Plutarch, *Tenets* (+ Ps.-Galen, *Philosophical History*); Stobaeus, *Anthology*

12. In what respect impression, impressor, imagination, figment are different[20]

1. Chrysippus[21] says that these four are different from one another. An impression (*phantasia*) is an affection coming about in the soul, which within itself reveals also what produced it (i.e., its cause). As when through sight we 5
observe something white, the affection is what has come about in the soul through seeing; and it is ‹on account of› this affection that we are able to say that there is a white object that affects us. And similarly, when we are affected through touch and smell.

The word impression (*pha-ntasia*) derives from "light" (*pha-os/phôs*);[22] just as light reveals itself and all the other 10
things that are embraced in it, so too the impression reveals itself and what produced it.

---

[20] All four terms have in common the root *phantas-*, but it is not possible to replicate this in English.

[21] Note that in this chapter there are no views of other Stoics, or of non-Stoics.

[22] This etymology is already present in Aristotle, *de An*. 3.3 429a3.

φανταστὸν δὲ τὸ ποιοῦν τὴν φαντασίαν· οἷον τὸ
λευκὸν καὶ τὸ ψυχρὸν | καὶ πᾶν ὅ τι ἂν δύνηται κινεῖν
τὴν ψυχήν, τοῦτ' ἔστι φανταστόν. |

φανταστικὸν δ' ἐστὶ διάκενος ἑλκυσμός, πάθος ἐν
15 τῇ ψυχῇ ἀπ' οὐδενὸς | φανταστοῦ γινόμενον, καθάπερ
ἐπὶ τοῦ σκιαμαχοῦντος καὶ κενοῖς ἐπιφέροντος | τὰς
χεῖρας· τῇ γὰρ φαντασίᾳ ὑπόκειταί τι φανταστόν, τῷ
δὲ | φανταστικῷ οὐδέν. |

φάντασμα δ' ἐστίν, ἐφ' ὃ ἑλκόμεθα κατὰ τὸν φαν-
ταστικὸν διάκενον | ἑλκυσμόν· ταῦτα δὲ γίνεται ἐπὶ
20 τῶν μελαγχολώντων καὶ μεμηνότων· | ὁ γοῦν τραγι-
κὸς Ὀρέστης ὅταν λέγῃ· |

ὦ μῆτερ, ἱκετεύω σε, μὴ 'πίσειέ μοι |
τὰς αἱματωποὺς καὶ δρακοντώδεις κόρας· |
αὗται γάρ, αὗται πλησίον θρώσκουσί μου. |

25 λέγει μὲν αὐτὰ ὡς μεμηνὼς ὁρᾷ δ' οὐδέν, ἀλλὰ δοκεῖ
μόνον· διὸ καί | φησιν αὐτῷ Ἠλέκτρα· |

μέν', ὦ ταλαίπωρ', ἀτρέμα σοῖς ἐν δεμνίοις· |
ὁρᾷς γὰρ οὐδὲν ὧν δοκεῖς σάφ' εἰδέναι, |

ὡς καὶ παρ' Ὁμήρῳ Θεοκλύμενος. (P) |

An impressor (*phantaston*) is what produces the impression, like the white or the cold or whatever is capable of affecting the soul, this is an impressor.

Imagination (*phantastikon*) is an empty reflex, an affection in the soul that does not arise from any impressor, as when someone shadowboxes or strikes his hands against thin air; for an impression has some impressor as its object, but the imagination has none. 15

A figment (*phantasma*)[23] is that to which we are attracted in an empty reflex of the imagination; it occurs in people who are melancholic and mad. When the tragic hero Orestes says: 20

> Mother, I beg you, don't urge upon me
> Those bloody-faced, snake-like maidens!
> Here they come leaping toward me,

he says this because he is mad, and he sees nothing but only believes that he does. That is why Electra also says to him: 25

> Poor man, keep still in your bed!
> You don't actually see anything you think you see!

Just like Theoclymenus in Homer too.[24]

---

[23] The meaning here differs from 4.11.1[16–24].
[24] Such quotations and allusions are typically Chrysippean.

4.13

Ps.-Plut. *Plac.* 4.13 (+ Ps.-Gal. *Hist. phil.* 94); Stob. *Ecl.*
1.52.1–8, 10–13

ιγ΄. Περὶ ὁράσεως, πῶς ὁρῶμεν (PS) |

1. Λεύκιππος Δημόκριτος Ἐπίκουρος κατὰ εἰδώλων
εἴσκρισιν οἴονται τὸ | ὁρατικὸν συμβαίνειν πάθος.
{καὶ κατά τινων ἀκτίνων εἴσκρισιν μετὰ τὴν | πρὸς τὸ
ὑποκείμενον ἔνστασιν πάλιν ὑποστρεφουσῶν πρὸς
5 τὴν ὄψιν}.⁴⁹ | (PS) |
2. Τιμαγόρας, εἷς τῶν παραχαραξάντων ἐν συχνοῖς
τὴν Ἐπικούρειον | αἵρεσιν, ἀντὶ τῶν εἰδώλων ταῖς
ἀπορροίαις χρῆται. (S) |
3. Στράτων χρώματά φησιν ἀπὸ τῶν σωμάτων φέρε-
σθαι συγχρῴζοντ᾽ | αὐτοῖς τὸν μεταξὺ ἀέρα. (S) |
10 4. Ἀρίσταρχος σχήματα συνδιατυποῦντά πως αὐτοῖς
τὸν ἀέρα. (S) |

§1 Leucippus at Democritus A29; Epicurus fr. 318
§2 Timagoras —   §3 Strato fr. 64   §4 Aristarchus —
⁴⁹ καὶ . . . ὄψιν secl. Wachsmuth

4.13

The primary and standard diaphonia is between diaereti-cally listed forms of intromission, or receptivity ($§§1–4$), and of extramission, or intentionality ($§§5–6$), followed by various compromise positions ($§§7–13$).

Ps.-Plutarch, *Tenets* (+ Ps.-Galen, *Philosophical History*); Stobaeus, *Anthology*

13. On sight, how we see

1. Leucippus, Democritus, and Epicurus believe that the visual sensation is the result of the penetration of images.   5
2. Timagoras, one of those who debased the Epicurean school on many issues, employs effluences instead of images.
3. Strato says that colors travel from bodies and give their color to the intermediate air.
4. Aristarchus says that it is shapes that travel from bodies   10 and somehow give the air the same form as themselves.

5. Ἵππαρχος ἀφ᾽ ἑκατέρου φησὶ τῶν ὀφθαλμῶν ἀπο-
τεινομένας ἀκτῖνας | τοῖς πέρασιν αὐτῶν, οἱονεὶ χει-
ρῶν ἐπαφαῖς, περικαθαπτούσας τοῖς | ἐκτὸς σώμασι
τὴν ἀντίληψιν αὐτῶν πρὸς τὸ ὁρατικὸν ἀναδιδόναι.
| (PS) |

15 6. ἔνιοι καὶ Πυθαγόραν τῇ δόξῃ ταύτῃ συνεπιγράφου-
σιν, ἅτε δὴ | βεβαιωτὴν τῶν μαθημάτων· καὶ πρὸς
τούτῳ Παρμενίδην ἐμφαίνοντα | τοῦτο διὰ τῶν ποιη-
μάτων. (S) |

7. Πλάτων συναύγειαν τοῦ μὲν ἐκ τῶν ὀφθαλμῶν φω-
τὸς ἐπὶ ποσὸν | ἀπορρέοντος εἰς τὸν ὁμογενῆ ἀέρα,
20 τοῦ δὲ ἀπὸ τῶν σωμάτων | ἀντιφερομένου, τοῦ δὲ περὶ
τὸν μεταξὺ ἀέρα, εὐδιάχυτον ὄντα καὶ | εὔτρεπτον,
συντεινομένου τῷ πυρώδει τῆς ὄψεως. αὕτη λέγεται |
Πλατωνικὴ συναύγεια. (PS) |

8. Ἀλκμαίων κατὰ τὴν τοῦ διαφανοῦς ἀντίληψιν. (S) |

9. Ἀριστοτέλης κατὰ κίνησιν τοῦ κατ᾽ ἐνέργειαν δια-
φανοῦς. (S) |

25 10. τῶν Ἀκαδημαικῶν τινες κατά τι⟨νων⟩ ἀκτί⟨νων⟩[50]
ἔκχυσιν μετὰ τὴν πρὸς | τὸ ὑποκείμενον ἔνστασιν
πάλιν ὑποστρεφουσῶν πρὸς τὴν ὄψιν. (S) |

§§5–6 cf. Archytas A25B   §5 Hipparchus —
  §6 Pythagoras —; Parmenides A48   §7 Plato cf. *Tim.*
45b–46a   §8 Alcmaeon A10   §9 Aristotle cf. *de An.*
2.6 418a31–b10, *Sens.* 2 438b2–5   §10 Academics —

[50] τι⟨νων⟩ ἀκτί⟨νων⟩ coni. MR

5. Hipparchus says that rays stretching from each of the eyes deliver apprehension of external bodies to the visual faculty by fastening onto them with their extremities like the touch of hands.[25]

6. Some ascribe this doxa to Pythagoras as well, since he is an authority for mathematics, and in addition to him to Parmenides, who shows this through his verses.[26]

7. Plato says that we see through coillumination, the light from the eyes streaming out over a certain distance into the congeneric air, whereas the light traveling from bodies is borne in the contrary direction, and the light in the air in between, which (sc. air) is easily diffused and flexible, and extends itself together with the fiery element of vision. This is called Platonic coillumination.

8. Alcmaeon says that we see through the perception of the transparent.

9. Aristotle says that we see according to the movement of what is actually transparent.

10. Some of the Academics say that we see through the effusion of certain ⟨rays⟩ that turn around again to the visual faculty after their contact with the underlying object.

[25] He may have seen pictures of the Egyptian god Atun.

[26] This is unlikely for Parmenides, in spite of the reference to the poem.

11. Ποσειδώνιος ⟨αὐ⟩γ⟨ῶ⟩ν[51] αὐτὴν σύμφυσιν ὀνομά-
ζει. (S) |

12. Ἐμπεδοκλῆς καὶ πρὸς τὸ διὰ τῶν ἀκτίνων καὶ
πρὸς τὸ διὰ τῶν εἰδώλων | ἐκδοχὰς παρέχεται· πλεί-
30   ους δὲ πρὸς ⟨τὸ⟩[52] δεύτερον· τὰς γὰρ ἀπορροίας | ἀπο-
δέχεται. (PS) |

13. Ἑστιαῖος ὁ Περίνθιος[53] τοῖς εἰδώλοις τὰς ἀκτῖνας
ἀνέμιξε, προσαγορεύσας | τὸ γιγνόμενον "ἀκτινείδω-
λον" συνθέτως. (PS) |

§11 Posidonius F194   §12 Empedocles A90
§13 Hestiaeus fr. 4

4.14

Ps.-Plut. *Plac.* 4.14 (+ Ps.-Gal. *Hist. phil.* 95); Stob. *Ecl.*
1.52.14–16

ιδ'. Περὶ κατοπτρικῶν ἐμφάσεων (PS) |

1. Ἐμπεδοκλῆς κατ' ἀπορροίας τὰς συνισταμένας μὲν
ἐπὶ τῆς ἐπιφανείας | τοῦ κατόπτρου, πιλουμένας δ'

§1 Empedocles A88

[51] ⟨αὐ⟩γ⟨ῶ⟩ν coni. Wachsmuth: γοῦν S
[52] ⟨τὸ⟩ add. Diels
[53] Ἑστιαῖος ὁ Περίνθιος S: Ἐμπεδοκλῆς falso ex 28 P

11. Posidonius calls it (sc. this manner of seeing) a natural fusion of light rays.

12. Empedocles provides evidence both for the view that we see through rays and for the view that we see through images; but more in relation to the latter, for he accepts the effluences. 30

13. Hestiaeus of Perinthos combined the rays with the images, calling the result by combination "ray-image."

4.14

Diaphonia between effluences and optical reflection, as in 4.13.

Ps.-Plutarch, *Tenets* (+ Ps.-Galen, *Philosophical History*); Stobaeus, *Anthology*

14. On reflections in mirrors

1. Empedocles says they come about by the effluences that come together on the surface of the mirror and are com-

ὑπὸ τοῦ ἐκκρινομένου ἐκ τοῦ κατόπτρου | πυρώδους
καὶ τὸν προκείμενον ἀέρα, εἰς ὃν φέρεται τὰ ῥεύματα,
5 συμμεταφέροντος. | (PS) |

2. Λεύκιππος Δημόκριτος Ἐπίκουρος τὰς κατοπτρι-
κὰς ἐμφάσεις γίνεσθαι | κατ' εἰδώλων παραστάσεις,[54]
ἅτινα φέρεσθαι μὲν ἀφ' ἡμῶν, συνίστασθαι | δὲ ἐπὶ
τοῦ κατόπτρου, κατ' ἀντιπεριστροφήν. (PS) |

3. οἱ ἀπὸ Πυθαγόρου καὶ τῶν μαθηματικῶν κατ' ἀντ-
10 ανακλάσεις τῆς | ὄψεως· φέρεσθαι μὲν γὰρ τὴν ὄψιν
τεταμένην[55] ὡς ἐπὶ τὸν χαλκόν, | ἐντυχοῦσαν[56] δὲ
πυκνῷ καὶ λείῳ πληχθεῖσαν ὑποστρέφειν αὐτὴν ἐφ' |
ἑαυτήν, ὅμοιόν τι πάσχουσαν τῇ ἐκτάσει τῆς χειρὸς
καὶ τῇ ἐπὶ τὸν ὦμον | ἀντεπιστροφῇ. (PS) |

4. δύναταί τις πᾶσι τούτοις τοῖς κεφαλαίοις χρῆσα-
15 σθαι ἐπὶ τοῦ "πῶς | ὁρῶμεν." (PS) |

§2 Leucippus at Democritus A31; Epicurus fr. 320
§3 Pythagoreans and mathematicians cf. Archytas A25A
§4 —

[54] παραστάσεις MR cf. 5.2.1: ὑποστάσεις P, ἐπιστάσεις G,
ἐμφάσεις S
[55] τεταμένην P: τεταγμένην S
[56] ἐντυχοῦσαν SG: στειχοῦσαν P

pacted by the fiery stuff discharged from the mirror, which
transports across with itself the air lying before it toward
which the streams travel.　　　　　　　　　　　　　　　　5

2. Leucippus, Democritus, and Epicurus say the reflections in mirrors come about through the manifestations of the images, which move away from us but arise on
the mirror that sends them back.

3. The successors of Pythagoras and of the mathematicians[27] say they come about by backward reflections of　10
vision. For they say that the visual beam is carried along
and extends toward the bronze mirror, but turns back on
itself when it encounters a dense and smooth object and
is repulsed, undergoing something akin to stretching out
a hand and then bending it back to the shoulder.

4. One can apply all these summary statements (kephalaia) to the question of "how we see."[28]　　　　　　　15

[27] Here in contrast to elsewhere, e.g., in 2.15, the term
μαθηματικός should be translated "mathematician" or perhaps
"scientist."

[28] A rare authorial remark, pertaining to the way that the
views expressed in the first three doxai (here called kephalaia)
relate to 4.13.

4.15

Ps.-Plut. *Plac.* 4.15 (+ Ps.-Gal. *Hist. phil.* 96); Stob. *Ecl.* 1.52.17–18

ιε΄. Εἰ ὁρατὸν τὸ σκότος (P) |

1. Σφαῖρος ὁ Στωικὸς ὁρατὸν εἶναι τὸ σκότος, ἐκ γὰρ τῆς ὁράσεως προχεῖσθαί | τινα εἰς αὐτὸ αὐγήν· καὶ οὐ ψεύδεται ἡ ὅρασις, βλέπεται γὰρ ταῖς | ἀληθείαις, ὅτι ἔστι σκότος. προέρχονται δὲ ἐκ τῆς ὄψεως ἀκτῖνες
5 ὁμιχλώδεις· | τὸ μὲν σκότος συνάγει πως καὶ συγκρί- νει[57] τὴν ὅρασιν καὶ ἀμβλύνει, | τὸ δὲ φῶς διακρίνει καὶ ποδηγεῖ τὴν ὅρασιν ἡμῶν ἐπὶ τὰ ὁρατὰ διὰ τοῦ | μεταξὺ ἀέρος. διὰ τοῦτο μὴ ὁρᾶν ἡμᾶς ἐν τῷ σκότει ἀλλ᾽ αὐτὸ μόνον τὸ | σκότος.[58] (PSG) |

2. Χρύσιππος κατὰ τὴν συνέντασιν τοῦ μεταξὺ ἀέρος
10 ὁρᾶν ἡμᾶς, νυγέντος | μὲν ὑπὸ τοῦ ὁρατικοῦ πνεύμα- τος, ὅπερ ἀπὸ τοῦ ἡγεμονικοῦ μέχρι τῆς | κόρης δι- ήκει, κατὰ δὲ τὴν πρὸς τὸν περικείμενον ἀέρα ἐπιβο-

§1 Sphaerus 1.627; Stoics 2.869
§2 Chrysippus 2.866

[57] συγκρίνει corr. Voss.: συγκινεῖ G
[58] 4–8 προέρχονται . . . σκότος G: om. PS

4.15

Two contrasting Stoic tenets, Chrysippus' being the stan-
dard view one would have expected in 4.13.

Ps.-Plutarch, *Tenets* (+ Ps.-Galen, *Philosophical History*);
Stobaeus, *Anthology*

15. Whether darkness is visible

1. Sphaerus the Stoic says that darkness is visible, since a
sort of beam of light is poured into it from the visual faculty. And the visual faculty does not err, for in very truth
it is seen that there is darkness. Misty rays proceed from
the organ of vision; darkness somehow compacts and com-   5
presses and dulls our sight, while light dilates our sight and
guides it through the intervening air that is in between
toward the things that are seen. This is why we do not see
in the dark but only darkness itself.[29]
2. Chrysippus says we see by the tension of the intervening
air, when it is pierced by the visual *pneuma* that extends   10
from the regent part to the pupil, and through projection
toward the surrounding air stretches it (sc. the visual

---

[29] The passage from "Misty rays" to the end of the lemma is
found only in Ps.-Galen, who here preserves an original section
of the text that was later lost. Its authenticity is guaranteed by the
diaphonic opposition to parts of the following Chrysippean doxa.

λὴν ἐντείνοντος | αὐτὸν κωνοειδῶς, ὅταν ᾖ ὁμογενὴς ὁ
ἀήρ. προχέονται δ' ἐκ τῆς ὄψεως | ἀκτῖνες πύριναι,
οὐχὶ μέλαιναι καὶ ὁμιχλώδεις· διόπερ ὁρατὸν εἶναι τὸ
σκότος. | (PS) |

4.16

Ps.-Plut. *Plac.* 4.16 (+ Ps.-Gal. *Hist. phil.* 97); Stob. *Ecl.*
1.53.1–4

ιϛ'. Περὶ ἀκοῆς (PS) |

1. Ἐμπεδοκλῆς τὴν ἀκοὴν γίνεσθαι κατὰ πρόσπτωσιν
πνεύματος τῷ | χονδρώδει,[59] ὅπερ φησὶν ἐξηρτῆσθαι
ἐντὸς τοῦ ὠτὸς κώδωνος δίκην | αἰωρούμενον καὶ τυ-
πτόμενον. (PS) |

5   2. Ἀλκμαίων ἀκούειν ἡμᾶς τῷ κενῷ τῷ ἐντὸς τοῦ ὠτός·
τοῦτο γὰρ εἶναι τὸ | διηχοῦν κατὰ τὴν τοῦ πνεύματος
ἐμβολήν· πάντα γὰρ τὰ κενὰ[60] ἠχεῖ. | (PS) |
3. Διογένης τοῦ ἐν τῇ κεφαλῇ ἀέρος ὑπὸ τῆς φωνῆς
τυπτομένου καὶ | κινουμένου. (PS) |

§1 Empedocles A93   §2 Alcmaeon A6
§3 Diogenes A21

[59] χονδρώδει corr. Diels: χόνδρῳ δι' G, χρονιώδει sive κο-
χλιώδει P, χόνδρῳ S   [60] κενὰ P: κοῖλα S

pneuma) in the shape of a cone, whenever the air is of the same kind as it. Fiery rays are poured forth from the visual faculty, not black and misty ones; for this reason darkness is visible.

4.16

Diaeresis between inside and outside, and also between full and empty.

Ps.-Plutarch, *Tenets* (+ Ps.-Galen, *Philosophical History*); Stobaeus, *Anthology*

16. On hearing

1. Empedocles says that hearing occurs when *pneuma* falls against the cartilaginous body that he says is suspended inside the ear, hanging and struck in the manner of a bell.
2. Alcmaeon says that we hear by means of the empty 5 space that is inside the ear. This is in fact what reverberates when *pneuma* enters; for all hollow spaces reverberate.
3. Diogenes says that we hear when the air in the head is struck and moved by the sound.

10   4. Πλάτων καὶ οἱ ἀπ' αὐτοῦ πλήττεσθαι τὸν ἐν τῇ κεφαλῇ ἀέρα, τοῦτον δ' | ἀνακλᾶσθαι εἰς τὰ ἡγεμονικὰ καὶ γίγνεσθαι τῆς ἀκοῆς τὴν αἴσθησιν. | (PS) |

§4 Plato cf. *Tim.* 67a–b

4.17

Ps.-Plut. *Plac.* 4.17 (+ Ps.-Gal. *Hist. phil.* 98); Stob. *Ecl.* 1.54.1–2

ιζ'. Περὶ ὀσφρήσεως (PS) |

1. Ἀλκμαίων ἐν τῷ ἐγκεφάλῳ εἶναι τὸ ἡγεμονικόν· τούτῳ οὖν ὀσφραίνεσθαι | ἕλκοντι διὰ τῶν ἀναπνοῶν τὰς ὀσμάς. (PS) |

2. Ἐμπεδοκλῆς ταῖς ἀναπνοαῖς ταῖς ἀπὸ τοῦ πνεύμο-
5   νος συνεισκρίνεσθαι | τὴν ὀσμήν· ὅταν γοῦν ἡ ἀναπνοὴ βαρεῖα γίνηται, κατὰ τραχύτητα μὴ | συναισθάνεσθαι, ὡς ἐπὶ τῶν ῥευματιζομένων. (PS) |

§1 Alcmaeon A8
§2 Empedocles A94

4. Plato and his successors say that the air in the head   10
receives a blow, and this air is reflected (i.e., bent back)
onto the ruling parts, and so the perception of hearing
arises.

4.17

Weak contrast between two views.

Ps.-Plutarch, *Tenets* (+ Ps.-Galen, *Philosophical History*);
Stobaeus, *Anthology*

17. On smelling

1. Alcmaeon says that the ruling part is in the brain.[30]
Smell then occurs with this part when it draws in the odors
through inhalation.
2. Empedocles says that the odor is introduced together
with the inhalations of the lung. But when breathing be-   5
comes heavy, the sensation (i.e., smell) no longer occurs
together with it due to hoarseness, as happens in the case
of those who have colds.

[30] Cf. 5.3.3.

4.18

Ps.-Plut. *Plac*. 4.18 (+ Ps.-Gal. *Hist. phil.* 99); Stob. *Ecl.* 1.55

ιη΄. Περὶ γεύσεως (PS) |

1. Ἀλκμαίων τῷ ὑγρῷ καὶ τῷ χλιαρῷ τῷ ἐν τῇ γλώττῃ πρὸς τῇ μαλακότητι | διακρίνεσθαι τοὺς χυμούς. (P) |
2. Διογένης τῇ ἀραιότητι τῆς γλώττης καὶ τῇ μαλα-
5 κότητι καὶ διὰ τὸ | συνάπτειν τὰς ἀπὸ τοῦ σώματος εἰς αὐτὴν φλέβας διαχεῖσθαι τοὺς | χυμοὺς ἑλκομένους ἐπὶ τὴν αἴσθησιν καὶ τὸ ἡγεμονικόν καθάπερ ἀπὸ | σπογγιᾶς. (P) |

§1 Alcmaeon A9
§2 Diogenes A22

4.18

Weak contrast between two views.

Ps.-Plutarch, *Tenets* (+ Ps.-Galen, *Philosophical History*);
Stobaeus, *Anthology*

18. On tasting

1. Alcmaeon says the flavors are distinguished by the moisture and warmth in the tongue as well as by its softness.
2. Diogenes (sc. of Apollonia) says that this happens
through the porousness of the tongue and its softness, and
because the veins from the body are connected to it, the   5
flavors are diffused and attracted to the perceptive faculty
and [or: i.e.] the ruling part, as from a sponge.

Ps.-Plut. *Plac.* 4.19 (+ Ps.-Gal. *Hist. phil.* 100); Stob. *Ecl.* 1.57

ιθ′. Περὶ φωνῆς (PS) |

1. Πλάτων τὴν φωνὴν ὁρίζεται πνεῦμα διὰ στόματος ἀπὸ διανοίας | ἠγμένον· καὶ πληγὴν ὑπὸ ἀέρος δι' ὤτων καὶ ἐγκεφάλου καὶ αἵματος | μέχρι ψυχῆς δια-διδομένην· (PS) |

5　2. λέγεται δὲ καὶ καταχρηστικῶς ἐπὶ τῶν ἀλόγων ζῴων "φωνὴ" καὶ τῶν | ἀψύχων, ὡς χρεμετισμοὶ καὶ ψόφοι· (PS) |

3. κυρίως δὲ φωνὴ ἡ ἔναρθρός ἐστιν ὡς φωτίζουσα τὸ νοούμενον. (PS) |

4. Ἐπίκουρος τὴν φωνὴν εἶναι ῥεῦμα ἐκπεμπόμενον ἀπὸ τῶν φωνούντων ἢ | ἠχούντων ἢ ψοφούντων· τοῦτο

10　δὲ τὸ ῥεῦμα εἰς ὁμοιοσχήμονα | θρύπτεσθαι θραύ-σματα· ("ὁμοιοσχήμονα" δὲ λέγεται τὰ στρογγύλα τοῖς | στρογγύλοις καὶ σκαληνὰ καὶ τρίγωνα τοῖς

§1 Plato cf. *Tht.* 206d　　§2 cf. Plato *Soph.* 263e; *Tim.* 67a–c　　§3 —　　§4 Epicurus fr. 321

4.19

Voice is here presented as corporeal, the primary diaphonia being between the discrete substrate of the Atomists and the continuous substance of the Stoics. The views of Anaxagoras and Plato fail to fit this distinction.

Ps.-Plutarch, *Tenets* (+ Ps.-Galen, *Philosophical History*); Stobaeus, *Anthology*

19. On voice[31]

1. Plato defines voice/sound as a *pneuma* (breath) directed from the intellect through the mouth, and as a blow by air through ears and brain and blood as far as the soul.

2. The word "voice" is used analogically of animals without 5
reason and inanimate things, designating for example neighs and noises.

3. But in its proper sense it is articulate voice, as it illuminates what is thought.[32]

4. Epicurus says voice/sound is a stream sent out from entities that speak, reverberate, or make noises. This stream is broken up into small particles of the same shape 10
("of the same shape" is said of globular with globular, and of irregular and triangular with what is of the same kind).

---

[31] Voice is presented not only as produced but also as received, heard (φωνή also means "sound"). What in Plato pertains to spoken or thought *logos*, or to hearing, has been rearranged to suit a heading pertaining to voice.

[32] Cf. 5.20.3.

ὁμοιογενέσι)· τούτων δ' | ἐμπιπτόντων ταῖς ἀκοαῖς
ἀποτελεῖσθαι τὴν αἴσθησιν τῆς φωνῆς· | φανερὸν δὲ
τοῦτο γίνεσθαι ἀπὸ τῶν ἀσκῶν ἐκρεόντων καὶ τῶν |
ἐμφυσώντων κναφέων τοῖς ἱματίοις. (P) |

15 5. Δημόκριτος καὶ τὸν ἀέρα φησὶν εἰς ὁμοιοσχήμονα
θρύπτεσθαι σώματα | καὶ συγκαλινδεῖσθαι τοῖς ἐκ
τῆς φωνῆς θραύσμασι· "κολοιὸς" γὰρ "παρὰ | κολοιὸν
ἱζάνει," καί "ὡς αἰεὶ τὸν ὁμοῖον ἄγει θεὸς ὡς τὸν
ὁμοῖον." καὶ γὰρ | ἐν τοῖς αἰγιαλοῖς αἱ ὅμοιαι ψῆφοι
κατὰ τοὺς αὐτοὺς τόπους ὁρῶνται, | κατ' ἄλλο μὲν αἱ
σφαιροειδεῖς, κατ' ἄλλο δ' αἱ ἐπιμήκεις· καὶ ἐπὶ τῶν |
20 κοσκινευόντων ἐπὶ τὸ αὐτὸ συναλίζεται τὰ ὁμοιο-
σχήμονα, ὥστε χωρὶς | εἶναι τοὺς κυάμους καὶ ἐρεβίν-
θους. ἔχοι δ' ἄν τις πρὸς τούτους εἰπεῖν· | πῶς ὀλίγα
θραύσματα πνεύματος μυρίανδρον ἐκπληροῖ θέα-
τρον; (P) |

6. οἱ δὲ Στωικοὶ φασι τὸν ἀέρα μὴ συγκεῖσθαι ἐκ
θραυσμάτων, ἀλλὰ | συνεχῆ δι' ὅλου μηδὲν κενὸν
25 ἔχοντα· ἐπειδὰν δὲ πληγῇ πνεύματι, | κυματοῦται
κατὰ κύκλους ὀρθοὺς εἰς ἄπειρον, ἕως πληρώσῃ τὸν |
περικείμενον ἀέρα, ὡς ἐπὶ τῆς κολυμβήθρας τῆς πλη-
γείσης λίθῳ· καὶ | αὕτη μὲν κυκλικῶς κινεῖται, ὁ δ'
ἀὴρ σφαιρικῶς. (P) |

§5 Democritus A128; 17 Homer *Od.* 17.218; Plato *Lys.* 214a–
b; Aristotle *EE* 7.1 1235a6–9, *Rhet.* 1.11 1371b16–17, Ps.-Arist.
MM 2.11.2
§6 Stoics 2.425

When these fall upon the ears, the perception of voice results. This is clear from a comparison with the skins that let out water and the fullers who blow air into garments. 5. Democritus says that the air too is broken up into corpuscles of the same shape, and these roll along with the small particles of voice/sound, "for jackdaw sits beside jackdaw" and "God always brings like to like."[33] Thus on beaches the same pebbles are seen in the same spots, the round ones in one place and the elongated ones in another. Also in the case of people using sieves similarly shaped things gather together to the same place, so that beans and lentils are separate.—But one could say in response to those who hold this opinion:[34] how do a few particles of breath fill a theater that seats tens of thousands of men? 6. The Stoics say that the air is not composed of small particles but, having no empty space, is wholly continuous. Whenever it is struck by breath, it undulates endlessly in concentric circles until it fills the surrounding air, as when a diving pool is struck by a stone. However, the diving pool moves in circles, whereas the air moves in spheres.[35]

[33] The first of these quotes is a proverb, the second a quotation from Homer. The former is also found in Plato and the two together in Aristotle and Ps.-Aristotle.

[34] Rare example of an explicit dialectical objection.

[35] This doxa relates to hearing and is displaced from 4.16.

7. Ἀναξαγόρας τὴν φωνὴν γίνεσθαι πνεύματος ἀντι-
πεσόντος μὲν | στερεμνίῳ ἀέρι, τῇ δ' ὑποστροφῇ τῆς
30 πλήξεως μέχρι τῶν ἀκοῶν | προσενεχθέντος· καθὸ καὶ
τὴν λεγομένην ἠχὼ γίνεσθαι. (P) |

§7 Anaxagoras A106

4.20

Ps.-Plut. *Plac.* 4.20 (+ Ps.-Gal. *Hist. phil.* 101); Stob. *Ecl.*
1.57

κ'. Εἰ ἀσώματος ἡ φωνὴ καὶ πῶς ἠχὼ γίνεται (PS) |

1. Πυθαγόρας Πλάτων Ἀριστοτέλης ἀσώματον· οὐ
γὰρ τὸν ἀέρα, ἀλλὰ τὸ | σχῆμα τὸ περὶ τὸν ἀέρα καὶ
τὴν ἐπιφάνειαν κατὰ ποιὰν πλῆξιν γίνεσθαι | φωνήν·
πᾶσα δ' ἐπιφάνεια ἀσώματος. συγκινεῖται μὲν γὰρ
5 τοῖς σώμασιν, | αὐτὴ δ' ἀσώματος πάντως καθέστη-
κεν, ὥσπερ ἐπὶ τῆς καμπτομένης | ῥάβδου ἡ μὲν ἐπι-
φάνεια οὐδὲν πάσχει ἡ δ' ὕλη ἐστὶν ἡ καμπτο-
μένη. (P) |

§1 Pythagoras —; Plato cf. *Tim.* 67b–c; Aristotle cf. *de An.* 2.8
419b4–420a2

7. Anaxagoras says voice/sound occurs when breath encounters solid air and, reverberating because of the impact, is carried to the ears; in this manner the so-called echo also occurs. 30

4.20

Clear and standard diaphonia between corporealists and incorporealists.

Ps.-Plutarch, *Tenets* (+ Ps.-Galen, *Philosophical History*); Stobaeus, *Anthology*

20. Whether voice is incorporeal and how echo occurs

1. Pythagoras, Plato, and Aristotle say voice/sound[36] is incorporeal. For not the air but the shape around the air and its surface becomes voice/sound through a certain sort of striking. Every surface is incorporeal, for it moves together with the bodies, though it itself remains wholly 5 incorporeal, just as when a cane is bent the surface is not affected, but the matter is bent.

[36] Cf. 4.19 n. 31.

2. οἱ δὲ Στωικοὶ σῶμα τὴν φωνήν· πᾶν γὰρ τὸ δρῶν[61]
ἢ καὶ ποιοῦν σῶμα, ἡ | δὲ φωνὴ ποιεῖ καὶ δρᾷ· ἀκούο-
μεν γὰρ αὐτῆς καὶ αἰσθανόμεθα προσπιπτούσης | τῇ
ἀκοῇ καὶ ἐκτυπούσης καθάπερ δακτυλίου εἰς κηρόν.
10 ἔτι πᾶν | τὸ κινοῦν καὶ ἐνοχλοῦν σῶμά ἐστι, κινεῖ δ'
ἡμᾶς ἡ εὐμουσία ἐνοχλεῖ δ' ἡ | ἀμουσία. ἔτι πᾶν τὸ
κινούμενον σῶμά ἐστι· κινεῖται δ' ἡ φωνὴ καὶ | προσ-
πίπτει εἰς τοὺς λείους τόπους καὶ ἀντανακλᾶται,
καθάπερ ἐπὶ τῆς | σφαίρας τῆς βαλλομένης εἰς τοῖ-
χον· ἐν γοῦν ταῖς κατ' Αἴγυπτον | πυραμίσιν ἔνδον
μία φωνὴ ῥηγνυμένη τέτταρας ἢ καὶ πέντε ἤχους |
15 ἀπεργάζεται. (P) |

§2 Stoics 2.387

4.21

Ps.-Plut. *Plac.* 4.21 (+ Ps.-Gal. *Hist. phil.* 102); Stob. *Ecl.*
1.57

κα΄. Πόθεν αἰσθητικὴ γίνεται ἡ ψυχὴ καὶ
τί αὐτῆς τὸ ἡγεμονικόν | (PS) |

1. οἱ Στωικοὶ φασιν εἶναι τῆς ψυχῆς ἀνώτατον μέρος
τὸ ἡγεμονικὸν τὸ | ποιοῦν τὰς φαντασίας καὶ συγ-

§1 1–21 Stoics 2.836; 16–19 1.150

[61] δρῶν G: δρώμενον P

2. The Stoics say voice/sound is body. For everything that acts and causes is corporeal and the voice/sound causes and acts. For we hear it and perceive it hitting our hearing and molding it like a ring pressed into wax. Moreover, ev- 10 erything that affects and distresses (sc. something else) is body, and good music affects us while bad music distresses us. Again, everything that is moved is body; the voice is moved and when encountering smooth places reverber- ates, like a ball thrown against a wall. Indeed in the case of the pyramids in Egypt a single voice/sound released inside produces four to five echoes. 15

4.21

Another Stoic theory only (as in 4.11–12), supplementing the previous account of soul.

Ps.-Plutarch, *Tenets* (+ Ps.-Galen, *Philosophical History*); Stobaeus, *Anthology*

21. How the soul comes to be sentient and what its regent part is

1. The Stoics say that the soul's highest part is its regent part, that which causes impressions, agreements, sensa-

5 καταθέσεις καὶ αἰσθήσεις καὶ ὁρμάς· καὶ | τοῦτο "λο-
γισμὸν" καλοῦσιν. ἀπὸ δὲ τοῦ ἡγεμονικοῦ ἑπτὰ μέρη
ἐστὶ τῆς | ψυχῆς καὶ ἐκτεινόμενα εἰς τὸ σῶμα, καθά-
περ αἱ ἀπὸ τοῦ πολύποδος | πλεκτάναι· τῶν δ' ἑπτὰ
μερῶν τῆς ψυχῆς πέντε μέν εἰσι τὰ αἰσθητήρια, | ὅρα-
σις ἀκοὴ ὄσφρησις⁶² γεῦσις καὶ ἁφή· |

ὧν ἡ μὲν ὅρασίς ἐστι πνεῦμα διατεῖνον ἀπὸ τοῦ
10 ἡγεμονικοῦ μέχρις | ὀφθαλμῶν, ἀκοὴ δὲ πνεῦμα δια-
τεῖνον ἀπὸ τοῦ ἡγεμονικοῦ μέχρις των | ὤτων, ὄσφρη-
σις δὲ πνεῦμα διατεῖνον ἀπὸ τοῦ ἡγεμονικοῦ μέχρι |
μυκτήρων, {λεπτῦνον}⁶³ γεῦσις δὲ πνεῦμα διατεῖνον
ἀπὸ τοῦ ἡγεμονικοῦ | μέχρι γλώττης, ἁφὴ δὲ πνεῦμα
διατεῖνον ἀπὸ τοῦ ἡγεμονικοῦ μέχρις | ἐπιφανείας εἰς
θίξιν εὐαίσθητον τῶν προσπιπτόντων. |

15 τῶν δὲ λοιπῶν τὸ μὲν λέγεται σπερματικόν,⁶⁴ ὅπερ
καὶ αὐτὸ πνεῦμά | ἐστι διατεῖνον ἀπὸ τοῦ ἡγεμονικοῦ
μέχρι τῶν παραστατῶν· τὸ δέ | "φωνᾶεν" ὑπὸ τοῦ
Ζήνωνος εἰρημένον, ὃ καὶ "φωνητικὸν"⁶⁵ καλοῦσιν,
ἐστὶ | πνεῦμα διατεῖνον ἀπὸ τοῦ ἡγεμονικοῦ μέχρι
φάρυγγος καὶ γλώττης καὶ | τῶν οἰκείων ὀργάνων. |

20 αὐτὸ δὲ τὸ ἡγεμονικὸν ὥσπερ ἐν κόσμῳ <σφαιρο-
ειδεῖ ὁ θεὸς>⁶⁶ κατοικεῖ ἐν τῇ ἡμετέρᾳ | σφαιροειδεῖ
κεφαλῇ. (P) |

---

⁶² ἀκοὴ ὄσφρησις coni. MR: ὄσφρησις ἀκοὴ P
⁶³ {λεπτῦνον} non hab. Q, secl. Reiske
⁶⁴ σπερματικόν G: σπέρμα P
⁶⁵ φωνητικὸν G: φωνὴν P
⁶⁶ coni. MR²

tions and impulses, and this they call the "power of reason-   5
ing." The soul has seven (sc. further) parts, which grow
from the ruling part and stretch out toward the body like
tentacles from an octopus. Of the seven parts of the soul
five are sense organs: sight, hearing, smell, taste, and
touch.

Of these sight is *pneuma* extending from the ruling part
to the eyes, hearing *pneuma* extending from the ruling   10
part to the ears, smell *pneuma* extending from the ruling
part to the nostrils, taste *pneuma* extending from the ruling part to the tongue, and touch *pneuma* extending from
the ruling part to the body's surface for sensitive touching
of things that encounter it.

Of the remaining parts one is called seminal, which is   15
itself also *pneuma* stretching from the ruling part to the
testicles; the other, called the "vocal" part by Zeno and
which they also call "speaking part," is *pneuma* stretching
from the ruling part to the trachea and tongue and its appropriate organs.

The ruling part itself, just as <the god> in the <spheri-   20
cal> heaven, dwells in our spherical head.[37]

---

[37] This is a minority Stoic view; cf. 4.5.7, which wrongly claims
that all the Stoics locate the ruling part in the heart. Without the
conjectural addition, the doxa does not make good sense.

4.22

Ps.-Plut. *Plac.* 4.22 (+ Ps.-Gal. *Hist. phil.* 103); Stob. *Ecl.* 1.60

κβ′. Περὶ ἀναπνοῆς (PS) |

1. Ἐμπεδοκλῆς τὴν πρώτην ἀναπνοὴν τοῦ πρώτου ζῴου γενέσθαι τῆς | ⟨μὲν⟩[67] ἐν τοῖς βρέφεσιν ὑγρασίας ἀποχώρησιν λαμβανούσης, πρὸς δὲ τὸ | παρακενωθὲν ἐπεισόδου {τῆς ἔξωθεν}[68] τοῦ ἐκτὸς ἀερώδους
5 γινομένης εἰς | τὰ παρανοιχθέντα τῶν ἀγγείων· τὸ δὲ μετὰ τοῦτο ἤδη τοῦ ἐμφύτου | θερμοῦ τῇ πρὸς τὸ ἐκτὸς ὁρμῇ τὸ ἀερῶδες ὑπαναθλίβοντος, τὴν | ἐκπνοήν, τῇ δ᾽ εἰς τὸ ἐντὸς ἀνθυποχωρήσει τῷ ἀερώδει τὴν ἀντεπείσοδον | παρεχομένου, τὴν εἰσπνοήν.

τὴν δὲ νῦν κατέχουσαν φερομένου τοῦ | αἵματος ὡς πρὸς τὴν ἐπιφάνειαν καὶ τὸ ἀερῶδες διὰ τῶν ῥινῶν
10 ταῖς | ἑαυτοῦ ἐπιρροίαις ἀναθλίβοντος κατὰ[69] τὴν ἐκχώρησιν αὐτοῦ γίνεσθαι | τὴν ἐκπνοήν, παλινδρομοῦντος δὲ καὶ τοῦ ἀέρος ἀντεπεισιόντος εἰς τὰ |

§1 Empedocles A74

[67] ⟨μὲν⟩ add. Diels ex 5.15.3
[68] τῆς ἔξωθεν om. Q, secl. Diels conl. 5.15.3
[69] κατὰ emend. corr. Voss.: καὶ P

4.22

Some physico-mechanical explanations, with Asclepiades
admitting that it is also voluntary.

Ps.-Plutarch, *Tenets* (+ Ps.-Galen, *Philosophical History*);
Stobaeus, *Anthology*

22. On respiration

1. Empedocles says that the first breath of the first living
being took place as the moisture that is in newborns was
excreted and the outside air entered into the slightly
opened vessels to fill the void. Right after this, as the in-　5
nate heat squeezed up the air from below by rushing to
the outside, exhalation took place, and when its corresponding reversion inward provided a reciprocal entrance
to the air, inhalation occurred.[38]

As for the breathing that prevails now, when the blood
moves toward the surface and forces the air up through
the nostrils by its influxes, the exhalation occurs through　10
the departure of the air, and when the blood runs back and
the air enters in turn into the gaps left by it, the inhalation.

[38] Cf. 5.15.3. The first half of the lemma gives a protological
account, i.e., what happened in the beginning, the second half
what happens now.

διὰ τοῦ αἵματος ἀραιώματα τὴν εἰσπνοήν. ὑπομιμνή-
σκει δ᾽ αὐτὸ ἐπὶ τῆς | κλεψύδρας. (P) |

2. Ἀσκληπιάδης τὸν μὲν πνεύμονα χώνης δίκην συνί-
15 στησιν, αἰτίαν δὲ τῆς | ἀναπνοῆς τὴν ἐν τῷ θώρακι
λεπτομέρειαν ὑποτίθεται, πρὸς ἣν τὸν | ἔξωθεν ἀέρα
ῥεῖν τε καὶ καθαίρεσθαι⁷⁰ παχυμερῆ ὄντα, πάλιν δ᾽ |
ἀπωθεῖσθαι μηκέτι τοῦ θώρακος οἵου τ᾽ ὄντος μήτ᾽
ἐπεισδέχεσθαι μήθ᾽ | ὑποστέγειν· ὑπολειπομένου δέ
τινος ἐν τῷ θώρακι λεπτομεροῦς ἀεὶ | βραχέος (οὐ
γὰρ ἅπαν ἐκκρίνεται), πρὸς τοῦτο πάλιν τὸ εἴσω ὑπο-
20 μένον | ⟨τὴν⟩⁷¹ βαρύτητα τοῦ ἐκτὸς ἀντεπεισφέρεσθαι.
ταῦτα δὴ ταῖς σικύαις | παρεικάζει· τὴν δὲ κατὰ προ-
αίρεσιν ἀναπνοὴν γίνεσθαί φησι | συναγομένων τῶν
ἐν τῷ πνεύμονι λεπτοτάτων πόρων καὶ τῶν βραγχίων
| στενουμένων· τῇ γὰρ ἡμετέρᾳ ταῦθ᾽ ὑπακούει προ-
αιρέσει. (P) |

3. Ἡρόφιλος δυνάμεις ἀπολείπει περὶ τὰ σώματα τὰς
25 κινητικὰς ἐν νεύροις | ἐν ἀρτηρίαις ἐν μυσί· τὸν οὖν
πνεύμονα νομίζει πρῶτον⁷² ὀρέγεσθαι διαστολῆς | τε
καὶ συστολῆς φυσικῶς· εἶτα δὲ καὶ τἆλλα. ἐνέργειαν
μὲν οὖν⁷³ | εἶναι τοῦ πνεύμονος τὴν ἔξωθεν τοῦ
πνεύματος ὁλκήν· ὑπὸ δὲ τῆς | πληρώσεως τῆς θύρα-
θεν γινομένης ἐφέλκεται· παρακειμένως δὲ διὰ τὴν |

§2 Asclepiades cf. p. 724   §3 Herophilus fr. 143b

⁷⁰ καθαίρεσθαι G: φέρεσθαι P   ⁷¹ ⟨τὴν⟩ add. Diels
⁷² πρῶτον coni. Diels: μόνον P   ⁷³ οὖν G: om. P

He illustrates this in the passage with the example of the clepsydra (water clock).

2. Asclepiades constructs the lung in the manner of a funnel. He supposes that the cause of respiration is the filter in the chest, toward which air flows in from outside, and which is cleaned because it is thick. It is pushed back again when the chest is unable to receive more or to sustain it. A small amount of fineness always remains in the chest (for it is not all excreted), and it is toward this, which remains inside, that ⟨the⟩ weighty mass from outside is brought back in again. He likens the process to what happens with cupping glasses. Voluntary respiration he says takes place when the finest pores in the lung are contracted and the bronchial passages narrowed. For these obey our will.

3. Herophilus admits motor capacities for bodies in the nerves, arteries and muscles. He thus thinks that only the lung has a natural tendency for dilation and contraction, and the other parts have this tendency as a consequence. The drawing in of *pneuma* from outside, he says, is accordingly the activity of the lung, and it draws it in through the filling process, which occurs from without. Next, because

δευτέραν ὄρεξιν ἐφ' αὑτὸν ὁ θώραξ τὸ πνεῦμα μετ-
30 οχετεύει, πληρωθεὶς | δὲ καὶ μηκέτι ἐφέλκεσθαι δυνά-
μενος πάλιν εἰς τὸν πνεύμονα τὸ | περιττὸν ἀντιμεταρ-
ρεῖ, δι' οὗ πρὸς τὰ ἐκτὸς τὰ τῆς ἀποκρίσεως γίνεται,
| τῶν σωματικῶν μερῶν ἀντιπασχόντων ἀλλήλοις. ὅτε
μὲν γὰρ διαστολὴ | ⟨ὅτε δὲ συστολὴ⟩[74] γίνεται πνεύ-
μονος, ταῖς ἀλλήλων ἀντιμεταλήψεσι | πληρώσεώς τε
καὶ κενώσεως γινομένης, ὡς τέσσαρας μὲν γίνεσθαι |
35 κινήσεις περὶ τὸν πνεύμονα, τὴν μὲν πρώτην καθ' ἣν
ἔξωθεν ἀέρα | δέχεται, τὴν δὲ δευτέραν καθ' ἣν τοῦθ'
ὅπερ ἐδέξατο θύραθεν ἐντὸς | αὑτοῦ πρὸς τὸν θώρακα
μεταρρεῖ, τὴν δὲ τρίτην καθ' ἣν τὸ ἀπὸ τοῦ | θώρακος
συστελλόμενον αὖθις εἰς αὑτὸν ἐκδέχεται, τὴν δὲ τε-
τάρτην | καθ' ἣν τὸ ἐξ ὑποστροφῆς ἐν αὑτῷ γινόμενον
40 θύραζε ἐξερᾷ. τούτων δὲ | τῶν κινήσεων δύο μὲν εἶναι
διαστολάς, τήν τ' ἔξωθεν τήν τ' ἀπὸ τοῦ | θώρακος·
δύο δὲ συστολάς, τὴν μὲν ὅταν ὁ θώραξ ἐφ' αὑτὸν τὸ
πνευματικὸν | ἑλκύσῃ, τὴν δ' ὅταν αὐτὸς εἰς τὸν ἐκτὸς
ἀέρα ἀποκρίνῃ· δύο γὰρ | μόναι γίνονται περὶ τὸν
θώρακα, διαστολὴ μὲν ὅταν ἀπὸ τοῦ πνεύμονος |
ἐφέλκηται, συστολὴ δ' ὅταν τούτῳ πάλιν ἀνταπο-
διδῷ. (P) |

[74] ⟨ὅτε δὲ συστολὴ⟩ add. Diels, cf. Q

of a second natural tendency, the thorax diverts the breath
to itself, and when it is full and can no longer draw it in, it   30
lets the excess flow back again into the lung, through
which what is excreted passes outward. The parts of the
body are thus affected inversely to one another.[39] For now
a dilation, ⟨then a contraction⟩ of the lung occurs, since
filling up and emptying occur through reciprocal ex-   35
change, so that there are in fact four movements that occur in the lung: the first is the one by which it accepts air
from outside, the second that by which the *pneuma*, which
it has received from outside, changes its flow internally
toward the thorax; the third that by which it receives again
into itself the contracted *pneuma* from the thorax, the
fourth the one by which it evacuates to the outside that
which is in it after the turnaround. Of these motions, he
says, two are dilations, one from the outside and one from   40
the thorax, and two contractions, namely one when the
thorax draws the pneumatic substance to itself, the other
when the lung itself excretes *pneuma* into the external air.
Only two motions, you see, occur in the thorax: dilation
when it draws in *pneuma* from the lung, contraction when
it delivers it back again to the lung.

[39] That is, the one accepts air as the other emits it.

4.23

Ps.-Plut. *Plac.* 4.23 (+ Ps.-Gal. *Hist. phil.* 104); Stob. *Ecl.* 1.60

κγ΄. Περὶ παθῶν σωματικῶν καὶ εἰ
συναλγεῖ τούτοις ἡ ψυχή (PS) |

1. οἱ Στωικοὶ τὰ μὲν πάθη ἐν τοῖς πεπονθόσι τόποις,
τὰς δὲ αἰσθήσεις ἐν τῷ | ἡγεμονικῷ. (P) |
2. Ἐπίκουρος καὶ τὰ πάθη καὶ τὰς αἰσθήσεις ἐν τοῖς
5 πεπονθόσι τόποις· τὸ | γὰρ ἡγεμονικὸν ἀπαθές. (P) |
3. Στράτων καὶ τὰ πάθη τῆς ψυχῆς καὶ τὰς αἰσθήσεις
ἐν τῷ ἡγεμονικῷ οὐκ | ἐν τοῖς πεπονθόσι τόποις συν-
ίστασθαι. ἐν γὰρ ταύτῃ κεῖσθαι τὴν ὑπομονήν, |
ὥσπερ ἐπὶ τῶν δεινῶν καὶ ἀλγεινῶν καὶ ὥσπερ ἐπὶ
τῶν ἀνδρείων | καὶ δειλῶν. (P) |

§1 Stoics 2.854
§2 Epicurus fr. 317
§3 Strato fr. 63A

4.23

The soul can be, or is, independent of what happens in the body. The diaeretic structure is more than usually obvious.

Ps.-Plutarch, *Tenets* (+ Ps.-Galen, *Philosophical History*); Stobaeus, *Anthology*

23. On bodily affections and whether the soul experiences pain along with these

1. The Stoics say that the affections are in the places that have been affected, but the sensations of them are in the ruling part.

2. Epicurus says that both the affections and the sensations are in the places that have been affected, for the ruling part is free from affection.[40]

3. Strato says that both the affections and the sensations exist together in the ruling part, not in the affected places. For in this location steadfastness is situated, just as in the case of terrible and painful circumstances, and just as in the case of brave and cowardly actions.

[40] Aptly placed in between §1 and §3.

BOOK V

PHYSIOLOGY

INTRODUCTION

Transmission

Book 5 is the most poorly attested of the five books that
make up Aëtius compendium. Regrettably, we are almost
wholly dependent on Ps.-Plutarch for our textual material.
From the evidence of the pinax in the Laurentianus manuscript and of Photius' index, it is certain that Stobaeus
also made extensive excerpts from this book, but these
were almost totally excised by later Byzantine redactors.
Of the ten Stobaean lemmata that remain, only two are
not found in the *Epitome*, and even they appear to dupli-
cate other doxai. The contents of this book were not useful
for Theodoret's apologetic enterprise, and he makes no
reference to them. The archetype from which the Byzantine manuscripts of Ps.-Plutarch derive appears to have
been damaged toward the end. Fortunately, missing material can be supplied from the Arabic translation of Quṣṭā
and from the epitome of Ps.-Galen, who is very assiduous
in his use of this book. The result of this poor state of
transmission is that Book 5 has a lower average of lemmata

401

per chapter (3.8) than any other. In terms of length, only Book 3 is shorter, but it has far fewer chapters (eighteen as opposed to thirty). Through statistical analysis, it can be calculated that most likely fifty-five to sixty lemmata of its original contents are missing.[1]

In this book there are a number of passages where the textual evidence is confused or uncertain. The additional evidence in Qusṭā and Ps.-Galen that supplements the text in the manuscripts of Ps.-Plutarch also gives rise to various questions. These issues are further discussed in Appendix II, to which the reader is adverted at the relevant points in the apparatus criticus.

Contents

There is no introductory section explaining the contents of the book. Apparently, it continues the treatment of "the particular phenomena" (*ta kata meros*) that began at 4.1. The division between the two final books can be fairly neatly described as between psychology, that is, the soul and its role in perception and thought, and physiology, in which the role of the body and its processes comes more to the fore. But this is clearly not an absolute divide, since many bodily processes occur with the participation of soul. So the division of the two books is a bit messy. The first two chapters of Book 5, on divination and dreams, would have been better placed in Book 4.

The main body of the book gives an overview of the de-

---

[1] For statistics on the length of books, see MR 5.97; on the missing lemmata, Jeremiah, "Statistical Explorations," 293–95, 347–52.

velopment of the human being, from conception to adulthood, amounting to a minitreatise on spermatology (chs. 3–5), conception (6–10), heredity (11–13), and embryology (15–18, 21–22), and concluding with chapter 23, on when the human being attains maturity. As in Plato's *Timaeus*, the focus is almost wholly on human beings, but the sequence is broken by three chapters that broaden the subject to include the wider category of living beings (14, on mules; 19–20, on the animal genera). The final chapters can best be regarded as an appendix treating related subjects on sleep and death, nourishment, health, disease, and old age. There is only one specifically medical chapter, on fever (29).

Name-Labels

In terms of name-labels, Book 5 is the least diverse of all, containing thirty-five different names in total, with a concentration on the fifth to third centuries BC. Important Presocratics are strongly represented: Parmenides (five doxai), Alcmaeon (six), Pythagoras (five), and, most remarkably, Empedocles (seventeen, all included in the sequence chs. 7–28). The high presence (nineteen doxai) of doctors—notably, Diocles, Erasistratus, Herophilus, and Asclepiades—is related to the book's subject matter.[2] The lack of diversity may be partly explained by the poor transmission but is also due to the fact that many philosophers did not pronounce on subjects treated in this book.

[2] More detailed analysis of the presence of doctors in the *Placita* may be found in Runia, "The *Placita* Ascribed to Doctors."

Chapter Headings

Another striking feature of this book is that it has very few chapters with a heading using the general formula *peri* x, or inquiring after the substance (*ousia*) of anything. The majority of chapters use the formulae *pôs* (how), *dia ti* (for what reason), or *pothen* (whence). In addition, quite a few chapters ask the *ei* (whether) question, inviting either a yes or a no answer structured in terms of a diaphonia. Book 5 is thus overwhelmingly focused on a quest for the cause of physiological and biological processes. These are very often schematically answered by means of prepositional phrases using *dia*, *kata*, and *para* (see, for example, chs. 6, 8, 9, and 13). In one case (5.8.1), Aëtius claims that an Empedoclean doxa virtually exhausts all the causes that can be given. Not surprisingly, therefore, most chapters are organized by means of the dialectical techniques of the diaeresis, the diaphonia, and the ordered list. This tendency may have been increased through the abridgment process employed by Ps.-Plutarch, for it is evident that he understood the importance of these techniques. Conversely, Book 5 stands out in its lack of historiographical material, with very little information given on the name-labels it contains. For example, it is silent on the role of Hippocrates as the father of medicine, mentioning him only once, with the formula *hoi peri* X, which refers both to him and to his followers (5.18.4).

Absences

Two further brief observations can be made on the book's contents. First, we note what is absent. Aside from chaper

1, on divination, it is striking how little reference there is to any theological or eschatological themes, with only a single rather obscure reference to the cosmic god (in 5.20.1). Also absent are references to epistemology (e.g., the truth value of dreams in ch. 2) or arithmology (e.g., with reference to the length of pregnancy). It is rather unexpected, however, to find in chapters 19 and 26 reference to cosmogonic and protological events, mostly in doxai attributed to Empedocles. These appear to be fossils dating back to the early period of Greek scientific explanation preserved in the doxographical tradition.

Comparative Material

For purposes of comparison, there are two texts belonging to the proximate tradition containing material that casts a great deal of light on the contents of Book 5. The first is the *Birthday Book* of Censorinus, dated to AD 238, which contains copious doxographies on topics relating to human life, from its start in conception to its end in death. The other is a section in the medical compilation *Definitiones medicae*, falsely attributed to Galen (§§439–52), which contains brief doxographical summaries of doctrines on spermatology, embryology, and gynecology. Other authors who provide useful parallels are Aulus Gellius, Tertullian, and Lactantius. It is likely that these authors, writing in Latin, including Censorinus, did not derive their material from Aëtius or similar doxographical compendia, but rather from the first-century BC Roman author Varro, whose writings appear to have made extensive use of the earlier doxographical tradition. For the views of doctors, that is, medical scientists, there existed specifically medical compendia. The most interesting of these is the *Iatrika* by the author called the Anonymus Londiniensis. It contains much early material, but there are very few overlaps with Aëtius' work. Finally, we observe the presence of physiological doctrines in Lucretius, and before him, Epicurus, which suggest they may have drawn on doxographical material. For the entirety of the doxographical tradition, in light of the prominence of Presocratic views (especially those of Empedocles) and also the telltale use of early cosmogonic themes, it would appear that the Peripatos of Aristotle and Theophrastus is the most logical place where this material was first assembled.

Sources

Other sources that contributed to the contents of Book 5 are the Hippocratic corpus (very little) and Plato's *Timaeus* (more, but the material available was limited). Of much greater significance are the biological treatises of Aristotle, notably *De generatione animalium*, but also *De partibus animalium* and *Historia animalium*. It is above all in the organization and general outline of biological and physiological topics that Aristotle's influence on the book's contents is most marked. For the majority of the chapter headings, there are parallels in his works. For the actual content of the reported doxai, however, the number of specific parallels is quite limited. The *Placita* are thus proof of the continuing influence of the Stagirite's biological works in the Hellenistic period. But the compendium also reveals that intermediate stages of doctrinal reception have taken place. It is likely that the Stoics made a significant contribution to this process, as suggested by the Stoic overlay of the *physikos logos* that we have discovered elsewhere in the work, but also on account of the prominence of Stoic doxai (thirteen references). But the sources at our disposal are too meager to allow further detective work. The influence of incipient Middle Platonism on the book is also limited. At most one can point to the theological reference in 5.20.1, which runs parallel to the Platonic doxa at 1.7.22, and also to the presence of the name-label Pythagoras in conjunction with Plato in 5.20.4 (with Aristotle's name added in 5.4.2).

ΑΕΤΙΟΥ ΠΕΡΙ ΤΩΝ ΑΡΕΣΚΟΝΤΩΝ
ΤΟ Ε′,[2] |

ἐν ᾧ κεφάλαια τάδε· |

〈Index〉

Ps.-Plut. *Plac.*

---

[1] Ps.-Plut. *Plac.* 5; Theod. *Cur.* 4.31, cf. 2.95, 5.16
[2] tit. T: Τῶν ἀρεσκόντων φιλοσόφοις φυσικῶν δογμάτων ἐν ἐπιτομῇ P (v. l. Περὶ τοῖς φιλοσόφοις βιβλίον)

AETIUS
ON THE PLACITA

BOOK V

in which the following chapter headings are found:[1]

[1] On the title and the list of chapter headings, or pinax, see above on Book 1 and the General Introduction 1.3.

θ΄. Διὰ τί γυνὴ πολλάκις συνουσιάζουσα οὐ συλλαμβάνει |

ι΄. Πῶς δίδυμα καὶ τρίδυμα γίνεται |

ια΄. Πόθεν γίνεται τῶν γονέων ἡ ὁμοίωσις καὶ τῶν προγόνων |

ιβ΄. Πῶς ἄλλοις ὅμοιοι γίνονται οἱ γεννώμενοι καὶ οὐ τοῖς γονεῦσιν |

15 ιγ΄. Πῶς στεῖραι γίνονται αἱ γυναῖκες καὶ ἄγονοι οἱ ἄνδρες |

ιδ΄. Διὰ τί αἱ ἡμίονοι στεῖραι |

ιε΄. Εἰ τὸ ἔμβρυον ζῷον |

ιϛ΄. Πῶς τρέφεται τὰ ἔμβρυα |

ιζ΄. Τί πρῶτον τελεσιουργεῖται ἐν τῇ γαστρί |

20 ιη΄. Διὰ τί τὰ ἑπταμηνιαῖα γόνιμα |

ιθ΄. Περὶ ζῴων γενέσεως, πῶς ἐγένοντο ζῷα, καὶ εἰ φθαρτά |

κ΄. Πόσα γένη ζῴων καὶ εἰ πάντα αἰσθητικὰ καὶ λογικά |

κα΄. Ἐν πόσῳ χρόνῳ μορφοῦται τὰ ζῷα ἐν τῇ γαστρὶ ὄντα |

κβ΄. Ἐκ ποίων συνίσταται στοιχείων ἕκαστον τῶν ἐν ἡμῖν γενικῶν μορίων |

25 κγ΄. Πότε ἄρχεται ὁ ἄνθρωπος τῆς τελειότητος |

κδ΄. Πῶς ὕπνος γίνεται καὶ θάνατος |

κε΄. Ὁποτέρου ἐστὶν ὕπνος καὶ θάνατος, ψυχῆς ἢ σώματος |

κϛ΄. Πῶς ηὐξήθη τὰ φυτὰ καὶ εἰ ζῷα |

κζ΄. Περὶ τροφῆς καὶ αὐξήσεως |

30 κη΄. Πόθεν αἱ ὀρέξεις γίνονται τοῖς ζῴοις καὶ αἱ ἡδοναί |

κθ′. Πῶς γίνεται πυρετὸς καὶ εἰ ἐπιγέννημά ἐστιν |
λ′. Περὶ ὑγείας καὶ νόσου καὶ γήρως |

5.1

Ps.-Plut. *Plac*. 5.1 (+ Ps.-Gal. *Hist. phil*. 105)

α′. Περὶ μαντικῆς (P) |

1. Πλάτων καὶ οἱ Στωικοὶ τὴν μαντικὴν εἰσάγουσι κατὰ
τὸ θεόπεμπτον | εἶναι,³ ὅπερ ἐστὶν ἐνθεαστικόν, καὶ κατὰ
θειότητα τῆς ψυχῆς, ὅπερ ἐστὶν | ἐνθουσιαστικόν· καὶ
5 τὸ ὀνειροπολικὸν καὶ τὸ ἀστρομαντικὸν καὶ τὸ | ὀρ-
νεοσκοπικὸν καὶ τὸ ἱεροσκοπικόν.⁴ οὗτοι τὰ πλεῖστα
μέρη τῆς | μαντικῆς ἐγκρίνουσι. (P) |
2. Ξενοφάνης καὶ Ἐπίκουρος ἀναιροῦσι τὴν μαντι-
κήν. (P) |
3. Πυθαγόρας δὲ μόνον τὸ θυτικὸν οὐκ ἐγκρίνει. (P) |

§1 Plato cf. *Tim*. 71e, *Phdr*. 244b–c; Stoics 2.1190
§2 Xenophanes A52; Epicurus fr. 395
§3 Pythagoras —

³ κατὰ τὸ . . . εἶναι MR: καὶ γὰρ . . . εἶναι G, κατὰ τὸ
ἔνθεον P, cf. Q
⁴ 4–5 καὶ¹ . . . ἱεροσκοπικόν MR Primavesi sec., vid. app.
sec.

5.1

*The main division is between accepting divination in its
various forms or rejecting it entirely, followed by intermediate views accepting certain parts of the practice.*

Ps.-Plutarch, *Tenets* (+ Ps.-Galen, *Philosophical History*)

1. On divination[2]

1. Plato and the Stoics admit divination in that it is sent by
a god, which is its visionary (i.e., prophetic) element, and
also because of the divinity of the soul, which is the element of divine possession; they also admit the interpreta-
tion of dreams, the divination of the stars, the inspection   5
of birds and the inspection of sacrificial victims.[3] These
thinkers include them as the most important parts of
divination.
2. Xenophanes and Epicurus reject divination.
3. But Pythagoras excludes only the sacrificial aspect as
part of divination.

[2] For this doxography compare the more detailed account at
Cicero *De divinatione* 1.4–7. But he also includes later philosophers Carneades, Panaetius, and Posidonius not found here.

[3] The listing of all four additional kinds of divination is found
only in the papyrus of Ps.-Plutarch. The Byzantine manuscripts
retain only the first. The next two are also found in Ps.-Galen and
Qusṭā. See further the additional notes to the text of Book 5 in
Appendix II.

4. Ἀριστοτέλης καὶ Δικαίαρχος τὸ κατ᾽ ἐνθουσιασμὸν
10 μόνον παρεισάγουσι | καὶ τοὺς ὀνείρους, ἀθάνατον μὲν
εἶναι οὐ νομίζοντες τὴν ψυχήν, θείου δέ | τινος μετέχειν
αὐτήν. (P) |

§4 Aristotle cf. *Div.somn.* 1 463b12–14; Dicaearchus fr. 30B

5.2

*The first two doxai distinguish between dreams with an
external or an internal origin. The third introduces a new
distinction between divinely inspired and natural dreams,*

Ps.-Plut. *Plac.* 5.2 (+ Ps.-Gal. *Hist. phil.* 106)

β΄. Πῶς ὄνειροι γίνονται (P) |

1. Δημόκριτος τοὺς ὀνείρους γίνεσθαι κατὰ τὰς τῶν
εἰδώλων παραστάσεις. | (P) |
2. Στράτων ἀλόγῳ φύσει τῆς διανοίας ἐν τοῖς ὕπνοις
5 αἰσθητικωτέρας μὲν | πως γινομένης, παρ᾽ αὐτὸ δὲ
τοῦτο τῷ γνωστικῷ κινουμένης. (P) |
3. Ἡρόφιλος τῶν ὀνείρων τοὺς μὲν θεοπνεύστους⁵ κατ᾽
ἀνάγκην γίνεσθαι, | τοὺς δὲ φυσικοὺς ἀνειδωλοποιου-
μένης τῆς ψυχῆς τὸ συμφέρον αὐτῇ καὶ | τὸ πρὸς τούτοις

§1 Democritus A136   §2 Strato fr. 68
§3 Herophilus T226

⁵ θεοπνεύστους P, cf. Q: θεοπέμπτους GL

4. Aristotle and Dicaearchus introduce only the aspect of divine possession and dreams as parts of divination, not regarding the soul as immortal, but as sharing in something of the divine.   10

5.2

but then adds a mixed type involving images internal to the soul.

Ps.-Plutarch, *Tenets* (+ Ps.-Galen, *Philosophical History*)

2. How dreams occur[4]

1. Democritus says that dreams occur through the manifestations of *eidôla*.
2. Strato says that they occur by an irrational nature in the mind when during sleep it somehow becomes more sensitive, and through this very fact is affected by the cognitive element.   5
3. Herophilus says that of the various kinds of dreams, those that are divinely inspired occur of necessity, whereas those that are natural occur when the soul forms an image

---

[4] Note that in this chapter the focus is on the physical and psychological mechanisms of dreams, not their origin (whether divine or human) and truth-value, as in most other ancient accounts.

ἐσόμενον, τοὺς δὲ συγκραματικοὺς ἐκ τοῦ αὐτομάτου |
κατ' εἰδώλων πρόσπτωσιν, ὅταν ἃ βουλόμεθα βλέπω-
10 μεν, ὡς ἐπὶ τῶν τὰς | ἐρωμένας ὁρώντων⁶ ἐν ὕπνῳ γίνε-
ται. (P) |

5.3

Ps.-Plut. *Plac.* 5.3 (+ Ps.-Gal. *Hist. phil.* 107)

γ'. Τίς ἡ οὐσία τοῦ σπέρματος (P) |

1. Ἀριστοτέλης· σπέρμα ἐστὶ τὸ δυνάμενον κινεῖν ἐν
ἑαυτῷ εἰς τὸ ἀποτελέσαι | τι τοιοῦτον, οἷόν ἐστι τὸ ἐξ οὗ
συνεκρίθη. (P) |
2. Πυθαγόρας ἀφρὸν τοῦ χρηστοτάτου αἵματος τὸ
5 σπέρμα, περίττωμα τῆς | τροφῆς, ὥσπερ τὸ αἷμα καὶ
μυελόν. (P) |
3. Ἀλκμαίων ἐγκεφάλου μέρος. (P) |
4. Πλάτων μυελοῦ τοῦ νωτιαίου ἀπόρροιαν. (P) |

§1 Aristotle cf. *GA* 4.1 766b12   §2 Pythagoras —
§3 Alcmaeon A13   §4 Plato cf. *Tim.* 74a

⁶ ὁρώντων coni. Diels, cf. Q: ἐχόντων P, ἐρώντων G

of what is advantageous for itself and will subsequently happen, but those that are mixed occur spontaneously through the impact of images,[5] whenever we see what we wish, as occurs in the case of those who see their lovers   10 while sleeping.

5.3

A first "metaphysical" view is contrasted with five physical views covering the three main ancient theories, hemato-genic (§2), encephalomyelogenic (§§3–4) and pangenetic (§§5–6).

Ps.-Plutarch, *Tenets* (+ Ps.-Galen, *Philosophical History*)

3. What the substance of semen is

1. Aristotle: semen is that which is able within itself to move to the production of such a thing as that from which it was itself secreted.
2. Pythagoras says that the semen is foam from the most useful kind of blood, a residue of food, like blood and   5 marrow.[6]
3. Alcmaeon says that it is a part of the brain.
4. Plato says that it is an effluence from the marrow in the backbone.

---

[5] The term is *eidôla* (images), as in the first doxa, but here the source is internal to the soul, and not external, as presumably in the case of the Atomist (though this is not made explicit).

[6] The three basic types of spermatological theories—hemato-genic, encephalomyelogenic, and pangenetic—are all represented in this chapter.

5. Ἐπίκουρος⁷ ψυχῆς καὶ σώματος ἀπόσπασμα. (P) |

6. Δημόκριτος ἀφ᾽ ὅλων τῶν σωμάτων καὶ τῶν κυρι-
10 ωτάτων μερῶν, οἷον | ὀστῶν⁸ σαρκῶν ἰνῶν. (P) |

§5 Epicurus fr. 329   §6 Democritus A141

5.4

Ps.-Plut. *Plac.* 5.4 (+ Ps.-Gal. *Hist. phil.* 108)

δ΄. Εἰ σῶμα τὸ σπέρμα (P) |

1. Λεύκιππος καὶ Ζήνων σῶμα· ψυχῆς γὰρ εἶναι ἀπό-
σπασμα. (P) |

2. Πυθαγόρας Πλάτων Ἀριστοτέλης ἀσώματον μὲν
εἶναι τὴν δύναμιν τοῦ | σπέρματος ὥσπερ νοῦν τὸν
κινοῦντα, σωματικὴν δὲ τὴν ὕλην τὴν προχεομέ-
5 νην. | (P) |

3. Στράτων καὶ Δημόκριτος καὶ τὴν δύναμιν σῶμα·
πνευματικὴ γάρ. (P) |

§1 Leucippus A35; Zeno 1.128
§2 Pythagoras —; Plato —; Aristotle cf. *GA* 2.3 737a7–12
§3 Strato fr. 70; Democritus A142

⁷ Ἐπίκουρος vid. app. sec.
⁸ οἷον ὀστῶν G: ὁ γόνος τῶν PQ

5. Epicurus says that it is a detached portion of soul and body.[7]
6. Democritus says that it comes from the bodies in their entirety and their most important parts, such as bones, tissues and sinews. 10

5.4

A progression of three views, the first stating semen is corporeal, the second distinguishing between its incorporeal power and corporeal substance, the third affirming that its power is also corporeal.

Ps.-Plutarch, *Tenets* (+ Ps.-Galen, *Philosophical History*)

4. Whether semen is a body[8]

1. Leucippus and Zeno say that it is a body, for it is a fragment of soul.[9]
2. Pythagoras, Plato, and Aristotle say that the power of the semen is incorporeal just like the mind that sets it in motion, but that the matter that is ejaculated is corporeal. 5
3. Strato and Democritus say that the power of the semen is a body as well, for it is pneumatic.

[7] The doxographer makes a mistake here. This is the view of the Stoics, also stated in 5.4.1 and 5.11.3. Epicurus followed the atomist views recorded in the next lemma. See further additional notes to the text in Appendix II. [8] Puzzlingly, the papyrus places the number 42 in front of the chapter's title, which may point to an early edition with a different numbering system.
[9] Cf. the corporealist views in 4.3.7 and 4.3.3 respectively.

5.5

Ps.-Plut. *Plac.* 5.5 (+ Ps.-Gal. *Hist. phil.* 109)

ε΄. Εἰ καὶ αἱ θήλειαι προΐενται σπέρμα (P) |

1. Πυθαγόρας καὶ Ἐπίκουρος καὶ Δημόκριτος καὶ τὸ θῆλυ προΐεσθαι | σπέρμα· ἔχει γὰρ παραστάτας ἀπεστραμμένους· διὰ τοῦτο καὶ ὄρεξιν | ἔχει περὶ τὰς χρήσεις. (P) |

5 2. Ἀριστοτέλης καὶ Ζήνων ὕλην μὲν ὑγρὰν προΐεσθαι οἰονεὶ ἀπὸ τῆς συγγυμνασίας | ἱδρῶτας, οὐ μὴν σπέρμα πεπτικόν. (P) |

3. Ἵππων προΐεσθαι μὲν σπέρμα τὰς θηλείας οὐχ ἥκιστα τῶν ἀρρένων, μὴ | μέντοι εἰς ζῳογονίαν τοῦτο συμβάλλεσθαι διὰ τὸ ἐκτὸς πίπτειν τῆς | ὑστέρας· ὅθεν ἐνίας[9] προΐεσθαι πολλάκις δίχα τῶν ἀνδρῶν

10 σπέρμα, καὶ | μάλιστα τὰς χηρευούσας. (P) |

4. <***>[10] καὶ εἶναι τὰ μὲν ὀστᾶ παρὰ τοῦ ἄρρενος τὰς δὲ σάρκας παρὰ τῆς | θηλείας. (P) |

§1 Pythagoras —; Epicurus fr. 330; Democritus A142
§2 Aristotle cf. *GA* 1.19 727a27–30, 2.4 738a34–b4; Zeno 1.129   §3 Hippo A13   §4 —

[9] ἐνίας coni. Diels, cf. Q et 5.9.1[2]: ὀλίγας P
[10] lac. pos. MR (secl. καὶ . . . θηλείας Kranz VS)

5.5

The first two doxai form an opposition, with the third introducing a compromise view. A fourth appears to contradict the third and follows on from the first.

Ps.-Plutarch, *Tenets* (+ Ps.-Galen, *Philosophical History*)

5. Whether females too release semen

1. Pythagoras, Epicurus, and Democritus say that the female releases semen as well as the male, for she has concealed testicles.[10] For this reason she also has desire for sexual intercourse.

2. Aristotle and Zeno say that she releases moist matter 5 just like sweat from doing exercise, but not semen that results from concoction.

3. Hippo says that females release semen no less than males. However, he says, this semen does not contribute to conception of life because it falls outside the womb. Hence some females often release seed apart from males, and it is especially widows who do this. 10

4. *** and the bones derive from the male but the flesh from the female.[11]

[10] This refers to the ovaries. The role of the female ovum in reproduction was not discovered until 1827 (by K. A. von Baer).

[11] Because the second part of the doxa contradicts the view of Hippo, it is likely that one or more name-labels have fallen out.

5.6

Ps.-Plut. *Plac.* 5.6 (+ Ps.-Gal. *Hist. phil.* 110); Stob. *Ecl.* 1.42.2

ϛʹ. Πῶς αἱ συλλήψεις γίνονται (PS) |

1. Ἀριστοτέλης τὰς μὲν συλλήψεις γίνεσθαι προανελκομένης μὲν ὑπὸ τῆς | καθάρσεως τῆς μήτρας, τῶν δὲ καταμηνίων συνεπισπωμένων ἀπὸ τοῦ | παντὸς ὄγκου μέρος τι τοῦ καθαροῦ αἵματος, ᾧ[11] συμβαίνειν τὸν τοῦ
5 | ἄρρενος γόνον· μὴ γίνεσθαι δὲ τὰς κυήσεις παρ᾽ ἀκαθαρσίαν τῆς μήτρας | ἢ ἐμπνευμάτωσιν ἢ φόβον ἢ λύπην ἢ δι᾽ ἀσθένειαν τῶν γυναικῶν ἢ δι᾽ | ἀτονίαν τῶν ἀνδρῶν. (P) |

§1 Aristotle cf. *HA* 9.2 582b11, *GA* 2.4 739a26

[11] ᾧ coni. Reiske: ὡς PGQ

5.6

A very uncommon example of a chapter with only a single doxa, though containing an opposition between successful conception and failure within it. It is likely incomplete.

Ps.-Plutarch, *Tenets* (+ Ps.-Galen, *Philosophical History*); Stobaeus, *Anthology*

6. How conceptions occur[12]

1. Aristotle says that conceptions occur when the womb has been drawn forward through the process of purification (i.e., menstruation), and the menses have brought along from the entire mass of the body a part consisting of pure blood, which the male seed then encounters. But he 5 says that pregnancies fail to occur from the lack of purification of the womb (i.e., cessation of menstruation) or its inflation or fear or pain or through weakness of the women or through lack of condition of the men.

[12] The first of many chapter headings in this book asking the "how" question, i.e., the cause of biological phenomena. Such headings are rare in the other books.

5.7

Ps.-Plut. *Plac.* 5.7 (+ Ps.-Gal. *Hist. phil.* 111); Stob. *Ecl.* 1.42.5

ζ΄. Πῶς ἄρρενα γεννᾶται καὶ θήλεα (P) |

1. Ἐμπεδοκλῆς[12] ἄρρενα καὶ θήλεα γίνεσθαι παρὰ θερμότητα καὶ ψυχρότητα· | ὅθεν ἱστορεῖται τοὺς μὲν πρώτους ἄρρενας πρὸς ἀνατολῇ καὶ | μεσημβρίᾳ γεγενῆσθαι μᾶλλον ἐκ τῆς γῆς, τὰς δὲ θηλείας πρὸς
5 ταῖς | ἄρκτοις. (P) |
2. Παρμενίδης ἀντιστρόφως· τὰ μὲν πρὸς ταῖς ἄρκτοις ἄρρενα βλαστῆσαι, | τοῦ γὰρ πυκνοῦ μετέχειν πλείονος· τὰ δὲ πρὸς ταῖς μεσημβρίαις θήλεα | παρὰ τὴν ἀραιότητα. (P) |
3. Ἵππων[13] παρὰ τὸ συνεστός τε καὶ ἰσχυρὸν ⟨ἢ⟩
10 παρὰ τὸ ῥευστικόν τε καὶ | ἀσθενέστερον σπέρμα. (P) |

§1 Empedocles A81   §2 Parmenides A53
§3 Hippo A14

[12] post nom. καὶ Ἀσκληπιάδης add. G
[13] Ἵππων coni. MR, cf. 5.5.3: Ἱππῶναξ PQ

5.7

The first two doxai record opposed explanations with reference to an original cosmology. The remaining views are based on various factors involved in (present-day) sexual intercourse.

Ps.-Plutarch, *Tenets* (+ Ps.-Galen, *Philosophical History*); Stobaeus, *Anthology*

7. How males and females are engendered[13]

1. Empedocles says that males and females come into being in relation to heat and cold. Hence it is recounted that the first males were born from the earth more in the east and the south, whereas the first females were born in the 5 north.[14]
2. Parmenides has it the other way around: the males grew in the north, for they share more in the dense element, the females in the south on account of their lightness.
3. Hippo says that males and females are engendered from the compacted and strong seed ⟨or⟩ from the fluid and weaker seed. 10

[13] The term "engendered" is chosen because it can be used for both sexes, in contrast to "beget" and "conceive."
[14] Here for the first time in Book 5, protological explanations are given for present-day biological phenomena. This was a feature of early Presocratic thought and is particularly well represented in doxai attributed to Empedocles.

4. Ἀναξαγόρας Παρμενίδης τὰ μὲν ἐκ τῶν δεξιῶν καταβάλλεσθαι εἰς τὰ | δεξιὰ μέρη τῆς μήτρας, τὰ δ᾽ ἐκ τῶν ἀριστερῶν εἰς τὰ ἀριστερά· εἰ δ᾽ | ἐναλλαγείη τὰ τῆς καταβολῆς, γίνεσθαι θήλεα. (P) |

5. Λεωφάνης, οὗ μέμνηται Ἀριστοτέλης, τὰ μὲν ἐκ τοῦ
15 δεξιοῦ διδύμου τὰ | δ᾽ ἐκ τοῦ ἀριστεροῦ. (P) |

6. Λεύκιππος διὰ τὴν παραλλαγὴν τῶν μορίων, καθ᾽ ἣν ὁ μὲν καυλὸν ἡ δὲ | μήτραν ἔχει· τοσοῦτον γὰρ μόνον λέγει. (P) |

7. Δημόκριτος τὰ μὲν κοινὰ μέρη ἐξ ὁποτέρου ἂν τύχῃ, τὰ δ᾽ ἰδιάζοντα κατ᾽ | ἐπικράτειαν. (P) |

20 8. Ἵππων,[14] εἰ μὲν ἡ γονὴ κρατήσειεν, ἄρρεν· εἰ δ᾽ ἡ τροφή, θῆλυ. (P) |

§4 Anaxagoras A111; Parmenides 28A53
§5 Leophanes cf. Arist. *GA* 4.1 765a21–25
§6 Leucippus A36
§7 Democritus A14
§8 Hippo A14

[14] Ἵππων coni. MR, cf. 5.5.3: Ἱππῶναξ PQ

4. Anaxagoras and Parmenides say that males are engendered when the seed from the right parts [i.e., testicle] is deposited on the right side of the womb and the seed from the left parts is deposited on the left side; but if the deposition is reversed, then females come into being.

5. Leophanes, who is mentioned by Aristotle,[15] says that males are engendered with seed from the right testicle, females with seed from the left testicle.   15

6. Leucippus says that males and females are engendered through the differentiation of the parts (i.e., sex organs), in accordance with which the male has a penis and the female has a womb. This is all that he says on the subject.

7. Democritus says that the parts held by males and females in common derive from either kind as it happens, but the parts that are specific to the two sexes through dominance.

8. Hippo says that if the seed dominates, a male is engendered, if the womb dominates, a female is engendered.[16]   20

[15] This reference proves that the sources Aëtius used for his compendium had access to the biological works of Aristotle.

[16] The doxa here is quite different from that in §3. Some confusion of name-labels in the tradition, e.g., between Hippo/Hipponax and Hippocrates, may be suspected.

427

5.8

Ps.-Plut. *Plac*. 5.8 (+ Ps.-Gal. *Hist. phil*. 112); Stob. *Ecl*. 1.42.6

η′. Πῶς τέρατα γίνεται (PS) |

1. Ἐμπεδοκλῆς τέρατα γίνεσθαι παρὰ πλεονασμὸν σπέρματος ἢ παρ' | ἔλλειψιν ἢ παρὰ τὴν τῆς κινήσεως ταραχὴν ἢ παρὰ τὴν εἰς πλείω | διαίρεσιν ἢ παρὰ τὸ
5 ἀπονεύειν· οὕτω προειληφὼς φαίνεται σχεδόν τι | πά-σας τὰς αἰτιολογίας. (P) |
2. Στράτων παρὰ πρόσθεσιν ἢ ἀφαίρεσιν ἢ μετάθεσιν ἢ ἐμπνευμάτωσιν. (P) |
3. τῶν ἰατρῶν τινες παρὰ τὸ διαστρέφεσθαι τότε τὴν μήτραν ἐμπνευματουμένην. | (P) |

§1 Empedocles A81
§2 Strato fr. 74
§3 —

5.8

The ten causes given relate either to the nature and activity of semen or to the movements of the womb. They are divided (with some overlap) between three doxai, of which the second forms a bridge between the first and the third.

Ps.-Plutarch, *Tenets* (+ Ps.-Galen, *Philosophical History*); Stobaeus, *Anthology*

8. How monstrous births[17] occur

1. Empedocles says that monstrous births occur from excess of semen or from lack of semen or from the disturbance of movement of the semen or from the division into more parts or from the inclining away of the womb. In this way he plainly anticipates almost all the causes that can be given. 5

2. Strato says that they occur from addition to the semen or subtraction from the semen or transposition or inflation of the womb.

3. Some of the doctors say that they occur from the twisting of the womb sometimes when it is inflated.

---

[17] The Greek term connotes the portentous, rather than the defective, nature of the birth.

5.9

Ps.-Plut. *Plac.* 5.9 (+ Ps.-Gal. *Hist. phil.* 113); Stob. *Ecl.* 1.42

θ′. Διὰ τί γυνὴ πολλάκις συνουσιάζουσα οὐ
συλλαμβάνει (PS) |

1. Διοκλῆς ὁ ἰατρὸς ἢ παρὰ τὸ μηδ᾽ ὅλως ἐνίας
σπέρμα προΐεσθαι ἢ παρὰ | τὸ ἔλαττον τοῦ δέοντος ἢ
διὰ τὸ τοιοῦτον, ἐν ᾧ τὸ ζῳοποιητικὸν οὐκ | ἔστιν· ἢ
διὰ θερμασίας ἢ ψύξεως ἢ ὑγρασίας ἢ ξηρότητος ἔν-
5 δειαν ἢ κατὰ | παράλυσιν τῶν μορίων. (P) |
2. οἱ δὲ Στωικοὶ κατὰ λοξότητα τοῦ καυλοῦ, μὴ δυ-
ναμένου τὸν γόνον εὐθυβολεῖν· | ἢ παρὰ τὸ ἀσύμ-
μετρον τῶν μορίων ὡς πρὸς τὴν ἀπόστασιν τῆς |
μήτρας. (P) |
3. Ἐρασίστρατος παρὰ τὴν μήτραν, ὅταν τύλους ἔχῃ
10 καὶ σαρκώσεις ἢ | ἀραιοτέρα τοῦ κατὰ φύσιν ἢ μικρο-
τέρα τυγχάνῃ οὖσα. (P) |

§1 Diocles fr. 42
§2 Stoics 2.751
§3 Erasistratus fr. 57

5.9

The doxai are fairly neatly divided into causes related to (1) female semen, (2) the male member, or (3) the female womb. But there are problems of attribution.

Ps.-Plutarch, *Tenets* (+ Ps.-Galen, *Philosophical History*); Stobaeus, *Anthology*

9. Why a woman, although frequently having intercourse, does not conceive[18]

1. Diocles the doctor says that it occurs because some women do not release any semen at all or less than is required, or because the semen is such that it is not productive of life, or through a lack of heating or cooling or moistening or dryness or through paralysis of the parts (i.e., sex   5
organs).
2. But the Stoics say that it occurs through a slanting of the penis, which is unable to project the seed in a straight line, or from the disproportion of the parts (i.e., testicles) in relation to the distance of the womb.[19]
3. Erasistratus says that it occurs because of the womb, whenever it has tumors or fleshy growths or is feebler or   10
smaller than what is natural.

[18] This chapter interrupts the sequence of 5.7–10 and appears to be misplaced. There is also obvious overlap with the topic of 5.13.
[19] In 5.13 the causes in this doxa are also attributed to Diocles, and a different explanation is attributed to the Stoics. The name-label of the Stoics here is likely to be mistaken.

431

5.10

Ps.-Plut. *Plac.* 5.10 (+ Ps.-Gal. *Hist. phil.* 114); Stob. *Ecl.* 1.42.10

ιʹ. Πῶς δίδυμα καὶ τρίδυμα γίνεται (PS) |

1. Ἐμπεδοκλῆς οἴεται δίδυμα καὶ τρίδυμα γίνεσθαι κατὰ πλεονασμὸν καὶ | περισχισμὸν τοῦ σπέρματος. (P) |

2. Ἀσκληπιάδης παρὰ τὴν τῶν σπερμάτων διαφοράν,
5 ὥσπερ τὰς κριθὰς | τὰς διστίχους καὶ τριστίχους· εἶναι γὰρ σπέρματα γονιμώτατα. (P) |

3. Ἐρασίστρατος διὰ τὰς ἐπισυλλήψεις, ὥσπερ ἐπὶ τῶν ἀλόγων ζῴων· | ὅταν γὰρ ἡ μήτρα ᾖ κεκαθαρμένη, τότε ἐπισύλληψιν δέχεσθαι.[15] (P) |

4. οἱ Στωικοὶ παρὰ τοὺς ἐν τῇ μήτρᾳ τόπους· ὅταν γὰρ εἰς πρῶτον καὶ | δεύτερον ἐμπέσῃ τὸ σπέρμα,
10 τότε γίνεσθαι τὰς ἐπισυλλήψεις καὶ τὰ | δίδυμα καὶ τὰ τρίδυμα. (P) |

§1 Empedocles A81   §2 Asclepiades pp. 721, 725
§3 Erasistratus fr. 58   §4 Stoics 2.750

[15] δέχεσθαι corr. Diels: ἔρχεται (sc. ἐπὶ σύλληψιν) P

5.10

The division covers the three main ancient theories, with the second doxa introducing a variation on the first.

Ps.-Plutarch, *Tenets* (+ Ps.-Galen, *Philosophical History*); Stobaeus, *Anthology*

10. How twins and triplets occur

1. Empedocles thinks that twins and triplets occur as the result of multiplication and division of the semen.
2. Asclepiades says that they occur from the difference of the semen, as in the case of barley with double and triple 5 stalks. For there are, he says, highly productive semen.
3. Erasistratus says that they occur through superfetations, as occurs in the case of the irrational animals. For he says that whenever the womb is in a state of having been purified, it then admits superfetation.
4. The Stoics say that they occur on account of the locations in the womb; for whenever semen settles in a first and a second location, then they say additional conceptions occur, i.e., twins and triplets.[20] 10

[20] Translating the first *kai* in the text as epexegetic.

Ps.-Plut. *Plac*. 5.11 (+ Ps.-Gal. *Hist. phil.* 115); Stob. *Ecl*. 1.42.7

ιαʹ. Πόθεν γίνεται τῶν γονέων ὁμοίωσις καὶ
τῶν προγόνων (PS) |

1. Ἐμπεδοκλῆς ὁμοιότητα γίνεσθαι κατ᾽ ἐπικράτειαν
τῶν σπερματικῶν | γόνων, ἀνομοιότητα δὲ τῆς ἐν τῷ
σπέρματι θερμασίας ἐξατμισθείσης. | (P) |

5   2. Παρμενίδης, ὅταν μὲν ἀπὸ τοῦ δεξιοῦ μέρους <εἰς
τὰ δεξιὰ μέρη>[16] τῆς μήτρας ὁ γόνος ἀποκριθῇ, | τοῖς
πατράσιν· ὅταν δ᾽ ἀπὸ τοῦ ἀριστεροῦ <εἰς τὰ ἀρι-
στέρα>,[17] ταῖς μητράσιν. (P) |

3. οἱ Στωικοὶ ἀπὸ τοῦ σώματος ὅλου καὶ τῆς ψυχῆς
φέρεσθαι τὸ σπέρμα, | καὶ τὰς ὁμοιομερείας[18] ἀνα-
πλάττεσθαι ἐκ τῶν αὐτῶν γενῶν τοὺς τύπους | καὶ
τοὺς χαρακτῆρας, ὥσπερ ἂν εἰ ζωγράφου ἀπὸ τῶν

§1 Empedocles A81   §2 Parmenides A54
§3 Stoics 2.749

[16] <εἰς τὰ δεξιὰ μέρη> coni. MR²
[17] <εἰς τὰ ἀριστέρα> coni. MR²
[18] ὁμοιομερείας G, cf. Q: ὁμοιότητας P

5.11

Again a division into three significant theories, but little attempt at consistency with 5.7, on sex differentiation.

Ps.-Plutarch, *Tenets* (+ Ps.-Galen, *Philosophical History*); Stobaeus, *Anthology*

11. Where resemblance to parents and ancestors comes from

1. Empedocles says that similarity occurs in accordance with dominance of the seminal seeds, but that dissimilarity occurs when the heat in the semen has vaporized.

2. Parmenides says that, whenever the seed is separated out from the right part of the womb ⟨to the right parts⟩, resemblance to the fathers occurs, but whenever this happens from the left part ⟨to the left parts⟩,[21] resemblance to the mothers occurs.

3. The Stoics[22] say that the semen is conveyed from the entire body and the soul, and that the *homoiomereiai* (things with like parts) form the outlines and the markings from the same kinds, as when a painter forms an image of

---

[21] The conjectures are probable in light of 5.7.4 above.

[22] In the light of 5.5.2, the name-label must be wrong. Given the reference to *homoiomereiai* (cf. 1.3.4), the doxa may be that of Anaxagoras.

10 ὁμοίων χρωμάτων | εἰκόνα τοῦ βλεπομένου. προίεσθαι
δὲ καὶ τὴν γυναῖκα σπέρμα· | κἂν μὲν ἐπικρατήσῃ τὸ
τῆς γυναικός, ὅμοιον εἶναι τὸ γεννώμενον τῇ | μητρί,
ἐὰν δὲ τὸ τοῦ ἀνδρός, τῷ πατρί. (P) |

5.12

Ps.-Plut. *Plac.* 5.12 (+ Ps.-Gal. *Hist. phil.* 116); Stob. *Ecl.*
1.42.8

ιβ΄. Πῶς ἄλλοις ὅμοιοι γίνονται οἱ γεννώμενοι καὶ
οὐ τοῖς γονεῦσιν | (PS) |

1. οἱ μὲν πλεῖστοι τῶν ἰατρῶν τυχικῶς καὶ αὐτομάτως,
ὅταν διαψυγῇ τὸ | σπέρμα καὶ τὸ τοῦ ἀνδρὸς καὶ τὸ
5 τῆς γυναικός, ἀνόμοια γίνεσθαι τὰ | παιδία. (P) |
2. Ἐμπεδοκλῆς τῇ κατὰ τὴν σύλληψιν φαντασίᾳ τῆς
γυναικὸς μορφοῦσθαι | τὰ βρέφη· πολλάκις γὰρ ἀν-
δριάντων καὶ εἰκόνων ἠράσθησαν γυναῖκες, | καὶ
ὅμοια τούτοις ἀπέτεκον. (P) |

§1 doctors —
§2 Empedocles A81

what is seen from similar colors. But they say that the   10
woman too releases semen; and if the semen of the woman
dominates, the child that is born is similar to the mother,
but if the semen of the man dominates, it is similar to the
father.

5.12

*A division between the first view, which gives a general
physiological explanation, and the remaining two, which
introduce various psychological factors.*

Ps.-Plutarch, *Tenets* (+ Ps.-Galen, *Philosophical History*);
Stobaeus, *Anthology*

12. How it happens that those who are born resemble
others and not their parents

1. Most of the doctors say that it occurs by chance and
spontaneously, whenever the seed—both that of the man
and that of the woman—has become chilled, that the resultant children become dissimilar to their parents.   5
2. Empedocles says that the babies are shaped by the
imagination of the woman during conception. For often
women fell in love with statues and images, and they gave
birth to children who resemble these.

3. οἱ Στωικοὶ συμπαθείᾳ τῆς διανοίας κατὰ ῥευμάτων
10 εἰσκρίσεις καὶ | ἀκτίνων ⟨ἢ καὶ⟩[19] εἰδώλων[20] γίνεσθαι
τὰς ἄλλων ὁμοιότητας. (P) |

§3 Stoics 2.753

5.13

Ps.-Plut. *Plac.* 5.13 (+ Ps.-Gal. *Hist. phil.* 117); Stob. *Ecl.*
1.42

ιγ΄. Πῶς στεῖραι γίνονται αἱ γυναῖκες καὶ
ἄγονοι οἱ ἄνδρες (PS) |

1. οἱ ἰατροὶ στείρας γίνεσθαι παρὰ τὴν μήτραν ἢ
παρὰ τὸ πυκνοτέραν εἶναι | ἢ παρὰ τὸ ἀραιοτέραν ἢ
παρὰ τὸ σκληροτέραν ἢ παρά τινας ἐπιπωρώσεις |
ἢ σαρκώσεις ἢ παρὰ μικροφυΐαν[21] ἢ παρ᾽ ἀτροφίαν ἢ
5 παρὰ καχεξίαν | ἢ παρὰ τὸ διαστρέφεσθαι τὸν σχη-
ματισμὸν ἢ διὰ παρασπασμόν. (P) |
2. Διοκλῆς ἀγόνους τοὺς ἄνδρας ἢ παρὰ τὸ μηδ᾽ ὅλως

§1 doctors —   §2 Diocles fr. 43

[19] ἢ καὶ coni. Diels: οὐκ PQ (om. G)
[20] εἰδώλων vid. app. sec.
[21] μικροφυΐαν coni. Kronenberg, cf. Q: μικροθυμίαν P

3. The Stoics say that the similarities to others occur by coaffection of the mind in accordance with penetrations of streams and rays ⟨or indeed⟩ of *eidôla*.[23] 10

5.13

A straightforward division explaining sterility through female causes, male causes, and the incompatibility of female and male together.

Ps.-Plutarch, *Tenets* (+ Ps.-Galen, *Philosophical History*); Stobaeus, *Anthology*

13. How it occurs that women are infertile and men without offspring

1. The doctors say that infertility occurs in women because of the womb, either from it being denser or lighter or rougher or from having formed calluses or fleshy growths, or from being small in size or from lack of nourishment or from being in poor condition or from its shape being 5
twisted or through distension.
2. Diocles says that men do not have offspring from the

---

[23] Here too (cf. 5.11.3) the attribution is likely to be wrong. The terminology is atomist. See further Appendix II.

ἐνίους σπέρμα προΐεσθαι | ἢ παρὰ τὸ ἔλαττον τοῦ
δέοντος· ἢ παρὰ τὸ ἄγονον εἶναι τὸ | σπέρμα ἢ κατὰ
παράλυσιν τῶν μορίων ἢ κατὰ λοξότητα τοῦ καυλοῦ,
μὴ | δυναμένου τὸν γόνον εὐθυβολεῖν, ἢ παρὰ τὸ
10 ἀσύμμετρον τῶν μορίων | πρὸς τὴν ἀπόστασιν τῆς
μήτρας. (P) |

3. οἱ Στωικοὶ αἰτιῶνται τὰς ἀσυμφύλους εἰς ἑκάτερον
τῶν πλησιαζόντων | δυνάμεις τε καὶ ποιότητας· αἷς
ὅταν συμβῇ χωρισθῆναι μὲν ἀπ᾽ ἀλλήλων | συνελθεῖν
δ᾽ ἑτέροις ὁμοφύλοις, συνεκρατήθη τὸ κατὰ φύσιν καὶ
| βρέφος τελεσιουργεῖται. (P) |

§3 Stoics 2.752

5.14

Ps.-Plut. *Plac.* 5.14 (+ Ps.-Gal. *Hist. phil.* 118); Stob. *Ecl.*
1.42.9

ιδ΄. Διὰ τί αἱ ἡμίονοι στεῖραι (PS) |

1. Ἀλκμαίων τῶν ἡμιόνων τοὺς μὲν ἄρρενας ἀγόνους
παρὰ τὴν λεπτότητα | τῆς "θορῆς," ὅ ἐστι σπέρματος,
καὶ ψυχρότητα· τὰς δὲ θηλείας παρὰ τὸ | μὴ "ἀναχά-

§1 Alcmaeon B3

440

fact that some of them do not emit seed at all or less than
is required, or from the infertility of their seed or from the
paralysis of the organs or from the slanting of the penis,
which is unable to offer the seed straight passage, or from
the disproportion of the parts (i.e., sex organs) in relation   10
to the distance of the womb.[24]

3. The Stoics determine as cause the incompatibility of the
powers and qualities of each of the partners with each
other; when it happens that they (sc. women) have been
separated from their partner and joined up with others (sc.
men) with whom they are compatible, then the natural
process has prevailed and a fetus is brought to completion.

5.14

In contrast to the previous chapter (and despite the chapter heading), first a male and then a female explanation.

Ps.-Plutarch, *Tenets* (+ Ps.-Galen, *Philosophical History*);
Stobaeus, *Anthology*

14. Why female mules are infertile

1. Alcmaeon says that of the mules the males are infertile
because of the thinness of the "sperm" (*thorê*), i.e., of the
semen, and its coldness. In the case of the females it is
from the wombs not "gaping wide" (*anachaskein*), which

---

[24] On the relation to the very similar views in the parallel
chapter 5.9, see the note ad loc.

σκειν" τὰς μήτρας, ὅ ἐστι ἀναστομοῦσθαι. οὕτω γὰρ
5 αὐτὸς | εἴρηκεν. (P) |

2. Ἐμπεδοκλῆς διὰ τὴν σμικρότητα καὶ ταπεινότητα
καὶ στενότητα τῆς | μήτρας, κατεστραμμένως προσ-
πεφυκυίας τῇ γαστρί, μήτε τοῦ σπέρματος | εὐθυβο-
λοῦντος εἰς αὐτὴν μήτε, εἰ καὶ φθάσειεν, αὐτῆς ἐκδε-
χομένης. | (P) |

10 3. Διοκλῆς δὲ μαρτυρεῖ αὐτῷ λέγων· "ἐν ταῖς ἀνατο-
μαῖς πολλάκις ἑωράκαμεν | τοιαύτην μήτραν τῶν ἡμι-
όνων·" καὶ ἐνδέχεσθαι διὰ τὰς τοιαύτας | αἰτίας καὶ
τὰς γυναῖκας εἶναι στείρας. (P) |

§2 Empedocles A82   §3 Diocles fr. 24

5.15

Ps.-Plut. *Plac.* 5.15 (+ Ps.-Gal. *Hist. phil.* 119); Stob. *Ecl.*
1.42.11

ιε΄. Εἰ τὸ ἔμβρυον ζῷον (PS) |

1. Πλάτων ζῷον τὸ ἔμβρυον· καὶ γὰρ κινεῖσθαι ἐν τῇ
γαστρὶ καὶ τρέφεσθαι | καὶ αὔξεσθαι.[22] (P) |

§1 Plato cf. *Tim.* 91d2–5

[22] καὶ αὔξεσθαι G: om. PQ

means "opening up their entrance." For this is how he
himself has spoken of it.[25]   5

2. Empedocles says that it occurs through the small size
and low position and narrowness of the womb, which has
reversed and grown next to the belly, with the result that
neither does the seed have a direct passage to it, nor, even
if it were to reach it, does the womb accept it.

3. But Diocles bears witness to him (i.e., the view of Em-   10
pedocles) when he says: "in the dissections we have often
observed the womb of mules like this"; and he adds that it
is possible that women too are infertile for reasons of such
a kind.

5.15

The first two doxai form opposed answers to the question,
followed by three more nuanced versions of the negative
view, each emphasizing the role of respiration.

Ps.-Plutarch, *Tenets* (+ Ps.-Galen, *Philosophical History*);
Stobaeus, *Anthology*

15. Whether the embryo is a living being

1. Plato says that the embryo is a living being. For he says
it moves in the womb, is nourished, and grows.

25 The quoted terms are archaic and indeed likely to go back
to Alcmaeon's treatise as claimed.

2. οἱ Στωικοὶ μέρος εἶναι αὐτὸ τῆς γαστρός, οὐ ζῷον·
5 ὥσπερ γὰρ τοὺς | καρποὺς μέρη τῶν φυτῶν ὄντας
πεπαινομένους ἀπορρεῖν, οὕτω καὶ τὸ | ἔμβρυον. (P) |
3. Ἐμπεδοκλῆς μὴ εἶναι μὲν ζῷον τὸ ἔμβρυον ἀλλ'
ἄπνουν ὑπάρχειν ἐν τῇ | γαστρί· πρώτην δ' ἀναπνοὴν
τοῦ ζῴου γίνεσθαι κατὰ τὴν ἀποκύησιν, | τῆς μὲν ἐν
τοῖς βρέφεσιν ὑγρασίας ἀποχώρησιν λαμβανούσης,
10 πρὸς δὲ | τὸ παρακενωθὲν ἐπεισόδου τοῦ ἐκτὸς ἀε-
ρώδους γινομένης εἰς τὰ | παρανοιχθέντα τῶν ἀγ-
γείων. (P) |
4. Διογένης γεννᾶσθαι μὲν τὰ βρέφη ἄψυχα, ἔνθερμα
δέ·[23] ὅθεν τὸ ἔμφυτον | θερμὸν εὐθέως προχυθέντος
τοῦ βρέφους τὸ ψυχρὸν εἰς τὸν πνεύμονα | ἐφέλκε-
ται. (P) |
15 5. Ἡρόφιλος κίνησιν ἀπολείπει φυσικὴν τοῖς ἐμ-
βρύοις, οὐ πνευματικήν· | τῆς δὲ κινήσεως αἴτια
νεῦρα· τότε δὲ ζῷα γίνεσθαι, ὅταν προχυθέντα | προσ-
λάβῃ τι τοῦ ἀέρος. (P) |

§2 Stoics 2.756
§3 Empedocles cf. A74
§4 Diogenes of Apollonia A28 (but could be Diogenes the
Stoic)
§5 Herophilus fr. 202

[23] ἔνθερμα δέ coni. MR, cf. Q Diels *DG* 853: ἐν θερμασίᾳ P

2. The Stoics say that it is a part of the womb, not a living being. For they say just as fruits are parts of plants and when they have ripened, they fall off, so the same happens with the embryo.

3. Empedocles says that the embryo is not a living being but exists without breathing in the womb. The living being's first breath occurs,[26] he says, at the time of the birth, when the moisture in the newborn babies[27] is excreted and in the space thus vacated entry of the external air occurs in the vessels that have opened up.

4. Diogenes[28] says that that the newborn babies are conceived without life, but do possess heat. For this reason, when the newborn baby is delivered, the innate heat draws the cold into the lung.

5. Herophilus grants the fetuses natural movement, but not movement that is pneumatic. The tendons are the causes of their movement. They become living beings at the moment when they are delivered and take in some of the air.

[26] The doxa here is almost word for word identical to the first section of 4.22.1.

[27] *Brephos* in Greek can mean both "fetus" and "newborn baby."

[28] It is uncertain whether this is the Presocratic or the Stoic. There are arguments in favor of both.

5.16

Ps.-Plut. *Plac.* 5.16 (+ Ps.-Gal. *Hist. phil.* 120); Stob. *Ecl.* 1.42.12

ιϛ´. Πῶς τρέφεται τὰ ἔμβρυα (PS) |

1. Δημόκριτος Ἐπίκουρος τὸ ἔμβρυον ἐν τῇ μήτρᾳ διὰ τοῦ στόματος | τρέφεσθαι· ὅθεν εὐθέως γεννηθὲν ἐπὶ τὸν μαστὸν φέρεσθαι τῷ στόματι· | εἶναι γὰρ καὶ ἐν τῇ μήτρᾳ θηλάς τινας καὶ στόματα, δι᾽ ὧν τρέφε-
5 σθαι. | (P) |

2. οἱ Στωικοὶ διὰ τοῦ χορίου καὶ τοῦ ὀμφαλοῦ· ὅθεν τοῦτον εὐθέως ἀποδεῖν | τὰς μαιουμένας καὶ ἀνευρύνειν τὸ στόμα, ἵνα ἑτέρα γένηται ἡ μελέτη | τῆς τρο-φῆς.[24] (P) |

3. Ἀλκμαίων δι᾽ ὅλου τοῦ σώματος τρέφεσθαι· ἀνα-
10 λαμβάνειν γὰρ αὐτό, | ὥσπερ σπογγιά, τὰ ἀπὸ τῆς τροφῆς θρεπτικά. (P) |

§1 Democritus A144; Epicurus fr. 332
§2 Stoics 2.754
§3 Alcmaeon A17

[24] ἑτέρα . . . τροφῆς P, cf. Q: διὰ τοῦ στόματος αἰσθητῶς τρέφηται G, cf. Ps

5.16

Two alternative views involving nourishment in the womb are opposed to a rather strange third view.

Ps.-Plutarch, *Tenets* (+ Ps.-Galen, *Philosophical History*); Stobaeus, *Anthology*

16. How embryos are nourished

1. Democritus and Epicurus say that the embryo is nourished in the womb through the mouth. For this reason as soon as it is born it moves with its mouth to the breast. For, they say, in the womb too there are nipples and mouths through which it is fed. 5

2. The Stoics say that the embryo is nourished through the placenta and the navel. For this reason the midwives immediately bind it up and open up the baby's mouth, so that another method of nourishment may occur.

3. Alcmaeon says that the embryo is nourished from the body in its entirety.[29] For he says it takes up the nourishing elements from the food, just like a sponge does. 10

[29] This view seems more appropriate for the nourishment supplied by the mother to the placenta, as already described by Aristotle at *GA* 2.7 745b23–45.

5.17

Ps.-Plut. *Plac.* 5.17 (+ Ps.-Gal. *Hist. phil.* 121); Stob. *Ecl.* 1.42.4

ιζʹ. Τί πρῶτον τελεσιουργεῖται ἐν τῇ γαστρί (PS) |

1. οἱ Στωικοὶ ἅμα ὅλον²⁵ γίνεσθαι (P) |

2. Ἀριστοτέλης πρῶτον τὴν ὀσφὺν ὡς τρόπιν νεώς. (P) |

3. Ἀλκμαίων τὴν κεφαλήν, ἐν ᾗ ἔστι τὸ ἡγεμονικόν. (P) |

5 4. οἱ ἰατροὶ τὴν καρδίαν, ἐν ᾗ αἱ φλέβες καὶ αἱ ἀρτηρίαι. (P) |

5. οἱ δὲ τὸν μέγαν δάκτυλον τοῦ ποδός. (P) |

6. ἄλλοι δὲ τὸν ὀμφαλόν. (P) |

§1 Stoics 2.755
§2 Aristotle cf. *GA* 2.1 735a14–15, *Met.* 5.1 1013a4
§3 Alcmaeon A13
§4 doctors —
§§5–6 anonymi —

²⁵ ἅμα ὅλον GQ: τοῖς πολλοῖς P

5.17

The question invites answers in the form of a list, but their sequence seems rather disorganized, in contrast to the similar chapter 4.5.

Ps.-Plutarch, *Tenets* (+ Ps.-Galen, *Philosophical History*); Stobaeus, *Anthology*

17. What is fully formed first in the womb

1. The Stoics say that it occurs all together as a whole.
2. Aristotle says that the loins are first formed like the keel of a ship.
3. Alcmaeon says that the head is first formed, in which the ruling part resides.
4. The doctors say that the heart is first formed, in which 5
the veins and the arteries have their source.
5. But others say that the large toe of the foot is first formed.
6. And yet others say that the navel is first formed.

Ps.-Plut. *Plac.* 5.18 (+ Ps.-Gal. *Hist. phil.* 122); Stob. *Ecl.* 1.42.13

ιη΄. Διὰ τί τὰ ἑπταμηνιαῖα γόνιμα (PS) |

1. Ἐμπεδοκλῆς, ὅτε ἐγεννᾶτο τὸ τῶν ἀνθρώπων γένος
ἐκ τῆς γῆς, | τοσαύτην γενέσθαι τῷ μήκει τοῦ χρόνου
διὰ τὸ βραδυπορεῖν τὸν ἥλιον | τὴν ἡμέραν, ὁπόση
νῦν ἐστιν ἡ δεκάμηνος· προϊόντος δὲ τοῦ χρόνου |
5 τοσαύτην γενέσθαι τὴν ἡμέραν, ὁπόση νῦν ἐστιν ἡ
ἑπτάμηνος· διὰ τοῦτο | καὶ τὰ δεκάμηνα γόνιμα καὶ
τὰ ἑπτάμηνα, τῆς φύσεως τοῦ κόσμου οὕτω | μεμελε-
τηκυίας αὔξεσθαι ἐν μιᾷ ἡμέρᾳ τῇ τότε καὶ νυκτὶ τὸ
βρέφος. (P) |
2. Τίμαιος καὶ δωδεκάμηνα φησιν τινα κύεσθαι[26]
παρὰ τὰς ἐπισχέσεις τῶν | μηνιαίων τὰς πρὸ τῆς συλ-
10 λήψεως· οὕτω καὶ τὰ ἑπτάμηνα νομίζεσθαι, | οὐκ ὄντα

§1 Empedocles A75
§2 Timaeus —

[26] καὶ . . . κύεσθαι G, cf. Q: οὐ δώδεκα μῆνάς φησιν, ἐννέα
δὲ νομίζεσθαι P

5.18

The narrowly defined question receives more broadly for-
mulated answers, with protological and astrological views
at the beginning and the end of the chapter, and various
physiological solutions placed in between.

Ps.-Plutarch, *Tenets* (+ Ps.-Galen, *Philosophical History*);
Stobaeus, *Anthology*

18. Why seven-month babies are viable

1. Empedocles says that when the human race was first
generated from the earth, because of the slow movement
of the sun the day was the same in length of time as ten
months now.[30] As time advanced, the day became the   5
same in length as seven months now. For this reason both
ten-month- and seven-month-olds are viable, the nature
of the cosmos having ensured that the baby will grow to
maturity in the womb in a single day and night of that time.
2. Timaeus says that some twelve-month-olds too are conceived beyond the cessation of the menstrual periods that
occurred before the conception. And seven-month-olds
may be considered in the same way, not really in fact being   10

[30] On this protological explanation, see n. 14 to chapter 5.7.

ἑπτάμηνα· γίνονται γὰρ καὶ μετὰ τὴν σύλληψιν πο-
σαί | καθάρσεις. (P) |

3. Πόλυβος Διοκλῆς οἱ Ἐμπειρικοὶ καὶ τὸν ὄγδοον
μῆνά φασι γόνιμον, | ἀγονώτερον²⁷ δέ πως τῷ πολ-
λάκις διὰ τὴν ἀτονίαν πολλοὺς φθείρεσθαι· | καθολι-
κώτερον δὲ μηδένα βούλεσθαι τὰ ὀκτάμηνα τρέφειν·

15 γεγενῆσθαι | δὲ πολλοὺς ὀκταμηνιαίους ἄνδρας. (P) |

4. οἱ περὶ τὸν Ἀριστοτελῆ καὶ Ἱπποκράτην φασίν, ἐὰν
ἐκπληρωθῇ ἡ μήτρα | ἐν τοῖς ἑπτὰ μησί, τότε προκύ-
πτειν καὶ γεννᾶσθαι γόνιμα· ἐὰν δὲ προκύψῃ | μὲν μὴ
τρέφηται δέ, ἀσθενήσαντος τοῦ ὀμφαλοῦ διὰ τὸ ἐπί-
πονον | αὐτῷ γεγενῆσθαι τὸ ἔκκριμα, τότε ἔμβρυον

20 ἄτροφον εἶναι· ἐὰν δὲ μείνῃ | τοὺς ἐννέα μῆνας ἐν τῇ
μήτρᾳ, προκύψαν τότε ὁλόκληρόν ἐστι. (PS) |

5. Πόλυβος ἐν ἑκατὸν ὀγδοήκοντα δύο καὶ ἡμίσει
ἡμέραις γίνεσθαι γόνιμα | τὰ ἔμβρυα· εἶναι γὰρ
ἑξάμηνα, ὅτι καὶ τὸν ἥλιον ἀπὸ τροπῶν ἐν τοσούτῳ |
χρόνῳ παραγίνεσθαι· λέγεσθαι δ᾽ ἑπταμηνιαίους διὰ
τὸ τὰς ἐλλειπούσας | ἡμέρας τούτου τοῦ μηνὸς ἐν τῷ

25 ἑπτὰ προσλαμβάνεσθαι· τὰ δ᾽ | ὀκταμηνιαῖα μὴ ζῆν,
ὅταν προκύψῃ μὲν τῆς μήτρας τὸ βρέφος, ἐπὶ | πλεῖον
δ᾽ ὁ ὀμφαλὸς βασανισθῇ· ἄτροφον γὰρ γίνεται, ὡς
τοῦ τρέφοντος | αἴτιος ὁ ὀμφαλός. (P) |

§3 Polybus —; Diocles fr. 48; Empiricists fr. 133
§4 Aristotle *HA* 7.4 584b2; Hippocrates *Oct.*, cf. *Carn.* 19
§5 Polybus cf. *Oct.* 1–2, 10

²⁷ ἀγονώτερον coni. Grensemann: ἀτονώτερον mss.

seven-month-olds. For even after the conception a number of purgings take place.

3. Polybus, Diocles, and the Empiricists say that the eighth-month-old can be viable too,[31] but is less viable somehow on account of many of them perishing through their poor condition. In general terms, they say, no one wishes to rear the eight-month-olds, but nevertheless many eight-month-olds have become full-grown men.   15

4. Aristotle and Hippocrates and their followers say that, if the womb reaches its full term in seven months, then those babies that emerge and are born are viable. But if it emerges but is not nourished, because the umbilical cord had grown weak on account of its secretion having become difficult, then as embryo it is malnourished. But if it remains the full nine months in the womb, then it emerges   20 as a complete being.

5. Polybus says that that one hundred and eighty-two-and-a-half days are required for embryos to be viable. This is a six-month period, he says, because the sun too moves from solstice to solstice in this length of time. But they are called seven-month-olds through the addition of the remaining days of this month to make up the seven. The   25 eight-month-olds do not live, since the baby emerges from the womb but the umbilical cord is excessively strained. As the umbilical cord is the cause of its nourishment, it remains unnourished.

[31] The strange view that, in contrast to seven-month-old fetuses, eight-month-olds are not viable, was widely held in antiquity. The parallel doxography in Censorinus (ch. 7) states that only Hippo, Aristotle, and Diocles disagree. The presentation here is less emphatic on this point.

6. οἱ δὲ μαθηματικοὶ τοὺς ὀκτὼ μῆνας ἀσυνδέτους φα-
σὶν εἶναι πάσης | γενέσεως, τοὺς δ' ἑπτὰ συνδετικούς·
30 τὰ δ' ἀσύνδετα ζῴδια ἐστιν, ἐὰν | τῶν οἰκοδεσποτούν-
των ἀστέρων τυγχάνῃ· ἐὰν γάρ τις τούτων τὴν ζωὴν
| καὶ τὸν βίον κληρώσηται, δυστυχεῖς καὶ ἀχρόνους
σημαίνει· ἀσύνδετα δ' | ἐστὶ ζῴδια <κατ'>[28] ὀκτὼ ἀριθ-
μούμενα, οἷον Κριὸς πρὸς Σκορπίον ἀσύνδετος, | Ταῦ-
ρος πρὸς Τοξότην ἀσύνδετος, Δίδυμοι πρὸς Αἰγόκε-
ρων, | Καρκίνος πρὸς Ὑδροχόον, Λέων πρὸς Ἰχθύας,
35 Παρθένος πρὸς Κριόν· διὰ | τοῦτο καὶ τὰ ἑπτάμηνα
ὄντα καὶ δεκάμηνα γόνιμα εἶναι· τὰ δ' ὀκτάμηνα | διὰ
τὸ ἀσύνδετον τοῦ κόσμου φθείρεσθαι. (P) |

§6 astrologers —

[28] κατ' coni. MR

6. But the astrologers[32] say that eight-month periods are incompatible with all generation, but seven months are compatible. The incompatible zodiacal signs occur if they   30
result in heavenly bodies that are predominant (i.e., that are malevolent). For if any of these should allot the life and span of any persons, they signify that those persons will be unfortunate and untimely. The incompatible zodiacal signs are numbered by eight, i.e., Aries is incompatible with Scorpio, Taurus incompatible with Sagittarius, Gemini with Capricorn, Cancer with Aquarius, Leo with Pisces, Virgo with Aries. For this reason they say both the   35
seven-month- and the ten-month-olds are viable, but the eight-month-olds perish because of their incompatibility with the cosmos.

[32] The term here is again *mathêmatikoi* (cf. the note to ch. 2.15), but the context justifies the translation "astrologers." The ancients did not distinguish between astronomers and astrologers as moderns do.

5.19

The sequence of questions on fetuses is interrupted by two chapters on living beings (zoia) in general. The first two doxai form an opposition, followed by a famous poetic

Ps.-Plut. *Plac.* 5.19 (+ Ps.-Gal. *Hist. phil.* 123); Stob. *Ecl.* 1.42

ιθʹ. Περὶ ζῴων γενέσεως, πῶς ἐγένοντο ζῷα, καὶ εἰ φθαρτά (PS) |

1. καθ᾽ οὓς μὲν γενητὸς ὁ κόσμος, γενητὰ τὰ ζῷα καὶ φθαρτά εἰσιν. (P) |

2. {οἱ περὶ Ἐπίκουρον}²⁹ καθ᾽ οὓς ⟨δὲ⟩ ἀγένητος, ἐκ μεταβολῆς τῆς ἀλλήλων | γεννᾶσθαι τὰ ζῷα· μέρη γὰρ εἶναι τοῦ κόσμου ταῦτα. (P) |

5   3. ὡς καὶ Ἀναξαγόρας καὶ Εὐριπίδης·

θνήσκει δ᾽ οὐδὲν τῶν γιγνομένων,
διακρινόμενον δ᾽ ἄλλο πρὸς ἄλλο
μορφὰς ἑτέρας ἀπέδειξεν. (P)

4. Ἀναξίμανδρος ἐν ὑγρῷ γεννηθῆναι τὰ πρῶτα ζῷα,
10 φλοιοῖς περιεχόμενα | ἀκανθώδεσι· προβαινούσης δὲ

§§1–2 anonymi—
§3 Anaxagoras A112; Euripides fr. 839
§4 Anaximander A30

²⁹ verba οἱ περὶ Ἐπίκουρον ut gloss. del. et δὲ inser. MR

5.19

quote illustrating the latter view. The remaining three doxai support the former view with protological material.

Ps.-Plutarch, *Tenets* (+ Ps.-Galen, *Philosophical History*); Stobaeus, *Anthology*

19. On the birth of living beings, how they were born as living beings and whether they are perishable

1. According to those thinkers who say that the cosmos is generated, living beings are generated and perishable.

2. <But> according to those who say that the cosmos is ungenerated, the living beings are born as the result of changing from each other. For these, they say, are parts of the cosmos.

3. As both Anaxagoras and Euripides have said: 5

> None of those things that come into being ever dies,
> but the one distinguished in relation to the other
> revealed different forms.[33]

4. Anaximander says that the first living beings were born in the moist substance and were covered with spiky bark.   10

[33] These lines are also quoted by the Alexandrians Philo and Clement. Lucretius 2.1002–1006 adapts them to support the first view rather than the second.

τῆς ἡλικίας ἀποβαίνειν ἐπὶ τὸ ξηρότερον[30] | καὶ πε-
ριρρηγνυμένου τοῦ φλοιοῦ ἐπ' ὀλίγον χρόνον μετα-
βιῶναι. (P) |

5. Δημόκριτος καὶ Ἐπίκουρος γεγενημένα εἶναι τὰ
ζῷα συστάσει εἴδει | ἐνδεεστέρων πρῶτον τοῦ ὑγροῦ
ζῳογονοῦντος. (GQ) |

6. Ἐμπεδοκλῆς τὰς πρώτας γενέσεις τῶν ζῴων καὶ
15 φυτῶν μηδαμῶς | ὁλοκλήρους γενέσθαι, ἀσυμφυέσι
δὲ τοῖς μορίοις διεζευγμένας, τὰς δὲ | δευτέρας συμ-
φυομένων τῶν μερῶν εἰδωλοφανεῖς, τὰς δὲ τρίτας τῶν
| ὁλοφυῶν·[31] τὰς δὲ τετάρτας οὐκέτι ἐκ τῶν στοι-
χείων,[32] οἷον ἐκ γῆς καὶ | ὕδατος, ἀλλὰ δι' ἀλλήλων
ἤδη, τοῖς μὲν πυκνωθείσης <τῆς> τροφῆς, τοῖς | δὲ καὶ
τῆς εὐμορφίας τῶν γυναικῶν ἐπερεθισμὸν τοῦ σπερ-
20 ματικοῦ | κινήματος ἐμποιησάσης. τῶν δὲ ζῴων πά-
ντων τὰ γένη διακριθῆναι διὰ | τὰς ποιὰς κράσεις· τὰ
μὲν ὑγρότερα εἰς τὸ ὕδωρ τὴν ὁρμὴν ἔχειν, τὰ δ' | εἰς
ἀέρα ἀναπτῆναι, ὅσ' ἂν πυρῶδες ἔχῃ τὸ πλέον, τὰ δὲ
βαρύτερα ἐπὶ | τὴν γῆν, τὰ δ' ἰσόμοιρα τῇ κράσει
πᾶσι τοῖς χωρίοις σύμφωνα εἶναι.[33] | (P) |

§5 Democritus A139, fr. 514 Luria; Epicurus—
§6 Empedocles A72

30 9–10 deest in P, ex GQ reconstr. Luria
31 ὁλοφυῶν Diels Karsten sec., cf. Emped. B62.4: ἀλληλο-
φυῶν PQ
32 στοιχείων Q: ὁμοίων P
33 21–23 vid. app. sec.

But as they got older, they moved away to the drier part and, when the bark had broken up, they lived a different life for a short time.

5. Democritus and Epicurus say that the living beings have come into being first in a composition of elements lacking in form, with the aid of the life-generating moisture.

6. Empedocles says that the first generations of the living beings and plants certainly did not occur in their complete   15
form, but they were disjoined with their parts not grown together. The second generations, which did have parts grown together, were like dream images, while the third generations did consist of beings that had grown as wholes. The fourth generations were no longer generated directly from the elements such as earth and water but now from each other, in the one case [e.g., plants] when their nourishment became solid, in another case (i.e., human beings) when the shapeliness of the women caused the seminal movement to be stimulated. The species of all the living   20
beings were separated out according to the various kinds of mixture, the more moist ones having an impulse toward the water, others flying up to the air, namely those in which the fiery element predominates, while the heavier ones went to the earth, but those with a more balanced mixture were in harmony with all the different environments.

5.20

*The chapter divides into two, corresponding to the two
questions posed. For the first there is a clearly formulated
opposition. The division of views in the second part is less*

Ps.-Plut. *Plac.* 5.20 (+ Ps.-Gal. *Hist. phil.* 124); Stob. *Ecl.*
1.43

κʹ. Πόσα γένη ζῴων καὶ εἰ πάντα αἰσθητικὰ καὶ
λογικά (PS) |

1. Πλάτων καὶ Ἀριστοτέλης³⁴ τέσσαρα γένη ζῴων·
χερσαῖα ἔνυδρα πτηνὰ | οὐράνια· καὶ γὰρ τὰ ἄστρα
ζῷα λέγεσθαι καὶ τὸν κόσμον καὶ τὸν θεὸν | ζῷον
λογικὸν ἀθάνατον. (PS) |

5 2. Δημόκριτος Ἐπίκουρος τὰ οὐράνια ‹οὐκ ἐγκρί-
νουσι›.³⁵ (P) |

3. Ἀναξαγόρας πάντα τὰ ζῷα λόγον ἔχειν τὸν ἐνερ-

§1 Plato *Tim.* 40a; Aristotle cf. *De phil.* fr. 22 Ross
§2 Democritus fr. 547 Luria; Epicurus fr. 342
§3 Anaxagoras A101

³⁴ Πλάτων καὶ Ἀριστοτέλης GQS: ἔστι πραγματεία Ἀρι-
στοτέλους ἐν ᾗ P
³⁵ coni. MR

5.20

clear-cut. All living things admit some measure of rational-
ity, but it is impaired through various factors.

Ps.-Plutarch, *Tenets* (+ Ps.-Galen, *Philosophical History*);
Stobaeus, *Anthology*

20. How many kinds of living beings[34] there are and
whether they all possess sense perception and reason

1. Plato and Aristotle say that there are four kinds of living
beings: those living on land and in the water, those that fly
in the air, and those that inhabit the heavens. In addition
the heavenly bodies and the cosmos are stated to be living
beings, and also the god, a living being who is endowed
with reason and is immortal.[35]
2. Democritus and Epicurus ⟨do not include⟩ the heav-   5
enly beings as living beings.
3. Anaxagoras says that all the living beings possess the

---

[34] "Living being" renders the term *zôion*. In the ancient perspective it may include heavenly beings (or even the cosmos, cf.
2.3) and plants (cf. 5.26), so the translation "animals" is too narrow.

[35] The formulation here recalls the views of the two philosophers on theology in 1.7.22–23.

γητικόν, τὸν δ᾽ οἱονεὶ | νοῦν μὴ ἔχειν τὸν προφορι-
κόν,[36] τὸν λεγόμενον τοῦ νοῦ ἑρμηνέα. (P) |

4. Πυθαγόρας Πλάτων λογικὰς μὲν εἶναι καὶ τῶν ἀλό-
γων ζῴων καλουμένων | τὰς ψυχάς, οὐ μὴν λογικῶς
10 ἐνεργούσας παρὰ τὴν δυσκρασίαν τῶν | σωμάτων καὶ
τῷ μὴ ἔχειν τὸ φραστικόν, ὥσπερ ἐπὶ τῶν πιθήκων
καὶ τῶν | κυνῶν· νοοῦσι[37] μὲν γὰρ οὗτοι οὐ φράζουσι
δέ. (P) |

5. Διογένης μετέχειν μὲν αὐτὰ τοῦ νοητοῦ καὶ ἀέρος,
διὰ δὲ τὸ τὰ μὲν | πυκνότητι τὰ δὲ πλεονασμῷ τῆς
ὑγρασίας, μήτε διανοεῖσθαι μήτ᾽ | αἰσθάνεσθαι,
προσφερῶς δὲ αὐτὰ διακεῖσθαι τοῖς μεμηνόσι, παρ-
15 επταικότος | τοῦ ἡγεμονικοῦ. (P) |

§4 Pythagoras —; Plato —;
§5 Diogenes A30

[36] προφορικόν emend. Lachenaud: παθητικόν PQ
[37] νοοῦσι G, cf. Q: λαλοῦσι P

active (*energêtikos*) *logos*, but their equivalent of the intellect (i.e., this *logos*) does not have the *logos* that gives utterance (*prophorikos*),[36] the so-called interpreter of the intellect.[37]

4. Pythagoras and Plato say that the souls of the so-called irrational living beings are rational too, but that they do not exercise reason on account of the poor mixture of their 10 bodies and because they do not have the ability to speak, as we see in the case of monkeys and dogs;[38] for these think but do not speak.

5. Diogenes says that they (i.e., irrational living beings) share in the intelligible and air, but because some do so with a dense nature and others with a surfeit of moisture they neither think nor perceive properly, but their condition resembles those human beings who are deranged because their ruling part has stumbled. 15

---

36 Or if the emendation is not accepted, "does not have the passive (*pathetikos*) *logos*." For this and the following doxa, cf. 4.19.2–3.

37 Cf. 4.19.3, where the phrase "articulate voice" is used for the same phenomenon.

38 This perhaps alludes to the fate of Thersites in *Resp.* 10.620c. But Aëtius never refers to the doctrine of reincarnation.

Ps.-Plut. *Plac.* 5.21 (+ Ps.-Gal. *Hist. phil.* 125)

κα΄. Ἐν πόσῳ χρόνῳ μορφοῦται τὰ ζῷα ἐν τῇ
γαστρὶ ὄντα (P) |

1. Ἐμπεδοκλῆς ἐπὶ μὲν τῶν ἀνθρώπων ἄρχεσθαι τῆς
διαρθρώσεως ἀπὸ | ἕκτης καὶ τριακοστῆς, τελειοῦσθαι
δὲ τοῖς μορίοις ἀπὸ πεντηκοστῆς | μιᾶς δεούσης. (P) |
5 2. Ἀσκληπιάδης ἐπὶ μὲν τῶν ἀρρένων διὰ τὸ θερ-
μότερα εἶναι τὴν διάρθρωσιν | γίνεσθαι ἀπὸ ἕκτης καὶ
εἰκοστῆς, πολλάκις δὲ καὶ ἐνδοτέρω· | πληροῦσθαι δ᾽
ἐντὸς τῆς πεντηκοστῆς ‹τοῖς›³⁸ μορίοις· ἐπὶ δὲ τῶν
θηλυκῶν | ἐν διμήνῳ διαρθροῦσθαι, ἐν τετραμήνῳ δὲ
τελειοῦσθαι διὰ τὸ ἐνδεῖν | τοῦ θερμοῦ· τὰ δὲ τῶν ἀλό-
10 γων ζῴων ὁλοτελῆ παρὰ τὰς συγκράσεις | τῶν στοι-
χείων. (P) |

§1 Empedocles A83
§2 Asclepiades pp. 721, 725

³⁸ τοῖς add. Reiske

5.21

The two doxai, which differ considerably in scope and detail, implicitly establish two oppositions: (1) between human beings and males–females; (2) between human beings and other living beings.

Ps.-Plutarch, *Tenets* (+ Ps.-Galen, *Philosophical History*)

21. In what length of time living beings are formed when they are in the womb

1. Empedocles says that in the case of human beings the articulation of the parts in the womb begins from the thirty-sixth day and is completed for the constituent parts from the forty-ninth day.
2. Asclepiades says that in the case of males because of 5 their greater heat the articulation occurs from the twenty-sixth day, and quite often even earlier within that period, and that for the constituent parts it is fulfilled within the fiftieth day. But in the case of the females they are articulated in a two-month period and are not completed till the fourth month because of a lack of heat.[39] As for the irrational living beings, however, they become complete depending on the mixtures of the elements. 10

[39] The differentiation between male and female conception through the factor of internal heat goes back to Empedocles(!) (see 5.7.1) and the Hippocratic corpus.

Ps.-Plut. *Plac.* 5.22 (+ Ps.-Gal. *Hist. phil.* 126)

κβ′. Ἐκ ποίων συνίσταται στοιχείων ἕκαστον τῶν
ἐν ἡμῖν γενικῶν | μορίων (P) |

1. Ἐμπεδοκλῆς τὰς μὲν σάρκας γεννᾶσθαι ἐκ τῶν
ἴσων τῇ κράσει | τεττάρων στοιχείων· τὰ δὲ νεῦρα ἐκ
5   πυρὸς καὶ γῆς ὕδατι διπλασίονι | μιχθέντων· τοὺς δ᾽
ὄνυχας τοῖς ζῴοις γεννᾶσθαι τῶν νεύρων καθ᾽ ὃ τῷ |
ἀέρι συνέτυχε περιψυχθέντων· ὀστᾶ δὲ ἐκ δυεῖν μὲν
ὕδατος καὶ τῶν | ἴσων γῆς, τεττάρων δὲ πυρός, ‹ἔσω
γῆς› τούτων συγκραθέντων μερῶν· | ἱδρῶτα δὲ καὶ
δάκρυον γίνεσθαι τοῦ αἵματος τηκομένου καὶ παρὰ τὸ
| λεπτύνεσθαι διαχεομένου.[39] (P) |

§1 Empedocles A78, B96

[39] vid. app. sec.

5.22

The single doxa points to a truncated chapter. One might have expected at least one other different view, e.g., based on Plato's Timaeus *73–76.*

Ps.-Plutarch, *Tenets* (+ Ps.-Galen, *Philosophical History*)

22. Out of what elements is each of the generic parts in us composed[40]

1. Empedocles says that the fleshy parts are generated from the four elements in an equal mixture, but the sinews are generated from fire and earth with a double amount of water mixed in. The nails that living beings have are   5 generated when the sinews insofar as they meet up with the air are cooled all around. The bones are generated from two parts of water, the same parts of earth and four parts of fire when these are mixed together ⟨within the earth⟩. Perspiration and tears occur when the blood melts and flows more easily from being thinned.

[40] A similar formulation, "how each of the parts is composed," is found at Aristotle *GA* 2.6 745b21.

Ps.-Plut. *Plac.* 5.23 (+ Ps.-Gal. *Hist. phil.* 127)

κγ΄. Πότε ἄρχεται ὁ ἄνθρωπος τῆς
τελειότητος (P) |

1. Ἡράκλειτος καὶ οἱ Στωικοὶ ἄρχεσθαι τοὺς ἀνθρώ-
πους τῆς τελειότητος | περὶ τὴν δευτέραν ἑβδομάδα,
περὶ ἣν ὁ σπερματικὸς κινεῖται ὀρρός· τὰ | γὰρ δέν-
δρα τότε τελειοῦται, ὅταν ἄρχηται γεννᾶν τὰ σπέρ-
5   ματα, ἀτελῆ | δ' ἐστὶ καὶ ἄωρα καὶ ἄκαρπα ὄντα. (P) |
2. Ἀριστοτέλης δὲ κατὰ τὴν πρώτην ἑβδομάδα, καθ'
ἣν[40] ἔννοια γίνεται | καλῶν τε καὶ αἰσχρῶν καὶ τῆς
διδασκαλίας ἀρχή. (P) |
3. ⟨ἄλλοι⟩[41] δὲ τελειοῦσθαι ἡμᾶς τῇ τρίτῃ ἑβδομάδι,
ὅταν καὶ γένεια σχῶμεν | καὶ τῇ ἰσχύι χρώμεθα. (G) |

§1 Heraclitus A18; Stoics 2.764
§2 Aristotle cf. *Pol.* 7.17
§3 anonymi cf. Solon fr. 27.5–6, Arist. *HA* 7.1 582a33–34

[40] Ἀριστοτέλης . . . καθ' ἣν G: al. P τέλειος οὖν τότε ἄν-
θρωπος· περὶ δὲ τὴν δευτέραν ἑβδομάδα
[41] coni. MR: ἕτεροι G (lemma deest in P)

5.23

A division of three answers, corresponding to the second, first, and third ages of life measured in periods of seven years.

Ps.-Plutarch, *Tenets* (+ Ps.-Galen, *Philosophical History*)

23. When does a human being commence maturity

1. Heraclitus and the Stoics say that human beings commence their maturity around the second hebdomad,[41] at the time that the seminal fluid starts to move. Trees by way of comparison attain maturity at the time that they begin to produce their seeds, whereas the immature ones are   5 without both blooms and fruits.

2. But Aristotle says that human beings commence maturity at the first hebdomad, at the time that understanding of things both good and disgraceful occurs and there is a beginning of instruction on such things.[42]

3. Other thinkers, however, say that we become mature in the third hebdomad, when we develop beards and are at full strength.[43]

[41] That is, period of seven years. The Athenian lawgiver Solon's famous poem divided the life of human beings into ten periods of seven years.   [42] Cf. the view attributed to the Stoics at 4.11.1[14–15].   [43] The final lemma is preserved only by Ps.-Galen. The final pages of the archetype of the Byzantine manuscripts of Ps.-Plutarch were patently damaged.

5.24

Ps.-Plut. *Plac.* 5.24 (+ Ps.-Gal. *Hist. phil.* 128); Stob. *Ecl.* 1.44

κδ′. Πῶς ὕπνος γίνεται καὶ θάνατος (PS) |

1. Ἀλκμαίων ἀναχωρήσει τοῦ αἵματος εἰς τὰς αἱμόρ-
ρους φλέβας ὕπνον | γίνεσθαί φησι, τὴν δ᾽ ἐξέγερσιν
διάχυσιν, τὴν δὲ παντελῆ ἀναχώρησιν | θάνατον. (P) |
5 2. Ἐμπεδοκλῆς τὸν μὲν ὕπνον κατὰ ψύξιν τοῦ ἐν τῷ
αἵματι θερμοῦ | σύμμετρον γίνεσθαι, κατὰ δὲ ἀσύμ-
μετρον καὶ παντελῆ ἐπαγγέλλειν | θάνατον. (P) |
3. Διογένης, εἰ ἐπὶ πᾶν τὸ αἷμα διαχεόμενον πληρώ-
σει μὲν τὰς φλέβας τὸν | δ᾽ ἐν αὐταῖς περιεχόμενον
10 ἀέρα ὤσει εἰς τὰ στέρνα καὶ τὴν ὑποκειμένην | γα-
στέρα, ὕπνον γεγενῆσθαι καὶ θερμότερον ὑπάρχειν
τὸν θώρακα· ἐὰν | δ᾽ ἅπαν τὸ ἀερῶδες ἐκ τῶν φλεβῶν
ἐκλίπῃ, θάνατον συντυγχάνειν. (P) |

§1 Alcmaeon A18
§2 Empedocles 31A85
§3 Diogenes A29

5.24

Two sets of binary oppositions, between (1) blood and air/ pneuma, and (2) single and twin principles (heat/cooling and blood/air). Intensification of the oppositions results in death.

Ps.-Plutarch, *Tenets* (+ Ps.-Galen, *Philosophical History*); Stobaeus, *Anthology*

24. How sleep and death occur

1. Alcmaeon says that sleep occurs by withdrawal of the blood to the veins that flow with blood, while waking up is the pouring forth of the blood back again, but the complete withdrawal of the blood is death.

2. Empedocles says that sleep occurs through a commensurate cooling of the heat in the blood, but if the cooling is incommensurate and total, sleep announces the occurrence of death.

3. Diogenes says that, if the blood expands and completely fill the veins but pushes the air contained in them to the breast and the stomach lying beneath it, then sleep will have occurred and the chest is quite warm; but if all that is airy departs from the veins, then this is when death takes place.

4. Στράτων[42] οἱ Στωικοὶ τὸν μὲν ὕπνον γίνεσθαι ἀνέ-
σει τοῦ αἰσθητικοῦ | πνεύματος οὐ κατ᾽ ἀναχαλασμόν,
καθάπερ ἐπὶ τῆς ‹μέθ›ης,[43] φερομένου | δ᾽ ὡς ἐπὶ τὸ
ἡγεμονικὸν ‹ἢ›[44] μεσόφρυον· ὅταν δὲ παντελὴς γένη-
15   ται ἡ | ἄνεσις τοῦ αἰσθητικοῦ πνεύματος, τότε γεγενῆ-
σθαι θάνατον. (P) |

§4 Strato fr. 66; Stoics 2.767

5.25

Ps.-Plut. *Plac.* 5.25 (+ Ps.-Gal. *Hist. phil.* 129); Stob. *Ecl.*
1.44

κεʹ. Ὁποτέρου ἐστὶν ὕπνος καὶ θάνατος, ψυχῆς
ἢ σώματος (PS) |

1. Ἀριστοτέλης κοινὸν μὲν τὸν ὕπνον σώματος καὶ
ψυχῆς· αἴτιον δὲ αὐτοῦ | τὸ ἀναθυμιαθὲν ὑγρὸν ἀπὸ
τοῦ θώρακος εἰς τοὺς περὶ τὴν κεφαλὴν | τόπους ἐκ

§1 Aristotle cf. *Somn.Vig.* 1 454a8–11, 3 456b17–29; *Iuv.* 4
469b13–20

42 Στράτων edd., cf. 4.5.3, 5.2.2: Πλάτων mss.
43 μέθης MR: γῆς PQ, γηράνσεως Sharples
44 ἢ coni. Corsinus (sed ἡγεμονικὸν ‹ἢ› fort. glossa)

4. Strato[44] and the Stoics say that sleep occurs by the remission of the sensory spirit, not through a slackening, as in the case of ‹drunkenness›, but when it is borne along to the regent part ‹or› what is in between the eyebrows. But when there is a total relaxation of the sensory spirit, then death has occurred.

15

5.25

All views embrace the four elements in the title, involving various causes and creating a number of oppositions, but without a clear diaeretic structure.

Ps.-Plutarch, *Tenets* (+ Ps.-Galen, *Philosophical History*); Stobaeus, *Anthology*

25. Whether sleep and death pertain to the soul or the body

1. Aristotle says that sleep is common to body and soul. Its cause is the moist exhalation that rises from the chest to the regions in the head from the nourishment located be-

---

[44] Plato's name has replaced that of Strato in the manuscripts, as often occurs elsewhere. The parallels in Tertullian *De an*. 43.2 and above at 4.5.3 prove that the view must be attributed to the Peripatetic philosopher.

τῆς ὑποκειμένης τροφῆς ἢ τὸ ἐν τῇ καρδίᾳ περι-
5 ψυχθὲν | θερμόν· τὸν δὲ θάνατον εἶναι παντελῆ κατά-
ψυξιν· θάνατον δ' εἶναι μόνου | τοῦ σώματος οὐ ψυχῆς·
ταύτης γὰρ οὐχ ὑπάρχει θάνατος. (P) |
2. Ἀναξαγόρας κατὰ κόπον τῆς σωματικῆς ἐνεργείας
γίνεσθαι τὸν ὕπνον· | σωματικὸν γὰρ εἶναι τὸ πάθος
οὐ ψυχικόν· εἶναι δὲ καὶ ψυχῆς θάνατον | τὸν διαχω-
ρισμόν. (P) |
10 3. Λεύκιππος οὐ μόνον κόπῳ⁴⁵ σώματος γίνεσθαι,
ἀλλὰ ἐκκρίσει τοῦ λεπτομεροῦς | πλείονι τῆς εἰσκρί-
σεως τοῦ ψυχικοῦ θερμοῦ, καὶ τὸν πλεονασμὸν |
αἴτιον θανάτου· ταῦτα δ' εἶναι πάθη σώματος οὐ ψυ-
χῆς. (P) |
4. Ἐμπεδοκλῆς τὸν θάνατον γεγενῆσθαι διαχωρισμὸν
τοῦ ‹γεώδους καὶ | ὑδατώδους καὶ ἀερώδους καὶ›⁴⁶
15 πυρώδους, ἐξ ὧν ἡ σύγκρισις τῷ | ἀνθρώπῳ συν-
εστάθη· ὥστε κατὰ τοῦτο κοινὸν εἶναι τὸν θάνατον |
σώματος καὶ ψυχῆς· ὕπνον δὲ γίνεσθαι διαχωρισμὸν
τοῦ πυρώδους. (P) |

§2 Anaxagoras A103
§3 Leucippus A34
§4 Empedocles A85

⁴⁵ κόπῳ MR, cf. Q: om. P
⁴⁶ γεώδους . . . καὶ add. MR, cf. Diels VS

low, or the heat in the heart that has been chilled. But death he says is complete chilling. Death, however, is of the body only, not of the soul, for of this latter death does not exist.[45] 5

2. Anaxagoras says that sleep occurs through tiredness resulting from bodily activity, for the affection is somatic and not psychic. But of the soul too there is death, namely its separation from the body.

3. Leucippus says that sleep occurs not only through tiredness of the body, but also by a secretion of the light-particled substance that is greater than the influx of the psychic heat, and that the excess of this secretion is the cause of death. These are affections of the body and not of the soul. 10

4. Empedocles says that death has occurred as the separation of ⟨the earthly and the watery and airy and⟩ the fiery elements, out of which the human composition has been established. So in accordance with this he says death is common to body and soul. But sleep occurs as separation of the fiery element only. 15

[45] The focus of the chapter is purely physiological, and its views on the possible death of the soul do not cohere well with the differing psychological perspective in 4.7.4 above.

5.26

The first three doxai form a division with a simple dialectical scheme involving two factors, similar to 2.3–4. Their subject continues the topic of 5.20. The final doxa intro-

Ps.-Plut. *Plac.* 5.26 (+ Ps.-Gal. *Hist. phil.* 130); Stob. *Ecl.* 1.45.1–2

κϛʹ. Πῶς ηὐξήθη τὰ φυτὰ καὶ
εἰ ζῷα (PS) |

1. Πλάτων Θαλῆς καὶ τὰ φυτὰ ἔμψυχα ζῷα· φανερὸν δὲ καὶ ἀπὸ τοῦ | σαλεύεσθαι καὶ ἐντεταμένους ἔχειν τοὺς κλάδους καὶ ἐν ταῖς ἐπαναγωγαῖς | εἴκειν καὶ πάλιν σφοδρῶς ἀναχαλᾶσθαι, ὥστε καὶ συνέλκειν |
5 βάρη. (PS) |
2. Ἀριστοτέλης ἔμψυχα μέν, οὐ μὴν ζῷα· τὰ γὰρ ζῷα ὁρμητικὰ εἶναι καὶ | αἰσθητικά, ἔνια δὲ καὶ λογικά. (PS) |

§1 Plato cf. *Tim.* 77a–c; Thales fr. 359, 405 Wöhrle
§2 Aristotle cf. *de An.* 2.2 413a21–b10

5.26

duces the aspect of origin, hence the past tense in the heading, which reverses the chapter's two parts.

Ps.-Plutarch, *Tenets* (+ Ps.-Galen, *Philosophical History*); Stobaeus, *Anthology*

26. How plants grew and whether they are living beings[46]

1. Plato and Thales say that plants too are ensouled living beings. This is evident from the fact that they move to and fro and hold their branches extended, and also that they yield when they are gathered together and then powerfully released again, so that they even pull up weights.   5
2. Aristotle says that they are ensouled, but are not in fact living beings. For he says living beings have impulses and sense perception, and some are even endowed with reason.

[46] The term *zôion* literally means "being with life," translated here as "living being," while the term *empsychos* is rendered "ensouled." The views turn on what these two terms entail in the case of plants, i.e., how do plants relate to defining characteristics of soul involving self-motion and perception. The ambiguity in the term *empsychos* is similar to that in the English "animate." In modern parlance, plants are animate, but not animals. Cf. also 5.20 above.

3. οἱ Στωικοὶ δὲ καὶ Ἐπικούρειοι οὐκ ἔμψυχα· τινὰ γὰρ ψυχῆς ὁρμητικῆς | εἶναι καὶ ἐπιθυμητικῆς, τινὰ
10 δὲ καὶ λογικῆς· τὰ δὲ φυτὰ αὐτομάτως πως | κεκινῆσθαι[47] οὐ διὰ ψυχῆς. (P) |

4. Ἐμπεδοκλῆς πρῶτα τὰ δένδρα τῶν ζῴων ἐκ γῆς ἀναφῦναί φησι, πρὶν | τὸν ἥλιον περιαπλωθῆναι καὶ πρὶν ἡμέραν καὶ νύκτα διακριθῆναι· διὰ δὲ | συμμετρίαν τῆς κράσεως τὸν τοῦ ἄρρενος καὶ τοῦ θήλεος περιέχειν | λόγον· αὔξεσθαι δ' ἀπὸ τοῦ ἐν τῇ γῇ θερ-
15 μοῦ διαιρουμένου, ὥστε γῆς | εἶναι μέρη, καθάπερ καὶ τὰ ἔμβρυα τὰ ἐν τῇ γαστρὶ τῆς μήτρας μέρη· | τοὺς δὲ καρποὺς περιττεύματα εἶναι τοῦ ἐν τοῖς φυτοῖς ὕδατος καὶ | πυρός· καὶ τὰ μὲν ἐλλιπὲς ἔχοντα τὸ ὑγρόν, ἐξικμαζομένου αὐτοῦ τῷ | θέρει, φυλλορροεῖν, τὰ δὲ πλεῖον παραμένειν ἀεὶ φύλλοις τεθηλότα, | ὥσπερ ἐπὶ τῆς δάφνης καὶ τῆς ἐλαίας καὶ τοῦ φοίνι-
20 κος· τὰς δὲ διαφορὰς | τῶν χυμῶν παραλλαγὰς τῆς ⟨γῆς⟩[48] πολυμερείας καὶ τῶν φυτῶν | γίνεσθαι, διαφόρους ἑλκόντων τὰς ἀπὸ τοῦ τρέφοντος ὁμοιομερείας, | ὥσπερ ἐπὶ τῶν ἀμπέλων· οὐ γὰρ αἱ διαφοραὶ τούτων χρηστικὸν οἶνον | ποιοῦσιν, ἀλλ' αἱ τοῦ τρέφοντος ἐδάφους. (P) |

§3 Stoics 2.708; Epicureans fr. 309 Usener
§4 Empedocles A70

[47] κεκινῆσθαι edd.: γεγενῆσθαι mss.
[48] γῆς coni. Diels VS

3. But the Stoics and Epicureans say that they are not ensouled. For they say that some living beings share in the impulsive and desiderative soul, and some even in the rational soul. But the plants move spontaneously somehow in a way not involving soul. 10

4. Empedocles says that the plants, as first of the living beings, sprung up from the earth, before the sun was spread around and before day and night had been separated.[47] Because of the commensurability of their mixture he says they contained the structure of the male and the female within themselves. They grow from the heat that has been separated out in the earth, so that they are parts 15 of the earth, just like embryos in the belly too are parts of the womb. The fruits are superfluities of the water and the fire in the plants. Some have a lack of moisture, and after it has evaporated in the summer, lose their leaves, while others that have more moisture remain as they are and continue to be in bloom with leaves, as is the case for the laurel, the olive and the palm. But the differences in fla- 20 vors result from the variation of the particles <of earth> and of the plants, which draw varieties of flavors from the *homoiomereiai* (things with like parts) of that which nourishes them, as in the case of vines. For it is not the differences in the vines that make serviceable wine, but differences in the terrain that nourishes them.

47 Here, as in 5.7, 5.18–19, the Empedoclean doxa begins with a protological account.

5.27

Ps.-Plut. *Plac.* 5.27, Qusṭā 5.27; Stob. *Ecl.* 1.46

κζ΄. Περὶ τροφῆς καὶ αὐξήσεως (PS) |

1. Ἐμπεδοκλῆς τρέφεσθαι μὲν τὰ ζῷα διὰ τὴν ὑπό-
στασιν τοῦ ὑγροῦ, | αὔξεσθαι δὲ διὰ τὴν παρουσίαν
τοῦ θερμοῦ, μειοῦσθαι δὲ καὶ φθίνειν διὰ | τὴν ἔκλει-
ψιν ἑκατέρων· τοὺς δὲ νῦν ἀνθρώπους τοῖς πρώτοις
5 συμβαλλομένους | βρεφῶν ἐπέχειν τάξιν. (P) |
2. Ἀναξαγόρας τρέφεσθαι μὲν [. . .] (P) |

انقساغورس يرى ان الحيوانات تغتذى بالرطوبة التى يجذبها
كل واحد من اعضائها بالرعى والاغتذاء وتنمى اذا كان ما
يصير اليها من الغذاء كثيرا وتهرم وتذبل اذا كان ما ينحلّ
عنها كثيرا.[49] (Q)

10

§1 Empedocles 31A77, cf. B62
§2 Anaxagoras fr. 78 Gemelli Marciano

[49] 6–10 vid. app. sec.

480

5.27

A weak division between views involving similar and dissimilar causes.

Ps.-Plutarch, *Tenets*, Qusṭā 5.27; Stobaeus, *Anthology*

27. On nourishment and growth

1. Empedocles says that the living beings are nourished by the settling down of the moisture and they grow through the presence of heat, whereas they diminish and perish through the failure of each of these. But the present-day human beings, compared to those who were first, have the status of infants.
2. Anaxagoras says that the animals (i.e., living beings) are nourished *by the moisture that each of their organs draws in by consumption and nourishment. They grow if the food that enters them is abundant but become decrepit and wither if what decomposes from them (i.e., is excreted by them) is abundant.*[48]

5

10

[48] The damage to the archetype of the Byzantine manuscripts worsens (see the note to 5.23.3 above), but here and in 5.29 the evidence of the Arabic translation can assist. Translation of the Arabic text by Robert Turnbull.

5.28

Ps.-Plut. *Plac.* 5.28; Stob. *Ecl.* 1.46, 1.50.25

κη΄. Πόθεν αἱ ὀρέξεις γίνονται τοῖς ζῴοις
καὶ αἱ ἡδοναί (PS) |

1. Ἐμπεδοκλῆς τὰς μὲν ὀρέξεις γίνεσθαι τοῖς ζῴοις
κατὰ τὰς ἐλλείψεις | τῶν ἀποτελούντων ἕκαστα στοι-
χείων, τὰς δ᾽ ἡδονὰς ἐξ ὑγροῦ κατὰ τὰς | τῆς αὐξή-
σεως τῶν γένει ὁμοίων κινήσεις,[50] τὰς δ᾽ ὀχλήσεις
5 κατὰ τὰς τῶν | ἐναντίων συγκρίσεις καὶ κράσεις.[51] (P) |
2. Παρμενίδης Ἐμπεδοκλῆς ἐλλείψει τροφῆς τὴν ὄρε-
ξιν. (S) |

§1 Empedocles A95
§2 Parmenides A50; Empedocles cf. A95

[50] κατὰ . . . κινήσεις MR, cf. Q: text. P non sanus
[51] κατὰ . . . κράσεις Wolfsdorf, cf. Q; vid. app. sec.

5.28

With effectively only a single lemma, this chapter is imperfectly preserved.

Ps.-Plutarch, *Tenets*; Stobaeus, *Anthology*

28. From where do the appetites arise in living beings and also pleasures

1. Empedocles says that the appetites occur in the living beings in accordance with the deficiencies of the elements required to complete each of them, but that pleasures occur from moisture through the motions involving increase of things that are similar in kind, whereas annoyances occur through the combinations and mixtures of things that are opposite in kind.

2. Parmenides and Empedocles declare that the appetite arises from a deficiency of food.[49]

[49] This doxa, preserved only in Stobaeus, appears to be a doublet of the first, though with a little extra information.

5.29

Ps.-Plut. *Plac.* 5.29 (+ Ps.-Gal. *Hist. phil.* 131), Qusṭā 5.29

κθ'. Πῶς γίνεται πυρετὸς καὶ εἰ
ἐπιγέννημά ἐστιν (P)[52] |

1. Ἐρασίστρατος ὁρίζεται τὸν πυρετὸν οὕτως· πυρε-
τός ἐστι κίνημα αἵματος | παρεμπεπτωκότος εἰς τὰ
τοῦ πνεύματος ἀγγεῖα ἀπροαιρέτως | γινόμενον· καθά-
περ γὰρ ἐπὶ τῆς θαλάττης, ὅταν μηδὲν αὐτὴν κινῇ, |
5   ἠρεμεῖ, ἀνέμου δ' ἐμπνέοντος βιαίου παρὰ φύσιν,
τότε ἐξ ὅλης κυκᾶται,[53] | οὕτω καὶ ἐν τῷ σώματι ὅταν
κινηθῇ τὸ αἷμα, τότε ἐμπίπτει μὲν εἰς τὰ | ἀγγεῖα τοῦ
πνεύματος, πυρούμενον δὲ θερμαίνει τὸ ὅλον σῶμα.
ἀρέσκει | δ' αὐτῷ καὶ ἐπιγέννημα εἶναι τὸν πυρε-
τόν, (P) |

وهو يرى فى الحمى انها توليد
10   لانها عن ورم يعرض فى الات الروح مع الغذاء الذى يسيل اليها. (Q) |

§1 Erasistratus fr. 195

[52] vid. app. sec.
[53] κυκᾶται Lachenaud, cf. Diels *DG*: κυκλεῖται P

5.29

After the initial definition, the chapter focuses on the second question in its heading and presents a simple opposition pro and contra.

Ps.-Plutarch, *Tenets* (+ Ps.-Galen, *Philosophical History* 131), Qusṭā

29. How fever occurs and whether it is an after-symptom

1. Erasistratus defines fever as follows: fever is a motion that occurs involuntarily when blood is diverted into the vessels of the *pneuma*. For just as in the case of the sea, it is at rest when nothing stirs it, but when a violent wind   5
blow contrary to what naturally occurs, it is then all churned up, in the same way in the body too, when the blood has been moved, it then plunges into the vessels of the *pneuma*, heats up the entire body and makes it enflamed. He is also of the view that fever is an after-symptom *because it arises from a swelling in the organs of the* pneuma *together with the nourishment that flows to them.*[50]   10

[50] Here again the Greek text falters and we have to turn to the Arabic translation of Qusṭā (in italics). Translation Robert Turnbull. For the remains of the chapter in Ps.-Galen, see Appendix II.

2. Διοκλῆς δέ φησιν· ὄψις ἀδήλων τὰ φαινόμενα· ἐστι δέ, οἷς φαινομένοις | ὁρᾶται ἐπιγενόμενος ὁ πυρετός, τραύματα καὶ φλεγμοναὶ καὶ βουβῶνες. (P) |

فيجب اذن اضطرارا ان
تقول ان الحمى تكون عن اشياء وإن خفيت فهى إما ورم
وإما غذاء او جسم اخر سخن. (Q)[54]

17 3.

واما ايروفيلس فيبطل ذلك ويرى ان الورم الحارّ ليس
يتقدم الحمى لكن الحمى تتقدمه وعلى هذا تكون الحمى فى
الامر الاكثر. وكثيرا ما تكون من غير ان يظهر بها سبب. وتحدث
22   علّتُها حركات الامراض القديمة وتولد الاورام الحارّة. (Q, cf. G) |

§2 Diocles fr. 56
§3 Herophilus fr. 217

54 Herophilus Q: Ἡρόδοτος G

2. Diocles says: the appearances are the sight of what is unclear.[51] The appearances in which fever is seen to occur as an after-symptom are wounds, boils and swollen glands. *Therefore, you must necessarily say that the fever can arise from several things (i.e., causes), even if they be hidden; these are either a swelling, or nourishment, or another hot body.*

3. *Herophilus refutes this and says that the hot swelling*   17
does not precede the fever, but the fever precedes it. That is how the fever occurs on most occasions. It often occurs without a cause for it being apparent. Its cause brings about the movements of the old diseases and generates the hot swellings.   22

[51] It seems that Diocles cites a well-known saying, which Sextus Empiricus, *M.* 7.140, attributes to Anaxagoras and Democritus.

5.30

Ps.-Plut. *Plac.* 5.30 (+ Ps.-Gal. *Hist. phil.* 132–133); Stob.
Flor. 4.36.29–31, 4.37.2, 4.50.30

λ′. Περὶ ὑγείας καὶ νόσου καὶ γήρως (PS) |

1. Ἀλκμαίων τῆς μὲν ὑγείας εἶναι συνεκτικὴν τὴν ἰσο-
νομίαν τῶν δυνάμεων, | ὑγροῦ ξηροῦ ψυχροῦ θερμοῦ
πικροῦ γλυκέος καὶ τῶν λοιπῶν· τὴν δ’ ἐν | αὐτοῖς
μοναρχίαν νόσου ποιητικήν· φθοροποιὸν γὰρ ἑκα-
5 τέρου μοναρχία. | (PS) |
2. Ἡρόφιλος⁵⁵ τὰς νόσους· συμπίπτειν⁵⁶ ὡς μὲν ὑφ’ οὗ
ὑπερβολῇ θερμότητος | ἢ ψυχρότητος· ὡς δ’ ἐξ οὗ διὰ
πλῆθος τροφῆς ἢ ἔνδειαν· ὡς δ’ ἐν οἷς | ἢ αἷμα ἢ
μυελὸν ἢ ἐγκέφαλον· γίνεσθαι δέ ποτε καὶ ὑπὸ τῶν
ἔξωθεν | αἰτιῶν, ὑδάτων ποιῶν ἢ χώρας ἢ κόπων ἢ
10 ἀνάγκης ἢ τῶν τούτοις παραπλησίων· | τὴν δὲ ὑγείαν
τὴν σύμμετρον τῶν ποιῶν κρᾶσιν. (PS) |

§1 Alcmaeon B4
§2 Herophilus cf. Leith (2014) 604

⁵⁵ Ἡρόφιλος Q: om. PS
⁵⁶ τὰς νόσους συμπίπτειν S, cf. Q: καὶ νόσων αἰτία P

5.30

The chapter falls into two parts, in accordance with the topics in the heading. The views give various causes but are not tightly structured.

Ps.-Plutarch, *Tenets* (+ Ps.-Galen, *Philosophical History*); Stobaeus, *Anthology*

30. On health and disease and old age[52]

1. Alcmaeon says that the sustaining cause of health is the equilibrium of the powers, namely the wet, dry, cold, hot, bitter, sweet, and the rest; but predominance among these is productive of disease, for predominance of either opposite produces destruction.   5

2. Herophilus[53] says that diseases occur when the agent cause is an excess of heat or cold, the material cause is an abundance or lack of food, and the location where it takes place is the blood or the marrow or the brain. It can also happen through the agency of external causes, such as the bad quality of water, or locality or stresses or necessity or factors similar to these. But health occurs as the balanced   10
mixture of qualities.

[52] The chapter has two unusual features: it is divided in two in Ps.-Galen's epitome; and the Stobaean material is not found in the *Eclogae*, but is from the final part of *Florilegium* Book 4.

[53] Herophilus' name is found in Qusṭā only, but it is likely to be correct, given the strong Peripatetic flavor of the doctrine attributed to him. The Peripatos was the dominant philosophical influence in early Alexandria, where the doctor was based.

3. Διοκλῆς τὰς πλείστας τῶν νόσων δι' ἀνωμαλίαν γίνεσθαι τῶν ἐν τῷ | σώματι στοιχείων καὶ τοῦ κατα- στήματος ἀέρος.[57] (PS) |

4. Ἐρασίστρατος τὰς νόσους διὰ πλῆθος τροφῆς καὶ δι' ἀπεψίας καὶ | φθορᾶς, τὴν δ' εὐταξίαν καὶ αὐτάρ- κειαν εἶναι ὑγείαν. (PS) |

15 5. Παρμενίδης γῆρας γίγνεσθαι παρὰ τὴν τοῦ θερμοῦ ὑπόλειψιν. (S) |

6. οἱ Στωικοὶ καὶ οἱ ἰατροὶ συμφώνως τὸ γῆρας γεγενῆσθαι διὰ τὴν τοῦ | θερμοῦ ἔλλειψιν· οἱ γὰρ {αὐτοὶ}[58] πλέον τὸ θερμὸν ἔχοντες ἐπὶ πλεῖον | γηρῶ- σιν. (P) |

7. Ἀσκληπιάδης Αἰθίοπάς φησι ταχέως γηράσκειν 20 ἐτῶν τριάκοντα διὰ τὸ | ὑπερθερμαίνεσθαι τὰ σώματα ὑπὸ τοῦ ἡλίου διαφλεχθέντας· ἐν Βρεττανίᾳ | ἑκατὸν εἴκοσιν ἐτῶν γηρᾶν διὰ τὸ κατεψῦχθαι μὲν τοὺς τό- πους, ἐν | ἑαυτοῖς δὲ στέγειν τὸ πυρῶδες· τὰ μὲν γὰρ τῶν Αἰθιόπων σώματά εἰσιν | ἀραιότερα διὰ τὸ ἀνα- χαλᾶσθαι ὑπὸ τοῦ ἡλίου, τὰ δ' ὑπὸ τῶν ἄρκτων | πυ- κνά, διὰ τοῦτο οὖν καὶ πολυχρόνια. (P) |

§3 Diocles fr. 51   §4 Erasistratus fr. 168
§5 Parmenides A46a   §6 Stoics 2.769
§7 Asclepiades p. 725

[57] ἀέρος GQ: om. P
[58] αὐτοὶ secl. MR, cf. αὐτὸ πλέον {τὸ θερμὸν} Diels

3. Diocles says that most diseases occur through a variability of the elements in the body and of the constitution of the air.

4. Erasistratus says that diseases occur through an abundance of food, and through indigestion and corruption of food, but health is a well-ordered regimen and sufficiency of food.

5. Parmenides says that old age occurs from the deficiency   15
of heat.

6. The Stoics and the doctors are in agreement that old age has occurred on account of the insufficiency of heat; for those who have a greater amount of heat live to a more advanced old age.

7. Asclepiades says that Ethiopians become old quickly at the age of thirty years because their bodies are overheated   20
when they are burned by the sun. In Britain people live to the age of one hundred and twenty through their localities being chilled and the protection of the fiery element in themselves. The bodies of Ethiopians are in fact thinner because they are distended by the sun, whereas those of the dwellers in the northern regions are stockier, and so for this reason they also live longer.

APPENDIX I

LIST OF CHANGES TO THE TEXT
IN THIS EDITION

As mentioned in the Preface and the General Introduction
(§3.2), the text of the work in this Loeb edition is virtually identical to the text in the major edition, *Aëtiana V*.
The following listing gives the passages where changes
have been introduced, as indicated by the sigla MR (*editio
maior*) and MR² (*editio minor*). With one exception, this
list does not include changes in punctuation. Due to the
conventions of the Loeb Classical Library, many sets of
quotation marks have been added to the text, especially
in Books 1 and 4. They exactly correspond to quotations
marks in the translation.

I.index before [5] $\beta^{+\prime}$. Περὶ κινήσεως κόσμου, on which
see below on 2.2a.

1.1.2[11]. ἡ φύσις ἀρχὴ ⟨καὶ⟩ τὸ πρῶτόν ἐστι· καὶ added
MR²

1.5.3[13]. Quotation marks in MR removed, since not a
literal quote from Plato; also question mark added after
ἔστι.

2.2a. This entire chapter has been added (also to the Index or pinax). See further the notes to the translation.

2.15.8. In MR this lemma was placed at the end of 2.16, as 2.16.7.

3.1.11[22]. μανώτεραν (reading S) MR²: μανώτερον MR

3.1.11[23]. πυκνώτεραν (reading S) MR²: πυκνώτερον MR (reading P)

3.3.8[27]. ποιοῦντος (emendation Natorp) MR²: ποιοῦν MR (reading S)

3.4.2[8]. ἀποψυχόμενα MR²: corrects MR ἀποψυχούμενα

3.14.1[2]. ἀναλόγως τῇ τοῦ {παντὸς} οὐρανοῦ σφαίρᾳ: παντὸς bracketed MR²

4.21.1[20]. τὸ ἡγεμονικὸν ὥσπερ ἐν κόσμῳ ‹σφαιροειδεῖ ὁ θεὸς› κατοικεῖ: σφαιροειδεῖ ὁ θεὸς added MR²

5.11.2[5–6]. ὅταν μὲν ἀπὸ τοῦ δεξιοῦ μέρους ‹εἰς τὰ δεξιὰ μέρη› τῆς μήτρας ὁ γόνος ἀποκριθῇ, τοῖς πατράσιν· ὅταν δ' ἀπὸ τοῦ ἀριστεροῦ ‹εἰς τὰ ἀριστέρα›: εἰς τὰ δεξιὰ μέρη and εἰς τὰ ἀριστέρα added MR²

APPENDIX II

ADDITIONAL NOTES TO THE TEXT

In the following notes, we give alternative readings for passages where the textual evidence of the two main witnesses differs significantly and cannot be easily set out in a compact critical apparatus (on such "irreducible texts," see General Introduction 2.2.2).

BOOK II

2.3.2[4–5]. The printed text is based on Stobaeus.

Ps.-Plutarch reads: Δημόκριτος δὲ καὶ Ἐπίκουρος καὶ ὅσοι τὰ ἄτομα εἰσηγοῦνται καὶ τὸ κενὸν οὔτ᾽ ἔμψυχον οὔτε προνοίᾳ διοικεῖσθαι, φύσει δέ τινι ἀλόγῳ. (But Democritus and Epicurus and those who introduce the atoms and the void say that it is neither ensouled or administered by providence but by an unreasoning natural force.)

2.4.1–2. The printed text combines elements from Stobaeus and Ps.-Plutarch.

Ps.-Plutarch reads: Πυθαγόρας καὶ οἱ Στωικοὶ γενητὸν ὑπὸ θεοῦ τὸν κόσμον. (Pythagoras and the Stoics say that the cosmos is generated through the agency of God.)

Stobaeus reads: Πυθαγόρας φησὶ γενητὸν κατ' ἐπίνοιαν τὸν κόσμον, οὐ κατὰ χρόνον. Ἡράκλειτος οὐ κατὰ χρόνον εἶναι γενητὸν τὸν κόσμον, ἀλλὰ κατ' ἐπίνοιαν. Ἐπίδικος ὑπὸ φύσεως γεγενῆσθαι τὸν κόσμον. (Pythagoras says the cosmos is generated in thought, and not in time. Heraclitus says the cosmos is generated not in time, but in thought. Epidicus says that the cosmos has come into being through the agency of nature.)

Theodoret paraphrases as follows: καὶ οἱ μὲν κατ' ἐπίνοιαν γενητὸν, οὐ κατὰ χρόνον. (And some philosophers say it is generated in thought and not in time.)

Another possibility for the second doxa is to read ‹κατὰ χρόνον›, which introduces a better contrast with the first lemma and gives suitable information on Stoic doctrine. The translation could be: The Stoics say that through the agency of God ‹it has come into being in time›.

2.4.13. The lemma as printed is based on the text of Stobaeus.

Ps.-Plutarch has a shorter text: Ἐπίκουρος φθαρτόν, ὅτι καὶ γενητόν, ὡς ζῷον καὶ ὡς φυτόν. (Epicurus says it is destructible, because it is also generated, just like an animal and like a plant.) This lemma is placed not at the end, as in Stobaeus, but after a doxa combining the views of Pythagoras, Plato, and the Stoics. It is easier to see how Ps.-Plutarch might have derived this text from that preserved in Stobaeus than vice versa, so preference should be given to the longer text.

2.5.3[6–7]. τὸ μὲν ... τὸ δὲ is found in GS[1]. The alternative τότε μὲν ... τότε δὲ, found in PS[2], i.e., "at the one time ... at the other," is equally possible. Most unusually, S cited this lemma twice (indicated by S[1] and S[2]).

2.16.6. Ps.-Plutarch has abbreviated the text: ἰσοδρόμους εἶναι τὸν ἥλιον τὸν ἑωσφόρον τὸν στίλβοντα (that the sun, the Dawn-bringer and the Gleamer run an equal course).

2.20.12[25–28]. The printed text is based on Stobaeus.

Ps.-Plutarch reads: διηθοῦντα δὲ πρὸς ἡμᾶς τὸ φῶς, ὥστε προσεοικέναι ἡλίῳ τὸ ἐν τῷ οὐρανῷ πυρῶδες τό τε δὴ ἀπ᾽ αὐτοῦ καὶ ἐσοπτροειδές, καὶ τρίτον ... (on the other hand pushing the light through toward us, so that both the fiery one in the heaven and the mirror-like one derived from it have the appearance of a sun, and thirdly ...)

2.25.1[2–5]. The printed text is based on Stobaeus.

Ps.-Plutarch reads: ... ὥσπερ ⟨τὸν⟩ τοῦ ἡλίου πλήρη πυρός· ἐκλείπειν δὲ κατὰ τὰς ἐπιστροφὰς τοῦ τροχοῦ· ὅμοιον γὰρ εἶναι ἁρματίου τροχῷ κοίλην ἔχοντι τὴν ἁψῖδα καὶ πλήρη πυρός, ἔχοντι μίαν ἐκπνοήν. (... like the circle of the sun full of fire; and it undergoes eclipse in accordance with the turnings of the wheel; for it resembles the wheel of a chariot with a rim that is hollow and full of fire, and it has a single blowhole.)

2.25.3. The printed text combines readings in the mss. of
Ps.-Plutarch and its tradition, Stobaeus, and Theodoret.
Ps.-Plutarch (ms. Moscow), Ps.-Galen, Lydus, and Qustā
read πεπυρωμένον (incandescent); Stobaeus, Ps.-Plutarch
(Planudean mss.), and Eusebius read πεπιλημένον (compressed); Ps.-Plutarch (ms. Venice) combines these in
the nonsensical πεπυρωλημένον. In the papyrus there is
room for only one participle, but it is unclear which one.
Theodoret combines Xenophanes' doxai on the sun and
the moon and reads νέφη πεπυρωμένα (incandescent
clouds).

BOOK V

5.1.1[4–5]. Of the four additional parts of divination
printed in the text, P reads only the first, τὸ ὀνειροπολικόν.
G, confirmed by Q, retains two more, τὸ ἀστρομαντικὸν
and τὸ ὀρνεοσκοπικόν. But the papyrus, as reconstructed
by O. Primavesi in an unpublished paper, provides evidence that the sentence ended with a fourth part, τὸ
ἱεροσκοπικόν. The reasons for the omissions will have
been haplography.

5.3.5–6. It is possible that words, including a name-label,
have fallen out and that the text was originally: Ἐπίκουρος
⟨ἀφ' ὅλων τῶν σωμάτων φέρεσθαι. οἱ Στωικοὶ⟩ ψυχῆς
καὶ σώματος ἀπόσπασμα. But in this case the Epicurus
doxa is basically a doublet of the Democritus view that
follows, so it might be better to conjecture: ⟨οἱ Στωικοὶ⟩
ψυχῆς καὶ σώματος ἀπόσπασμα. Δημόκριτος ⟨'Επί-
κουρος⟩ ἀφ' ὅλων τῶν σωμάτων . . .

5.12.3. Another possibility, rejected in MR ad loc., is that two original lemmata have been coalesced in P. Given the evidence of G, who records οἱ Στωικοὶ κατὰ συμπάθειαν τῆς διανοίας καὶ ῥευμάτων καὶ ἀκτίνων εἴσκρισιν, this must have happened early, perhaps already in Aët. The editions of Mau and Lachenaud suggest οἱ Στωικοὶ συμπαθείᾳ τῆς διανοίας <. . .> <. . .> κατὰ ῥευμάτων εἰσκρίσεις καὶ | ἀκτίνων <ἢ καὶ> εἰδώλων γίνεσθαι τὰς ἄλλων ὁμοιότητας, where the second lacuna could be filled in with <᾿Επίκουρος> vel sim.

5.19.6[21–23]. The text of P worsens toward the end of Book 5. It is evident that for these lines Q had a superior text, which allows the following readings (G omitted this lemma):

21 ὑγρότερα Q (was von ihnen feuchter ist): οἰκειότερα P
22 ἀναπτῆναι Q (was in der Luft fliegt): ἀναπνεῖν P
23 τοῖς χωρίοις σύμφωνα εἶναι Q (ist ebenmässig an allen Orten): τοῖς θώραξι πεφωνηκέναι P

In addition to MR, see further the text of Primavesi in MP p. 456.

5.22.1. Here too the text in P is seriously defective and can be greatly improved by taking into account the evidence of G and Q. In addition to MR, see further the text of Primavesi in MP pp. 498–500.

5.27.1. As the state of P's text deteriorates, Q has additional material not present in P. However, the order of the sentences differs. P places the Empedoclean lemma first, followed by the words Ἀναξαγόρας μὲν τρέφεσθαι and a lacuna of 1¾ lines. Q begins with the Anaxagorean lemma, to which he attaches the final part of the Empedocles lemma, followed by the remainder of that lemma. The reconstruction is based on the order in P. The reference to cosmogonic themes in the disputed phrase τοὺς δὲ . . . τάξιν is consistent with other Empedoclean doxai in Books 2 and 5; cf. 2.8.2, 5.7.1, 5.18.1, etc.

5.28.1. Here again the text in P is seriously corrupt. The emended text, based on the evidence of Q, must be regarded as tentative. For the final phrase, see Wolsdorf, "Empedocles," 31.

5.29. Here once again Q is needed to complement the defective remains of P. This time G provides evidence of all three lemmata, but his text is strongly reduced. It reads as follows (text Diels):

Ps.-Galen *Historia philosopha* c. 131 Πῶς γίνεται πυρετὸς καὶ ἐπιγίνεται (How fever occurs and occurs afterward)

1. Ἐρασίστρατος ὁρίζεται τὸν πυρετὸν κίνημα αἵματος παρεμπεπτωκότος εἰς τὰ τοῦ πνεύματος ἀγγεῖα ἀπροαιρέτως γινόμενον καθάπερ ἐπὶ τῆς θαλάττης, ὅταν μηδὲν αὐτὴν κινῇ πνεῦμα, ἠρεμεῖ. (Erasistratus defines fever as a motion that occurs involuntarily when blood is diverted into the vessels of the *pneuma*, just as, in the case of the sea, it is at rest when no *pneuma* stirs it.)

2. Διοκλῆς ἐπιγέννημα εἶναι τὸν πυρετόν· ἐπιγίνεται δὲ τραύματι καὶ βουβῶνι. (Diocles says
that fever is an after-symptom; it occur afterward in
a wound and a swollen gland.)

3. Ἡρόδοτός [sic] φησιν ἐνίοτε μηδεμιᾶς αἰτίας
προηγησαμένης πυρέττειν τινάς. (Herodotus [sic]
says that people sometimes have a fever without any
preceding cause.)

GLOSSARY OF TERMS

antithesis: Significant contrast.
archê, archai: First principle(s).
archetype: Extant or hypothetical text commencing a textual tradition.
areskonta: What it pleases (one) to think or believe.

categories: "Things said of," classification deriving from Aristotle, of
  entities that can be the subject or predicate in a proposition, into
  ten sets, namely, substance, quantity, quality, relative, place or
  where, time or when, being-in-a-position, having or condition, doing or action, and being affected. Used in the *Placita* to order series of chapters or issues in individual chapters according to topics
  treated.
coalesce: Collecting different but related items from various places
  and combining them into a single cluster.
compendium: Treatise containing concise information.
compromise (view): Compatible with distinctions or contraries or
  contradictories in a diaeresis or diaphonia; combining opposite attributes.
corporealism: The view that ultimate reality is corporeal, or material.

decad: See *tetraktys*
definition: *See* nominal (definition); real (definition)
diaeresis: Division or sorting of an overarching concept into underlying concepts characterized by strongly or gradually contrasting
  substances or properties; division of an entity, e.g., philosophy, into
  parts.
diaeretic: Pertaining to a diaeresis.
dialectic(al): Method of arranging a variety of related views according to question types and diaeresis and/or diaphonia, with room for
  compromises and exceptions; in Stoicism, logical part of philosophy.

503

GLOSSARY OF TERMS

diaphonia: Opposition (disagreement, conflict) among entities or attributes that exclude each other.

difference: Contrast among entities or attributes.

distinction: Defining contrast between similar entities.

division: *See* diaeresis

doxa(i): Tenet(s), opinion(s), view(s) of a philosopher or scientist or author or school.

dyad, Dyad: "Twoness," number two, set of two, principle of duality or plurality.

efficient cause: Immediate agent in producing an effect.

eidôla: Images.

ellipsis: Suppression of verbs of saying or of the subject of views that are cited.

enclave: Section of text or microenvironment containing excerpts from a different source than its surroundings.

entelecheia, entelechy: Realization.

epitomator: Someone who abridges a text.

epitome, *Epitomê*: Shorter version of larger work.

ethnicon: Adjective indicating the name of city or country of origin.

example: Item representing a set of similar items.

finitist: Someone who holds that the principles and/or elements are limited in number.

fossil: Isolated remnant of earlier version.

genesis: Generation, creation.

hêgemonikon: Ruling part.

homoiomereiai, homoiomerê: Things with like parts.

incorporealism: The view that the incorporeal, or immaterial, is an important component of ultimate reality.

infinitist: Someone who holds that the principles and/or elements are unlimited in number.

intermediate: Being in between opposed entities.

lemma(ta): Paragraph(s) in a chapter.

list (*noun*): Arrangement of gradually contrasting items in a division or a process of sorting.
list (*verb*): Enumerate one after the other.
logos: Account; reason.

macrostructure: Argumentative structure of treatise or one or more books.
mathêmatikos: Astronomer, astrologer, mathematician, scientist.
metarsia: "Things on high" (in the atmosphere), in between *ourania* and *prosgeia*.
microstructure: Argumentative structure of a chapter or part of a chapter.
mixed view: Combining opposite attributes.
monad, Monad: "Oneness," unity, number one, principle of oneness or unity.
monism: The view that there is only one ultimate reality.

name-label: Name used to identify a person or persons propounding or subscribing to a doxa.
nominal (definition): Definition of the everyday, or the technical meaning of a word.

opposition, opposed view: View or tenet contrasting with another one in a diaeresis.
ourania: Things in the heavens.

patronymic: Adjective indicating name of father.
physikos logos: Account of physics or natural philosophy.
pinax: Table of contents.
placita (Latin, translates *areskonta*): Tenet(s), opinion(s), view(s) of a philosopher or scientist or author or school.
Placita: General title of doxographical treatises, e.g., the compendium of Aëtius.
pluralism: The view that there is more than one ultimate reality.
pneuma, pneumata: Breath(s).
primary division: Division providing the main structure of a chapter.
prosgeia: Things on the earth.
protological: Relating to origins or beginnings.

GLOSSARY OF TERMS

quaestiones: *See* questions

question types: The four standard research issues deriving from Aristotle, concerning existence ("whether it is"), substance or definition ("what it is"), attribute or fact ("the that"), and cause ("the why"). Utilized in a chapter or string of chapters in the *Placita* for systematic inquiry into issues. The question of existence pertains to the category of substance, but may also be put forward in regard to other categories, and that concerned with the attribute or fact pertains not only to quality (including shape) but also to quantity, place, time, motion etc.

questions: Issues or problems that are the theme of a chapter or string of chapters.

real (definition): Definition of the essence or substance according to a person or persons or school.

series: *See* list

subdivision: Further or secondary diaeresis of a concept underlying the primary division.

subsidiary division: *See* subdivision

succession: Sequence in master-pupil relationship of individual heads of a philosophical or other school (or traditional occupation) deriving from a (purported) founding father, e.g., Thales or Pythagoras.

syllogism: Form of argument according to which two premises necessarily produce a conclusion.

tenet: Opinion held on a particular question or topic. *See* doxa(i); *placita*

tetrad: "Fourness," set of four.

tetraktys, Tetraktys: Pythagorean principle, primary set of four comprising the primary numbers 1, 2, 3, and 4, adding up to the decad, or primary "ten."

topic: Theme of a chapter or series of chapters.

transition: Term or quality linking two different items.

triad: "Threeness," set of three.

typhôn(es): Typhoon(s).

views on: Various doxai in a chapter.

INDEX OF NAME-LABELS AND
OTHER NAMES

This index combines listings of the following groups of names:

1. All the name-labels in the *Placita* (including names of schools and also group descriptions).
2. All other non-mythical names of persons mentioned within the doxai, indicated in each case with an added asterisk.
3. The names of witnesses to the text of the *Placita* and other philosophers relevant to its use and reception as mentioned in the General Introduction, Introductions to the five books, and notes to the translation.

For each philosopher, school, or witness, a brief description is provided, followed where applicable by a listing of doxai grouped according to main themes. Numbers at the end indicate the sum total of doxai for each name-label (or group description).

Testimonia and Fragment collections are given for authors whose writings are not preserved. For full details see the Abbreviations (p. lxxi). The collection first mentioned is the one used for the *apparatus testimoniorum* under the Greek text.

Dates are BC unless otherwise indicated.

ABBREVIATIONS

Name-labels attached to doxai are listed under the following rubrics:

Intro.	Book 1, chs.1–10	Introduction
Princ.	Book 1, chs. 11–30	Principles, Foundational Concepts
Cosm.	Book 2, chs. 1–32	Cosmology

INDEX

Academics: members of the New Academy, school of Plato, during its "skeptical" phase, from Arcesilaus (q.v., head ca. 273–ca. 242) to Philo of Larissa (head ca. 110–ca. 79). *Psych.* 4.8.13, 4.9.19, 4.13.10 (3)

Academy: founded by Plato (q.v.), one of the four main Hellenistic schools in Athens. Often divided into Old Academy, up to the death of Polemon (q.v.), and the New Academy, from the headship of Arcesilaus (*see* Academics).

Academy, successors of the: group designation for later followers of the philosophers of the New Academy. *Psych.* 4.9.2 (1)

Achilles: lived in Alexandria, probably early in the third century AD. Wrote a work still extant entitled *De universo* with most likely the purpose of serving as an introduction to the poem of Aratus (q.v.) (ed. Di Maria [1996]). See General Introduction 1.6, 2.1.4, 2.2.1.

Alcmaeon of Croton (fl. 470–440): early Western Greek philosopher. Wrote a wide-ranging treatise on natural philosophy (no longer extant), with extensive sections on the makeup of the human being. Testimonia and Fragments: DK 24; also LM 37. *Cosm.* 2.16.2, 2.22.1, 2.29.3; *Psych.* 4.2.2, 4.13.8, 4.16.2, 4.17.1, 4.18.1; *Physio.* 5.3.3, 5.14.1, 5.16.3, 5.17.3, 5.24.1, 5.30.1 (14)

Alexander of Aphrodisias (fl. AD 200–210): taught Peripatetic philosophy at Athens and wrote extensive commentaries on the works of Aristotle, as well as many other writings on philosophical topics. The second book of his *On the Soul*, also called the *Mantissa*, includes material that may not be authentic but comes from his school.

All others: group designation, contrasted with one particular other group of philosophers, i.e., Atomists. *Cosm.* 2.3.1 (1)

All who assume matter is passive: group designation. *Princ.* 1.24.3 (1)

All who create a world through aggregation: group designation indicating Atomist philosophers. *Princ.* 1.24.2 (1)

All who propose atoms and void: group designation indicating Atomist philosophers. *Cosm.* 2.3.2 (1)

Anaxagoras of Clazomenae (ca. 500–428/7): early Ionian philosopher, active in Athens. Wrote only a single treatise (no longer extant) devoted to natural philosophy. Testimonia and Fragments: DK 59; also MP 8; LM 25; Sider (2005). *Intro.* 1.3.4, 1.7.1*, 1.7.6; *Princ.* 1.14.3, 1.24.2, 1.29.4, 1.30.2; *Cosm.* 2.1.2, 2.4.7, 2.8.1, 2.13.3, 2.16.1, 2.20.8, 2.21.3, 2.23.2, 2.25.10, 2.28.6, 2.29.7, 2.29.8, 2.30.3; *Meteor.* 3.1.7, 3.2.3, 3.2.10, 3.3.4, 3.4.2, 3.5.8; *Earth-sea* 3.15.4, 3.16.2; *Nile* 4.1.3; *Psych.* 4.3.2, 4.7.1, 4.7a.1, 4.9.1, 4.9.6, 4.19.7; *Physio.* 5.7.4, 5.19.3, 5.20.3, 5.25.2, 5.27.2 (39)

Anaxagoras and successors: general designation for philosophers who posit the existence of elemental parts; linked with Democritus and his successors (q.v.). *Princ.* 1.17.2 (1)

Anaximander of Miletus (610/9–ca. 540): early Ionian philosopher, disciple of Thales. Wrote a treatise on natural philosophy (no longer extant). Testimonia and Fragments: DK 12; also MP 2; LM 6; Wöhrle (2012). *Intro.* 1.3.2, 1.7.3; *Cosm.* 2.1.3, 2.1.4, 2.4.7, 2.11.3, 2.13.7, 2.15.6, 2.16.4, 2.20.1, 2.21.1, 2.24.3, 2.25.1, 2.28.1, 2.29.1; *Meteor.* 3.3.1, 3.7.1; *Earth-sea* 3.10.2, 3.16.1; *Psych.* 4.3.2; *Physio.* 5.19.4 (21)

Anaximenes of Miletus (ca. 585–ca. 515): early Ionian philosopher, disciple of Anaximander. Wrote a treatise on natural philosophy (no longer extant). Testimonia and Fragments: DK 13; also MP 3; LM 6; Wöhrle (2012). *Intro.* 1.3.3, 1.7.4; *Cosm.* 2.1.3, 2.2a.2, 2.4.7, 2.11.1, 2.13.9, 2.14.3, 2.16.5, 2.19.2, 2.20.3, 2.22.1, 2.23.1, 2.25.2; *Meteor.* 3.3.2, 3.4.1, 3.4.7; *Earth-sea* 3.10.3, 3.15.3, 3.15.8; *Psych.* 4.3.2 (21)

Ancients, successors of: very general group designation. *Psych.* 4.8.9 (1)

Anonymi: group designation, usually through the designations "those," "some," "others." *Princ.* 1.15.11–13, 1.23.5–6; *Cosm.* 2.2.2–3, 2.4.6, 2.14.4, 2.23.7, 2.24.6, 2.26.4, 2.27.6, 2.30.2, 2.32.2, 2.32.3, 2.32.4–7, 2.32.10; *Meteor.* 3.1.4; *Earth-sea* 3.13.1, 3.15.9; *Psych.* 4.3.1, 4.5.10–12, 4.8.11, 4.9.8, 4.9.17, 4.10.6, 4.13.6; *Physio.* 5.17.5–6, 5.19.1–2, 5.23.3 (38)

Anonymus Londiniensis (ca. 1st c. AD): author of the *Iatrika* (ed. Manetti [2011]), a compilation of medical doctrines that contains doxographical material going back to the early Peripatos. Preserved on an Egyptian papyrus perhaps by the author's own hand.

Antipater of Tarsus (ca. 210–ca. 130): Stoic philosopher, head of the school in Athens. The titles of about twelve books are known, treating the three parts of philosophy according to the Stoics. Testimonia and Fragments: *SVF* 3.244–58. *Princ.* 1.27.6 (1)

Antiphon of Rhamnus: Athenian sophist, probably to be identified with the orator and politician (ca. 480–411). Philosophical writings include treatises *On Truth* (substantial papyrus fragments) and *On Concord*. Testimonia and Fragments: DK 87, Pendrick (2002); also Decleva Caizzi et al. (1989); LM 37. *Princ.* 1.22.7; *Cosm.* 2.20.4, 2.28.4, 2.29.3; *Earth-sea* 3.16.4 (5).

Apollodorus of Athens (ca. 180–ca. 110): scholar with an interest in philosophy. Disciple of the Stoic philosopher Diogenes of Babylon. Wrote an important poem, *Chronika*, on chronology from the fall of Troy to his own time. Testimonia and Fragments: *FGrH* 244. *Cosm.* 2.15.8 (1)

Apollodorus of Corcyra: nothing known about him. Mentioned nowhere else in extant ancient literature. *Earth-sea* 3.17.8 (1)

Apollophanes of Antioch (fl. ca. 250): Stoic philosopher. Of his writings, two titles are known, including a *Physics*. Testimonia and Fragments: *SVF* 1.90. *Psych.* 4.4.5 (1)

Aratus of Soli (fl. ca. 275): Hellenistic poet, author of the extant *Phaenomena*, the most famous poem of the Hellenistic period. When living in Athens, attended lectures of Zeno the Stoic (q.v.). The poem gave rise to a rich commentary literature, including the work of Achilles (q.v.). *Cosm.* 2.19.3 (1)

Arcesilaus of Pitane (316/15–241/40): Academic philosopher, founder of the New Academy. Not mentioned in the *Placita*.

Archedemus of Tarsus (fl. ca. 170): Stoic philosopher, disciple of Diogenes of Babylon. Testimonia and Fragments: *SVF* 3.262–64. *Cosm.* 2.5a.3 (1)

Archelaus of Athens (or Miletus; fl. ca. 450): early Greek natural philosopher, disciple of Anaxagoras, and reputedly teacher of Socrates. According to the *Suda*, wrote a *Physiologia* and some other works. Testimonia and Fragments: DK 60; LM 26. *Intro.* 1.3.5, 1.7.5; *Cosm.* 2.1.3, 2.4.4, 2.4.7, 2.13.6; *Meteor.* 3.3.5; *Psych.* 4.3.2 (8)

Aristarchus of Samos (ca. 310–ca. 230): Greek astronomer, famous for his heliocentric view of the universe. According to *Plac.* 1.15.5, disciple of Strato the Peripatetic (q.v.). Only work extant is *On the Sizes and Distances of the Sun and the Moon*. Testimonia and Fragments: not collected but discussed in Heath (1913). *Princ.* 1.15.5, 1.15.9; *Cosm.* 2.24.7; *Psych.* 4.13.4 (4)

INDEX

Aristotle of Stagira (384–322): studied with Plato in the Academy. After the latter's death founded the Lyceum, or Peripatos, one of the four main Hellenistic schools in Athens. With Theophrastus and other disciples, collected and critiqued many doctrines of early Greek philosophy. Aside from the extant corpus of his writings, wrote many other works now lost; see listing at Diog. Laert. 5.42–48. Testimonia and Fragments: Rose (1886); Ross (1955); but neither includes the doxai of the *Placita*; also Gigon (1987), who does include them grouped together in double Dielsian columns as fr. 19. *Intro.* 1.prooem.3, 1.1.2, 1.3.21, 1.7.23 1.9.5, 1.10.4; *Princ.* 1.11.3, 1.12.3, 1.15.10, 1.16.3, 1.18.6, 1.19.2, 1.21.2a, 1.23.2, 1.29.2; *Cosm.* 2.1.2, 2.3.4, 2.4.10, 2.5.1, 2.7.5, 2.9.4, 2.10.1, 2.11.5, 2.13.13, 2.16.3, 2.17.5, 2.20.11, 2.23.8, 2.25.8, 2.26.3, 2.28.2, 2.29.4*, 2.29.7, 2.30.7; *Meteor.* 3.1.9, 3.2.4, 3.3.13, 3.7.4; *Earth-sea* 3.15.5, 3.17.1; *Psych.* 4.2.6, 4.4.3, 4.5.7, 4.6.2, 4.7.4, 4.8.6, 4.9.3, 4.10.2, 4.13.9, 4.20.1; *Physio.* 5.1.4, 5.3.1, 5.4.2, 5.5.2, 5.6.1, 5.7.5*, 5.17.2, 5.20.1, 5.23.2, 5.25.1, 5.26.2 (59)

Aristotle and followers: group designation for Peripatetic school. *Intro.* 1.2.1 (1)

Aristotle and Hippocrates and their followers: group designation, probably inspired by the contents of the doxa in which it occurs. *Physio.* 5.18.4 (1)

Arius Didymus (fl. ca. 10): probably to be identified with the Stoic philosopher from Alexandria, court philosopher of Augustus. Excerpts from doxographical writings preserved by Eusebius (q.v.) and Stobaeus (q.v.). Fragments on physics edited by Diels; see also Runia (1996). See General Introduction 1.2, 2.2.1.

Arrian: author of brief excerpts on astronomy and meteorology preserved by Stobaeus (q.v.). Probably to be identified with Arrian of Nicomedia (ca. AD 85–ca. 165).

Asclepiades of Bithynia (ca. 150–ca. 80): doctor with philosophical interests, active in Rome. No writings survive. Testimonia and Fragments: Vallance (1993, listing of references only). *Princ.* 1.23.10; *Psych.* 4.2.8, 4.22.2; *Physio.* 5.10.2, 5.21.2, 5.30.6 (6)

Astronomers (*mathēmatikoi*): group designation for scientists engaged in astronomical studies with an emphasis on calculation. *Cosm.* 2.15.5, 2.16.2, 2.16.6, 2.30.8, 2.31.2; *Physio.* 5.18.6 (6)

Athenagoras: early Christian apologist who composed a still extant address to the emperors Marcus Aurelius and Commodus in about AD 176 (ed. Marcovich [1990]). See General Introduction 1.1, 1.6.

511

INDEX

INDEX

Demetrius the Laconian (fl. ca. 100): Epicurean philosopher, active in both Miletus and Athens. Parts of some of his wide-ranging writings have been uncovered in Herculaneum. Testimonia and Fragments: Gigante in Puglia (1988); also De Falco (1923). *Princ.* 1.18.3 (1)

Democritus of Abdera (ca. 460–ca. 370): Atomist philosopher, disciple, and collaborator of Leucippus (q.v.). Prolific and wide-ranging writer; see the listing at Diog. Laert. 9.46–49, but no writings extant. Testimonia and Fragments: DK 68, Luria (2007); also MP 9; LM 27. *Intro.* 1.3.14, 1.3.16*, 1.7.7; *Princ.* 1.12.6, 1.15.8, 1.18.3, 1.23.3, 1.24.2, 1.25.3, 1.26.2, 1.29.4; *Cosm.* 2.1.3, 2.2.4, 2.3.2, 2.4.12, 2.7.2, 2.13.5, 2.15.3, 2.16.1, 2.17.3*, 2.20.8, 2.23.5, 2.25.10, 2.30.4; *Meteor.* 3.1.8, 3.2.3, 3.3.11; *Earth-sea* 3.10.5, 3.12.2, 3.13.4, 3.15.1, 3.15.7; *Nile* 4.1.4; *Psych.* 4.3.5, 4.4.7, 4.4.8, 4.5.1, 4.7.4, 4.7a.2, 4.8.5, 4.8.10, 4.9.1, 4.9.6, 4.9.9, 4.10.4, 4.10.5, 4.13.1, 4.14.2, 4.19.5; *Physio.* 5.2.1, 5.3.6, 5.4.3, 5.5.1, 5.7.7, 5.16.1, 5.19.5, 5.20.2 (55)

Democritus and his successors: group designation for philosophers who posit the existence of elemental parts; linked with Anaxagoras and his successors (q.v.). *Princ.* 1.17.2 (1)

Democritus, successors of: group designation for philosophers in the atomist tradition after Democritus. *Intro.* 1.9.3 (1)

Diagoras of Melos (ca. 480–ca. 410): lyric poet, notorious for his atheistic views and opposition to cults of the gods. Testimonia and Fragments: Winiarczyk (1981). *Intro.* 1.7.1*

Dicaearchus of Messina (ca. 375–ca. 310): Peripatetic philosopher, member of the Lyceum during Aristotle's lifetime, but also traveled widely. Many writings on psychology, ethics, and politics, all lost. Testimonia and Fragments: Mirhardy (2001); also Wehrli (1967). *Earth-sea* 3.17.2; *Psych.* 4.2.7; *Physio.* 5.1.4 (3)

Diocles of Carystos (fl. 350–320): doctor and medical scientist. Writings on a wide range of medical subjects, none extant. Testimonia and Fragments: Van der Eijk (2000–2001). *Physio.* 5.9.1, 5.13.2, 5.14.3, 5.18.3, 5.29.2, 5.30.2 (6)

Diodorus Cronus (fl. 320–300): dialectical philosopher of the Megarian school. Of his writings no titles are known. Testimonia and Fragments: Döring (1972); also Giannantoni (1990). *Intro.* 1.3.18; *Princ.* 1.13.3, 1.23.7 (3)

Diodorus of Tyre (fl. 110): Peripatetic philosopher, disciple of Critolaus (q.v.) and his successor as head of the school in Athens. Very few fragments remain, collected in Wehrli (1969). *Intro.* 1.7.12 (1)

514

INDEX

Diogenes Laertius (fl. AD 200–250): obscure author of the *Vitae philosophorum*, a rich compendium of information on the biographies and doxographies of the ancient philosophers (ed. Dorandi [2013]). See General Introduction 1.5.

Diogenes of Apollonia (fl. 430): early Greek philosopher, one of the last Presocratics. Main treatise *On nature*, but also other writings, all lost. Testimonia and Fragments: DK 64; also Laks (2008); LM 28. *Intro.* 1.3.10, 1.7.8; *Cosm.* 2.1.3, 2.1.8, 2.4.7, 2.8.1, 2.13.4, 2.13.10, 2.20.10, 2.23.3, 2.25.11; *Meteor.* 3.2.9, 3.3.8; *Psych.* 4.3.2, 4.3.8, 4.5.8, 4.7.1, 4.9.9, 4.16.3, 4.18.2; *Physio.* 5.15.4, 5.20.5, 5.24.3 (23)

Diogenes of Babylon (ca. 240–ca. 150): Stoic philosopher, followed Zeno of Tarsus as head of the school in Athens. Many and wide-ranging writings, especially on rhetoric, none extant. Often possible confusion with Diogenes of Apollonia, e.g., at 1.7.8, 4.5.8, 5.15.4. Testimonia and Fragments: SVF 3.210–43. *Cosm.* 2.32.9 (1)

Diogenes of Oenoanda (fl. 2nd c. AD): Epicurean philosopher from Oenoanda in Lycia, who erected a huge wall recording writings of Epicurus and himself in stone. Many pieces of the wall survive, preserving its text.

Diotimus of Tyre (fl. ca. 400–370): obscure philosopher, probably follower of Democritus. Testimonia and Fragments: DK 76. *Cosm.* 2.17.3 (1)

Doctors: group designation for doctors or medical scientists. *Physio.* 5.8.3, 5.12.1, 5.13.1, 5.17.4, 5.30.6 (5)

Ecphantus of Syracuse (or Croton) (fl. ca. 420): Pythagorean, younger contemporary of Philolaus. Known mainly through the doxographical tradition (the work *On kingship* is pseudonymous). Testimonia and Fragments: DK 51; LM 16; also in MP 3. *Intro.* 1.3.17; *Cosm.* 2.1.2, 2.3.3; *Earth-sea* 3.13.3 (4)

Empedocles of Agrigentum (484/3–424/3): early Western Greek philosopher. Author of two didactic poems, the *Katharmoi* and the *Physika* (both lost, but many fragments), the former proclaiming a divine revelation, the latter focusing on themes of natural philosophy. Testimonia and Fragments: DK 31; also MR 7; LM 22; Wright (1981). *Intro.* 1.3.19, 1.5.2, 1.7.19; *Princ.* 1.13.1, 1.15.3, 1.17.3, 1.18.2, 1.24.2, 1.26.1, 1.30.1; *Cosm.* 2.1.2, 2.1.6, 2.4.11, 2.6.3, 2.7.7, 2.8.2, 2.10.2, 2.11.2, 2.13.2, 2.13.11, 2.20.13, 2.21.2, 2.23.4, 2.24.2,

515

2.25.6, 2.27.5, 2.28.6, 2.31.1, 2.31.4; *Meteor.* 3.3.7, 3.8.1; *Earth-sea* 3.16.3; *Psych.* 4.3.12, 4.5.9, 4.7.1, 4.7a.2, 4.9.1, 4.9.6, 4.9.15, 4.13.12, 4.14.1, 4.16.1, 4.17.2, 4.22.1; *Physio.* 5.7.1, 5.8.1, 5.10.1, 5.11.1, 5.12.2, 5.14.2, 5.15.3, 5.18.1, 5.19.6, 5.21.1, 5.22.1, 5.24.2, 5.25.4, 5.26.4, 5.27.1, 5.28.1, 5.28.2 (61)

Empiricists: group designation referring to the medical school founded ca. 250 by Philemon of Cos (or Serapion of Alexandria), one of the three main medical schools of antiquity. Testimonia and Fragments: Deichgräber (1930). *Physio.* 5.18.3 (1)

Ephorus of Kyme (Asia Minor) (ca. 400–ca. 330): historian. Many writings, including the *Historiae* in thirty books, all lost. Regarded as the founder of universal history. Testimonia and Fragments: *FrGH* 70. *Nile* 4.1.6 (1)

Epicureans: group designation for followers of Epicurus (q.v.). *Psych.* 4.13.2*; *Physio.* 5.26.3 (1)

Epicurus of Samos (342/1–270): Athenian philosopher, founder of the Garden, one of the four main Hellenistic schools in Athens. Prolific author; writings listed at Diog. Laert. 10.24–28. Three summaries of his own doctrines in physics and ethics, and also two collections of maxims, are extant. Of his chief work, *On Nature* in thirty-seven books, extensive fragmentary sections found in Herculaneum. Testimonia and Fragments: Usener (1887); Arrighetti (1973). *Intro.* 1.3.16, 1.5.4*, 1.7.25, 1.8.3; *Princ.* 1.12.5, 1.15.9, 1.18.3, 1.20.2, 1.22.6, 1.23.4, 1.24.2, 1.29.3; *Cosm.* 2.1.3, 2.1.5, 2.2.5, 2.3.2, 2.4.13, 2.7.3, 2.13.14, 2.20.14, 2.21.5, 2.22.4; *Meteor.* 3.4.5; *Earth-sea* 3.15.11; *Psych.* 4.3.11, 4.4.7, 4.5.6, 4.7.4, 4.8.2, 4.8.10, 4.9.5, 4.9.6, 4.9.12, 4.9.20, 4.13.1, 4.14.2, 4.19.4, 4.23.2; *Physio.* 5.1.2, 5.3.5, 5.5.1, 5.16.1, 5.19.5, 5.20.2 (43)

Epidicus: wholly unknown philosopher, mentioned only in Aëtius. The name must be considered suspect. *Cosm.* 2.4.3 (1)

Epigenes of Byzantium (fl. 2nd c.): astrologer, who wrote a book on the Chaldeans. *Meteor.* 3.2.7 (1)

Erasistratus of Cos (ca. 330–ca. 255): doctor and medical scientist, contemporary of Herophilus. Resided in Alexandria, where he conducted medical research. A wide range of writings, including general principles of medicine, none extant. Testimonia and Fragments: Garofalo (1988). *Psych.* 4.5.4; *Physio.* 5.9.3, 5.10.3, 5.29.1, 5.30.3 (5)

Eratosthenes of Cyrene (ca. 275–ca. 195): versatile scientist and philologist. Moved from Athens to Alexandria, where he became Head of the Library. Many writings on a wide range of subjects, including philosophy, none extant. Testimonia and Fragments: Bernhardy (1822). *Princ.* 1.21.3; *Cosm.* 2.31.3 (2)

Eudemus of Rhodes (fl. 320–300): Peripatetic philosopher, disciple and colleague of Aristotle. Writings included histories of mathematics, astronomy, and theology. Testimonia and Fragments: Wehrli (1969).

Eudoxus of Cnidus (ca. 390–ca. 337): celebrated astronomer and mathematician with wide-ranging interests, including philosophy. Resided for a time in Athens, where he had contact with Plato and his school. Many writings, all lost. Testimonia and Fragments: Lasserre (1966). *Cosm.* 2.19.3; *Nile* 4.1.7 (2)

Euhemerus of Messina (but according to Aëtius from Tegea) (ca. 340–260): author of a travel narrative in which the Olympian gods were discovered to have been great kings in their day. Famed as originator of Euhemeristic theology. Testimonia and Fragments: Winiarczyk (1991); also *FGrH* 63. *Intro.* 1.7.1*

Euripides (ca. 480–406): Athenian tragedian. Of his ninety-two plays, nineteen have survived; many fragments of others. Renowned as the "philosopher of the stage" due to his philosophizing pronouncements. Testimonia and Fragments: Kannicht (2004). *Intro.* 1.7.1*; *Physio.* 5.19.3 (1)

Eusebius of Caesarea (ca. AD 260–ca. 340): Christian bishop and writer. Author of the *Praeparatio evangelica*, containing numerous excerpts from ancient philosophers and doxographies (ed. Mras [1982–1983]). See General Introduction 1.1–2, 1.6, 2.1.2.

Euthymenes of Massilia (fl. 500?): famed seafarer and explorer. His lost work *Periplous* is known only from its theory on the source of the Nile. Testimonia and Fragments: *FGrH* 647. *Nile* 4.1.2 (1)

Gorgias of Leontini (ca. 480–ca. 380): celebrated sophist and rhetor, but also with philosophical interests. Made a start in recording the contrasting views of philosophers. Testimonia and Fragments: DK 82; LM 32. See General Introduction 1.5.

Hecataeus of Abdera (fl. 300): philosopher, reportedly disciple of Pyrrhon; also historian/ethnographer. Writings on Egypt and other topics, all lost. Testimonia and Fragments: DK 73; also *FGrH* 264. *Cosm.* 2.20.6 (1)

Heraclides of Pontus (ca. 390–ca. 310): philosopher, disciple of Plato,

authorities. Testimonia and Fragments: DK 86; LM 36. See General Introduction 1.5.

Hippo of Metapontum (alternatively, Rhegium or Croton or Samos) (fl. ca. 450–430): reportedly Pythagorean in late authors. Interests in natural philosophy and medicine. Testimonia and Fragments: DK 38; also LM 24. *Psych.* 4.3.9; *Physio.* 5.5.3, 5.7.3, 5.7.8 (4)

Hippocrates of Chios (fl. 450–400): mathematician with philosophical interests, associated with the Pythagorean school.

Hippocrates of Cos (ca. 460–ca. 380/60): the most famous doctor of antiquity, known as the "father of Medicine." A corpus of sixty treatises survives under his name, though none can be attributed to him with certainty. *Psych.* 4.5.2 (1)

Hippocrates and followers. *See* Aristotle and Hippocrates and their followers

Hippolytus: early Christian author of the work *Refutation of All Heresies* in ten books. It contains much discussion of earlier philosophers and in Book 1 a collection of doxographies on key early Greek philosophers that shares source material with the tradition of the *Placita*. The author is often identified with Hippolytus, the schismatic Bishop of Rome (170–236), but the attribution is controversial.

Homer (fl. ca. 750–700): celebrated poet, author of the *Iliad* and the *Odyssey*. *Intro.* 1.3.1*

Homoiomerê, Those who posit: group designation for thinkers who postulate the existence of "things with like parts." *Psych.* 4.9.10 (1)

Iamblichus (ca. AD 240–ca. 325): Neoplatonist philosopher with a strong interest in the Pythagorean tradition.

Infinitesimals, those who posit: group designation for thinkers who postulate the existence of infinitesimals. *Psych.* 4.9.10 (1)

Ion of Chios (ca. 480–423/2): lyric poet and tragedian, who spent time in Athens. Also wrote prose works with philosophical themes. Testimonia and Fragments: DK 36. *Cosm.* 2.25.12 (1)

John Lydus. *See* Lydus
John of Stobi. *See* Stobaeus

Lactantius (ca. AD 250–ca. 325): Christian Latin rhetorician and apologist. His extant writings furnish useful evidence for the broader doxographical tradition.

INDEX

Leophanes: early Greek natural philosopher, about whom almost nothing is known but is cited by Aristotle and Theophrastus. Testimonia and Fragments: not in DK. *Physio.* 5.7.5 (1)

Leucippus (fl. ca. 450–420): early Greek natural philosopher, founder of atomism. Birthplace uncertain. His basic ideas further developed by Democritus (q.v.). Probably wrote just the one book, unless the title at *Plac.* 1.25.4 refers to a separate work. Testimonia and Fragments: DK 67; also MP 9; LM 27. *Intro.* 1.3.13; *Princ.* 1.18.3, 1.25.4; *Cosm.* 2.1.3, 2.2.4, 2.3.2, 2.4.7, 2.7.2; *Meteor.* 3.3.10; *Earth-sea* 3.10.4, 3.12.1; *Psych.* 4.3.7, 4.7.1, 4.7a.1, 4.8.5, 4.8.10, 4.9.1, 4.9.9, 4.13.1, 4.14.2, 4.19.7; *Physio.* 5.4.1, 5.7.6, 5.25.3, 5.20.3 (25)

Leucippus, successors of: group designation for philosophers in the atomist tradition. *Princ.* 1.14.4 (1)

Lydus, also Johannes Lydus (ca. AD 490–ca. 560): early Byzantine government official interested in antiquarian topics. In his extant *On the Months* he makes limited use of material from Ps.-Plutarch's epitome of the *Placita*.

Macrobius (fl. ca. AD 410–ca. 430): Latin author of the *Saturnalia* in seven books, which contains a vast amount of antiquarian, scientific, and philosophical material, and also of a Commentary on Cicero's *Dream of Scipio*.

Majority, the: group designation for the holders of a majority view, as opposed to the view of a single individual. *Princ.* 1.22.8 (1)

Manilius (fl. ca. AD 10–35): Roman didactic poet, author of the *Astronomica*, which in five books presents a comprehensive account of the ancient science of astrology.

Materialists: group designation for philosophers who hold that matter is body. *Intro.* 1.9.6 (1)

Mathematicians (*mathêmatikoi*), successors of: group designation for members of a tradition of scientists engaged in mathematical studies. *Psych.* 4.14.3 (1). *See also* Astronomers

Melissus of Samos (fl. ca. 440): early Greek philosopher, follower of Parmenides (q.v.), and member of the Eleatic school. Wrote just a single treatise, not extant. Testimonia and Fragments: DK 30; also LM 21. *Intro.* 1.7.18; *Princ.* 1.24.1; *Cosm.* 2.1.2, 2.1.8, 2.4.5; *Psych.* 4.9.1 (6)

Metrodorus of Chios (fl. 400–350): philosopher, follower of Democ-

Pliny the Elder (AD 23/24–79): Roman author of the still extant *Natural History*, a vast compilation of information on the universe and its contents in thirty-seven books.

Polemon of Athens (ca. 350–ca. 270): philosopher, member of the Academy and its head after Xenocrates (q.v.). Little known about his writings. Testimonia and Fragments: Gigante (1977). *Intro.* 1.7.20 (1)

Polybus of Cos (fl. ca. 400–ca. 370): doctor and medical scientist, disciple, and son-in-law of Hippocrates (q.v.). Possibly author of one or more writings in the corpus Hippocraticum. *Physio.* 5.18.3, 5.18.5 (2)

Polycrates: ruler (tyrant) of Samos from 540 to 522. *Intro.* 1.3.8*

Porphyry (AD 234–ca. 305): Neoplatonist philosopher, disciple of Plotinus. Author of a large corpus of writings, including commentaries and works on earlier Greek philosophy. His *Philosophical History*, of which only fragments survive, contained both doxographical and biographical information on philosophers up to and including Plato and is mentioned by Theodoret (q.v.).

Posidonius (ca. 135–51): Stoic philosopher, disciple of Panaetius, but not his successor as head of the school. Active on Rhodes, where he founded his own school. Author of some thirty writings, none extant. Testimonia and Fragments: Edelstein-Kidd (1972); also Theiler (1982). *Intro.* 1.7.10; *Princ.* 1.28.5; *Cosm.* 2.9.3, 2.25.5; *Meteor.* 3.1.11; *Earth-sea* 3.17.4; *Psych.* 4.13.11 (7)

Protagoras of Abdera (ca. 490–ca. 420): renowned sophist, with substantial interests in philosophy. Spent time in Athens but fled when charged with atheism. Testimonia and Fragments: DK 80; also LM 31. *Psych.* 4.9.1 (1)

Psellus, Michael (AD 1018–ca. 1090): Byzantine scholar, rhetor, and polymath. Author of the *De omnifaria doctrina*, the structure of which is adapted from the *Epitome* of Ps.-Plutarch (ed. Westerink [1948]). See General Introduction 1.6, 2.1.2.

Ps.-Alexander *Mantissa*. *See* Alexander of Aphrodisias

Ps.-Aristotle *De inundacione Nili*: Latin translation of a short treatise *On the Flooding of the Nile*, which most likely is the product of the early Peripatos and shows affinities with early doxographical literature.

Ps.-Aristotle *De mundo* (*On the Cosmos*): treatise in the form of a letter from Aristotle to his pupil Alexander the Great presenting a comprehensive summary of the contents of the universe. Regarded by most scholars as inauthentic and to be dated to about the first century BC.

Ps.-Galen (date unknown, probably third or fourth century AD): unknown author of the *Philosophos historia*, the greater part of which is a further abridged version of the *Epitome* of Ps.-Plutarch (ed. Diels *DG*, and partly Jas [2018]). See General Introduction 1.2, 1.6, 2.1.2, 2.2.1, 3.2.

Ps.-Galen *Definitiones Medicae* (*Medical Definitions*): collection of short statements on a wide range of medical terms containing some valuable links to doxographical literature in the area of physiology. First modern critical edition just published (ed. Kollesch, 2023).

Ps.-Justin *Cohortatio ad Graecos* (*Exhortation to the Greeks*): treatise of a Christian apologist that makes incidental use of Ps.-Plutarch's epitome of the *Placita*. Usually dated to the third century AD, but an attribution to bishop Marcellus of Ancyra (AD ca. 285–374) has been suggested on philological grounds.

Ps.-Plutarch: unknown author of an epitome of Aëtius' *Placita*, to be dated to probably about AD 150 (ed. Mau [1971], Lachenaud [1993]). See General Introduction 1.1–3, 2.1.2, 2.2.1.

Ps.-Plutarch *Stromateis* (*Miscellanies*): collection of a dozen brief doxographies on early Greek philosophers preserved by Eusebius (q.v.). They contain many parallels to the doxographical material in the *Placita* but, as is the case in Hippolytus (q.v.), are organized by philosopher rather than by topic.

Pythagoras of Samos (ca. 570–ca. 490): early Greek philosopher. Though first active in Ionia, he migrated to Croton in Southern Italy. Earliest of the Western Greek philosophers. Founded the community of the Pythagoreans. Left no writings, but many impor-

through the dialogues of Plato and accounts in Xenophon (q.v.) and other Socratics. *Intro.* 1.3.20, 1.7.22, 1.10.2 (3)

Soranus of Ephesus (fl. AD ca. 100–ca. 130): doctor and prolific writer of medical treatises, of which the *Gynaecia* (*Women's Diseases*) is partially extant. Important source of medical doxography in later writers, including Tertullian (q.v.).

Speusippus of Athens (ca. 408–339): philosopher. Nephew of Plato, took over as head of the Academy on his death. Developed Plato's thought in new directions. Many writings listed in Diog. Laert. 4.4–5, but none survive. Testimonia and Fragments: Tarán (1981); also Lang (1911); Isnardi Parente (1980). *Intro.* 1.7.11 (1)

Sphaerus of Borysthenes (fl. ca. 260): Stoic philosopher, disciple of Zeno and Cleanthes. Many writings listed at Diog. Laert. 7.178, but none survive. Testimonia and Fragments: *SVF* 1.139–42. *Psych.* 4.15.1 (1)

Stobaeus (fl. AD 400–430): author (probably Christian) of the *Anthologion*, a vast collection of quotations and excerpts on natural philosophy and ethics compiled for educational purposes (ed. Wachmuth [1884] and Hense [1894–1916]). See General Introduction 1.1–2, 2.1.3.

Stoics: group designation for school founded by Zeno of Citium (q.v.), one of the four main schools of philosophy in the Hellenistic period. Fragments: Von Arnim, *SVF*, 4 vols. (1903–1924); Hülser, 4 vols. (1987–1988). *Intro.* 1.prooem.2, 1.5.1, 1.6.1, 1.7.24; *Intro.* 1.8.2, 1.9.2, 1.9.8, 1.10.5; *Princ.* 1.11.5, 1.11.7, 1.12.4, 1.14.5*, 1.22.2, 1.27.3, 1.28.4, 1.29.4; *Cosm.* 2.1.9, 2.2.1, 2.4.2, 2.4.8, 2.6.1, 2.9.2, 2.14.1, 2.15.2, 2.17.4, 2.22.3, 2.23.6, 2.25.5, 2.26.1, 2.27.1, 2.28.3, 2.29.7, 2.30.6; *Meteor.* 3.1.10, 3.3.15, 3.7.2, 3.8.1; *Earth-sea* 3.9.3, 3.10.1, 3.15.2; *Psych.* 4.3.3, 4.4.4, 4.5.7, 4.7.3, 4.8.1, 4.8.7, 4.8.8, 4.8.12, 4.9.4, 4.9.18, 4.10.1, 4.11.1, 4.19.6, 4.20.2, 4.21.1, 4.23.1; *Physio.* 5.1.1, 5.9.2, 5.10.4, 5.11.3, 5.12.3, 5.13.3, 5.15.2, 5.16.2, 5.17.1, 5.23.1, 5.24.4, 5.26.3, 5.30.5 (68)

Strabo of Amaseia, Pontus (64/63 BC–ca. AD 25): historian and geographer. His extant *Geography* in seventeen books contains information on questions of natural philosophy (esp. terrestrial phenomena).

Strato of Lampsacus (ca. 330–269/68): Peripatetic philosopher, third head of the school after Aristotle (q.v.) and Theophrastus (q.v.). Numerous writings, listed at Diog. Laert. 5.59–60, covering all the major areas of Hellenistic philosophy, none extant. Testimonia and Fragments: Sharples (2011); also Wehrli (1969). *Intro.* 1.3.24; *Princ.* 1.12.7, 1.15.5*, 1.18.4, 1.19.3, 1.22.5; *Cosm.* 2.11.4, 2.17.2; *Meteor.* 3.2.5, 3.3.14; *Psych.* 4.5.3, 4.13.3, 4.23.3; *Physio.* 5.2.2, 5.4.3, 5.8.2, 5.24.4 (16)

Suda: title of the famous tenth-century Byzantine lexicon. See General Introduction 1.2.

Tertullian of Carthage (fl. ca. AD 200–ca. 215): early Latin Christian theologian, apologist, and controversialist. His treatise *On the Soul* preserves much valuable doxographical material thought mainly to derive from Soranus (q.v.).

Thales of Miletus (ca. 625–ca. 547): Ionian philosopher, the first of the early Greek philosophers of nature. Recognized as the founder of the Ionian succession. Incipient philosophical and broad scientific interests. Uncertain whether he left behind any writings. Testimonia and Fragments: DK 11; also MP 1; LM 5; Wöhrle (2014). *Intro.* 1.2.2, 1.3.1, 1.3.6*, 1.7.2, 1.8.2; *Princ.* 1.11.6, 1.18.1, 1.25.1; *Cosm.* 2.1.2, 2.12.1, 2.13.1, 2.20.9, 2.24.1, 2.25.9, 2.28.5, 2.29.7; *Earth-sea* 3.10.1, 3.15.1; *Nile* 4.1.1; *Psych.* 4.2.1; *Physio.* 5.26.1 (20)

Thales and his successors: group designation for philosophers standing in the tradition of natural philosophy. *Princ.* 1.11.6, 1.17.1; *Earth-sea* 3.9.1 (3)

Thales, successors of: group designation for philosophers standing (1) in the Ionian succession or (2) more generally in the tradition of natural philosophy. *Intro.* 1.9.2; *Princ.* 1.16.1; *Earth-sea* 3.11.1 (3)

Theodore of Cyrene (fl. ca. 310): philosopher, known as "the atheist." Continued interests of Cyrenaic school in ethics. Treatise *On the Gods* and other writings, now lost. Testimonia and Fragments: Winiarcyck (1981). *Intro.* 1.7.1*

Theodoret of Cyrrhus (AD 393–ca. 458): Christian bishop and theologian. Author of *Graecarum affectionum curatio*, which in Books 2 to 5 makes substantial use of Aëtius' *Placita* (ed. Raeder [1904]). See General Introduction 1.1–3, 1.6, 2.1.4, 3.2.

Theophrastus of Eresos (372/71–288/87): philosopher, disciple, and collaborator of Aristotle. Succeeded him as head of the Peripatos. Prolific and wide-ranging author. Writings listed at Diog. Laert. 5.42–50, of which a few still survive. Testimonia and Frag-

INDEX